17.

(review copy)

WILLIAM WORDSWORTH
OF RYDAL MOUNT

'William Wordsworth, Esquire, of Rydal Mount, was one person, and the William Wordsworth whom he so heartily reverenced quite another.'

LOWELL, *Among My Books*.

William Wordsworth

Portrait by Inman

WILLIAM WORDSWORTH OF RYDAL MOUNT

An Account of the Poet and
his Friends in the Last Decade

by

FREDERIKA BEATTY

Illustrated with
eight plates

LONDON : J. M. DENT & SONS LTD

FOREWORD

No one who comes to know William Wordsworth can fail to feel the essential unity in his mind and work from first to last. That most of his best poetry was written before he was forty cannot be denied, but that there was a sharp break in his personality at the end of youth or even in old age may well be questioned. It is the purpose of this book to show that though Wordsworth, like many of us, became gradually less flexible with the years, the difference between the older and the younger man was far less marked than is usually thought.

The ultra-conservative, whom many people consider the true Wordsworth of the later years, is largely the creation of his nephew and biographer, the canon of Westminster. Despite Christopher Wordsworth's charms as nephew and cousin, it is unfortunate that the poet commissioned him to write his biography, for a narrow theologian was not the man to present Wordsworth to posterity.

Many of those living when the *Memoirs* were published regretted the book. Other biographers had been suggested, especially Edward Quillinan. The temporary estrangement between the poet and his son-in-law was probably responsible for the choice of his nephew as biographer, for the agreement was made in writing on 16th November 1847,[1] and Quillinan did not know of the existence of this document until a week after Wordsworth's death. He tried not to resent the choice which Wordsworth had made, and offered the appointed biographer what assistance he could. He even lent the manuscript notes that Miss Fenwick had made for Dora and given to him.

Crabb Robinson was afraid that the biography would not be adequate: 'I fear he will try to make W: appear as a Puseyite. But he cannot get rid of the Sonnet on Young

England.'[2] Robinson went to Rydal later in the summer, and from there wrote:

Dr Wordsworth . . . is one of the most bigotted [sic] high church-men I ever came near—This is ill expressed by me—I should say, whose books I ever looked into, for personally he is one of the most amiable of men—His unaffected softness of manner and kindness of disposition quite disarming those who come to him prepared to quarrel on account of his most intolerant & both absurd & offensive polemical writings.[3]

Quillinan also was afraid that the bias of Dr Wordsworth might warp the life.[4] The fears of Robinson and Quillinan were echoed by a good many other persons.

I have had some strange letters on the subject [wrote the son-in-law in May 1850]. One of them says 'I see with regret by an Advertise-ment in the Newspapers that the Life of your Father-in-law is to be written by a man *who did not know him!*'—I was rather struck and amused by the phrase, and the objection, though not in the same pithy words, has been made from other quarters. There is no doubt that you and I both knew Wordsworth much better than his nephew knew him; but in some respects he is quite the proper man.[5]

Throughout the year Quillinan tried to pretend to himself and to Crabb Robinson that it was not a bitter disappointment to be deprived of writing Wordsworth's life, but in January he wrote:

Had Dora survived, as you say, all this would have been different; and the Papist would in fact have written the Life, with Her & You for his Coadjutors. But two thirds of my literary ambition are buried yonder.[6]

Apparently Wordsworth had originally intended to have his son-in-law write his biography.

When the book came out Robinson wrote of the first volume that he had 'very little to object to, giving the writer his first principles.'[7] Reading further, he said: 'If not the whole man is given, portions are faithfully, tho' inevitably in magnitude disproportioned to the other portions of his character.'[8] He found that the Coleridges were 'no great admirers of the book,'[9] and that Miss Fenwick was 'not pleased with the Memoir of her friend the poet—tho' her religious opinions are those of the Doctor the Westminster Canon.'[10] Lady Richardson wrote to Robinson that she felt much as he did about Dr Wordsworth's *Memoirs*: 'He gives all he could, for he did not know much of his Uncle, except by hearsay, and that was not the way to know Wordsworth.'[11] Wordsworth's own son, William, said that he sincerely regretted the publication of the *Memoirs*.[12]

The comments of the more impersonal writers often agree with those of the poet's friends and family. Edward Paxton Hood wrote:

. . . A book has been produced, which fails to give an account of the life of the man. Some persons who knew Wordsworth well, seem to be strangely forgotten and slighted. . . . An ordinary reader feels that there is an evident, a very evident attempt to exhibit the poet in his aristocratical relationship. . . . In his life by his nephew, Wordsworth is like the portrait in the first volume [Pickersgill]; he looks too gentlemanly; too proper; the portrait wants the ease, the *abandonment*, the careless grace, which were certainly his if they were ever any man's, especially the eye longs to see him among his friends in his social undress.[13]

Even the conservative Austin and Ralph felt that Dr Wordsworth had made his uncle too orthodox in politics and religion, that the book 'is unfortunately far too much devoted to proving that Wordsworth was at last ashamed of his juvenile politics, and that if he was ever a Pantheist, he lived to be an orthodox High Churchman.'[14]

May this volume about Wordsworth in his later years, a man among his many friends, enable those of our generation to come a little nearer to William Wordsworth of Rydal Mount.

The author wishes to express her indebtedness to the Librarian and the Trustees of Dr Williams's Library, Gordon Square, London, for their permission to examine the Diaries of Henry Crabb Robinson. She wishes to state that the Trustees are not responsible for the selection made.

To Dr B. R. Johnston on behalf of the Trustees of Dove Cottage she is grateful for permission to use two letters written by Dora Wordsworth to Edward Quillinan, and to Mrs Dorothy Dickson for permission to use letters to herself from the late Gordon Wordsworth.

She wishes also to thank the Librarian and the Assistant Librarian of Cornell University for giving access to the Correspondence of Henry Reed with Wordsworth, Mrs Wordsworth, and others.

Acknowledgment to the owners of portraits reproduced in the book is made in the list of illustrations.

To the Carnegie Hero Fund Commission, Pittsburgh, Pennsylvania, she is deeply grateful for educational awards which facilitated the progress of this book.

For helpful criticism she wishes to thank Professor Ernest Hunter Wright, Professor Oscar James Campbell, and Professor Hoxie Neale Fairchild of Columbia University.

The typescript of Henry Crabb Robinson's Diary (22.338 C at Dr Williams's Library, Gordon Square) is indicated as Crabb Robinson, *Diaries*, the typed volumes designated by arabic numbers 18–22. Thomas Sadler's edition is called *Diaries and Correspondence*, of which only volume iii has been used. Miss Edith Julia Morley's *Correspondence of Henry Crabb Robinson with the Wordsworth Circle* is called *Correspondence*.

The Correspondence of Henry Reed with William Wordsworth, Mrs Wordsworth, and Others, 1836–1853, in the Wordsworth Collection at Cornell University, Ithaca, New York, I have examined in manuscript. Though my reading of some of the letters is slightly different from that of Professor Broughton, I have used his published edition in my notes, for the reader's convenience.

NEW YORK,   F. B.
    May 1939.

CONTENTS

ILLUSTRATIONS

I. WORDSWORTH HIMSELF

His bodily frame had been from youth to age
Of an unusual strength; his mind was keen,
Intense, and frugal, apt for all affairs. . . .

Michael.

WILLIAM WORDSWORTH was a rather tall man, personable, and of amazing vitality. His capacity for physical and intellectual enjoyment, for friendship and deeper affection, was above that of the ordinary man. Sorrow he felt keenly, but his strength enabled him to rise above it.

Wordsworth in his seventies was as hale as many men of fifty. Neighbours and less frequent visitors have described him as about five feet ten inches tall, his frame large but a little stooped, his brow and nose prominent, and his grey eyes of an unusual depth and luminousness.

'In person he is tall and largely framed,' said Thomas Powell.[1] 'In personal appearance,' said Jerdan, 'Wordsworth was a noticeable man; one of the few whom, having once seen, you remember as apart from the common herd.'[2] And Thomas Cooper, the Chartist, gave his first impression:

In another half minute I was in the presence of that majestic old man, and I was bowing with a deep and heartfelt homage for his intellectual grandeur—with which his striking form and the pile of his forehead seemed to congrue so fully—when he seized my hand, and welcomed me with a smile so paternal, and such a hearty 'How do you do? I am very happy to see you' that the tears stood in my eyes for joy.[3]

Those who saw the bard in his last decade were amazed at the vigour of his body and mind. 'Yes, I have seen the Poet! . . .' wrote Shairp to John Duke Coleridge. 'He seems very old; and yet it is a green old age.'[4] John Taylor Coleridge remembered walking with him 'on a drizzly, muddy day, the turf sponging out water at every step, through which he stalked as regardless as if he were of iron, and with the same fearless, unchanged pace over rough and smooth, slippery and sound.' [5] 'My strength,' said Wordsworth himself, 'exceeds that of most men of my years, and my general health continues to be, as it always has been, remarkably good.' [6]

The curate of Windermere wrote of Wordsworth's 'quite remarkable vigour of intellect and bodily powers' [7] on his seventy-fifth birthday, and Lady Richardson commented on his vigour eighteen months later. James T. Fields saw him when he was 'nearly eighty, but he seemed hale and quite as able to walk up and down the hills as ever.' [8] After speaking of Southey's pitiable condition, Doctor Arnold said: 'Wordsworth is in body and mind still sound and vigorous; it is beautiful to see and hear him.' [9] 'Wordsworth is remarkably well,' he wrote a fortnight later, 'and we see him daily.' [10] Of Wordsworth's 'pedestrian strength' Henry Taylor said: 'The fainting London tourist may still meet with him, robust and fresh, on the top of Helvellyn.' [11]

Sometimes the poet's son-in-law found him too little deterred by the weather:

I have been . . . walking about a considerable part of the morning through the waters and the mists with the Bard who seems to defy all weathers; and who called this a beautiful, soft solemn day; and so it was; though somewhat insidiously soft, for a mackintosh was hardly proof against its insinuation. He is in great force, and in great vigour of mind.[12]

But Wordsworth suffered much from inflamed eyes, and he had no sense of smell. Time and again he complained of his eyes: of inflammation of the lids, of aggravating the trouble by exposure to wind and storm, of excessive heat as painful, of strong light as insufferable, of the impossibility of reading at night, of various remedies tried. The trouble started about 1803, when he had overheated himself carrying John, 'a lusty infant,' to the top of Kirkstone.[13] Two letters in the British

Museum written about 1827 thank a friend [14] for a new remedy:

It gives me great pleasure to say, which I do with gratitude, that I have derived, I am persuaded, great benefit from your remedy. The Blue Stone was applied by Mrs W—— to my eyes, five or six times; it distressed them not a little for the time; but they have not been any thing like so well for many years as since. It is but justice to ascribe this to the virtues of the Stone; though it is proper to say that my having about the same period entirely left off wine (fermented or spirituous liquors have never made a part of my beverage) it is probable that this change may have concurred in producing the beneficial effect.[15]

The poet wrote later to the same benefactor that his eyes were

infinitely better than I ever expected they would be; indeed all but quite well, and perhaps if I had more courage in applying the remedy they would be entirely without inconvenience—I can now read two or three hours by candle light, a practice I had been obliged to abandon all together [sic] previous to the use of your remedy.[16]

He had told Henry Taylor in 1823 that the complaint was partly seasonal, that he was 'always much better in winter than in the summer season,'[17] and in 1830 he wrote to Charles Lamb that he had put off writing until longer days would allow him to write without candlelight—

but alas, when the days lengthened, my eyesight departed, and for many months I could not read three minutes at a time. You will be sorry to hear that this infirmity still hangs about me, and almost cuts me off from reading altogether.[18]

He continued to write intermittently of severe and frequent inflammations. And Mary Fletcher, describing him in the summer of 1839, said: 'At this time he wore a green shade, and his head was usually bent down, his eyes being weak.' [19]

The subject of Wordsworth's eyes has been treated at length by Miss Edith Batho,[20] who cites numerous instances from 1804 to 1840 of the intense suffering the poet endured from inflammation of the eyes. She shows him relatively free of this trouble after 1840, except in the summer of 1845. But the

old infirmity did not entirely leave him in his last decade, and
his letters refer to it now and then. Speaking of excuses, he
mentioned 'that old one of the state of my eyes, which never
leaves me at liberty either to read or write a tenth part as much
as I could wish, and as otherwise I ought to do.' [21] To Lady
Frederick Bentinck he wrote:

I have for these last few years been visited always with a serious
inflammation in my eyes about this season of the year, which causes
me to have fears about the fulfilment of any engagement, however
agreeable. [22]

He apologized to his nephew, Christopher, for a delay in
writing:

The inflammation in one of my eyes which seized me on my first
arrival in London kept it closed for a long time. I had your first
two pamphlets read to me. [23]

Carlyle, meeting Wordsworth at informal breakfasts and great
dinners in London, describes a device used by the poet:

The light was always afflictive to his eyes; he carried in his pocket
something like a skeleton brass candlestick, in which, setting it on
the dinner-table, between him and the most afflictive or nearest of
the chief lights, he touched a little spring, and there flirted out, at
the top of his brass implement, a small vertical green circle which
prettily enough threw his eyes into shade, and screened him from
that sorrow. [24]

This mechanical eye-shade is preserved in the Wordsworth
Museum at Grasmere.

'With regard to *fragrance*,' said the nephew in his *Memoirs*,
'Mr Wordsworth spoke from the testimony of others; he himself had *no sense of smell*.' Doctor Wordsworth even explains
away the one recorded instance of the poet's enjoying the smell
of flowers:

The incident occurred at Racedown, when he was walking with
Miss H——, who coming suddenly upon a parterre of sweet flowers,
expressed her pleasure at their fragrance, a pleasure he caught from
her lips, and then fancied to be his own.

The explanation is not entirely convincing. Southey thought that Wordsworth *smelled* the 'bed of stocks in full bloom; . . . it was like a vision of Paradise to him; but it lasted only a few minutes, and the faculty has continued torpid from that time.'[25] It seems more likely that the olfactory weakness was not congenital but the result of inflammation of the facial cavities, and that in the Racedown days the sensitiveness had not completely disappeared.

Once in a while the old man suffered from rheumatism.[26] Sometimes after working too steadily at revising his poems he had a nervous headache.[27] And when he was worried about the health of his daughter, he sometimes looked very old.[28] 'Wordsworth . . .' wrote Crabb Robinson in 1847, 'is always serene and uncomplaining; but I think he is somewhat less animated than he was.'[29] Robinson was disappointed that his old friend allowed him 'uncontradicted to state heresies which would not have been tolerated a few years ago.'[30] Even Miss Fenwick once gave 'an unpleasant account of W[ordsworth]'s mental health—perhaps strength would be the better term.'[31] These testimonies, rare even when the poet was in his late seventies, show that his friends hardly thought of Wordsworth as an old man, and were surprised when they found him so.

Several persons have recorded that Wordsworth was handsome. 'Mr Wordsworth talked and looked very handsome,' said Miss Airy to Mrs Clarkson.[32] She had 'never heard Mr Wordsworth talk so much before—She admired his Beauty and his talk also.'[33] Crabb Robinson described him at the Marshalls', one Sunday afternoon: 'The afternoon passed off very well—Wordsworth in very remarkable [*sic*] good health and looking quite handsome.'[34] Wordsworth's portraits do not show him as handsome, but his face, said Robinson, 'was of a kind that the likeness was hard to miss, and yet more hard to strike strongly and agreeably.'[35]

Of the impressive head, Thomas Cooper wrote: 'The dignity with which he uttered every sentence seemed natural

in a man whose grand head and face, if one had never known
of his poetry, would have proclaimed his intellectual superiority.' [36] Recalling in his old age the impressions of his youth,
Henry Taylor said:

Wordsworth's was a face which did not assign itself to any class.
It was a hardy weather-beaten old face which might have belonged
to a nobleman, a yeoman, a mariner, or a philosopher; for there was
so much of a man that you lost sight of super-added distinctions.
For my own part I should not, judging by his face, have guessed him
to be a poet. To my eyes there was more of strength than refinement
in the face. . . . Perhaps what was wanting was only *physical* refinement. It was a rough grey face, full of rifts and clefts and fissures,
out of which . . . you might expect lichens to grow. But Miss
Fenwick, who was familiar with the face in all its moods, could see
through all this; and so could I too at times. [37]

Emerson's first impression of Wordsworth was that he was
'a plain, elderly white-haired man, not prepossessing and dis-
figured by green goggles.' [38] Emerson saw him again and
continued the description fifteen years later: 'His face
sometimes lighted up, but his conversation was not marked
by special force or elevation. . . . He had a healthy look,
with a weather-beaten face, his face corrugated, especially the
large nose.' [39]

Wordsworth himself was conscious of the size of his nose.
He wrote to an artist about a portrait of himself:

The position of the head . . . cannot be favourable to *likeness* as
by shortening the upper lip so much it makes the nose seem much
larger than I will grant my own, though undoubtedly large, could in
any position appear to be. . . . I barely *ask* whether the *blackness*
under the nose might not be a little softened or mitigated with
some advantage. [40]

But it was the eyes and the general contour of the head that
gave distinction to Wordsworth's appearance. Powell called
his eyes 'the seat of contemplation, not observation,' Haydon
alluded to the 'internal vision,' Hazlitt to the 'preternatural
lustre.' Ellis Yarnall said:

His eyes, though not glistening, had yet in them the fire which betokened the greatness of his genius. This no painter could represent, and this it was that gave his countenance its high intellectual expression. His features were not good; indeed but for this keen grey eye with its wondrous light his face could hardly have been called pleasing; but this atoned for all.[41]

And even Leigh Hunt, who was not always friendly with Wordsworth, said:

Certainly I never beheld eyes that looked so inspired or supernatural. They were like fires half burning, half smouldering, with a sort of acrid fixture of regard, and seated at the further end of two caverns. One might imagine Ezekiel or Isaiah to have had such eyes.[42]

Thomas Arnold, brother of the poet, described Wordsworth's head. After admitting that 'the aquiline nose was too large and thick to be called beautiful,' and that 'the mouth and chin, though far from weak, were without distinction,' Arnold dwelt on

the beauty and nobility of the head, the width and poise of the forehead, the manifest adaptation of the 'tenement of clay,' to house a majestic and many-sided intellect, which atoned for all minor shortcomings, and fixed the gaze of the beholder. Clough's head, too, was beautiful, but Clough's head was not equal to Wordsworth's.[43]

In London Wordsworth wore the conventional attire, but his everyday dress in Westmorland was 'a loose brown frock-coat, trousers of shepherd's plaid, a loose black handkerchief for a necktie, a green and black shawl round the shoulders, and a wide-awake or straw hat, often with a blue veil attached to it.'[44] Ellis Yarnall found him a little more formally clothed:

One hand was generally thrust into his half-buttoned waistcoat. His dress was a black frock coat, grey trousers, a black waistcoat, and cravat of black silk carelessly tied; his appearance, in fact, was somewhat rough, but not slovenly; his clothes were not old-fashioned, nor did he dress as an old man in any peculiar way.[45]

The testimony of Carlyle, who cared little for the poet but

admired the strength and independence of the man, is perhaps more valuable than that of more partial observers:

A fine wholesome rusticity, fresh as his mountain breezes, sat well on the stalwart veteran, and on all he said and did. You would have said he was usually a taciturn man; glad to unlock himself to an audience sympathetic and intelligent, when such offered itself. His face bore marks of much, not always peaceful meditation; the look of it not bland or benevolent so much as close, impregnable, and hard; a man *multa tacere loquive paratus*, in a world where he had experienced no lack of contradictions as he strode along! The eyes were not very brilliant, but they had a quiet clearness; there was enough of brow and well-shaped; rather too much of cheek . . .; face of squarish shape and decidedly longish, as I think the head itself was . . .; he was large-boned, lean, but still firm-knit, tall, and strong-looking when he stood, a right good old steel-grey figure, with rustic simplicity and dignity about him and a vivacious strength looking through him.[46]

Multa tacere loquive paratus. When the mood was on him, Wordsworth was silent. He could be, in the chatter of a large dinner-party, apparently as much alone as in his mountain solitudes. Kenyon gave a dinner for twelve in Wordsworth's honour in May 1842; the guests included Rogers and Browning, as well as the ever-present Crabb Robinson. And yet, though the poet and Mrs Wordsworth had prolonged their stay in London to give Kenyon the evening, 'Wordsw[orth] was quite spent and hardly spoke during the whole time.'[47] A similar thing happened at Mrs Hoare's three years later.[48]

Crabb Robinson knew that his friend needed tactful handling. To Quillinan, who had suggested his offering himself as a companion on a journey into Wales in the autumn of 1843, he wrote: 'It will be quite enough to suggest anything . . . when Mr W: may begin to be unsettled And feel the nomadic disease upon him—And then the hint must be delicately given.'[49] When Brockedon wanted to do Wordsworth's portrait, Robinson 'advised him not to ask Wordsworth abruptly.'[50] In 1846 Harriet Martineau said:

While all goes on methodically he is happy and cheery and courteous and benevolent; so that one could almost worship him. But to secure this everybody must be punctual, the fire must be bright and all go orderly as his angel takes care that every thing shall as far as depends on her.[51]

Sometimes the poet became indignant.[52]

But he was never petty; he was not easily offended. On one ocasion he read a letter intended for his sister, a letter not complimentary to him, and it made not the slightest difference in the friendship between him and the correspondent. 'Offended!' he wrote to him, 'what could you be dreaming about!'[53] Robinson answered that he had never observed in Wordsworth or in any member of his family 'the slightest tendency to take offence at trifles.'[54] When Mary Russell Mitford visited Talfourd in 1836 and was so much fêted that her host became jealous and openly rude, Wordsworth was free from envy. 'Wordsworth, dear old man!' Miss Mitford wrote her father, 'aids it by his warm and approving kindness.'[55]

Crabb Robinson could sometimes twit his friend with impunity. After seeing a portrait of Wordsworth in Cottle's possession, he wrote: 'You have taken abundant care to let the world know that you did not marry Mrs W: for her beauty. Now this picture will justify the inference that she too had a higher motive for her acceptance of you.'[56] And once, Wordsworth was actually impish. He told Justice Coleridge in October 1836 how he got even with 'the Eastern traveller,' who was so bold as pompously to prefer the 'silent solitude of the Arabian Desert' to the sounding cataracts of the Lakes.

My mountain blood was up [said the old man]. I quickly observed that he had boots and a stout greatcoat on, and said: 'I am sorry you don't like this; perhaps I can show you what will please you more.' I strode away, and led him from crag to crag, hill to vale, and vale to hill, for about six hours; till I thought I should have had to bring him home, he was so tired.[57]

Wordsworth's nature was predominantly happy, often communicative.   Thomas Powell,[58] Gladstone,[59] and Mary Russell Mitford [60] saw the poet under different circumstances, and each has left a record of his geniality. Miss Mitford liked him better as she knew him better: 'I sat next him at dinner three following days, and had the pleasure of finding my old idolatry of the poet turned into a warm affection for the kind, simple, gracious man.' [61]

Wordsworth often dined or drank tea at the home of Mrs Fletcher, widow of the great Whig leader and herself a liberal of some reputation. 'He was in a very happy mood,' wrote Mary Fletcher in her note-book after Wordsworth had dined with them one evening in June 1840, 'and threw himself into the interests of our possession in a most engaging manner.' [62] The mother, though no less fond of her great neighbour, was more critical. 'Our excellent friend was in his happiest vein of cheerfulness,' she wrote, 'having left Mrs Quillinan much better and brought back his three Grandsons who came here with him and Mrs Wordsworth.' Then she added: 'I did not venture to provoke a *frown* or a harsh word against the Dissenters Bill.' [63]

In Crabb Robinson's diary and letters are numerous comments on the poet's amiability, his excellent spirits, his willingness to talk to every one—but usually with the slight undercurrent of surprise, the possibility that the complaisance may not last. Robinson gave a dinner in the poet's honour on 10th July 1841. Afterwards, he wrote in his diary: 'Wordsworth talked chiefly tête à tête but he seemed to be in a good mood—On the whole he is improved as a companion since his last being in London.'[64] The next May, he gave a breakfast and a dinner for him, and we can detect in the host's letters a certain breathless relief. 'The poet made himself very agreeable indeed,' he wrote of the dinner,   'He talked at his ease with everyone—Indeed he has been remarkable [*sic*] pleasant during his visit here.' [65] Robinson mentioned, too, Wordsworth's cordiality to Alsager, an intimate friend of Charles Lamb's and especially invited to meet the poet: 'Wordsworth . . . was particularly

pleased to see him.   Sat next him and was in excellent spirits—
but talked with almost everyone.' [66]

The poet was of many moods, and 'not always accessible'—
but, added Harriet Martineau, 'how *bewitching* Wordsworth
is when he is so!   And he very often—usually—appears
happy and gay.' [67]   After Wordsworth's death, Aubrey de
Vere said: 'His was pre-eminently a happy, and, in the main,
even a satisfied life.' [68]   Wordsworth himself regarded geniality
as essential to his nature.   Once when his spirits were depressed
for a long time, in 1832, he wrote to Professor Hamilton
that he was losing 'those genial feelings which, through life,
have not been so much accompaniments of my character as
vital principles of my existence.' [69]

Wordsworth was a great talker.   His voice was low—and a
little rough—'a deep and roughish but not unpleasing voice,
and an exalted mode of speaking.' [70]   'His deep guttural voice,'
said Powell, 'seems to come from the depths of his heart, and
the impressive tone he speaks in gives an emphasis even to the
commonest of commonplace.' [71]   Carlyle remembered the tone
of Wordsworth's voice and the resonance of certain phrases years
afterwards:

> The tone of his voice when I got him afloat on some Cumberland
> or other matter germane to him, had a braced rustic vivacity,
> willingness and solid precision, which alone rings in my ear when all
> else is gone. . . . His voice was good, frank and sonorous, though
> practically clear [*sic*] distinct and forcible rather than melodious; the
> tone of him businesslike, sedately confident; no discourtesy, yet no
> anxiety about being courteous.[72]

In duration, in variety, in richness, Wordsworth's conversation was remarkable.   Quoting what someone had said of
Burns, 'He is great in verse, greater in prose, and greatest in
conversation,' Rogers applied it to Wordsworth in 1842: 'So it
is of all great men—Wordsworth is greatest in conversation.' [73]

Many persons have commented on the ceaselessness of Wordsworth's flow of words, but with different feelings about it.   An
opinionated and highly eccentric Scotch lady, Mrs Anne Grant,

of Laggan, was disturbed that the poet did not spend all his time meditating: 'Wordsworth, they say, talks incessantly; his conversation has the perpetual flow of a stream—monotonous in sound and endless in duration.'[74] Of a breakfast given by Taylor about 1840 to bring together Carlyle and Wordsworth, the Scotchman said: 'Breakfast was pleasant, fairly beyond the common of such things. Wordsworth seemed in good tone, and, much to Taylor's satisfaction, talked a great deal.'[75] And Mary Fletcher gaily described in August 1841 what seems almost a marathon performance: 'Mr Wordsworth, Miss Fenwick, and Mrs Hill came to dine, and it rained the whole day, but happily the Poet talked on from two to eight without being weary, as we certainly were not.'[76]

Whether Wordsworth delivered monologues or conversed as with a friend depended a good deal on his interlocutors. Caroline Fox, the young Quaker who knew many literary men and women and recorded their talk in her journal, was apparently no more than an audience, but she realized that for others there was more give and take. Even before meeting the poet, she wrote down in 1841 what she could glean of his conversational habits:

To strangers whom he is not likely to see again he converses in the monologue style as the mood is upon him, but with his friends he is very willing, and indeed desirous, of hearing them state their own opinions.[77]

The next year, when she heard that he was staying at old Mrs Hoare's, she went immediately to see and hear him. Then she wrote in her journal:

When speaking earnestly, his manner and voice become extremely energetic; and the peculiar emphasis, and even accent, he throws into some of his words, add considerably to their force. He evidently loves the monologue style of conversation, but shows great candour in giving due consideration to any remarks which others may make.[78]

Two years later, in October 1844, she and her sister went to the Lakes and called twice at Rydal. 'He was in great force,'

she wrote, 'and evidently enjoyed a patient audience. . . .
The old man looks much aged; his manner is emphatic, almost
peremptory, and his whole deportment is virtuous and
didactic.' [79]

Crabb Robinson saw another side, and so did Julius Hare.
The diarist wrote from Rydal Mount at Christmas 1842 that
Wordsworth was no speaker of *bons mots*, but a conversationalist
and disputant.[80]   When the Hares visited the Arnolds in the
summer of 1844, Miss Hare said of the poet and her brother:
'He is most kind-hearted, with all the simplicity and love of
nature that his poetry bespeaks, and he and Julius have much
pleasant conversation together, to which we listen.' [81]   The
Fletchers, too, knew the other Wordsworth, for—orator though
he sometimes was—he was often a sympathetic listener.   Mrs
Davy, one of Mrs Fletcher's daughters, has preserved a
charming picture, that same July:

> . . . his venerable head; his simple, natural, and graceful attitude
> in his arm-chair; his respectful attention to the slightest remarks or
> suggestions of others in relation to what was spoken of, his kindly
> benevolence of expression as he looked round now and then on the
> circle in our little parlour . . . [82]

Mrs Sigourney said: 'His conversation has that simplicity
and richness for which you are prepared by his writings.' [83]

A youthful spirit often permeated Wordsworth's talk.   In
his seventies he still looked to the future, to possible journeys
and new experiences.   Italy lured him, and he cherished the
hope of making a second visit there.   'He still indulges the
hope of one day going to Naples,' wrote Robinson in his diary
in 1840.[84]   The air-castle began to take more definite shape,
part of the radiant scheme being to show the favourite spots
to his friend, Miss Fenwick.   With the companion of
his former Italian tour, Wordsworth discussed the matter
during the Christmas visit of 1841–2.[85]   The idea was not
abandoned by June, but indeed seemed to be gaining strength.
'Wordsworth talked about his own affairs with feeling,' said
Robinson.   Then he added—partly in shorthand, as if convey-

ing a great secret—'if he got a pension he expected he would be able to go abroad and live a year in Italy. In that case I would join him.' [86] The dream might have materialized had it not been for Miss Fenwick's losses through the failure of the Bank of the United States and the temporary defaulting of her Pennsylvania Bonds.

Wordsworth anticipated, also, another journey to France even when he was seventy-nine years old.[87]

The health of the poet and his disposition did much to form his tastes and habits, and these in turn contributed to his physical well-being. Frugally he lived and simply, eschewing strong drink and even tobacco, and his bodily vigour drove him to constant activity. His wife wrote casually of him at seventy-four, as excuse for his not writing, that he was 'too tired by hard work in the Hay-field.' [88] The next summer, Wordsworth wrote: 'I overlaboured and overheated myself with my axe and saw.' [89] Running up a hill was apparently nothing to the hardy septuagenarian.[90] Though he defended angling (contrary to his attitude toward hunting and other slaughterous sports),[91] and continued his skating into his old age, Wordsworth was pre-eminently a walker.

For hours he could walk, without fatigue, and he liked to converse while he walked. His habit was to go four or five steps and then turn to his companion to emphasize what he was saying. Crabb Robinson's diary and letters are full of walks with Wordsworth—in London, in the Lake District, in and around Bath, and at Malvern. Mrs Fletcher also records many walks with the poet, especially up Easedale behind her house. The following account of 21st December 1843 is typical:

Wordsworth and Miss Fenwick . . . came early, and, although it was misty and dingy, he proposed to walk up Easedale. We went by the terrace, and through the little gate on the fell, round by Brimmer Head, having diverged a little up from Easedale, nearly as far as the ruined cottage. . . . He said on the terrace: 'This is a striking anniversary to me; for this day forty-four years ago, my sister and I took up our abode at Grasmere, and three days after we found out this walk, which long remained our favourite haunt.' [92]

Henry Taylor wrote an account of a day in London with Wordsworth in May 1842:

Yesterday I almost spent the day with him, and it was well for me that I could walk pretty stoutly, for, beginning by telling me that he had a lame leg and could not walk as well as usual, he walked from Upper Spring Street . . . to Upper Grosvenor Street, from thence to the end of Grosvenor Place, then to the Colonial Office (where we dined . . .), then to the House of Lords, and when we came out of that (I having been long uneasy about the fatigue he was undergoing, not to mention the lameness) he proposed that we should take an omnibus to Baker Street, look in upon Mrs Wordsworth, and then take half an hour's walk in the Regent's Park. . . . And from the beginning of the day to the end never did he cease talking, and for much of the time with his best vivacity.[93]

'So long as his legs would carry him,' said Calvert, who saw the poet at Malvern the last summer of his life, 'Wordsworth never tired of rambling.' [94]

With Wordsworth, the line between an afternoon walk and a walking tour was vaguely drawn if drawn at all. In his old age he continued this larger wandering, sometimes walking, but often supplementing with a carriage. He repeated his Duddon tour in 1840, and again in 1844. When Dora was married, the poet revisited Tintern and Chepstow on the way to Bath, and Alfoxden afterwards. He and Mrs Wordsworth then went to Exeter and Plymouth, to Salisbury and Winchester, and to London, returning by way of Coleorton. They were away from home almost four months.[95]

The poet acknowledged his passion for *wandering*, in the Fenwick notes.[96] And Quillinan, the son-in-law, wrote to Crabb Robinson in June 1843: 'Once started, there is no telling whither he may wend, Here awa' there awa' wandering Willie.' [97]

It was not only for the exercise that Wordsworth wandered far and wide. That love of nature with which his poems

abound was one of the realities of his everyday life. Whether
in Rome or London, in Alfoxden or Inversnaid, or in his
beloved Lake District, he felt exquisite joy in observing the
world about him. He saw more than most men see, and in
what he saw he experienced greater happiness.

The beauties of nature in Rome he enjoyed far more than
records of history or works of art.[98] He spoke of the beauty
of the flowers and ferns that grew on the walls of the Coliseum
as its best attraction.[99] His keen pleasure in creeping laburnum
growing on some houses in London, in May 1842, surprised
Henry Taylor.[100]

In 1841 the poet searched out an old larch at Alfoxden which
he had known more than forty years earlier,[101] and near Liége
found 'a tree which he had reposed under forty-eight years
ago.'[102] Touring Scotland with his daughter in 1831, he
wrote of cloud and mist effects:

The rainbows and coloured mists floating about the hills were
more like enchantment than anything I ever saw, even among the
Alps. There was in particular, the day we made the tour of Loch
Lomond in the steam-boat, a fragment of a rainbow, so broad, so
splendid, so glorious, with its reflection in the calm water, it
astonished every one on board.[103]

Custom could not stale, for Wordsworth, the infinite variety
of the Lakes. Half the pleasure of wandering must have been
the return home. On the last Duddon trip, the effects of a
sleepless night were all forgotten in the ecstasy of discovering
a little bunch of harebell growing out of an old stone wall.[104]
In September 1840, after a visit at Lowther, Wordsworth took
Rogers home with him.

We alighted at Lyulph's Tower [he wrote to Lady Frederick] and
saw the waterfall in great power after the night's rain, the sun
shining full into the chasm, and making a splendid rainbow of the
spray. Afterwards . . . we saw the lake to the greatest possible
advantage. Mr R. left on Thursday, the morning most beautiful,
though it rained afterwards. I know not how he could tear himself
away from this lovely country.[105]

He loved every tarn and crag, every copse and terrace in the Lakes.

In his own back-yard, moreover, Wordsworth found stimulus for occasional poems and matter for days and days of quiet happiness. When Inman went to Rydal Mount in August 1844, to paint Wordsworth's portrait, he noticed the effect of light and shadow made by sunlight and glancing leaves. Calling the poet's attention to it, he was surprised that Wordsworth had already put the 'press of sunshine' into a poem.[106]

The Poet accompanied me twice on my sketching excursions [said the artist], and pointed out various points of view, which seemed favourable as subjects for the pencil. In walking over his own grounds he would pause occasionally to invite my attention to some fine old tree. . . . He would point to its gnarled and tortuous trunk with the same gusto with which the statuary might scan a fragment from the chisel of Phidias. . . . The moss-covered rock, the shining cascade, the placid lake, or splintered mountain-pinnacle seemed each to constitute for him a prideful possession.[107]

It was inevitable that Wordsworth should be interested in the arrangement of natural beauties to the best advantage, and he was all but a professional landscape-gardener. Early in his life he had helped Sir George Beaumont to lay out his extensive grounds at Coleorton, and even at Dove Cottage he had built a summer-house and a garden seat from which to view the lake.

Walking one day in the later years with the curate of Windermere, Wordsworth stopped suddenly—to view a favourite scene from just the right point—and then told the clergyman that there were three callings for which he had been especially fitted, 'the callings of poet, landscape-gardener, and critic of pictures and works of art.'[108]

A walk with Wordsworth in the Lake District was 'a real treat,' said Justice Coleridge, in 1836:

I never met with a man who . . . had such exquisite taste for rural scenery: he had evidently cultivated it with great care; he not only admired the beauties, but he could tell you what were the peculiar features in each scene, or what the incidents to which it

c

owed its peculiar charm. . . . He combined, beyond any man with whom I ever met, the unsophisticated poetic delight in the beauties of nature with a somewhat artistic skill in developing the sources and conditions of them. In examining the parts of a landscape he would be minute; and he dealt with shrubs, flower-beds, and lawns with the readiness of a practised landscape-gardener. . . .[109]

The poet's grandson, the late Gordon Wordsworth, told me in August 1931 that Wordsworth wanted his youngest son to be a landscape-gardener—'to go into it seriously as a profession.' Mr Wordsworth felt that this showed how much ahead of his time his grandfather was, for though modern gardening had been developing in England for a century or more, it was mainly a gentleman's hobby in Wordsworth's day. 'It is only very recently,' said Mr Wordsworth, 'that people have made anything at it.'

Wordsworth was always helping his friends in the planning and planting of their grounds, sometimes actually doing the work. He helped Dr Arnold to find and purchase the property and build the home at Fox How. He advised the carpenters about the chimneys; his sister-in-law, Sara Hutchinson, laid out the garden.[110] He helped Mrs Fletcher, the beautiful old lady from Edinburgh, and her daughter in every detail about the purchasing and building of Lancrigg.[111] When Harriet Martineau moved to Ambleside, Wordsworth gave her much advice, and Crabb Robinson wrote to Mrs Wordsworth: 'I hear she is building herself a cottage, in which case I have no doubt she has had the aid of one who can build other than the lofty rhyme.'[112]

Lady Richardson, Mrs Fletcher's daughter, has left a picture of the poet, in 1842, planting for the future:

Wordsworth and Miss F[enwick] came early to walk about and dine. He was in a very happy kindly mood. We took a walk on the terrace, and he went as usual to his favourite points. On our return he was struck with the berries on the holly tree, and said: 'Why should not you and I go and pull some berries from the other side of the tree, which is not seen from the window? . . .' We pulled the berries, and set forth with our tool. I made the holes, and the Poet put in the berries. He was as earnest and eager about it, as if it had been a matter of importance; and as he put the seeds in, he every now and then muttered, in his low solemn tone, that beautiful verse from Burns's 'Vision':

> 'And wear thou this, she solemn said,
> And bound the holly round my head. . . .'

He clambered to the highest rocks in the 'Tom Intake,' and put in the berries in such situations as Nature sometimes does with such true and beautiful effect. He said: 'I like to do this for posterity . . . the past does much for us.' [113]

Occasionally Wordsworth's interest in improving a bit of ground was not shared by his visitors. W. R. Greg, a friend of Harriet Martineau's, did not enjoy Wordsworth; the poet was, 'in external manner and habit, too much of the peasant for Greg's intellectual fastidiousness. He called on one occasion at Rydal Mount, and Wordsworth, who had been regravelling his little garden walks, would talk of nothing but gravel, its various qualities, and their respective virtues.' [114]

At home, Wordsworth built three terraces, two in the grounds of Rydal Mount and another in the piece of land adjoining, which he bought and later gave to Dora that she and her husband might build on it. Terraces he particularly liked, as vantage points from which to view the lakes and the winding Rotha, and also as esplanades on which to pace while composing verses.

In April 1830 Dorothy wrote to Crabb Robinson: 'My Brother . . . has lately been busied day after day out of doors among workmen who are making us another new and most delightful Terrace.' [115] Since the last one at the Mount was not built until after the sister's health had failed—an easy, low place where her invalid's chair might be comfortably wheeled—this was apparently the terrace in the beautiful sloping ground later called 'Dora's Field.'

Wordsworth wrote to George Huntly Gordon, an old friend of Sir Walter Scott's,[116] of his activities in reclaiming it:

You ask me what are my employments. According to Dr Johnson they are such as entitle me to high commendation, for I am not only making two blades of grass grow where only one grew before, but a dozen. In plain language, I am draining a bit of spungy ground. In the field where this goes on I am making a green terrace that commands a beautiful view of our two lakes, Rydal and Windermere, and more than two miles of intervening vale with the stream visible by glimpses flowing through it. I shall have great pleasure in showing you this.[117]

It was in this field that he had a little pool for goldfish; here, too, was the hollow tree with the wren's nest partly hidden by a primrose. Up the hillside Wordsworth made winding paths pleasing to the eye and agreeable to tread upon. When friends came to visit him, and even friendly strangers, he took them about these pleasant places, and showed them his favourite views, especially a glimpse of the lake with the island framed by trees.

Within the grounds of Rydal Mount, at the end of the upper terrace, he had a little summer-house. He used to lead visitors into this summer-house, and then suddenly throw open the rustic door, giving his guests an almost overwhelming view.

Wordsworth loved Rydal Mount, though he never owned it. He loved its terraces and summer-house, its garden and lawns, its holly and laurel, its grassy paths and simple flowers. In the note to *Poor Robin*, dictated to Miss Fenwick in 1843, he said:

I often ask myself, what will become of Rydal Mount after our day. Will the old walls and steps remain in front of the house and about the grounds, or will they be swept away with all the beautiful mosses and ferns and wild geraniums and other flowers which their rude construction suffered and encouraged to grow among them? . . . 'What a nice well would that be,' said a labouring man to me one day, 'if all that rubbish was cleared off.' The 'rubbish' was some of the most beautiful mosses, and lichens and ferns and other wild growths, as could possibly be seen.[118]

Rydal Mount and its grounds are still entailed in the Fleming family, but 'Dora's Field' was until 1935 the property of Gordon Wordsworth. On a summer afternoon in 1931 I

had the incomparable pleasure of strolling with Mr Wordsworth through this 'field' and into the grounds of Rydal
Mount, and 'Dora's Field' was much as it had been in the
eighteen-forties.

'The poet made these paths,' said his grandson.   He showed
me the terrace, the tree that had harboured the wren's nest
protected by the primrose, and the spot where the goldfish pool had been—now a bed of lilies.   He beckoned me
down a hillside across the grass from one path to another, and
said: 'You can't imagine the wealth of daffodils there, in the
springtime.'   With reference to one tree in the grounds of
Rydal Mount, Mr Wordsworth said: 'That tree was not here
in my grandfather's time, and he wouldn't have liked to see it
here. . . . He wouldn't have anything but native trees on
his place.' [119]

Mr Wordsworth showed me, too (as the poet had shown to
the fiery young Chartist, Thomas Cooper, to Justice Coleridge,
to Emerson, to the Queen Dowager Adelaide, and to many
others), 'the island framed,' the two terraces at the Mount,
the summer-house, and the sudden, breath-taking view.

Wordsworth did not put nature above people; he even went
so far as to caution his visitors against expecting too much.
The poet Clough, 'when a boy of eighteen,' was shocked to
hear Wordsworth say: 'People come to the lakes . . . and
are charmed with a particular spot, and build a house, and find
themselves discontented, forgetting that these things are only
the *sauce and garnish* of life.' [120]   Later we shall take up Wordsworth's relation to his family and friends, but here we may
say that he *was* social-minded, that he liked to drop in casually
on his neighbours, that he was glad to play a rubber of whist
in the evening—especially in the later years—that he enjoyed
breakfasts and dinners in London, and that he sometimes went
to the theatre and the opera.

Some mention must be made of his manner of composing
and his custom of reciting his own verses to any audience and
in any spot.   When a maid was asked by a stranger to be

shown the poet's study, she 'took him to the library, and said:
"This is master's *library*, but he *studies* in the fields."' [121]
And one of Coleridge's grandsons was told that 'Wordsworth
went "sounding on his way"—murmuring or booming his
verses as he paced up and down the level terrace.' [122]   An old
dame of Westmorland told Canon Rawnsley that 'many
times did she as a child walk to school at Ambleside alongside
of the poet, in his old blue military cape, who would
be "murmuring awt way and not *takking* a bit o' notish o'
nowt."' [123]

Once in a while Wordsworth must have composed indoors,
for Canon Rawnsley says: 'We may hear the crash of a plate,
which Mrs Wordsworth has ordered to be broken outside his
study door, to bring him to his dinner,' and then he quotes
the old dame again: '"for ya kna, Wudsworth was a careful
man, varra, and he could nat abide the brekking o' his chiney,
and nowt else would sarra to stir 'im, when he was deep i
study."' [124]   So intense was the poet's concentration that his
whole system felt the strain.   Once he found that an injured
foot did not get well until he gave up composing:

> Though I desisted from walking, I found that the irritation of the
> wounded part was kept up by the act of composition, to a degree
> that made it necessary to give my constitution a holiday.   A rapid
> cure was the consequence. [125]

Wordsworth did recite his poetry to friend and stranger
alike

> with an enthusiasm of wondering admiration that would have been
> profoundly comic but for its simple sincerity and for the fact that
> William Wordsworth, Esquire, of Rydal Mount, was one person,
> and the William Wordsworth whom he so heartily reverenced quite
> another. [126]

But his recitals were often at the definite request of his companions. [127]   William Ellery Channing was exalted by Wordsworth's reciting his own poetry at sunset, [128] and James T.
Fields urged him on to say poem after poem. [129]
Sometimes Wordsworth recited his verses spontaneously—

to the delight of his intimate friends.   At a party of Miss
Fenwick's, in 1839, Mary Fletcher asked him about Lancrigg,
the farm in Easedale which her mother was thinking of buying.
The poet became enthusiastic, and asked Mrs Wordsworth
to read the sonnet 'suggested to him there by the likeness of
a rock to a sepulchral stone in that hazel copse.   This she
did with much expression.' [130]   On the last Duddon excursion
Wordsworth felt the appreciation of his audience.   He

repeated several verses of his own, which he seemed pleased that
Serjeant Talfourd had repeated to him the day before.   He mentioned a singular instance of T. Campbell's inaccuracy of memory
in having printed as his own a poem of Wordsworth's, 'The Complaint': he repeated it beautifully as we were going up the hill to
Coniston. [131]

Drinking tea at Rydal Mount one autumn day in 1847, Mrs
Fletcher and Mrs Arnold begged Wordsworth to read *Lycoris*
to them, and 'he read the poem twice over, in his most
beautiful and impressive manner.' [132]

The zest of physical exercise, especially walking, a detailed
and fine appreciation of nature, the satisfaction of landscape-
gardening, the happiness of mixing with people, and the joy
of his own poetry—these were some of Wordsworth's pleasures.

Though others may have considered him somewhat aloof,
Wordsworth felt himself a part of whatever group he was
in, and usually enjoyed the companionship.   The dalesmen in
Westmorland he respected and liked; and they liked him too
—though sometimes with a mixture of condescension.   'Do
the people here . . . value Mr Wordsworth most because he
is such a celebrated writer?' Margaret Fuller asked her land-
lady.   'Truly, Madam,' she answered, 'I think it is because
he is so kind a neighbour.' [133]   Harriet Martineau, that none
too gentle critic, said: 'It is . . . as a neighbour among the
cottagers, that he is most genially remembered.' [134]   Dr
Chalmers said to Mrs Fletcher in 1846: 'I always felt attracted
to Wordsworth by his love for the common people.' [135]

Understanding the peasants as he did, the poet made an excellent go-between when one of his friends wanted to secure a piece of property. His trading with 'old Rowlandson' on Mrs Fletcher's behalf brought the original price down seventy pounds, and yet, wrote Dora, 'the price was very handsome, and more than he was likely to get from any other person.' [136] Wordsworth argued about the time, too, when Mrs Fletcher might move in. But when Rowlandson spoke of 'the custom of the country,' the Westmorland poet said that 'doubtless Mrs Fletcher would be willing to abide by the custom.' Though unwilling to be imposed upon, Wordsworth was no hard trader.

He made a point of upholding the rights of the villagers when some great lord enclosed what had been public property. Perhaps the injustice practised on his father by Sir James Lowther had deepened his tendency to resent encroachment on the rights of the people. Justice Coleridge tells of going through the Glenridding Walks with Wordsworth in 1836:

I remember well, asking him if we were not trespassing on private pleasure-grounds here. He said, no; the walks had, indeed, been inclosed, but he remembered them open to the public, and he always went through them when he chose. [137]

Later, at Lowther, a lord who had enclosed some public grounds near Penrith accused Wordsworth and the judge of having trespassed, and the poet answered him with great vigour. 'He had evidently a pleasure,' said Justice Coleridge, 'in vindicating these rights, and seemed to think it a duty.'

And yet the country folk did not usually feel that he was one of them.

Wordsworth . . . was a great poet [said Thomas Arnold], and his life was lived in a sense apart; and though he could discuss trivialities and domestic matters, and sometimes seem heartily amused by them, I suppose there was a general want of practicality . . . which raised a barrier between him and the Westmorland people. [138]

A few stories circulated about the poet reflect the attitude of the Westmorland folk toward the great man who dwelt among them. When Mary Fletcher, in 1841, urged one of the builders at Lancrigg to make the chimneys like those at Fox How because '"Mr Wordsworth thinks they are the best for this country, and we must do what he tells us," "Yes," said the man deliberately, "m'appen he *has* as much sense as most on us."' Charles Mackay's story is less complimentary. An American visitor inquired of a Westmorland woman the way to Rydal Mount. Though near the famous home, the poor woman did not seem to understand, until the stranger mentioned the word *poet*:

'Oh, the poet,' she replied; 'and why did you not tell me that before? I know who you mean now. I often meet him in the woods, jabbering his pottery (poetry) to hisself. But I'm not afraid of him. He's quite harmless, and almost as sensible as you or me.' [140]

When Wordsworth went murmuring along the road, the peasants did not dare to disturb the stones or bushes. Once, Hartley Coleridge greeted a man with 'Good morning, John, what news have you this morning?' and he answered: 'Why, nowte varry particler only old Wudswurth's brocken lowce ageen.' [141]

The peasants' grudging respect for Wordsworth is given by Canon Rawnsley:

Nivver a man as laughed not to saay right owt, but a decent quiet man, well spokken on by his sarvants at t' Mount, terble kind to fowkes as was badly and very highly thowt on, paid his way reglar, vara particler an aw about his accounts, and that was Mrs Wordsworth's doing ye kna, for she was a reglar manasher. Turble fond o' study out 'rwoads, specially at night time, and wi' a girt voice bumming awaay fit to flayte aw the childer to death ameaast. . . . Quite yan o' us ye kna, not a bit o' pride in him for o quality thowte ot warld on 'im. But he wasn't a man as was thowte a deal o' for his potry when he was hereabout. It had no laugh in it same as Lile Hartley's. . . . It was kept oer long in his head mappen.[142]

His more refined neighbours found Wordsworth more congenial. The poet and Mrs Wordsworth attended and gave large dinners, and sometimes had picnics on the Island in Lake Windermere, or informal gatherings in their own hay-

field.[143]   Robinson's diary through his Christmas visits is full
of casual calls made with the poet.[144]

   During Robinson's visits Wordsworth and Miss Fenwick,
Mrs Wordsworth and Crabb Robinson played whist almost
every evening.   Well ahead of Christmas time, Wordsworth
began to anticipate the card-playing, for in October 1841 he
wrote to 'the Crabb': 'Pray promise to come down for a
month at Christmas!   Miss F. consents to play whist, after
her fashion every evening—so do Mary and I.' [145]   One week
of Robinson's diary shows the frequency of 'rubbers' at
Rydal Mount:

Jan. 8, 1841. I found both Wordsworth and Miss Fenwick better.
. . . I read there and we played whist both before and after tea.

Jan. 9. The rest of the day was spent at home and up the hill—
No variety in one's occupation, reading at home and in the evening
a little whist.

Jan 12. A company of young people.   We seniors sat apart retired
playing whist.

Jan. 14. I dined and spent the evening at Wordsworth's.   We
played whist as usual.[146]

When the barrister was not there, Edward Quillinan often
made the fourth; sometimes, Dora.   Now and then an outsider filled in, such as the Rev. Mr Hill, Bertha Southey's
husband.   The card-playing continued year after year.   Wordsworth's 'great resource,' said Mary Russell Mitford, in 1846,

is whist—the great resource of age.   Somebody comes to see him and
brings two packs of cards, which last till the same somebody comes
again the following year.[147]

The 'somebody' was Crabb Robinson, who—teasing his own
brother about not playing whist—said: 'A great loss to yourself, as Wordsworth declared it would have been to him late
in life if he had not possessed it.' [148]   A set of whist markers
is still preserved at Dove Cottage.

   Mary Fletcher, dining at the Mount a few days before Christmas, 1846, with her nephew Henry, Mrs Arnold, Harriet

Martineau, and Crabb Robinson, was impressed with the neighbourliness and naturalness of their host:

He expressed himself very sweetly at dinner on the pleasant terms of neighbourly kindness we enjoyed in the valleys. It will be pleasant in after times to remember . . . his manner when he said this, it was done with such perfect simplicity and equality of feeling, without the slightest reference to self, and I am sure without thinking of himself at the time as more than one of the little circle whose friendly feeling he was commending.[149]

In his old age Wordsworth was called upon for various social duties: to stand godfather for infants, to give away young women in matrimony, to be present at opening of church or school. When Frederick Myers opened his parish school he had Wordsworth at his side, to increase the dignity of the ceremony, but 'nothing could induce the old poet to make a speech; he simply bowed and said: "I agree with every word that Mr Myers has spoken."'[150]

The old man's seriousness sometimes surprised children. On the last Duddon excursion, for instance, Wordsworth and his friends came upon 'a very tiny boy, with a can of water in his hand.' The child looked at them 'in speechless amazement, when the poet said: "Is there a well here, my little lad?"'[151] The little girl at Tynwald Hill whom he singled out to recite the Lord's Prayer must have wondered, too. She recited the prayer, and the poet then began to expound the meaning; 'but I was not at all satisfied with my own part,' he said. 'Hers was much better done; and I am persuaded that, like other children, she knew more about it than she was able to express, especially to a stranger.'[152]

Crabb Robinson remembered Wordsworth at Nîmes lost in contemplation of 'two very young children at play with flowers.' After a while Robinson heard him say: 'Oh! you darlings, I wish I could put you in my pocket and carry you to Rydal Mount.'[153] Harriet Martineau shows him mingling with the children of Westmorland:

It used to be a pleasant sight when Wordsworth was seen in the middle of a hedge, cutting switches for a half-a-dozen children, who were pulling at his cloak or gathering about his heels.[154]

Had Wordsworth not been fond of children and at least fairly popular with them, Miss Fenwick would hardly have celebrated his birthday on two consecutive years with a great party for children. When he was seventy-three, a 'tea-drink' was given in his honour to about a hundred and thirty little girls.[155] The next year, the poet's birthday came on Easter Sunday, and on the following Tuesday several hundred children, boys as well as girls, were entertained in the grounds of Rydal Mount. The reports of this party were so extensive that they even reached American newspapers. Mary Fletcher's pretty picture shows Wordsworth with the children:

We arrived at Rydal Mount about three o'clock, and found the tables all tastefully decorated on the esplanade in front of the house. The Poet was standing looking at them with a very pleased expression of face. . . . The Grasmere boys and girls came first, and took their places on the benches placed round the gravelled part of the esplanade; their eyes fixed with wonder and admiration on the tables covered with oranges, gingerbread, and painted eggs, ornamented with daffodils, laurels, and moss, gracefully intermixed. The plot soon began to thicken, and the scene soon became very animated. Neighbours, old and young of all degrees, ascended to the Mount to keep the Poet's seventy-fourth birth-day, and every face looked friendly and happy. Each child brought its own mug, and held it out to be filled with tea, in which ceremony all assisted. Large baskets of currant cakes were handed round and liberally dispensed; and as each detachment of children had satisfied themselves with tea and cake, they were moved off, to play at hide and seek among the ever-greens on the grassy part of the Mount. . . . Miss F—, the donor of the fête, looked very happy, and so did all the Poet's household. The children, who amounted altogether to above 300, gave three cheers to Mr Wordsworth and Miss F—. After some singing and dancing, and after the division of eggs, gingerbread, and oranges had taken place, we all began to disperse.[156]

With Londoners Wordsworth was also at ease. He made a continuous round of breakfasts and dinners, and had many friends among the nobility as well as among literary persons. He attended Serjeant Talfourd's box-party for the *première* of

Ion in 1836, when Landor, Southey, Miss Mitford, and other writers were also guests. He was present at the fashionable reception of Miss Burdett-Coutts in June 1842.

William Jerdan says that he was not unsophisticated and that De Quincey, 'in some fit of resentment,' did him 'gross injustice.' The bitterness, according to Crabb Robinson, arose from the fact that when De Quincey married his mistress, 'the Wordsworth ladies did not call on his wife.' [157] After taking up the separate points made by De Quincey, Jerdan says:

I must protest that there was no warrant for this caricature; but, on the contrary, that it bore no feature of resemblance to the slight degree of eccentricity discoverable in Cumberland, and was utterly contradicted by the life in London. . . . Mr Wordsworth was facile and courteous; dressed like a gentleman, and with his tall, commanding figure—no mean type of the superior order, well trained by education and accustomed to good manners.[158]

The letter accepting the Laureateship is that of a man adept in the social conventions.

It is not in London, however, that we most frequently think of Wordsworth. In his native Lake District he spent his boyhood and most of his maturity, and there—except for frequent journeys—he would spend his old age.

His cordiality to strangers and semi-strangers who came to Rydal Mount is proverbial, and his hospitality is the more remarkable when we realize that hundreds of people every summer made demands on his time and his apparently inexhaustible energy. Thomas Cooper presented himself at Rydal Mount without an introduction. Just out of jail, he was shabby and travel-stained, and the housemaid at Rydal Mount was not impressed by his appearance. But when the enthusiastic young Chartist, taking a scrap of paper from his hat, scribbled a note and sent it in to the poet, he was made welcome. The visit was all that Cooper could have wished for; he was invited 'to take some refreshment in the adjoining room,' and Wordsworth received him as a fellow-poet.

When I hastened to depart [said the young man]—fearing that I

had already wearied him—he walked with me to the gate, pressing
my hand repeatedly, smiling upon me so benevolently, and uttering
so many good wishes for my happiness and usefulness, that I felt
almost unable to thank him.[159]

Until more than thirty years old Wordsworth had been very
poor, and he continued to be thrifty throughout his life.   He
told the Fletchers in 1845 that in his youth 'he had only a
hundred a year.   Upon this he lived, and travelled, and
married.' [160]   The estate left by his father was for a time
illegally withheld from Wordsworth and his brothers and
sister by Sir James Lowther, Lord Lonsdale.   It is true
that in 1795 Raisley Calvert had left the poet a legacy of
£900, and that in 1803 Sir George Beaumont gave him a piece
of property at Applethwaite and in 1827 left him a bequest
of £100 a year for an annual tour.   But if Wordsworth had
received his rightful heritage promptly, these smaller sums
would have been unnecessary.

At the death of Lord Lonsdale [said Austin and Ralph], who had
so long doggedly refused to pay the debt due to Wordsworth's father,
his successor immediately disbursed not only the original sum,
£5,000, but also £3,500 as interest upon it.[161]

As Dorothy always made her home with her brother, her share
may be reckoned with his, their two-fifths of the total being
£3,400.   At the death of the sailor-brother, at least half of
his share would presumably go to William and Dorothy,
bringing their joint total up to £4,250.   January Searle, publishing his *Memoirs of William Wordsworth* only two years after
the poet's death, mentions £1,800 as the share of each bene-
ficiary,[162] and Professor de Selincourt accepts this figure.   This
would make the share of William and Dorothy, with half of
John's share, £4,500.

Lord Lonsdale died on 24th May 1802, but the money
was not divided for three more years,[163] and the proper legal
documents were not drawn by Wordsworth's eldest brother,
Richard, until shortly before his death in 1816.[164]

The second Lord Lonsdale, later the Earl of Lowther, did not stop when he had paid his predecessor's debt and the accrued interest. He used his influence to obtain for Wordsworth the post of Distributor of Stamps for Westmorland, a position with not very onerous duties and an annual stipend of £400 or more.[165] Wordsworth held the distributorship from March 1813 to July 1842, when he resigned the post to his youngest son, who had been serving under him for 'more than eleven years.' The new arrangement did not greatly please William, for he felt that he was taking from his father income which the latter could ill spare. Crabb Robinson wrote in his diary for 26th May 1842:

William Wordsworth walked back with me. He was not in spirits—He is about to succeed his father as Distributor of the stamps . . . and cannot take anything from his father's limited income—so for the present he rather loses than gains—The emoluments of the Office have been greatly reduced by the Whig economical reforms—However there are hopes *that W. will have a pension given him, but he will not accept less than has been given to any one that has three hundred pounds*.[166]

Wordsworth had come to London on 4th May to do what he could toward transferring the stamp distributorship to his son and winning a pension for himself. In June a Whig paper carried the notice of the transfer of the stamp office and the granting of the pension.[167] But the stamp office was transferred in July,[168] and the question of the pension dragged on for months. 'I have only faint hopes of success,' wrote Crabb Robinson in May;[169] and in June: 'W: will I fear suffer a disappointment.' Sir Robert Peel had given one literary person £150 'out of his own pocket,' which to Robinson proved 'the groundlessness of W's opinion that there may be every year £5,000 additional pensions given.'[170]

Lord Monteagle[171] and Lord Lonsdale were using their influence, but the strongest advocate was Gladstone.[172] Apparently the main obstacle was a memorandum given to the poet by the retiring Whig Government, and presented by Gladstone to Sir Robert Peel.

The writing of this memorandum [wrote Sir Robert on 10th October] was a very shabby act. The late Government did nothing for Mr Wordsworth . . . and now — wants to get for himself the credit of being instrumental in procuring a pension for Mr Wordsworth.

I wish I had never seen this paper, for it is difficult for me to overcome the obstacle which it presents in my mind. . . .

I wish you would be good enough to return it to Mr Wordsworth, and say that if the late Government had intended to grant a pension to him they had ample means of doing it . . . that I do not attach the slightest weight to this memorandum; and that I think it ought not to have been written and sent to Mr Wordsworth.

Can you tell me confidentially what are his circumstances? If they are very straitened, I should be disposed (forgetting the memorandum) to recognize his claim as a very strong one.[173]

Gladstone answered that the poet's circumstances were straitened,[174] and the pension was granted on 15th October 1842—£300 a year for Wordsworth's lifetime.

I need scarcely add [wrote Sir Robert] that the acceptance, by you, of this mark of favour from the Crown, considering the grounds on which it is proposed, will impose no restraint upon your perfect independence, and involve no obligation of a personal nature.[175]

Wordsworth and his friends were jubilant. In his diary Crabb Robinson wrote:

October 18. W: writes with great pleasure of it. I went at night to Mrs Quillinan to rejoice with her about it—She is quite delighted —Now probably Wordsworth will go in the Spring to Naples or rather in the autumn.

October 29. The pension of W: is now in all the parties [papers] and I rejoice to find that not a single paper as far as I can hear or a single person even, snears [sic] or snarls at it.

November 2. I breakfasted this morning with Sam Rogers tete a tete. . . . Very little said about Wordsworth's Pension which however Rogers said he rejoiced in.[176]

And he wrote gaily to Mrs Wordsworth:

I should have written yesterday to express the fullness of my pleasure, but I wished first to have a little chuckling in private with

Dorina—So I went to her last night And found her quite happy I learned too, to my sorrow, that she had given herself the trouble to come all the way to Russell Square to be the bearer of the glad tidings—

There is but one draw-back on *my* satisfaction A little bit of party shame—I am still a whig and have whig-predilections—And now my imagination is disturbed by very offensive combinations—

The Whig-ministry and Lady Morgan—!

The Tories and the Poet!!

But the mortification is not such as to stand in the way of my feeling real heart-felt joy at an incident that will remove every shadow of discomfort and apprehension from the most sensitive and delicate mind. . . .[177]

In 1843 Wordsworth was made Poet Laureate, an honour carrying the annual stipend of £150.[178] Southey had told James Montgomery that the income, 'after deducting fees of office, amounted to little more than ninety pounds a year.'[179]

What Wordsworth earned from the sale of his poems was variable. At first the financial returns were negligible. Matthew Arnold's familiar statement is more picturesque: 'I have myself heard him declare that, for he knew not how many years, his poetry had never brought him in enough to buy his shoe-strings.'[180] As late as 1820 Wordsworth wrote: 'I have never been much of a salesman in matters of literature (the whole of my returns—I do not say *net profits*, but *returns*— from the writing trade not amounting to seven score pounds.)'[181] But with the poet's increased fame and with the sale of edition after edition, the emoluments gradually increased, and Aubrey de Vere said in 1845 that Wordsworth told him he 'had within the last seven years been making two hundred per annum by his poems.'[182] This increase was probably due to the sale of the 1836–7 collected edition.

Meanwhile, the income from his patrimony must have fluctuated with the years. Some of his money was invested in National Provincial Bank shares. These he planned to sell in October 1841, having already lost more than one-fifth on what he had sold.[183] Two months later, Philip Courtenay,

D

one of Wordsworth's executors and a stockholder of the bank, 'was found dead at an hotel at Liverpool from an overdose of morphine.' [184]   Fearing that Courtenay had committed suicide and that knowledge of this would shake public confidence in the bank, Crabb Robinson made investigations. But the bank was declared to be in good condition, and Courtenay was said to have had little stock; the jury declared his death accidental. Wordsworth got rid of this bank stock the following spring, sustaining a loss of £300 through a speculation of Courtenay's. [185]   It was about this time that he resigned his position as stamp distributor, and allowed his friends to get him a Government pension.

In addition to whatever capital he had accumulated and the income from his investments, Wordsworth had in the later years a regular annual income of about £750: £300 from the pension, £150 as Laureate, £100 from Sir George Beaumont, and about £200 from the sale of his poems. Though never wealthy, Wordsworth had a competency in his old age.

There is no denying that Wordsworth's nature was predominantly solemn. I believe that this was true even of the younger Wordsworth, and his seriousness did not lessen with the years. 'There is a solemnity and an earnestness about W:,' said Crabb Robinson in 1833, 'which inspire respect.' [186] 'Here is W:,' he said later, 'every day affirming with the solemnity of a Hebrew prophet that he would rather dye [sic] a thousand deaths than consent to yield any part of the Established Church in Ireland.' [187]

Wordsworth took his mission as poet seriously. More than most arts, he felt, poetry could elevate the spirit. With all his veneration for science, he would never grant that 'that which acts upon spirit through matter . . . can be regarded as an agency of an equally high order with that which acts upon spirit through spirit.' [188] Crabb Robinson sometimes twitted him on his veneration for poetry. [189] With great solemnity and eloquence Wordsworth recited his own verses;

Mrs Hemans was impressed by his 'almost patriarchal simplicity.' [190] When he heard in 1837 that an edition of his poems had been published in Boston, Wordsworth rejoiced in the extension of his influence for good. 'An author in the English language,' he said, 'is becoming a great Power for good or evil—if he writes with spirit.' [191]

With these bardic qualities Wordsworth was, of course, no professional wit. Thomas Powell made the sweeping statement:

Of all the superior intellects who have spoken or written, Wordsworth is undoubtedly one of the most incapable of humour. He cannot understand a joke, either mental or practical. Even when explained to him, he lays it on his logical rack, and there dissects it scientifically.[192]

And Sara Coleridge said in 1847 that Wordsworth did not appreciate humour:

One great characteristic of that genius [Carlyle's] is *humour*, and Mr W. never in his life appreciated any genius in which that is a large element. Hence his disregard for Jane Austen's novels, which my Father and Uncle so admired.[193]

Certainly Wordsworth was no Tom Moore, but he had his lighter moments, and his wit was sometimes amusing to his friends. Long before his death Wordsworth had become the object of a cult; and worshippers tend to mould their idols into heroic form, leaving to posterity their weighty remarks, but not their lighter conversation. Only a few of Wordsworth's witticisms have come down to us, and these few have probably been made more serious in the telling.

The poet could be jocular about the honours heaped upon him. Writing of the LL.D. granted by the University of Durham in 1838 he said to Crabb Robinson: 'Therefore, you will not scruple when a difficult point of law occurs to consult me.' [194] Robinson was so often asked whether Wordsworth had ever written an epigram that he put the question to Mrs Wordsworth:

Did the author of the Excursion ever write an epigram? I hear

Dorina burst out 'Oh no   He could not'—On which you reprovingly
say—My dear You should say he would not. . . . I do recollect by
the bye a naughty joke of his which might have involved him in a
duel had it been found out. . . .[195]

Robinson does not tell the 'naughty joke,' but William
Jerdan says that Wordsworth was 'often sportive, and could
even go the length of strong . . . expressions in the off-hand
mirth of his own observations. . . .' With Wordsworth,
Jerdan went to an exhibition at the Royal Academy, 'wherein
Turner had indulged his most defiant whim in colour by painting a Jessica looking out of her father Shylock's window.'
Wordsworth looked at 'the unlovely Jessica,' and said: 'She
looks as if she had supped off underdone pork, and been unable
to digest it in the morning.' [196]
The weaknesses in Wordsworth's personality have been
elaborately pointed out, but the accounts do not agree, and
exaggerated blame is often followed by equally exaggerated
praise. 'His warmest admirers,' said Austin and Ralph,
'would find it difficult to defend him against the charges of
vanity, egotism, and obstinacy.' [197] Toynbee mentioned a
visit that Wordsworth paid to Lord Spencer's library at
Althorp, 'when, according to the librarian, the only volumes
that he looked at were his own poems!' [198] 'He lives too much
alone,' said Charles Mackay. 'He does not associate with his
fellow men. He has shut himself up for years among the
mountains . . . he has ended by worshipping himself.' [199]
But so many of Mackay's statements are palpably untrue that
the others may be questioned. 'I don't think Wordsworth
has any enemies,' he said. '. . . He only requires to mix a
little with the world to be one of the best fellows who ever
lived.' [200]
Speaking of Wordsworth in May 1850, Henry Taylor
said: 'A composite character will always be inscrutable to
the many, very often even to the few.' [201] Persons who did
not know Wordsworth often considered him vain. But the
objectionable traits were on the surface; the admirable

ones, deeper down. Those who knew him best loved him most.

It is amusing to witness Mary Russell Mitford's conscious effort to *admire* Wordsworth, in 1817:

> I do not mean by 'admire' merely to like and applaud those fine passages which all the world must like, but to admire *en masse*—all, every page, every line, every word, every comma; to admire all day long. This is what Mr Wordsworth expects of his admirers. . . . One's conscience may be pretty well absolved for not admiring this man: he admires himself enough for all the world put together.[202]

And yet in 1836, when she came to know him, she not only admired but loved him.

> I had heard that Wordsworth was vain and egotistical [said the young Chartist], but had always thought this very unlikely to be true, in one whose poetry is so profoundly reflective; and I now felt astonished these reports should ever have been circulated.[203]

Though rather dogmatic in his own field—in his opinions of poetic theory and poets both contemporary and traditional— Wordsworth did listen to the opinions of others, and some-times modified his own opinions accordingly.[204]

Harriet Martineau seemed to feel an affection for her neigh-bour, and—in many ways—a deep admiration, but she was determined not to fall under his powerful spell. Again and again, though admitting the greatness of the man, she delighted in picking flaws.

> He is very interesting [she said, rather condescendingly, in February 1846] merely as an old poet without any W-ism to those who have seen him oftener than once or twice — His mind must always have been essentially liberal, but now it is more obviously and charmingly so than I understand it used to appear—The mildness of age has succeeded to what used to be thought a rather harsh particularity of opinion and manners. His conversation can never be anticipated. Sometimes he flows on in the utmost grandeur, that even you can imagine, leaving a strong impression of inspiration. At other times we blush and are annoyed at the extremity of bad taste with which he pertinaciously dwells on the most vexatious and vulgar trifles—The first mood is all informed and actuated by

knowledge of man; the other, a strange and ludicrous proof of his want of knowledge of men.

She thought him blind to the vices of the Westmorland peasants, and even unaware what their actual virtues were:

> I dare say you need not be told how sensual vice abounds in rural districts. Here, it is flagrant beyond any thing I ever could have looked for and here while every justice of the peace is filled with disgust and every clergyman with almost despair at the drunkenness quarrels and extreme licentiousness with women—here is dear good old W. for ever talking of rural innocence and deprecating any intercourse with towns lest the purity of his neighbours should be corrupted. [205]

Miss Batho says that Wordsworth saw all that Harriet Martineau saw—and more—but was less concerned over the sensuality because he was less prudish.[206]

The poet's everyday companions often recognized the superiority of his mind. The invalid Carr, living at Ambleside, considered Wordsworth's occasional calls the intellectual stimulus of the week. When Miss Fenwick became a more and more satisfying companion, and Wordsworth went less frequently to call on Carr, the latter regarded Miss Fenwick 'as a sort of enemy.' [207] Miss Fenwick's cousin, Henry Taylor, spoke of the strength and elasticity of Wordsworth's mind in 1841.[208] Carlyle was struck with the keenness of Wordsworth's mind. The two were discussing the noted men of their day, and Carlyle remembered, years later,

> the excellent sagacity, distinctness and credibility of Wordsworth's little biographic portraitures of them. Never, or never but once, had I seen a stronger intellect, a more luminous and veracious power of insight, directed upon such a survey of fellow-men and their contemporary journey through the world. . . . You perceived it to be faithful, accurate, and altogether life-like, though Wordsworthian.[209]

Wordsworth was independent and honest, a man of the utmost integrity. When his opinion was asked he gave it—whether popular or not. Many of his admirers sent their own verses to him, and many received frank—even severe—criticism. To William Rowan Hamilton he wrote in 1827:

'You will have no pain to suffer from my sincerity'; but some of the specific criticism was not complimentary:

These are two of the worst lines in mere expression. . . . But the separation of the parts or decomposition of the word, as here done, is not to be endured.

Of the verses sent by Hamilton's sister Wordsworth said:

They are surprisingly vigorous for a female pen, but occasionally too rugged, and especially for such a subject; they have also the same faults in expression as your own, but not, I think, in quite an equal degree.[210]

Though in sympathy with Crabb Robinson on the Clarkson-Wilberforce affair, he frankly disapproved the publication of any of Southey's letters in June 1840,[211] because Southey, though mentally incompetent, was still alive. The poet was not in accord with his friend in 1844 on the Dissenters' Chapels Bill, a matter dear to Robinson. He wrote a long letter on the subject, and then would not let Mrs Wordsworth send it. When Crabb Robinson pressed him for his opinion, he wrote: 'I was averse to the Bill, and my opinion is not changed.'[212] He then began to list his reasons, and again was checked by love for his friend.

The poet's sensibility made him tolerant, and his sympathy was broad and deep. He was considerate of the feelings of others, and rejoiced in the affection bestowed upon him. 'The Giant Wordsworth—God love him!' Coleridge had said in 1798. 'When I speak in the terms of admiration due to his intellect, I fear lest these terms should keep out of sight the amiableness of his manners.'[213] His friend's unfailing sympathy Coleridge acknowledged six years later. Most well people, he said, are unsympathetic to an ill person—but not Wordsworth. 'Show me anyone,' he said, 'made better by blunt advice, and I may abate of my dislike to it, but I have experienced the good effects of the contrary in Wordsworth's conduct toward me.'[214]

Wordsworth became more tolerant with advancing years. He acted as peace-maker in 1841 between Southey's second wife and the estranged children.[215] 'My life here,' said Crabb Robinson in 1842, 'has been . . . very pleasant. W: is become more companionable being more tolerant than he used to be.'[216] Toward the religious fanatic, Richmond, as toward the Chartist, Thomas Cooper, the old man was friendly. His tolerance of the half-crazy Richmond, Crabb Robinson could hardly accept. When Quillinan wrote that the American had been at Rydal and had amused them all, Robinson wrote in his diary: 'How can W[ordsworth] tolerate a man who asserts that the six great English poets are Chaucer, Shakespeare, Spenser, Milton, Wordsworth and *Martin Tupper*!!!'[217]

To the end Wordsworth was vigorous in body, vigorous in mind, and vigorous in his emotional life. Though he never got over the shock of his daughter's death, and probably never would have done so had he survived a much longer time, he became more composed as time went on, and was able in company to be something of his former genial self. Miss Helen Darbishire says:

In reality his nature was first and last strongly passionate. It is not the mild and gentle who preach meekness as the saving quality of manhood, nor is it the innately conventional who feel the deeper values of law and custom. If he ever attained outward calm, it was the result of hard-won self-command, and if he came to seek the support of forms sanctioned by custom and tradition, it was not from weakness but, in part at least, from knowledge of rebellious energies in himself that needed control. The passionate intensity of his affections in youth was no whit relaxed in old age.[218]

And those who were in closest contact with him realized, or partly realized, his greatness. Crabb Robinson often regretted his inability to record important conversations— 'living in daily intercourse with the man whom I believe firmly posterity will recognize as the greatest English poet of the age.'[219]

II. WORDSWORTH'S FAMILY

Where'er my footsteps turned
Her voice was like a hidden Bird that sang;
The thought of her was like a flash of light
On an unseen companionship, a breath
Of fragrance independent of the Wind.'

The Recluse.

WORDSWORTH never forgot the debt he owed to Dorothy. Again and again throughout his poems he joyously acknowledged that she it was who sharpened his sensibilities, who saved him for poetry, who planted laughing flowers on an otherwise rugged rock. And when the beloved sister became only a shell of her former self, Wordsworth's affection never wavered. He seemed to love her even more when he could no longer depend on her devoted sympathy, but could only minister to her.

Dorothy Wordsworth was, in 1840, physically and mentally an invalid. Her health had given way in later middle life, but for a while her mind seemed unaffected. Always remarkable for her unselfishness, Dorothy was keeping house for her nephew, John Wordsworth, at Whitwick in Leicestershire, when she was attacked by the first serious illness of her life, 'an inflammation in the Bowels, caught by imprudent exposure, during a long walk.'[1] Mrs Wordsworth hurried to her, but apparently the danger was already past. This was in the spring of 1829, when Dorothy was fifty-seven.

She had been lonely at Whitwick, a loneliness which she valiantly denied even to herself. She missed the society of her brother, and longed to return to Rydal. When she was able to write, she spoke of the kindness of her brother and niece in sparing Mrs Wordsworth so long.[2] Mrs Wordsworth remained until 11th May, when the invalid was steadily improving.

Homesick as Dorothy was for Rydal Mount, she nevertheless went to Halifax to see old Mrs Rawson, who had mothered
her in her childhood and was now eighty-three years old.   At
Halifax she was ill again, and she did not reach home until
September.   From then on, she had a series of recoveries and
relapses, sinking gradually into the condition of a permanent
invalid.

When Dorothy first became ill, Wordsworth was unable to
contemplate life without her: 'Were She to depart, the Phasis
of my Moon would be robbed of light to a degree that I have
not courage to think of.' [3]

Writing about Coleridge to Professor Hamilton in June
1832, Wordsworth said: 'He and my beloved sister are the
two beings to whom my intellect is most indebted.' [4]

Not until the summer of 1835, when Dorothy was well over
sixty-three, do the letters carry any hint of her mental break-
ing.   On 23rd June,[5] Sara Hutchinson died, and Wordsworth wrote: 'One of our anxieties is over and not that which
we thought would first cease.' [6]   After this, Dorothy began to
be very difficult—made unreasonable requests, and emitted
wild sallies of wit and moanings almost simultaneously.
Though Mrs Wordsworth and Dora were considerate and even
affectionate, it was the poet who loved her most, and who
therefore suffered the keenest.

I feel my hand shaking [he wrote to Crabb Robinson], I have had
so much agitation to-day, in attempting to quiet my poor Sister,
and from being under the necessity of refusing her things that would
be improper for her.   She has a great craving for oatmeal porridge
principal[ly] for the sake of the butter that she eats along with it
and butter is sure to bring on a fit of bile sooner or later.   Her
memory is excellent; this morning I chanced to mutter a line from
Dyers Grongar Hill—she immediately finished the passage—reciting
the previous line and the two following.   Speaking of her faculties
she told me that Miss Hutchinson's vanishing had been a sad
shattering to them.[7]

Mrs Wordsworth urged Robinson to visit them at Christmas, that he might draw Wordsworth out of himself.   She

explained that with Dorothy's improved physical condition, the doctor was about to discontinue the use of opium. The new experiment, however, was so distressing to Wordsworth that he asked his friend to postpone the visit.[8]   When Crabb Robinson did make the trip a little later he wrote: 'Poor Miss W. is in a very melancholy state.   I have seen her once.' [9]

The radiant Dorothy—once known as Dolly and, by Coleridge, as Rotha[10]—had now become 'Aunty' and 'poor Miss Wordsworth.'   She spent most of her time in a wheel-chair or, latterly, in bed.   An attendant slept in the little room next to hers, the big front room on the first floor with the view of Lake Windermere.   Her condition was accepted so much as a matter of course that it was her lucid intervals that were chronicled rather than her debility, and the accounts are full of her improvement, her good health, her 'doing nicely.'   Now and then a newcomer would be shocked at Miss Wordsworth's condition, although another outsider might say that he could hardly tell that anything was wrong.   Despite daily fluctuations Dorothy's general condition remained unchanged.   When Joanna Hutchinson arrived at Rydal Mount in October 1836, she was shocked at the change in Dorothy.[11]

For a time Wordsworth thought of publishing his sister's Scotch tour, hoping that 'the taking it through the Press would be a profitable stirring of her mind'; he had even 'corrected and enlarged two little Poems which would have seen the light for the first time in this Publication.' [12]   But he abandoned the idea by the end of 1837, for it seemed indelicate to draw public attention to Dorothy 'in her present melancholy state.'

Three years later Crabb Robinson wrote in his diary:

Miss W. is amazingly improved—She can talk for a time rationally enough—but she has no command of herself and has the habit of blowing with her lips very loudly and disagreeably and sometimes of uttering a strange scream something between the noise of a turkey and a partridge but more shrill than ever [either].   She can be withdrawn from this only by being made to repeat verses which she does with great feeling, quite pathetically.[13]

He added on New Year's Day: 'Poor Miss W came down and sat a long time and was quite rational but unable to repress the impulse to make the noises above described.' He wrote to his brother that she could be drawn from the queer noises 'only by a request to repeat Verses—Which she does with affecting sweetness—She is fond of repeating her own pretty lines Which way does the wind blow?'[14]

'Friend Crabb' was always thoughtful of Dorothy. Sometimes, when writing a long, chatty letter, he would address it to the invalid sister, 'as dear Miss W: has a momentary pleasure in such things.'[15] Mrs Wordsworth would read it aloud to the family downstairs, and then send it upstairs—to Dorothy's great delight—and the invalid would then promise to answer it to-morrow.[16] She was not unaware of Robinson's attentions. Before the 1842 Christmas visit, Quillinan wrote: 'Miss Wordsworth counts the days till you come.—She is very well, and oftener merry than sad.'[17] And when Robinson was unable to be present the last Christmas of the poet's life, and sent a letter instead, Quillinan read the letter to the assembled family, and 'Miss Wordsworth . . . listened with more interest than she usually does to letters from any one.'[18]

It was Crabb Robinson who wrote of Dorothy Wordsworth when first he was told that her mind was beginning to fail: 'But the temporary obscurations of a noble mind can never obliterate the recollection of its inherent and essential worth.'[19]

Despite her childlike feebleness, her uncontrolled blowing with her lips, and her frequent irritability and unreasonableness, Dorothy was cherished always by her brother. His lasting affection for her was one of the beautiful things in his character. The late Dame Elizabeth Wordsworth, ten years old when her great-uncle died, said of the later relation between the poet and Dorothy: 'Others tell how his voice always softened at the mention of her name with a tenderness in which compassion for her present state never excluded gratitude for all she had once been.'[20] Harriet Martineau shows how the invalid was protected from prying eyes:

During the long years of this devoted creature's helplessness she was tended with admirable cheerfulness and good sense. Thousands of Lake tourists must remember the locked garden gate when Miss Wordsworth was taking the air, and the garden chair going round and round the terrace, with the emaciated little woman in it, who occasionally called out to strangers and amused them with her clever sayings.[21]

The Fenwick notes, dictated in the last decade of Wordsworth's life, are full of reminiscences of his sister. Now it is of her unusual sensibility, now a regret for something Dorothy has missed. The note to *Yarrow Visited*, for instance, reads:

I seldom read or think of this poem without regretting that my dear sister was not of the party, as she would have had so much delight in recalling the time when, travelling together in Scotland, we declined going in search of this celebrated stream, not altogether . . . for the reasons assigned in the poem.[22]

Constantly in conversation the poet mentioned his sister, and always with the deepest affection.

There is always something very touching [said Mrs Fletcher in December 1843] in his way of speaking of his sister; the tones of his voice become more gentle and solemn, and he ceases to have that flow of expression which is so remarkable in him on all other subjects. It is as if the sadness connected with her present condition was too much for him to dwell upon in connection with the past.[23]

Mary Fletcher reports his inability to sleep, on the 1844 Duddon excursion, because of 'the recollection of former days and people' crowding in upon him, 'and, most of all, my dear sister.'[24]

Sometimes Wordsworth pushed Dorothy's wheel-chair himself. Sometimes he led visitors quietly away so as not to disturb her. Now and then he introduced a guest to her. 'Our dear Sister,' wrote Mrs Wordsworth in June 1845, 'keeps in her usual way—her Br is at this moment drawing his Sister's Carriage in *the front*.'[25] Charles Mackay reports that when the invalid was wheeled near the place where he and the poet were chatting, Wordsworth took his arm and hurried him down a by-path. 'She does not like the presence of strangers,' he said, 'and I would not pain her for the world.' [26]   Thomas Cooper, however, Wordsworth presented to Dorothy during the same summer of 1846—possibly because the poet was himself attracted to the young Chartist.

The poet's aged and infirm sister [wrote Cooper] was being drawn about the courtyard in a wheeled chair, as we walked on the terrace. He descended with me, and introduced me to her—as a poet!—and hung over her infirmity with the kindest affection, while she talked to me. [27]

After the death of his daughter Wordsworth devoted himself even more sedulously to his sister, so that Dorothy sadly missed his presence whenever he was absent from home for even a brief visit. [28]   Crabb Robinson was amazed at the joy Wordsworth felt in his attendance on her. 'Poor Miss W:,' he wrote in January 1848, 'I thought sunk still deeper in insensibility—By the bye, Mrs W: says that almost the only enjoyment Mr W: seems to feel is in his attendance on her—and that her death would be to him a sad calamity!!!' [29]

This calamity the aged Wordsworth was spared, for his sister outlived him.   Strangely enough, as the poet's death approached, Dorothy seemed to regain her clarity of mind and to realize that the lifelong union was about to be broken. [30]

The late Mr Gordon Wordsworth told me, in August 1931, that posterity had not properly appreciated his grandmother. He spoke of her as a remarkable housekeeper and a gracious hostess.   It is difficult to evaluate Mary Wordsworth, for one is always comparing her with Dorothy, and few women can bear such comparison.   That the poet loved his wife cannot be doubted, nor that he depended on her for certain spiritual needs; but she was never the poetic inspiration which he found in his sister.   'She was the incarnation of good sense,' said Harriet Martineau, 'as applied to the concerns of the every-day world.' [31]   Mrs Basil Montagu, effusive and often undiscriminating, said: 'I have met with very few faultless people in my journey through life, but Mrs Wordsworth seemed to me faultless.' [32]   All who write of the poet's wife speak of her calm and—in the two great sorrows of her old age—her resignation.

Mrs Wordsworth was not beautiful, except in so far as the placidity of her character and the sweetness of her nature gave to her face a certain beatitude.   One of her eyes had a slight squint and was of no use to her, but she was strangely unaware of this until she was thirty years old.[33]

Dear Mrs Wordsworth [said Thomas Arnold] was universally beloved.   At the time when I first knew her she had lost all the beauty which made her in her prime 'a phantom of delight' to her poet; but the kindness of her looks, tones, and actions was rightly valued by all who knew her.   She spoke with a strong but very pleasing Westmoreland accent.[34]

Ellis Yarnall describes her after Dora's death:

She seemed most refined and simple mannered, about the same age as her husband, slender, her face much furrowed, features small; she was dressed in black.   I could see that she was still mistress of her household, presiding with dignity and natural grace. . . . There was tenderness in the tones of his voice when speaking with his wife.   'Peace settles where the intellect is meek' is a familiar line from one of the beautiful poems which Wordsworth addressed to her, and this seemed peculiarly the temper of her spirit—peace—the holy calmness of a heart to which love had been an 'unerring light.' [35]

Mrs Hare, visiting the Arnolds in July 1844, met the poet and his wife. 'I was most . . . attracted,' she said, 'by the sweet old face of Mrs Wordsworth.' [36]

Her voice was ever gentle, soft, and low; and it grew fainter with old age. In 1847, when the poet and his wife were almost seventy-seven, Sara Coleridge wrote: 'Dear Mrs Wordsworth is a wonderful person of her years—so active and so independent.   Her face is aged since I saw her last and her voice is fainter than it used to be, though it was always low.' [37]   She wrote later: 'Mrs Wordsworth reads so faintly that I could not catch the contents of your letter this morning distinctly.'

'Dear Mrs Wordsworth is what she always was,' wrote Crabb Robinson after Dora's death. 'I see no change in her, but that the wrinkles of her careworn countenance are somewhat deeper.' [38]   Mrs Wordsworth is quoted as having said 'that the worst of living in the Lake region was that it made one unwilling to die when the time came.' [39]   And the same calm satisfaction is mentioned again and again by those who saw the quiet little woman at the poet's side.

Mrs Wordsworth was more than a gracious hostess. Rydal Mount is not a small house, and it was often filled to overflowing. Dinner-parties and picnics were common, to say nothing of a round of whist. Even strangers who came to lionize her husband were invited in by Mrs Wordsworth to take a cup of tea or a glass of wine. House-guests were so frequent that it was subject for comment when no one was there. Some of Mrs Wordsworth's activities at seventy-two are described in a letter written by her son-in-law:

John and his three boys, and William and a friend of his are at Rydal, and what with looking after the children and entertaining her Son's guest, receiving visiters [sic], that swarm at this season, in spite of the wet, and visiting her poor Nephew John etc., etc. she is more than fully occupied just now. [40]

She also nursed the sick—kinsfolk and servants [41]—and quietly mothered irresponsible Hartley Coleridge. [42]   Margaret Fuller speaks of the admiration that the villagers felt for Mrs Wordsworth, [43] and Harriet Martineau bears elaborate testimony to her influence for thrift and orderliness. [44]

Carlyle paints Mrs Wordsworth as snobbish, anxious for her social position. Wordsworth, he says, accepted his lionism and was not affected by it, whereas

his wife, a small, withered, puckered, winking lady, who never spoke, seemed to be more in earnest about the affair, and was visibly and sometimes ridiculously assiduous to secure her proper place of precedence at table. [45]

Henry Taylor discounts Carlyle's criticism, [46] but Mrs Wordsworth's strange pride in her daughter and her condescension

Mrs Wordsworth

Miniature by Miss Gillies

toward the factory workers coming by rail to the Lake District were not free from superciliousness. Of the workers she said 'that a green field with buttercups would answer all the purposes of Lancashire operatives, and that they did not know what to do with themselves when they came among the mountains.' [47] And she felt that Dora should be shielded from experiences suitable enough for ordinary persons:

Mrs Wordsworth has all her life wished her daughter to be above both marriage and authorship, and finds it hard to submit to these vulgarities on her behalf in this stage of her life career.[48]

Much has been written of Mrs Wordsworth's devotion to her husband. 'His wife is perfectly charming,' wrote Harriet Martineau, 'and the very angel he should have to tend him.' [49] Another visitor spoke of 'that Christian calmness and gentleness and love which . . . made her almost like the Poet's guardian angel for near fifty years.' [50] She acted as his amanuensis even when suffering from rheumatism, and her joy in serving him was mingled with her innocent pride in his fame.

When the poet took James T. Fields in to sit by his dining-room fire, in 1847, Mrs Wordsworth rose to greet them. All through the visit she listened eagerly to everything that her husband had to say. Fields was impressed by her devotion. 'When she raised her eyes to his, which I noticed she did frequently, they seemed overflowing with tenderness.' And when Wordsworth took the guest into the library, 'Her spare little figure flitted about noiselessly, pausing as we paused, and always walking slowly behind us as we went from object to object in the room.' [51]

Mary Wordsworth was not, however, merely the worshipper. To Crabb Robinson she questioned her husband's opinion of his own health.[52] She knew, too, her ability to help him get the editions ready for the printer.[53] She even ventured to criticize his literary activities, urging Robinson, in 1836, not to encourage him in occasional poems, but gently to persuade him to work on the unfinished *Recluse*.[54]

E

Mrs Wordsworth told one story [55] which showed that, sometimes at least, she had a will of her own—especially when encouraged by the irrepressible Dora. The poet and Mrs Wordsworth had planned to go to Brigham to visit their grandchildren, and Dora had come over to stay with her invalid aunt. Then such a storm came up that Wordsworth and William considered the trip impracticable; whereupon Dora urged: 'Mother, let you and I go.' Mrs Wordsworth agreed, and was making arrangements with the servant James to drive them over, even though 'the Lord and Master at first said, *"remember you go against my consent."'* Finally Wordsworth compromised, putting them in James's care, 'to return or not, as our way was found to be practicable or otherwise—and we consented to this arrangement.'

It was natural that Mrs Wordsworth, understanding her husband as she did, should be able to soothe him. During the hard summer when his sister's illness began, the poet was frequently depressed in spirits, and Mrs Wordsworth, noticing that he was often revived by a visit to the rock at Thorney How, used to suggest his going there.[56]

When the beloved Dora lay dying, in July 1847, Mary Russell Mitford wrote: 'Mrs Wordsworth will feel her daughter's death more than her husband.' [57] But Miss Mitford was probably mistaken. Though deeply affected, Mrs Wordsworth was able to bear her own grief and share that of her husband.[58] His suffering seemed more appalling to her than her own.[59]

This meek little woman was throughout their life together a source of strength to Wordsworth. His affection for her is apparent. His joy at being honoured by a visit from the queen dowager in 1840 was doubled by her cordiality to Mrs Wordsworth.[60] Harriet Martineau tells the story of an old friend who insisted on talking to Wordsworth about De Quincey:

'He says your wife is too good for you.' The old Poet's dim eyes lighted up instantly, and he started from his seat, and flung himself against the mantelpiece, with his back to the fire, as he cried with loud enthusiasm—'And that's *true*! *There* he is right!'[61]

Knowing the old couple intimately, and loving them both, Sara Coleridge once said: 'I often think with shuddering of his Mr W[ordsworth]'s misery, should he survive his wife.'[62]

He not only loved and respected her, but relied on her judgment. When the painter, Henry Inman, did his portrait of Wordsworth, he noted

the close and kindly sympathy that seemed to bind the aged Poet and his wife together. . . . She sat close at his side, when the sittings were taken, and the good old man frequently, in the course of a conversation mainly addressed to myself, turned to her with an affectionate inquiry for her opinion respecting the sentiment he had just expressed, and listened with interest to her replies.[63]

Wordsworth sometimes deferred to Mrs Wordsworth's opinion in his critical comment on other writers,[64] and even in the arrangement of his own poems.[65]

Praise from his wife made the poet 'radiant with joy.' Miss Fenwick recounts an incident when he came to her cottage so happy that she knew 'something had occurred which had delighted him exceedingly.' To her challenge that he had been very successful that morning the old man agreed, and then added:

'And I must tell you what Mary said when I was dictating to her this morning. . . . "Well, William, I declare you are cleverer than ever,"' and the tears started into his eyes, and he added: 'It is not often I have had such praise; she has always been sparing of it.'[66]

It was his delight to credit Mrs Wordsworth with the composition of two lines in *I wandered lonely as a cloud*:

> They flash upon that inward eye
> Which is the bliss of solitude.[67]

'The two best lines in it,' he said to Miss Fenwick, 'are by Mary.'[68]

Wordsworth wrote many poems about his wife, and in most of them he commended her meekness, her resignation, the humility of her spirit.   Though he paid an occasional compliment to her appearance, many of the poems say that she was definitely not beautiful; sometimes, he even suggests that her plainness is an asset because his love has more to confer!

Fully two years before his marriage Wordsworth wrote, late in 1799 or early in 1800, the poem *To M. H.*—'Our walk was far among the ancient trees'; and two years later, when he and Dorothy were going to bring home the bride, he referred to her in *A Farewell* as 'a gentle maid whose heart is lowly bred.'

The best known of the poems to Mrs Wordsworth, *She was a phantom of delight*, had for its germ a fleeting glimpse of a young highland girl, probably fourteen years old, whom the poet saw at Inversnaid in 1803.[69]   There was evidently a good deal of question during the poet's lifetime as to the subject of this poem, for Wordsworth was continually making the statement that the poem was written to his wife.   Mrs Clarkson wrote to Crabb Robinson in May 1842:

. . . am quite sure that he told me that the first two lines were suggested to him by the sight of a young girl of whom I was speaking to him & who to look upon was indeed 'a phantom of delight.' . . . I may be wrong but if you think I am ask the Poet himself & let him decide betw. us.[70]

Crabb Robinson appended to Mrs Clarkson's letter the following note: 'N.B. The Poet expressly told me that the Verses were on his Wife.'   The editor, Miss Edith J. Morley, adds: 'This is confirmed by Mr Gordon Wordsworth.'

Shortly after the 1842 edition had come out Crabb Robinson called on Wordsworth and discussed the individual poems. He recorded in his diary on 12th May:

W: said that the poems 'Our walk was far among the antient [*sic*] trees,' ii. 297—then 'She was a phantom of delight'—next, 'Let other bards of angels sing,' i. 158—and finally, the two Sonnets, 'To a Painter' in the new volume, p. — [*sic*] but of which the first is only of value as leading to the second—should be read in succession as exhibiting the different phases of his affection for his wife.[71]

Robinson does not mention in this list the two (or perhaps

three) references to her in the *Prelude*, the short lyric, *O dearer far than light and life are dear*, or the two poems not published until 1845 and probably not written until then, *Forth from a jutting ridge* and *Yes, thou art fair, yet be not moved*.

In the *Prelude*, vi, lines 223–30, Wordsworth refers to his wife's 'placid under-countenance' and 'meek confiding heart.' In xiv, lines 266–75, he says of her:

> She came, no more a phantom to adorn
> A moment, but an inmate of the heart,
> And yet a spirit, there for me enshrined
> To penetrate the lofty and the low,

comparing her to the light that shines in 'the brightest of ten thousand stars' and in 'the meek worm.' In xii, lines 151–73,[72] the poet does not so obviously refer to Mrs Wordsworth, and yet he mentions her gentleness, her piety, her gratitude:

> She welcomed what was given, and craved no more.

The line

> Peace settles where the intellect is meek,

quoted so often in Mrs Wordsworth's life as epitomizing her, occurs in *O dearer far than light and life are dear*, and it is in this poem that Wordsworth urges his wife to strengthen his faith in immortality.

Of those verses cited by Wordsworth as 'exhibiting the different phases of his affection for his wife,' one has a very strange stanza which was later omitted. Professor Henry Reed has supplied in a footnote the second stanza of *Let other bards of angels sing*, which was excluded from the 1845, the 1850, and most subsequent editions.[73] The complete poem, both in its frank, unpoetic passages and in the beautiful tribute to his wife near the end, expresses Wordsworth's attitude toward Mrs Wordsworth:

> Let other bards of angels sing,
>   Bright suns without a spot;
> But thou art no such perfect thing:
>   Rejoice that thou art not!

Such if thou wert in all men's view,
  A universal show,
What would my fancy have to do?
  My feelings to bestow?

Heed not tho' none should call thee fair;
  So, Mary, let it be
If nought in loveliness compare
  With what thou art to me.

True beauty dwells in deep retreats,
  Whose veil is unremoved
Till heart with heart in concord beats,
  And the lover is beloved.

Of the five children born to the poet and Mrs Wordsworth, three were alive in 1840—John, Dora, and William. Catharine and Thomas had died in early childhood, but after thirty years their father often spoke as if they had recently gone.

In 1840 John was thirty-seven, a clergyman at Brigham, and the father of five children. He was not a fascinating individual, nor particularly considerate. He was always dropping in uninvited, often joining a breakfast party of Crabb Robinson's at 30 Russell Square to which he was especially unsuited. When he had accepted an invitation he would sometimes write a note postponing the visit, after the host had been waiting for hours.

After becoming rector of Moresby John Wordsworth married, on 11th October 1830, 'Isabella Christian Curwen, daughter of Henry Curwen, Esq., of Workington Hall, Cumberland, and of Curwen's Isle, Windermere.' [74] His Aunt Dorothy wrote, a year later: 'John is happily married, and lives at Moresby, near Whitehaven. . . . His Wife is one of the best of good creatures.' [75]

Their first child was born in 1833, their sixth in 1841, and in another year or so Mrs John Wordsworth's health began to fail. By 1843 the Wordsworth letters were full of anxiety about the daughter-in-law's condition, and no one seemed quite to know what the trouble was. For a while young Mrs

Wordsworth was thought to be pregnant again; then she seemed to have 'only some obstruction.'[76] Her husband took her to London to consult a doctor, and then to Tunbridge for her health. Quillinan thought that she was not so ill as she imagined,[77] but Sara Coleridge's opinion was very different: 'She talked of Mrs John Wordsworth who she thinks is in a very bad way and unlikely to live long.'[78]

Wordsworth was very much the grandfather. When Jane, the first grandchild, was born, he wrote a poem to her mother, *Upon the Birth of her First-born Child, March 1833*. After a year he was openly bragging about the baby.[79] He continued to be proud of little Jane, and said of her when she was almost ten years old:

The child upon whose birth these verses were written is under my roof, and is of a disposition so promising that the wishes and prayers and prophecies which I then breathed forth in verse are, through God's mercy, likely to be realised.[80]

When she was sixteen, Jane remained in the room while her grandfather entertained the American, Ellis Yarnall, and the latter noticed a particular gentleness in Wordsworth's voice when he spoke of her.[81]

The second grandchild was a boy, Henry, born in 1834. The third was the poet's namesake and godson, for Mrs Wordsworth wrote on 16th March 1836:

William has been . . . at Workington to *assist* at the Christening of William the 3d with whom and his Sister and Brother the old gentleman returned, as much delighted as any fond grandfather ever was since the world begun [*sic*].[82]

Three more sons, John, Charles, and Edward, were born to the John Wordsworths, and all the children stayed a good deal with their grandparents. 'A little troublesome Grandson,' wrote Mrs Wordsworth in August 1838, 'is at my elbow making it necessary that I should lay aside my pen.'[83]

William was a favourite with his grandfather. To Crabb

Robinson, who told the child fanciful tales and apparently gave him a magic lantern, Wordsworth wrote:

John and his family, stayed one day with us, on their passage home, last week—they took our Darling along with them—To our great regret the Magic Lantern was packed up—so that they could not get at it, that we might have witnessed the impression it made upon the Child—He well remembered not only the 'Peacock with the fairy tail'—but also your manner of repeating it—& made no bad attempt at an immitation [sic].[84]

Eighteen months later the poet wrote again of his namesake:

My Son John and his second Son Wm leave us to-morrow. The Boy is full as interesting as when you saw him. He charms us all by his sweet looks and ways, and his remarkable intelligence—We shall be truly grieved to part with him.[85]

This grandson was welcomed by Wordsworth's friends in London when still a lad. He was present at some of Rogers's breakfast parties, and when Robinson was unable to spend the Christmas of 1849 at Rydal Mount, the fourteen-year-old William called on the invalid on Christmas Eve.[86]

The mother of Jane, Henry, and William, of Johnny and Charley and little Edward, was in a serious condition. The father took Willy and John, early in July 1843, and left them with their grandparents. For a month or so the children visited back and forth between Rydal Mount and Belle Isle, Windermere, where the Curwens had lent a summer home to the Quillinans. Near the end of August Dora was summoned by her brother to keep house for all the children in Brigham,[87] while John Wordsworth took his wife to London. But Dora did not remain long at Brigham, for her husband fetched her home before the first of September, leaving the children 'to be taken care of by the Governess.' [88]

The doctor advised Isabella to go to Madeira, where John took her, and remained with her for a year or more. She did not seem to make any progress, and was next sent to Italy.

Meanwhile, Wordsworth and Mrs Wordsworth did what they could to fill the place of father and mother to their six grandchildren. They went to Brigham to see them, and brought some of them back to Rydal Mount.

We are Darby and Joan-ing it by ourselves [wrote Mrs Wordsworth in July], save that 3 of our Grandsons are come to make a sort of holiday—& tho' their company is at times somewhat troublesome, yet we delight in it—for they are 3 fine Lads as one would wish to see in their different ways—none of them much given to learning—but full of activity.[89]

For these grandchildren Wordsworth wrote *The Westmoreland Girl* on 6th June 1845, adding two stanzas in July.[90]

But Mrs John Wordsworth wanted her children with her, and their father returned to England for them. He took all six to Lucca in June, little Edward being only four years old at the time. In September Mrs Wordsworth wrote: 'Alas we have no good news from Lucca save that the Children are all well.'[91]

The father went back once more to England, to take up his duties as rector. The older boys were left with a clergyman who took pupils in Lucca and Pisa, and the mother with four of the children went to Rome for the winter, where she was under the doctor's care.

Even the good news that the children were well did not last, for in Rome three of them became ill with a fever, and the youngest—'as noble a boy of nearly five years as ever was seen'[92] —did not recover. He died of convulsions, and was buried in the Protestant cemetery, near the graves of Keats and Joseph Severn. This was toward the end of 1845.

Wordsworth wrote, in January 1846, the sonnet, *Why should we weep or mourn, Angelic boy?*[93] in which there seem to be echoes of Shelley's *Adonais* in

> Death has proved
> His might, nor less his mercy, as behoved—
> Death conscious that he only could destroy
> The bodily frame. That beauty is laid low
> To moulder in a far-off field of Rome. . . .

In 1931 Mr Gordon Wordsworth told me that because this little grandchild was buried near Joseph Severn, the Wordsworths and the Severns have been friends for generations.

John Wordsworth, 'in a distracted state of mind,' went again to Italy, 'and found his Children well tho' . . . looking miserably, his wife greatly shattered, but, in some respects better than when he left her.' [94]   He took the five surviving children back to England, leaving his wife with her mother in Italy.

From now on the Wordsworths and the Quillinans shared with John the responsibility of his children.   Even after Dora's death, in July 1847, the Wordsworths were able to make a happy home for their little grandsons.   Quillinan left the old couple, on 23rd July 1848, at tea with '"quite a family party" —Mr Monkhouse, my two girls, Jemima and Rotha, two of John Wordsworth's boys Johnny and Charley, Mr Herbert Hill and one of his little boys, and Mr *Hartley Coleridge*.'   The next day, an elaborate birthday party was to be given for the two grandsons, eleven and nine respectively:

It is Johnny Wordsworth's birthday & tomorrow is Charley's, & the Poet's two Grand-children have invited all the children in the country & some adults to celebrate the two birthdays to-morrow evening.   James Dixon has prepared a balloon which is to be sent up; & I know not what besides is to astonish the Country.   Poor Rydal & happy children.[95]

While the children were leading a normal, happy life with their grandparents in Westmorland, their mother, Isabella Wordsworth, was dying in Italy.   By August or September she was dead.[96]

Dora has been mentioned throughout this book.   It would be impossible to talk about her father, her mother, the aunt for whom she was named, or about either of her brothers without talking also about Dora.

From childhood, 'with her wild, flashing eyes, floating curls, and unrestrained gaiety,' [97] she was a joy to her Aunt Dorothy. She did not lose her prankishness when she grew up, for when she was twenty, Crabb Robinson sent a message 'to Miss D: saucy tho' she be.' [98]   A merry war continued intermittently between Dora and her father's friend. When she was thirty-seven she pretended to be hurt because Robinson had addressed her in too formal a manner.[99] To Hartley Coleridge she was flippant, though apparently pleased by his compliments. She wrote of him in 1829 to Edward Quillinan, her future husband: 'Hartley has given me a copy of the Winter's Wreath and with it such a pretty sonnet—but shockingly complimentary my head will be turned by daft verses from daft men.'[100]

How early her health began to be delicate is hard to determine. Already in her twenties, she was the cause of great anxiety to her parents and her aunt.[101] But despite her lack of physical vigour, Dora's nature continued buoyant, and when she was away from Rydal Mount her father missed the radiance of her personality. In April 1830 Dorothy wrote that her namesake was visiting John at his parish in Moresby, and would remain 'till fetched home by her Father—who finds a sad want of her.'[102]

Though not a walker like her mother and her aunt, Dora rode with her brother. She was apparently a good skater, too, for Thomas Arnold wrote of her:

From the first time that I ever saw her, when Rydal Lake was frozen over, and she gave my brother and me some useful hints with regard to skating upon it, the sense of unbounded confidence in her kind eyes, or rather in the tenderness and goodness which beamed from them, never left either of us.[103]

The understanding between Dora and her father was such that she could be mischievous and adoring, jealous for his reputation, and yet fearful of his becoming vain.[104] She apparently never stood in awe of him. She called him 'Daddy' now and then, and he called her 'Dorina.' It was of Dora that Robinson wrote: 'I only obeyed orders—*Dorina* commanded. . . . And having observed how she is obeyed at home I did not dare to refuse.'[105] And it was probably of Dora that the story arose: 'Some men . . . are hen-pecked—but Wordsworth is *chicken-pecked*.'[106]

One of her father's friends began gradually to interest Dora Wordsworth, the widower, Edward Quillinan. He had long admired Wordsworth's poetry, and in 1821, when he gave up military service, had 'settled in the vale of Rydal, in a house taken for him by Mr Wordsworth, for the sake of whose society, even more than for the beauty of the district, he became a resident at the lakes.' [107] At the tragic death of Mrs Quillinan, on 25th May 1822,[108] Dora—then only eighteen years old—had been inconsolable. Her father had written the first six lines of the epitaph to Mrs Quillinan in Grasmere church, and had stood godfather to the second baby, Rotha.

By 1829 Dora was writing to the thirty-eight-year-old widower in a vein of affectionate chiding:

You cruel wicked vagabondizer—nearly a fortnight elapsed and not even a line to inform us how you performed your journey, whether you escaped colds—broken limbs—and a thousand other perils . . . I have never once enquired after your little Darlings whom I trust you found well and happy as you could desire. All send their sincere love. Edith's too—the money came safe from Kendal blue bonnet's eyes did sparkle when I gave her your little present.[109]

Aubrey de Vere says that Quillinan and Dora were in love for years before Wordsworth suspected it. The poet and Quillinan, meanwhile, continued their friendship. The younger man would send poems which Dora would read to her father, and Wordsworth would say it was in Quillinan's power 'to attain a permanent place among the poets of England.' [110] Wordsworth asked Quillinan to read his 1837 edition,[111] and then he invited the widower to visit them. Quillinan came in December 1837, and remained two weeks.[112]

When the father finally realized the truth about Dora and Quillinan, his jealous love for his daughter struggled with his desire for her happiness. Quillinan was a widower, a good deal older than Dora, and a Roman Catholic. His finances, moreover, were in a precarious condition. Wordsworth idolized his only daughter, and depended on her in many ways. It is easy to understand his objections to the marriage.

Dora herself may have considered the religious difference an obstacle for a time. 'She is a staunch Anti-Papist, in a Woman's way,' said her father in April 1829, in a letter about the Catholic Relief Bill.[113] But Edward Quillinan was not dogmatic about his religion. According to Mr Gordon Wordsworth, he not only reared his two daughters in the religion of their mother, but even escorted them to church himself when no other suitable companion could be found. But Quillinan remained a Roman Catholic, and often referred to himself as a Papist.[114]

Crabb Robinson's letters and diary indicate that the marriage between Dora and Quillinan was expected to take place more than a year before its actual date, and was prevented—partly at least—by Quillinan's financial straits.

Dora went to London with Miss Fenwick about 11th January 1840.[115] She visited the Hoares and the Marshalls until well into April, seeing Quillinan constantly. Crabb Robinson makes two significant entries in his diary:

Feb. 21. Quillinan breakfasted with me—very friendly—It seems that the reason why the intended marriage was not carried into execution was the discovery that certain property of his is incumbered. Dora is in town and everything remains in the same unsettled state in which it has long been.

Feb. 22. I dined with H: N: Coleridge—no one there but Dora Wordsworth and Quillinan except a silent young Irishman. . . . I presume that Dora and Q: being thus invited together is a sort of public annunciation of the connection intended to be consummated between them. Qu: it seems insists that Wordsworth shall give his daughter away—This I think is going too far. W: I suppose does not actively oppose the marriage but submits to what he cannot successfully oppose.[116]

In the summer Quillinan and his elder daughter made the Duddon trip with the Wordsworths, Dora Wordsworth, Miss Fenwick, and Miss Fenwick's niece.[117]

In the same summer, on the last day of August, Dora and Quillinan accompanied the poet on a climb up Helvellyn. Dora rode the whole way. During the climb Wordsworth composed his *Sonnet on a Portrait of the Duke of Wellington, by Haydon.*[118]　Quillinan composed verses, too, merry verses to amuse the fun-loving Dora.[119]

Dora went to London again the next spring, apparently to be near Quillinan.　The two called on Crabb Robinson on 11th March.　Robinson entertained Dora and Quillinan at breakfast on 3rd April, and was then told of their approaching marriage.[120]　About a week longer Dora remained in London, and then with Miss Fenwick joined her parents at Tintern Abbey on 13th April.　From there they all journeyed on to Bristol and Bath, where Dora was to be married.

They stayed with Miss Fenwick at 12 North Parade, Bath. The date of the marriage was set, but no one seemed certain about it—even within a week of the day.　Henry Taylor has described the old man's struggles, the many sleepless nights spent in agony and conflict, and the fresh appearance at breakfast as if nothing were the matter.[121]　'Our marriage still stands for the 11th,' wrote Miss Fenwick on 6th May, 'and I do sincerely trust nothing will interfere with its taking place on that day, for all parties seem prepared for it.　Mr Wordsworth behaves beautifully.'[122]　On 8th May the bridegroom arrived.

On 11th May 1841 Dora Wordsworth was married to Edward Quillinan, 'in St James' Church at Bath, Wordsworth, his wife, and two of his sons being present, as well as Quillinan's brother John.'[123]

On the afternoon of the wedding day the bridal couple departed for Wells, to be overtaken the next day by the bride's parents and Miss Fenwick.[124]　The whole party then went on to Alfoxden.　At Bridgewater they separated, the Quillinans going by railway to the Lakes, and the others visiting Miss Fenwick's brother-in-law in Somersetshire, and then touring through Exeter to Plymouth, and finally by Salisbury and Winchester to London.

For Wells and Alfoxden they had two perfect days.　But Wordsworth's joy in once more viewing the loved scenes was clouded by disappointments in some of the old landmarks, and by remembering Dorothy, his joyous companion of the other days.

Dora and her husband went to Rydal to take care of the invalid Dorothy while the poet and Mrs Wordsworth visited in London. 'We find dear old Aunty very comfortable & delighted to see us,' wrote the bride, ' & it is most affecting to me to observe the childlike *fun* & pleasure she makes for herself in addressing me by my new name.' [125]

Mrs Quillinan visited her parents the first Christmas after her marriage. Accompanied by Crabb Robinson, she arrived on Christmas Eve, and stayed until 18th January.[126] Her brother William also spent Christmas at Rydal.

For a time the Quillinans, including Jemima and Rotha, lived in Upper Spring Street, London, where the poet and Mrs Wordsworth visited them in the spring of 1842. In the autumn they went to Rydal, while their lodgings in London were under repair,[127] and their temporary stay in Westmorland developed into a more or less permanent residence. Wordsworth's nephew says that the Quillinans moved to the Lakes in the winter of 1843–4, but the writer of Quillinan's memoir puts it a year earlier.[128] Crabb Robinson's correspondence, also, shows Quillinan at Ambleside early in 1843, and on Belle Isle in the summer.

Mrs Quillinan's health had long been a matter of comment. Even in 1842 Robinson had written:

Mar. 23. I dined with the Quillinans and Moxons. Poor Mrs Qu[illinan] looked very poorly.
May 11. Mrs Qu: is looking very poorly and her father is anxious about her.
Oct. 29. In the evening at the Quillinans—Mrs Qu: looked very poorly.[129]

By April 1843 numerous devices to improve her condition were being tried.

Mrs Wordsworth and William have just brought the carriage for Dora [wrote Quillinan], that she may get a warm shower-bath at

Rydal. She takes these baths about thrice a week, and thinks they are of much service to her—not so the homoeopathy which she thinks a humbug and so do I.[130]

An old man who had once been gardener's boy at Rydal Mount told Canon Rawnsley of Wordsworth's shower-bath:

I was ter'ble curious, and was like enough to hev bin drowned, for they had a bath, filled regular o' nights, up above, ya kna, with a sort of curtainment all round it. And blowed if I didn't watch butler fill it, and then goa in and pull string, and down came watter, and I was 'maazed as owt, and I screamed, and Mr. John come and fun' me, and saaved my life.[131]

Dora's illness was more pronounced in the summer of 1844, and with Jemima and Rotha Quillinan she went to the Cumberland coast. There she had 'a bad attack of her stomach complaint,' and, later, a cough.[132]   In the autumn she contracted a severe cold and influenza, which lasted a month or more.   While Quillinan and his daughters were at Belle Isle, Windermere, she remained with her parents at Rydal Mount, lying on a sofa most of the day.[133]

By April 1845 there was talk of Quillinan's taking his wife to a warmer climate. His brother had offered to lend them 'a pretty marine villa at the mouth of the Douro, 3 miles from Oporto,' and Quillinan was eager to try the new experiment.[134] Never embittered by weakness or ill-health, Dora was more like a radiant, eager child than a woman of forty. When the trip to Oporto was planned she was jubilant at the prospect. Then the thought of leaving 'Daddy and Mammy' distressed her so much that the idea was for a while abandoned.[135]   On 8th April Quillinan wrote, in some disgust:

We talked of Oporto, & all agreed that it was a most desirable experiment for D.—One person only said nothing—& it was too evident that she was very low on the subject—Mrs Wordsworth.— Dora when we came home intimated to me that she was thrown into an uncertainty about going by her Mother's fears & dislike of the scheme. I therefore at once advised her to give it up, for if she went it could do her no good to be fretting because she would feel that her Mother was fretting. Mrs W's anxiety is natural, & Dora's

Dora Wordsworth

Miniature by Miss Gillies

unwillingness to pain her, & to leave her at 75, is all right—but it is a pity that Mrs W. does not take more cheerfully to the only plan likely to restore her daughter's health.[136]

By 18th April, however, the details were definitely worked out, and Quillinan wrote to Crabb Robinson that he and his wife and two daughters would arrive early the following Thursday, that Dora would need 'a cup of coffee and a slice of very thin dry toast on her arrival and the use of the sofa that she may rest till your breakfast hour,' and that the party would remain with Crabb Robinson until noon, when Mrs Hoare's carriage would take them to her home.[137]

The poet also came to London to attend the queen's ball on 25th April and her levee on 7th May. He stayed first at Moxon's and then at the Hoares'. His recognition by the queen was little joy to him, however, because of his distress over his daughter's condition. 'Mrs Quillinan's health,' wrote Robinson, 'is so bad as to justify any apprehension on his part but she was looking better to-day.'[138]

As the time for Dora's departure drew nearer, her father's suffering became more patent. Dining with the poet at Mrs Hoare's a few days before the sailing, Crabb Robinson wrote:

He was in wretched spirits And spoke not a word to any one. Mrs Quillinan sets off for Lisbon on Wednesday And he is filled with anxious apprehensions concerning her health when there—He is besides indisposed from a complaint in his eyes—On the same day he ought to attend the Queen's Levee I have no expectation that he will be able to pluck up spirits for the exercise. A more uncomfortable dinner I have seldom had—The rest of the party all felt for him.[139]

On the 7th of May 1845 at three o'clock in the afternoon the Quillinans sailed in the *Queen* steamer for Portugal.

The trip apparently did all that was expected for Mrs Quillinan's health. For the first two or three months the accounts fluctuated, but by August all the letters were encouraging. 'She now rides a beautiful Andalusian Poney,' wrote her mother, 'and is in the 7th Heaven.'[140] As her health improved, Dora's childlike buoyancy overflowed in her letters. Planning an elaborate tour through Lisbon, Cintra, Cadiz, Seville, Gibraltar, Granada, she finished: 'This is all very easy but *I* am so ambitious as to ask, Cannot we go from Grenada to Madrid & thence home by the Pyrenees? Old Daddy, Mammy & dearest Miss F. you must give us the meeting among those mountains—.'[141] She wrote to Sara Coleridge 'that she had been brought to such a state by her foreign travel—That she slept like a top and ate like a plough-boy.'[142]

The Quillinans returned to England in June, visiting Miss Fenwick, the Hoares, and other friends before going on to Rydal. Quillinan had been ill, but the reports agree on Dora's radiant health and contagious enthusiasm. 'Yesterday,' wrote Sara Coleridge, 'I saw Dora, who called here and I went with her to dine at Mrs Hoare's at Hampstead. . . . Dora looks like a rose. The improvement in her is marvellous. I have not seen her look so well since her teenish girlhood.'[143]

The four Quillinans settled once more in Westmorland in July 1846—this time at Loughrigg Holme. Dora continued well, Quillinan convalescent. On 30th August Quillinan wrote: 'Dora quite well!!!! I gain strength slowly, slowly.'[144]

Dora's recovery was short-lived. In less than a year her body was laid to rest in Grasmere churchyard.

Meanwhile, she was joyous with her family—with her husband and stepdaughters at Loughrigg Holme, with her parents and aunt at Rydal Mount, with her brothers at Brigham and Carlisle, and with John's children both at Rydal Mount and in her own home. She was happily arranging her home and writing gay letters to her friends, especially to Crabb Robinson for his handsome house-warming present, two book-cases built into the new home, one in the drawing-room and one in Quillinan's little study.[145]

While Quillinan was working on his studies in Portuguese literature, Dora was finishing and getting ready for the press her *Journal of a Few Months' Residence in Portugal and Glimpses of the South of Spain*. The book came out the following spring, with the dedication: 'These notes are dedicated in all reverence and love to my Father and Mother, for whom they were written.'

Late in the year Dora went to Carlisle,

to assist in the preparation of the house of her youngest brother, who was about to marry. This winter journey resulted in a cold, the effects of which she never cast off. Shortly after her return she went to stay for a time at Rydal Mount, during the absence of Mr and Mrs Wordsworth at Westminster, when she became rapidly worse.[146]

It was about 10th April that the Wordsworths, then staying in Hampstead with the Hoares, began to be alarmed about Dora's illness.[147] Then the news was better. 'I dined with the Wordsworths at Mrs Hoare's,' said Crabb Robinson. 'He is looking much better and was cheerful and chatty. Mrs W: also cheerful. Good accounts from Mrs Quillinan.'[148] On 26th April, after the Wordsworths had gone to visit their nephew in the Westminster cloisters, came a distressing letter from Rydal Mount,[149] and the poet and Mrs Wordsworth returned home that evening.

The doctors apparently held out no hope, and Dora's husband wrote to Crabb Robinson four days later:

To you and three or four other friends I write, & to no one else, on an afflicting subject. You have been so kind a friend to Dora, & are so much esteemed by her, and by myself, that I know she would wish this melancholy attention paid to you, if she knew, which she does not yet, that her life is nearly at an end.—A cold caught on a rash journey to Carlisle before Christmas, on a visit of sisterly service to William, has never been shaken off, and has finally attacked her lungs. She is sinking rapidly—I need say no more. Do not trouble yourself to answer. Mr and Mrs Wordsworth and I know that you will feel for us.[150]

For eleven more weeks Dora Quillinan lingered. Her death, Robinson feared, would cause her mother's death.[151] Her father seemed, at first, fairly composed.

About the middle of May Dora was told that she had only a short time to live. Sara Coleridge was impressed by her serenity—'the heavenly composure, sweetness, and piety of her frame of mind.' Of the poet and Mrs Wordsworth she said: 'The parents are wonderfully supported, but deep, deep is their sorrow. Mr Wordsworth cannot speak of it without tears. Poor Mr Quillinan!'[152]

As the fatal illness dragged on and on, Mrs Arnold understood the desire of the parents to be alone, and refrained from calling on them, and even from directly inquiring about Dora's condition. When Wordsworth did come near Fox How, she joined him and walked about with him, enabling him to avoid the guests in her own home. Mrs Arnold felt that the long illness and Dora's unceasing courage had in a measure prepared the parents to bear their loss.[153]

The poet used to wander forth, sometimes, to get whey from the farm of Mrs Tyson, at one time a servant at the Mount. 'You *must* make it,' he told her, 'for if you do not my daughter will die before morning.' And Mrs Quillinan was kept alive for three weeks, according to the old woman, on whey and wine.[154]

During the many, many weeks of constantly facing death, Dora Quillinan's spirit did not falter. She received great comfort from a hymn sent her by her friend, Charlotte Oxenden, the hymn, *Just as I am*, with the refrain, 'O Lamb of God, I come.' Her cousin, Christopher Wordsworth, wrote of her last weeks:

But she who was the object of their care was cheerful. She knew that her end was near, and she looked steadily and calmly at it. None of her natural courage and buoyancy failed her, and it was invigorated and elevated by faith.[155]

She died on 9th July 1847 at one o'clock in the morning. She was buried in Grasmere churchyard, near the Rotha, and her childhood friend, Sara Coleridge, made the journey from London for the funeral.[156] Quillinan put up a monument in white marble, marked by a lamb and a cross, and the verse, 'Him that cometh to Me I will in no wise cast out.'[157] The monument apparently refers to Dora's hymn.

The first Christmas was almost unbearable for Wordsworth. Everything connected with the festive season was associated with Dora. Arriving as usual for the holiday, Crabb Robinson was struck with the darkness of the situation:

What I anticipated I have found confirmed. Both Mr and Mrs Wordsworth have received a blow, the effects of which I fear they will never be able to counteract—Neither of them has yet ventured to pronounce the name of their beloved daughter. . . . But at least Mrs W. is able to mix more with her friends And discharge as she has been accustomed the ordinary functions of her domestic life.

Mr W. keeps very much alone. And whichever room I may happen to be in, he goes into the other—All the ordinary occupations in which his daughter took a part are become painful to him—I brought as usual a pack of cards and proposed a hand of Whist to Mrs W: in his absence, but even she rejected it with a shudder—I have been able to draw him out of the house but for a short time—And when I this morning proposed a call on old Mrs Cookson at Grasmere, this produced a flood of tears. . . . Neither of them go anywhere. And very few of their friends even call.[158]

Robinson was able gradually to draw his friend out, but the results were fluctuating. 'There has been a sensible improvement in the spirits of my friend,' he wrote one day; and then, a week later: 'The poet I grieve to say does not rally. I hear that when alone he does but sigh and sob tho' I have drawn him out to make calls when he appears cheerful.' [159] To Miss Fenwick he wrote:

Mrs W. tells me that after such walks he would retire to his room sit alone and cry incessantly—I witnessed several such bursts of grief occasioned by the merest accidents, such as my proposing to call with him on Mrs Arnold—He was unable to take leave of me for sobbing when I came away.[160]

Though Robinson felt that there was little or no improvement yet, his faith in Wordsworth gave him hope for the future: 'He has a strong nature in body as well as mind And he may yet rally.' [161] A few days after Christmas Wordsworth wrote to Moxon: 'Our sorrow, I feel, is for life; but God's will be done.' [162]

One of the strange phases of the old man's grief was a disinclination to go to Loughrigg Holme, where Dora had lived. At first Quillinan resented Wordsworth's attitude, regarding it as a selfish display and 'an insult to his wife's memory.' Though the son-in-law continued to call and dine at Rydal Mount, an estrangement had begun by Christmas which Robinson feared 'might widen and lead to an entire alienation.' [163] Crabb's sympathies were with Wordsworth, and he persuaded Quillinan that the poet's 'refusal to go into his house was the effect of real feeling and pure grief, which Quillinan had doubted before.' [164] Miss Fenwick was distressed at 'the want of understanding' between Quillinan and the Wordsworth family:

Mr Q.—but for that *touchiness* which we lament in him—might have been the most *helpful* friend and the greatest comfort . . . Mr and Mrs W——could have had.[165]

After a while the breach seemed to be gradually healing.

Mr Wordsworth and I [wrote Quillinan in February] walk about together a good deal now, and he seems to seek and to take pleasure in my company. He talks constantly of my beloved Wife, and this suits my feelings, though it is so sad a theme. He comes to this house too occasionally.[166]

The poet contemplated a volume of the poems written to or about his daughter, and he invited her husband to contribute some of his verses. Quillinan unearthed a paper he had written to please Dora, and printed it in the July number of *Blackwood's* as 'Laurels and Laureates.' But the joint volume on Dora was apparently never published.

And yet as late as November 1848 Wordsworth seldom went to Loughrigg Holme. 'My husband,' wrote Mrs Wordsworth in June, 'still shrinks from turning his steps towards Loughrigg which *was* such a happy walk to us all—or to go beyond the Cookson's house in our *own* Vale of Grasmere.' [167]

Meanwhile, visitors began to come again to Rydal Mount —strangers 'coming from a distance with introductions,' and guests of friends in the neighbourhood. Emerson, visiting

Harriet Martineau in February, had an interview—'a valuable hour, and perhaps a half more, with Mr Wordsworth, who is in sound health at 77 years, and was full of talk.' [168] Quillinan thought that company did the poet good, that he was 'less disposed or less able to bear up when alone or only with his wife.' [169] Of the stream of pilgrims to Rydal Mount he said:

> I think such perpetual interruptions, which would drive some men mad, are rarely disagreeable to Mr Wordsworth; and in my opinion all these callers do him good, by taking him out of himself.[170]

A report started in one of the papers that Wordsworth had lost his mind. At first Mary Russell Mitford doubted the rumour, until Ruskin was refused admittance to Rydal Mount. But it hardly follows that Wordsworth was deranged because he did not wish to see, in his grief, this 'very elegant and distinguished-looking young man, tall, fair, and slender,' [171] this callow youth who had called the Lakes 'vile bits of woodland and pools of dirty water.' [172] Harriet Martineau pooh-poohed the journalistic reports.

> The Wordsworths are very well indeed [she wrote to Robinson in June 1848]. I need not tell *you* that the account in the papers of Mr W's imbecility is utter nonsense. I dare say Mr Quillinan has told you that the abominable statement was made by a trumpery intruder who went one day when Mr W. was in one of his silent moods. I saw him twice last Sunday, when he was very cheerful and amiable . . . we found Mr W. bringing up from Church three stranger ladies, to see his garden. . . . It is the best way of his (unconsciously) putting a stop to the reports of his imbecility, which, according to Mr Quillinan, have spread very widely.[173]

George S. Hillard, of Boston, saw Wordsworth in the summer of 1848, and wrote:

> His mind had not felt in the slightest degree the touch of time, and his health was good, his frame and countenance showing as few marks of age as those of any person, so old, that I have ever seen. . . . I left him with my ideal image unstained and unruffled. His daughter's death has thrown a deep and abiding shadow over his path. In speaking of her he said that the loss of her 'had taken the sunshine out of his life.' [174]

The second Christmas was very different from the first. 'In the two days I have spent already here,' wrote Robinson to his brother, 'I have had more conversation with the poet than during the whole of my last visit.' [175] With his old vigour Wordsworth discussed politics and literature, and Robinson felt that the grief was now 'softened down to an endurable sadness.' The poet could 'master his sorrows in society,' but Mrs Wordsworth told Robinson that 'when he is alone paroxysms of weeping and sighing are not infrequent.' [176]

Returning to London, Robinson wrote to Miss Fenwick:

The most agreeable circumstance is that he goes occasionally to Mr Quillinan's And that they stand in a friendly relation towards each other—Every unpleasant impression on the mind of Mr Qu: is quite removed.[177]

Quillinan had written to Robinson: 'Mr Wordsworth today came to me through snow and sleet, and sat for an hour in his most cheerful mood. . . . He was particularly interesting.' [178]

For the rest of Wordsworth's life, some fifteen or sixteen months more, it was the same: dark moods, resignation, cheerful spirits, despondency. 'I cannot speak of my departed child,' he wrote to Coleridge's nephew in February 1849, 'further than to thank you, in my own name and that of her mother, for the affectionate expression of your sympathy; "Thy will be done" is perpetually in my thoughts.' [179] And Quillinan wrote to Crabb Robinson in October:

You will find your old and faithful friend the poet pretty much as he was on your last visit. The same social cheerfulness—company cheerfulness—the same fixed despondency (uncorrected) I esteem him for both: I love him best for the latter.[180]

William was thirty in 1840. He had been delicate as a child, and had been removed from the Charterhouse at the age of twelve, and kept at home until he was eighteen. Then he was sent to Germany, where he studied under a clergyman at Bremen, and later became a student at Heidelberg. The young man had 'a strong bent to the Army,' but his father planned—through the influence of the Lowthers—to get him a Government position; and when in 1831 the stamp distributorship was extended, William was brought home from Germany and given the position as deputy for his father at Carlisle. Even in 1842 Wordsworth was arranging the life of his son, having his office of stamp distributor transferred to him.[181]

Crabb Robinson had been fond of William ever since the days when he used to go to see him at the Charterhouse and write to Wordsworth and Dorothy how the little boy was faring; and whenever the young man went to London he stayed with his father's friend. To Crabb Robinson, therefore, in February 1843, Quillinan wrote a piece of joyful news about William as soon as he heard it and before it was generally known.[182] William was engaged to Mary Monkhouse. She was pretty and amiable, and worth about £20,000. Furthermore, she was a close connection of the Wordsworths, her father's sister having married Mrs Wordsworth's brother, so that Mrs Thomas Hutchinson was aunt to both Mary and William, and it was she who broke the news to the delighted Wordsworths. 'Master Willy might have done worse,' wrote Quillinan.[183] And Crabb Robinson put in his diary: 'This reminds one of De Quincey's snear [sic] that everything succeeds to Wordsworth. This is in every respect an enviable occurrence.' [184]

But the engagement did not last two months. On 1st April Mrs Wordsworth wrote that it was broken, giving no particulars. Crabb Robinson called on the girl's uncle and guardian, and wrote to Mrs Wordsworth: 'Mr Monkhouse remarked that it is quite necessary that the cause should be known to be one of pure calamity involving no reproach on W: nor indeed on any one, being a case of undoubted disease.' [185] In his diary he wrote:

I began my morning calls by going to Mr Monkhouse with whom I found Mrs Hutchinson. Learned from him what I had heard hinted, that his niece had become melancholy (in her mother's family there is insanity) and therefore only has the intended marriage been broken off.[186]

The year passed, and the next, and the next. Little is said of William in the letters or journals of his father's friends. He lived at Carlisle as stamp distributor, visiting his parents now and then at Rydal Mount. In March 1846 he visited Crabb Robinson, who introduced him to his friends, and apparently enjoyed his companionship, but left him free to come and go as he chose.[187]

Just when William began to be interested in Fanny Graham does not appear, but on 17th August 1846 Quillinan wrote: 'William is at Brighton, on a visit to his betrothed, a Miss Graham, whom he is to marry next February, with the approbation of all parties concerned.'[188]   William went again to Brighton in November, remaining with his fiancée about eighteen days and then stopping in London. 'When I came home after 11,' said Robinson, casually, 'I found in my room W: Wordsworth junr. He had taken tea there—He came in the afternoon from Brighton.'[189]   William stayed only one night and one day with Robinson, returning to the Lakes by the night train on 1st December. 'William was in joyous spirits, as was natural,' wrote his host to Mrs Wordsworth.[190]

At the end of the year William took his fiancée to call on Crabb Robinson—evidently a definite engagement visit:

Having an empty space I may here note down that W: W: came here with his betrothed Miss Graham—They are to marry in January. He has given me a daguerrotipe [sic] copy of Miss Gillies miniature of Mrs Wordsworth—a much more agreeable picture than any I have seen before—[191]

Mr Gordon Wordsworth wrote to me, on 13th November 1932, of the affection between his parents and Crabb Robinson:

They had a most genuine affection for Crabb (as I invariably heard him called in my young days) and it is obvious that he liked my father, and I know he had a great admiration for my mother.

William Wordsworth junior and 'Fanny Elisa Graham, youngest daughter of Reginald Graham, Esq., of Brighton,' were married at Brighton on 20th January 1847.[192] On the 30th William took his bride to Rydal Mount.[193]

Mrs William Wordsworth junior was twenty-six years old, eleven years younger than her husband. 'She is a very nice person,' wrote Robinson a few years later, 'very amiable but also a delicate creature, who would excite the sympathy of you all being one of two children the survivors of eight, all the rest being the victims of pulmonary consumption.' [194] Gordon Graham Wordsworth, who survived until July 1935, was their youngest child.

Much has been made recently of the liaison between Wordsworth and Annette Vallon in 1791–2. The facts of this French affair were originally written into the official life of Wordsworth by his nephew, but his intimate friend and confidant, Crabb Robinson, insisted on deleting the passage. In 1851, when the *Memoirs* were almost ready for publication, Robinson recorded his anxiety:

March 18. Wordsworth [John] shewed me the proof sheets of the Life in which I am sorry to see a canting commonplace remark on the perils to which W: was exposed in his youth at Paris which might make one utterly ignorant of W's personal character imagine he had been guilty of some immorality. I wrote a short letter on this to Quillinan.

March 21. I called on Moxon about the Life. . . . Moxon is sure that the objectionable passage has been expunged and at all events it will be if Mrs W: requires it.

March 25. From Moxon I learned what provoked me—that the injudicious paragraph about Wordsworth's residence in France is retained, which I thought had been omitted and I wrote to Quillinan in consequence.

March 27. A call from John Wordsworth just after a letter from Quillinan. Qu: would submit to the Doctor's insertion of the offensive paragraph but I advise him [John W.] and his mother to prohibit it absolutely. Moxon will do what they wish.[195]

Robinson's insistence was effective, for though he wrote on 2nd April, 'I am sorry to find that Dr Wordsworth has not yielded to remonstrances,' [196] there is no mention of Annette

Vallon in the *Memoirs*. The public first read of the French affair in Professor Harper's *William Wordsworth, his Life, Works, and Influence* in 1916.

Had the details of this youthful episode been known just after the death of Wordsworth, the event would probably have fallen into its natural perspective. Wordsworth was twenty-one at the time, Annette several years older. The French Revolution was in progress, with the slackening of discipline consequent upon war, and the abolition of the functions of the Church. The only marriage possible in France at that time was a civil marriage, which to Annette—Roman Catholic as she was—would have been little better than no marriage at all. In the summer of 1802, just before his marriage with Mary Hutchinson, Wordsworth visited Annette for a month, taking his sister with him.[197] The sonnet, *It is a beauteous evening, calm and free*, refers to his little French daughter, Caroline, then ten years old:

> Dear Child! dear Girl! that walkest with me here . . .

Between Wordsworth and Annette a friendly feeling lasted throughout their lives. Mrs Wordsworth and Dorothy and the lawyer-friend, Crabb Robinson, knew of the early romance; Dorothy also told her intimate friend, Mrs Clarkson, and Crabb Robinson told Quillinan. The poet's sons were not informed.

In 1814, when Caroline was to be married to Jean Baptiste Baudouin, she and her mother were eager for Dorothy Wordsworth to attend the wedding. Professor de Selincourt shows how the poet's sister looked forward to the visit, and how Caroline—then twenty-one years old—kept putting off the date of her wedding in order that her Aunt Dorothy might come.[198] Disliking France and all things French, Dorothy yet felt a warm affection and pity for Annette and her daughter.

You would have been able [she wrote to Mrs Clarkson] to confirm or contradict the reports which we receive from Caroline's mother and Mr Baudouin of her interesting and amiable qualities. They both say that she resembles her Father most strikingly, and her letters give a picture of a feeling and ingenuous mind.[199]

The wedding was postponed to April 1815, and the young Frenchwoman kept urging her English aunt to come. Dorothy felt that it would be better to put the money on Caroline's dowry, but finally wrote to Annette that she would make the journey. Four days later news reached Ambleside that Napoleon had re-entered France. Letters went back and forth between Wordsworth's sister and the mother of his French daughter. There was talk of Caroline's visiting England.

Finally, in February 1816, the wedding was solemnized. Dorothy was not present, but her 'affection for Annette and Caroline was warm as ever, and she still clung to her plan of visiting them.' Neither Annette nor Caroline felt any bitterness toward her or toward Wordsworth: 'On 27th December 1816 when Caroline gave birth to her first child, William was godfather, and the baby was named after her grand-aunt, Louise Marie Caroline Dorothée.' [200]

When the poet, Mrs Wordsworth, and Dorothy made their continental tour in 1820 they stayed in Paris in the rue Charlotte, the street where the Baudouins lived. Eustace Baudouin, brother of Jean Baptiste, met Wordsworth and his sister, and took them to see Caroline and her little girl. 'During their stay,' says Mr de Selincourt, 'they spent a good deal of their time with Annette and the Baudouins.' [201]

We catch a glimpse in Crabb Robinson's letters of an occasional interchange of small gifts between the Vallons and the Wordsworths. The summer after the tour Annette sent a parcel to Dorothy.[202] And a few months later the latter sent needles and razors to Annette and the Baudouins.[203] On his Italian journey in 1837 Wordsworth procured for his 'friends in France' some rosaries, and left them to be blessed by the Pope. The following spring he sent them by Southey to Crabb Robinson, who was to forward them to Annette and her daughter. Mrs Wordsworth wrote the letter to Robinson:

The little parcel which accompanies this—is some certain Popish charm which has followed Wm from his Holiness from Rome and which you are to seize some favorable occasion to forward to his friends in Paris—You know their address and by doing this service you will add to the number of the innumerable kind things you have done for us. . . .

W. says, as they meant to change their residence you had best direct to Mon. Baudouin Mont de Piété.[204]

The poet wrote, later, to Robinson: 'The Chapelets have been received by my friends in France; and given them great pleasure; many thanks for the trouble you took upon the occasion.'[205]

Financially, also, Wordsworth had not neglected his French daughter. Miss Edith C. Batho, in an appendix to her *Later Wordsworth*, discusses at some length the poet's settlement on Caroline.[206] At the time of her marriage Wordsworth began to give her an annuity of £30, and continued this for about twenty years. He then gave her £400, and received from Caroline Baudouin and her husband a receipt that the financial obligation was settled. 'Caroline had received between £500 and £600 from her father since her marriage,' says Miss Batho, 'and the settlement of 1835 brought the sum to approximately £1,000—a large amount to a man of Wordsworth's financial standing and obligations to his other children.'

But Caroline's husband felt that his wife should continue to receive money from her distinguished father—even after she was fifty years old, and had been married twenty-six years, and had also accepted the final settlement. Baudouin wrote to Wordsworth and then to the poet's lawyer, Crabb Robinson. Returning from the north in August 1842, Robinson received 'a letter from Baudouin complaining of the conduct of Mr W: in not answering his letter.'[207] He turned the letter over to Quillinan, who discussed it with him, and then drafted 'a very sensible letter in French' for Robinson to use in reply.[208] After pondering the matter for ten days, Robinson wrote such a letter

that B: may not be tempted to write again—I giving B: to understand

Caroline Vallon
Portrait by Vauchelet

that W: had not the means of doing anything further and that his means had been reduced.[209]

Apparently the letter silenced the Frenchman for a number of years, but immediately after the death of Wordsworth Baudouin became more importunate, trying to win for his wife and himself part of her father's estate. Less than a fortnight after the poet's death Robinson recorded in his diary:

May 4, 1850. A letter from Mrs Wordsworth inclosing one from France.
May 6, 1850. I wrote to M. Baudouin at Paris No. 6 Rue Jacob informing him that Mrs Wordsworth had transmitted his letter to me and desiring that he would in future write to me.[210]

Baudouin threatened to come to England 'to look after his *interests* if necessary,' and Robinson sent a draft of his answer to Strickland Cookson, one of Wordsworth's executors, saying: 'This will be a troublesome business I fear, but I think the claims should be flatly refused.'[211] Cookson talked with the poet's biographer, Dr Christopher Wordsworth, and then wrote to Robinson:

I found that he did not consider it necessary, in the discharge of his duty as a biographer, to make any mention of the French entanglement of 1791–2, but he is now under the impression that the French people will try to get money from the family as the price of silence, and that failing in that, they will make up and publish a revelation, which will be made as romantic and attractive as French ingenuity in such matters can make it, and in which a small modicum of truth will be mixed up with just as much falsehood and perversion as may be considered necessary to make the revelation pleasing and acceptable to the French taste; and consequently that it will be better to anticipate the movement by giving in the memoir a true narrative of the facts, with the age of the actor, influence under which he was placed, state of society in France at the time, subsequent visit of his sister and himself to the parties (in 1802) and knowledge of the main fact by his sister and intended wife. . . .[212]

Baudouin continued to be a problem until the next year, and Dr Wordsworth kept the French episode in his book until April 1851. Finally, on 17th July, Crabb Robinson reassured

Mrs Wordsworth that 'she had no cause for fearing any annoyance from France.' [213]

But the friction was not between Annette and Wordsworth, nor yet between Caroline and her father, but rather between Annette's son-in-law and the heirs of Wordsworth.

The servants in the Wordsworth home were regarded as members of the family. John Carter was not exactly a servant, but an indispensable member of the household. A clerk, at first, in the office of the stamp distributor, he became amanuensis to the poet, and was one of his executors. Many of the manuscripts of the poems are in his handwriting.

Of all the servants he ever had Wordsworth was most devoted to and most dependent on James Dixon. For thirty years James served his beloved master, and the visitors to Rydal Mount tell of his versatility. Edwin Paxton Hood wrote:

The servant, who was to the poet gardener, groom, and something more, a loving and faithful, and watchful heart, cut his master's hair, but the locks were never thrown away from that venerable head, but found their way into hundreds of hands in every part of the Empire; he kept also a quantity of cards with the poet's autograph, and thus he sometimes comforted those who failed to see him, by either a lock of his hair, or a dash of his pen.[214]

As landscape-gardener, James sometimes opposed the opinion of his master. 'James and I . . . are in a puzzle here,' said Wordsworth to Sir John Taylor Coleridge one summer morning.

The grass here has spots which offend the eye; and I told him we must cover them with soap-lees. 'That,' he says, 'will make the green there darker than the rest.' 'Then,' I said, 'we must cover the whole.' He objected: 'That will not do with reference to the little lawn to which you pass from this.' 'Cover that,' I said. To which he replies, 'You will have an unpleasant contrast with the foliage surrounding it.' [215]

When Crabb Robinson fell down the stairs of his cottage at Rydal, it was James who dressed him and put him in Dorothy

Wordsworth's wheeled chair, it was James who drew him up the Mount and deposited him safely in the poet's home, and it was James who attended him night and day throughout the visit.[216] Robinson presented him with a silver watch when he left, and wrote afterwards that he would always consider James as 'particularly in the family.' The next Christmas Crabb Robinson brought James a chain and seal for the watch. [217] And when Robinson arrived for the 1845 Christmas visit, getting out of the Whitehaven mail 'at the foot of Mr Wordsworth's lane,' he found James waiting with the poet [218]—'my old friend James the *"child of fortune"* whose naïveté I hope you have not forgotten.' [219]

James attempted to comfort the aged poet in his grief over his daughter's death.

I was lamenting to James [said Robinson] his Masters [*sic*] inability to submit to the will of providence—'Ah! Sir And so I took the liberty of saying to Master—He merely said—"Oh she was such a bright creature"—And then I said *"But Sir don't you think she is brighter now than she ever was,"* And then Master burst into a flood of tears'—Those were not tears of unmixed grief— [220]

James attended Hartley Coleridge in his last illness.[221]

The last service James rendered his living master was described by a servant in another home in Westmorland:

Very shortly before his [the poet's] death it was thought he might be more comfortable if he were shaved. Accordingly, he was raised in the bed, and his faithful servant was about to minister to him in this way when Wordsworth said in his serious, calm voice, 'James, let me die easy.' [222]

Another member of the household at Rydal Mount was 'little Jane the house-maid.' The Wordsworths were so attached to her that when she died suddenly, in the autumn of 1843, Crabb Robinson wrote a note of sympathy to Mrs Wordsworth.[223]

Mrs Tyson, who supplied whey in Dora's last illness, was a former servant; another was Mary Fisher.

We went to drink tea [wrote Mrs Fletcher, in August 1840] with our cousins the Williamsons, at Mary Fisher's, where Mr and Mrs

G

Wordsworth joined us, walking from and back to Rydal Mount over the fell way. Mary Fisher had been their servant in their early days at the cottage at Town End. After tea the conversation turned on Crabbe and his poetry.[224]

Crabb Robinson mentions two visits to Mary Fisher in one week:

Dec. 26, 1841. After dinner I took a walk with W: to his old servant Mary—an annual Christmas call—He was very cordial and communicative.

Dec. 31. I went on to Grasmere joining Wordsworth at Mary Fishers. We took early tea.[225]

Wordsworth was a man to whom family ties meant much. Richard, his eldest brother, had died in 1816, but the widow and their only son, John, were alive in Wordsworth's later years. This nephew had gone as a doctor to the Ionian Isles. There he had contracted an illness which sent him home to the Lakes, where he lingered an invalid for several years, and died in 1846. He stayed for a while with the Harrisons at Green Bank, and then with his aunt and uncle at Rydal Mount for five or six weeks before joining his mother at Keswick.

Wordsworth had not been particularly congenial with his youngest brother, the Reverend Christopher Wordsworth, D.D., Master of Trinity College, Cambridge. Dr Wordsworth was a formal, stiff sort of person, who took his profession very seriously. In 1815 Crabb Robinson had said of him: 'He has all the elements of an high priest in him, tempered by domestic virtues.' [226] The undergraduates of Trinity used to call him 'the meezerable sinner,' because of the way he read the Litany. Crabb Robinson records a *bon mot* of one of the Fellows of Trinity. In a discussion of etymology Dr Wordsworth

prosily shewed that the *Canon* of the Church meant the rule and that the word came from *Cane* a reed used as a measure. Thompson whispered—'Does it require so much learning to prove that a canon may be a stick.' [227]

But as Wordsworth and his brother grew older they meant

more to each other.   Dr Wordsworth retired from Trinity in
the summer of 1841, after twenty years' service, and devoted
himself entirely to the parish of Buxted, Sussex.   In the
autumn of 1841 he visited at Rydal Mount, and the poet's
two sons joined their uncle there.   Again in 1844 Dr Wordsworth visited his brother, this time for three weeks.[228]   His
son Christopher was with him, as well as Thomas Hutchinson
and his sister.   Dr Christopher Wordsworth died on 2nd
February 1846.

His three sons, John, Charles, and Christopher, were all
clergymen—the two younger ones becoming, later, Bishop of
St Andrews and Bishop of Lincoln.   John died at Cambridge
at the end of the year 1839, while his father was still Master
of Trinity.   He had been a Fellow of Trinity and, according
to his uncle, 'one of the best scholars in Europe.' [229]   Wordsworth had hoped that this nephew would read the proofs of
his 1839–40 edition.   'He is the most accurate man I know,'
he wrote to his publisher, 'and if a revise of each sheet could
be sent to him the edition would be immaculate.' [230]

Charles and Christopher were both High Church theologians
—to Crabb Robinson's disgust.[231]   The poet and Mrs Wordsworth visited Charles at Winchester for two days just after
Dora's marriage, and the Winchester master and his little
motherless daughter, Charlotte Emily, stayed in the Quillinans' lodgings at Ambleside for part of the summer of 1845.
Charles Wordsworth gave up his post at Winchester in 1846
—'it is said on account of reproaches cast on him for confessing
the boys!!' [232]   Crabb Robinson continued to be disgusted by
the churchmanship of Charles Wordsworth.[233]

Young Christopher Wordsworth showed academic promise
at Cambridge, winning prizes and honours.[234]   He sent
Wordsworth, in 1834, a copy of his pamphlet *On the Admission
of Dissenters to graduate in the University of Cambridge*.   He
became Head Master of Harrow, and in 1844 Canon of
Westminster.[235]   The churchmanship of the future Bishop of
Lincoln was probably not so extreme as that of his brother.

And yet Crabb Robinson berated his *Theophilus Anglicanus* for five consecutive days, finally lending it to one of his High Church friends:

Oct. 15, 1844. At night I began the younger Dr Wordsworth's Theophilus Anglicanus which should be called Ecclesiaphobus Anglicanus. It is a very laboured exposition of High Church doctrines. . . . The appointment of Dr W: to a prebend of Westminster is a matter of reproach to the Government—under his government the school being reduced from 400 to 80!

Oct. 16. I went on with Dr Wordsworth's book and the further I get the more I am disgusted—At the same time I found more scriptural arguments than I expected—But that operates rather to make one doubt the scriptures than adopt the doctrine.

Oct. 17. I continued today reading *Theophilus Anglicanus*—it is much worse than I had any anticipation of.

Oct. 18. I was glad to get done with it for it only disgusted me and sets me at liberty for better reading.[236]

Though Christopher Wordsworth was a severe theologian, and probably a dogmatic schoolmaster, Dorothy loved him,[237] and Dora was fond of her 'Cousin Chris.' He asked Dora to stand sponsor to his second child, named his fourth child for Mrs Wordsworth, and after Dora's death named his seventh child for her. It is not strange that Christopher was something of a favourite with his uncle. Wordsworth even wrote a note to him at the time of Dora's death.

Christopher Wordsworth married Susanna Hatley Frere, and she bore him seven children: Elizabeth, Priscilla, John, Mary, Susan, Christopher, and Dora. Dame Elizabeth Wordsworth was the first Head of Lady Margaret Hall, Oxford,[238] and the first woman to receive the D.C.L. from Oxford, after Queen Victoria. She wrote a *Life of Wordsworth*, a volume of poems, and several other books. Priscilla fell heir to Dora Wordsworth's album, the book which Mrs Hemans had given her, and for which Wordsworth collected autographs from many of his famous friends.[239] John became Bishop of Salisbury, and Christopher, Canon of Salisbury. The latter survived until 30th January 1938.

But it was Mary, Christopher's fourth child, who particularly interested the poet when he made his last visit to London, and spent part of his time with his nephew in the Westminster cloisters. Mary was named for Mrs Wordsworth and the little two-year-old girl remembered — years later — 'being brought down to see her great uncle, who stood her on the table and looked at her solemnly.' She remembered gazing with awe at his large nose and grave countenance—He stroked me gently and said something, but I was rather relieved when he placed me on the floor and I felt free again. He was very absent, and one day came down in his slippers, and he had gone the length of the cloisters in them, before my mother could overtake him and bring him back.[240]

Not only to the whole Wordsworth connection had the poet come to be paterfamilias, but to his wife's relatives, too. Mary, Peggy, and Sara Hutchinson had been girlhood friends of Dorothy Wordsworth. Sara Hutchinson had lived in the Wordsworth home now and then for much of her life, and her lines, *To a Redbreast*, are included among Wordsworth's poems, with due acknowledgment.[241] Mary's eldest brother, Henry, also has a poem among those of his brother-in-law, the sonnet, *From early youth I ploughed the restless Main.*[242]

Thomas, George, and Joanna were alive in 1840. Thomas Hutchinson, Mrs Wordsworth's favourite brother, had married his first cousin, Mary Monkhouse. Though seventeen years Mrs Wordsworth's junior, Mrs Hutchinson was a great favourite with her, and used to visit often at Rydal Mount. She was a particular comfort at the time of Sara's death. In 1837 Thomas Hutchinson had a serious accident which left him a cripple, and the poet admired the fortitude of his brother-in-law.[243] The Thomas Hutchinsons lived at Brinsop, in Herefordshire, and had five children, three sons and two daughters.

It was for these two nieces, Elizabeth and Sara, and for his own daughter that Wordsworth was concerned about the Mississippi bonds. Sara Hutchinson had made the investment, and left it to her three nieces, each of whom received £40 annually.[244] When the State of Mississippi defaulted, just before Dora Wordsworth's wedding, Wordsworth was so disappointed that he wrote: 'I fear that the reputation for integrity in those Southern States is very low indeed.'[245] Again and again he referred to 'the dishonest State of Mississippi.' And in 1845 he said of his sister-in-law:

Often and often have I felt a sort of melancholy satisfaction that the dear Person died soon after that investment was made. She was a noble-minded Person, of a most generous spirit, and I fear to think how painful it would have been to her to be thrown, in destitution, upon her Friends for a maintenance.[246]

The money was, apparently, never recovered.

Mrs Wordsworth's youngest sister, Joanna, was the subject of two of Wordsworth's poems—*To Joanna*, written two years before the poet's marriage, and *Louisa*, beginning 'I met Louisa in the shade'—and probably of *To a Young Lady*, beginning 'Dear Child of Nature, let them rail.' Of her Robinson wrote:

Joanna is the laughing girl whose loud expression of joy roused all the echoes—The Poem is a famous one for the ridicule which the revilers have cast on it tho' I love it exceedingly. She is the subject of the poem which treats of the maiden '*ruddy fleet and strong*.' The very beau ideal of a stout hearted and stout bodied rustic girl.[247]

In July 1843 Joanna Hutchinson had a paralytic stroke while on a visit to Elton, near Stockton. 'She is a dear generous single-minded woman,' wrote Quillinan, 'and would be an irreparable loss to her family.'[248] At first she was thought not to be in great danger, but a month later Mrs Wordsworth became alarmed. Wordsworth and Quillinan had been planning a tour of the Duddon, and the Wordsworths were also looking forward to a visit with the Thomas Hutchinsons at Brinsop. Both trips were postponed, and on 29th August the poet and Mrs Wordsworth started for Elton.[249] They remained with Joanna for several weeks, and then went on to Brinsop, where they were joined by Crabb Robinson on 27th

September. Joanna's death occurred soon after her sister's departure.[250]

Six years afterwards, in the summer of 1849, the poet and Mrs Wordsworth—and their friend Miss Fenwick—visited Mrs Wordsworth's nephew at West Malvern. Thomas Hutchinson was visiting his son, and Crabb Robinson and Moxon joined the Wordsworths there. They were all very happy together, sight-seeing and going on picnics. About the end of June the Wordsworths returned to Rydal Mount, and two days later received word of Thomas Hutchinson's death.[251]

In his later years Wordsworth became more interested in the early history of his family. Edwin Paxton Hood says:

Although his father was only an attorney, and his mother the daughter of a draper, his family was ancient, and it was his delight to trace back its history, both on his father's and mother's side, beyond the times of the Norman Conquest.[252]

Wordsworth's maternal grandmother was Dorothy Crackanthorp, 'of the ancient family of that name, who from the times of Edward the Third had lived in Newbiggen Hall, Westmoreland.' The Wordsworths came into Westmorland only two generations before the poet, having settled 'at Peniston, in Yorkshire . . . probably before the Norman Conquest.'[253] According to Sir William Rowan Hamilton, Wordsworth claimed to be a lineal descendant of Alfred the Great.[254]

In 1840 the poet acquired an old cabinet made for a remote ancestor.

The chest, or rather Crypt which you kindly allude to [he wrote to Crabb Robinson in September] is arrived. It fully answered our expectations, being both curious, and in the carving, beautifuly [sic]; wholly uninjured and its age 315—years. It is much admired by everybody.[255]

The cabinet was much older. In the memorandum dictated in 1847 Wordsworth said:

I possess, through the kindness of Col. Beaumont, an almery made in 1325, at the expense of a William Wordsworth, as is expressed in a Latin inscription carved upon it, which carries the pedigree of the family back four generations from himself.[256]

Ellis Yarnall saw the old cabinet on 18th August 1849;[257] and on 10th August 1931 the writer saw it—still on the wall of Wordsworth's study, the big, dark room on the ground floor, with two huge oak beams in the ceiling.

The poet was proud of his mother's people, the Cooksons and the Crackanthorps. But he was also proud that he was a Wordsworth, and that the cabinet was carved for an ancestor in the fourteenth century, an earlier William Wordsworth.

III. HIS MOST INTIMATE FRIENDS

BETWEEN the poet's family and his close friends it is not always easy to draw the line. Quillinan, for instance, was long his admirer and devoted friend before he became his son-in-law. Miss Fenwick, though bound by no ties of blood or marriage to the Wordsworth family, became almost indispensable to the poet and Mrs Wordsworth, and seemed in many ways to supply the place of the beloved Dorothy. Crabb Robinson, a friend of the middle and later years, was so much a part of the Christmas festivities at Rydal Mount that all the Wordsworths were wont to quote Quillinan's 'No Crabb no Christmas.' To Hartley and Sara Coleridge, to Kate Southey, and in a smaller degree to Bertha, Edith, and Cuthbert Southey, the venerable Wordsworth stood *in loco parentis.*

Wordsworth had a great capacity for friendship. Willing to help his friends whenever he could, he did not scruple to accept favours from those who loved him. Perhaps this is one of the reasons why his friends enjoyed him. Reading the Dedication of the *Descriptive Sketches* in 1840, Samuel Rogers said: 'What a pity it would have been had this been left out! —Every man who reads this must love Wordsworth more and more. Few know *how* he loves his friends!' [1]

The closest friends of Wordsworth's old age were, perhaps, Isabella Fenwick, Henry Crabb Robinson, and two of the children of Samuel Taylor Coleridge, Hartley and Sara.

Isabella Fenwick, of Somersetshire, is still spoken of by the living members of the Wordsworth family with great affection, as if she were a favourite aunt. In Dove Cottage, her picture hangs among those of the 'Women of the Wordsworth household and their friends,' and in Mr Gordon Wordsworth's living-room it hung by the fireplace opposite the poet's.

'Her face might have been called handsome,' wrote Henry Taylor, 'but that it was too noble and distinguished to be

89

disposed of by that appellative. Her manners, her voice, and everything about her, harmonized with her face, and her whole effect was simple and great, and at the same time distinctly individual.' [2]   Miss Fenwick was strong and unselfish, intense in her affections, and of such great sensibility that her happiness was seldom unalloyed.

In all her affections [said Taylor, who knew her perhaps as well as any one] there was an element of diffidence and disturbance working up and betraying itself from time to time, as well as a profounder element of peace—profounder far—the peace of the deep sea . . .

Perhaps there are no natures, having a rare and extraordinary large-ness of love, which can hold themselves in a constant and invariable contentment with the objects of their love. [3]

Despite her high moral rectitude, [4] Miss Fenwick was tolerant of poor, wayward Hartley Coleridge. She tried to reconcile the daughters of Robert Southey and their step-mother, Caroline Bowles. 'Such a heavenly-minded woman,' wrote Quillinan, in 1843, '*must* succeed.' [5] She it was who had persuaded Wordsworth to give his daughter to Edward Quillinan, and from her home in Bath the couple had gone to the church to be married.

'She is a woman of a large and noble heart,' wrote Aubrey de Vere, in 1845, 'with a peculiar spirit of self-sacrifice; and her imagination and feeling alike are as fresh as they could have been at twenty.' [6]   To Henry Taylor de Vere wrote:

What a noble being she is! In conversing with her, as in inter-course with Wordsworth, I am perpetually reminded of the per-petual youth that belongs to true excellence. . . . I have seen her face kindle with animation such as she may have felt at twenty. Wordsworth was reading poetry at the moment, and I felt inclined to fancy that it might have been to her that he had written those lines, 'How rich that forehead's broad expanse.' [7]

Miss Fenwick was about fifty when she met Wordsworth, and almost sixty when she began to know him well. She was cousin and intimate friend of Henry Taylor's stepmother, and early became Taylor's confidante. She kept house for him during the winter season in London, and through him met first

Southey and then Wordsworth. When Miss Fenwick first went to Rydal Mount, she said of Wordsworth that she would be 'content to be a servant in the house to hear his wisdom.'[8]

It was eight years later, in June 1838, that she took a cottage in Ambleside. At first she was awed by the friendship given unreservedly, especially when Wordsworth began to read her *The Prelude*, which he was then revising. Perhaps it was more than diffidence that made Miss Fenwick feel overwhelmed by the bard's reciting his autobiographical poem to her:

> But at present I am not sufficient for these things, though they are not lost upon me *altogether*. From time to time I have heard portions of that marvellous work of his which is to appear when he ceases to be, and I am to hear it all. . . . After hearing it, I think I must have felt as the Queen of Sheba felt after hearing all the wisdom of Solomon—'there was no more spirit in her'; and so it was with me. I wish you could hear it as I did; though you, I trust, may live to read it, it is something more to hear him recite it, or, as his little grandson says, 'Grandpapa reading without a book.'[9]

By August she was able to take him more casually, and to see how 'droll' he could be about the slightest indisposition.[10] Wordsworth had already begun to escape to her house from the many daily visitors at Rydal Mount. Miss Fenwick comprehended the poet's enjoyment of the beauty around him, and also the integrity of his poetry:

> Every day that I am with him I am more and more struck with the *truth* of his writings; they are from the abundance of his heart; yet (as he said last night) how small a portion of what he has felt or thought has he been able to reveal to the world; and he will leave it, his tale still untold.[11]

She realized, now, the depth of their mutual friendship: 'Perhaps no one has ever seen him in greater intimacy, and I can truly say my admiration has kept pace with my knowledge of him, and my reverence even with this near view of his infirmities.'[12]

But when he began again to read *The Prelude*, Miss Fenwick saw in Wordsworth the glowing of such fire that she was once more awed by his present as well as his past greatness:

The beloved old poet has again begun to read me his MS., so in time I hope to hear it all. . . . It was almost too much emotion for me to see and hear this fervent old man, the passionate feelings of his youth all come back to him, making audible this 'linked lay of truth.' . . . He recognised his own greatness in the midst of the neglect, contempt, and ridicule of his fellow-creatures, which strikes one as what is most extraordinary in his character, when one keeps in view his ardent sympathies with them, and how alive he is in all his affections.[13]

She saw him practically every day, and was more and more aware of his emotional intensity, of his 'storms and darker moments,' and yet of the control superinduced by his intellect.

What strange workings are there in his great mind [she wrote in January], and how fearfully strong are all his feelings and affections! If his intellect had been less powerful they must have destroyed him long ago. . . . I have witnessed many a sad scene, yet my affection and admiration, even my respect, goes on increasing with my increasing knowledge of him.[14]

Early in January Miss Fenwick said: 'There are very few days that I do not see the poet for an hour or two.' Later in the month, when none of his own thirteen coats suited the day, the old man put on a cape of Dora's rather than miss his visit to Miss Fenwick. In February he and Mrs Wordsworth went to stay in her cottage 'for the sake of her society and change of air—and above all,' as the poet naïvely added, 'because it may not be prudent for me to walk to see her so often as I could wish.'[15] And in March he used to go to her in the evening and unburden himself of the strain and joy of composition.[16]

He was at this time revising The Prelude, getting it ready for publication after his death. Professor Ernest de Selincourt says that the bulk of the changes in The Prelude, in the D manuscript, 'were made early in 1839,' and cites Miss Fenwick's letter of 28th March to prove it:

Our journey was postponed for a week, that the beloved old poet might accomplish the work that he had in hand, the revising of his grand autobiographical poem, and leaving it in a state fit for publication. At this he has been labouring for the last month, seldom less than six or seven hours in the day, or rather one ought to say the whole day, for it seemed always in his mind—quite a possession; and much, I believe, he has done to it, expanding it in some parts, retrenching it in others, and perfecting it in all. I could not have imagined the labour that he has bestowed on all his works had I not been so much with him at this time.[17]

But Mr de Selincourt does not mention the earlier letter that shows the poet toiling also in the previous summer on his great poem:

He has been working hard this last month at this poem, that he may leave it in a state fit for publication so far as it is written—that is, fifteen books. May God grant him life to write many more! He seems still to have a great power of working; he can apply himself five, six, or seven hours a day to composition, and yet be able to converse all the evening.[18]

In the spring of 1839 Miss Fenwick went with Wordsworth to Cambridge, where he took delight in showing her his obscure nook in St John's College and how, from his bed, he could see 'the top of the window in Trinity College Chapel, under which stands that glorious statue of Sir Isaac Newton.'[19] This, said Miss Fenwick, was also in the poem. The poet went on to Oxford to receive an honorary degree, and his friend returned to Westmorland. But when the celebration was over, Wordsworth got off the coach at Ambleside to tell Miss Fenwick all about it—even before he returned home.[20]

Isabella Fenwick was happy in the Lakes. 'I must have been the very devil,' she wrote to Taylor in the spring of 1840, 'to retain my ill humour in the midst of all this beauty and the love that . . . harmonises all the feelings.' She had her house to the end of October, and would then probably move to Rydal Mount. Recalling her first impression of Wordsworth, she now said: 'I value his wisdom quite as much as I could have done then, and I love him ten thousand times more than I ever expected I should.'[21]

She was his frequent companion in walks about the country-side. The two often walked up Easedale, and stopped for tea with the Fletchers. It was Miss Fenwick who gave the 'tea-drink' in honour of the poet's seventy-third birthday [22] and the more elaborate party the following year. On Wordsworth's seventy-fifth birthday she entertained very simply in her own home the poet and Mrs Wordsworth, Dora, and Quillinan.[23]

Miss Fenwick was a woman of considerable means, and depended upon her friend for financial advice. In the correspondence between Wordsworth and his American editor, especially from 26th May 1840 to 28th August 1845, the investments of Isabella Fenwick in America bulk large. The financial depression subsequent to the panic of 1837 had lowered the value of her investments both in the loans of the State of Pennsylvania and in the Bank of the United States, and she was undecided whether to sell at a great sacrifice or to risk holding the shares until times should improve.

Reed was in a position to give authoritative advice, his brother being not only State Senator from Philadelphia but chairman of the Committee of Finance.[24]   Reed urged the poet, in August 1840, to reassure his friend.   And in September, after receiving from Wordsworth Miss Fenwick's name, the Philadelphian was more explicit:

The investment stands in Miss Fenwick's own name—'Isabella Fenwick, of Somersetshire England'—the amount thirty five thousand dollars . . . Pennsylvania Five per Cents—a loan of the year 1832 redeemable in 1860. . . . I was much relieved to learn by your letter, that she had not been induced to sell.[25]

About the Pennsylvania investment Reed was most encouraging, but he did not feel so sanguine about the Bank of the United States.

'Mrs W. and I rejoice in the good news more than she will,' wrote Wordsworth of Miss Fenwick. 'She is so charitable and benevolent a creature that every one who knows her would grieve at her means being curtailed.' [26]   But the poet's rejoicing was ill-timed. The next February the banks of Philadelphia failed, Miss Fenwick's stock (which had stood at eighty the previous April) dropped to thirty-three, and the Pennsylvania loan ceased to pay a dividend.[27]

Miss Fenwick was eager to get rid of her American investments, even at a sacrifice of half her property, and only the poet's confidence in Professor Reed prevented her. For three years there was the fluctuating hope every February and August that payments of the dividend would be resumed. And finally in February 1845 the interest was paid again.[28]

Meanwhile the Wordsworths and Miss Fenwick had been planning a trip to Italy. They wanted to go in the summer of 1843 (Wordsworth having received his pension the previous autumn), and remain through the following winter. But with the continued default of the Pennsylvania loan, the plan was abandoned. To Wordsworth and his friend the disappointment was not so much the loss of the journey as the lost opportunity to see Italy together.[29]

Wordsworth felt a personal debt of gratitude to Professor Reed for all that the latter had done for Miss Fenwick, and when the professor's brother made a visit to Rydal Mount, Wordsworth sent by him one of his own valued books—a gift from Crabb Robinson—as a token of the appreciation felt by Miss Fenwick and himself.[30]

Miss Fenwick knew Wordsworth too well to overburden him with material gifts. She did, however, give him a cuckoo clock, knowing his keen delight in the bird. Wordsworth had written four poems about the cuckoo, had modernized *The Cuckoo and the Nightingale*, and had been particularly happy when he heard the cuckoo's twofold call in Italy. He hung the clock on the stairway, just outside his bedroom, wrote a poem about it, and said of it in his manuscript notes: 'It must be here recorded that it was a present from the dear friend for whose sake these notes were chiefly undertaken, and who has written them from my dictation.' [31] The cuckoo clock was striking twelve when Wordsworth died. It is now in Dove Cottage.

Realizing his special interest in Chatterton, Miss Fenwick

bought for Wordsworth, also, the only known portrait of the marvellous boy, an oil painting given by Chatterton's sister, Mrs Newton, to Southey. It represents Chatterton 'as a boy of twelve with a charming, odd, sulky, querulous face. . . . The boy wears a red coat, and has long auburn-brown hair.' [32] When Southey's possessions were sold, Miss Fenwick commissioned Quillinan to buy this portrait. She gave it to Wordsworth, 'with a reversion to Henry Taylor.' It was hung in her sitting-room at Rydal Mount, [33] and later passed to Sir Henry Taylor.

At the time of Dora's marriage Miss Fenwick sustained the parents. She and Dora met them on 13th April at Tintern Abbey, and the party journeyed to Bristol and Bath, where Miss Fenwick entertained them. Immediately after the wedding she toured with the old couple for about three weeks, taking them to visit her married sister at Taunton. 'Tomorrow Mg,' wrote Mrs Wordsworth, on 31st May, 'we shall part with our dear friend at Charmouth. . . . We have had a most delightful tour . . . but feel very sad just now at the thought of parting with our dear friend.' [34]

Again in 1847 the Wordsworths visited their friend at Bath. Crabb Robinson joined them there, and Sara Coleridge came later. [35] From this visit the poet and Mrs Wordsworth went to London, where they received the news in April of Dora's alarming condition. It was Miss Fenwick who kept Sara Coleridge informed of Dora's gradual decline.

But for Isabella Fenwick, we should not have had the notes dictated by Wordsworth in his last decade. Late in 1842 Miss Fenwick suggested that the poet should dictate to her the circumstances which gave rise to the different poems. He did so—largely in 1843—and Miss Fenwick promised the manuscript to Dora Quillinan. Though a man of seventy-three can seldom recapture the poetic experience of his youth, the Fenwick manuscript notes are invaluable for the factual information they contain. [36] After Dora's death Miss Fenwick gave the notes to Quillinan, and perhaps she did much to

Miss Fenwick
Miniature by Miss Gillies

cement the broken friendship between Wordsworth and his son-in-law.

The friendship between Wordsworth and Isabella Fenwick was not exclusive. 'Mrs Wordsworth . . .,' said Henry Taylor, 'attached herself to Miss Fenwick with a warmth and energy of nature which took no account of years; and it can seldom have happened that a friendship of three persons first formed in advanced life has been so fervent and so inward.' [37]

Isabella Fenwick was no blind worshipper. 'I feel quite sure that I know *all his* faults,' she said early in her acquaintance with Wordsworth—'all that they have done, are doing, and may do.' She did not presume to understand his whole intellectual nature, but said of his weaknesses: 'I think I never love a person thoroughly till I know how far they are liable to take the wrong way. I always want to have as little room for my imagination to work in as possible.' [38] She found no obsequiousness at Rydal Mount. Coming from Greta Hall, where Kate and Bertha Southey ministered silently to their dazed father, she considered 'the storms that sometimes visit the Mount . . . more healthful and invigorating than such calms.' [39] The openness and sincerity that she found at Rydal Mount she regarded 'as of infinite value in the regulation of Wordsworth's life and mind.' She once told Henry Taylor, 'There is no domestic altar in that house,' and he added, 'If she found none there, neither did she set up one.' [40] She even ventured to tell the poet what she disliked in his verse. One line in the sonnets on *Personal Talk* she 'always stigmatised . . . as vulgar, and worthy only of having been composed by a country squire.' Far from resenting her criticism, Wordsworth perpetuated it, adding a facetious slur of his own:

By the bye, I have a spite at one of this series of sonnets (I will leave the reader to discover which), as having been the means of nearly putting off for ever our acquaintance with dear Miss Fenwick. [41]

Miss Fenwick told Aubrey de Vere, visiting her in March 1845, 'several instances of Wordsworth's strange vehemence and waywardness of temper. No degree of intimacy, she

H

said, can diminish your reverence for him, though you would discover a small . . . man in the midst of the great and noble man—he has in fact two natures, though the better one prevails.' She had told Henry Taylor of the poet's intense emotions; now she said that Wordsworth 'could not trust himself to write any but severe poetry.' [42]

Her respect for Wordsworth's character was strained in 1847. When, in the preoccupation of his own grief, Wordsworth forgot that of others, and became estranged from his son-in-law, Miss Fenwick was on the side of Quillinan. Crabb Robinson called on her at Mortlake and wrote in his diary on 30th September:

> She spoke with great kindness of Mr Quillinan to whom she is going to give the notes to Wordsworth's poems which he dictated to her . . . for she had promised them to Mrs Quillin: and she wishes W: would appoint Qu: literary executor. . . . *She has lost something of her respect for the great poet himself, at least as concerns his moral character, on the ground of this same want of liberality.*[43]

And yet, the next day, Robinson wrote: 'She is very confidential towards me in matters of delicacy as well as importance— She is the most warm of friends towards Wordsworth.' [44] And he referred to her the next year as 'Wordsworth's most intimate friend.' [45]

Though Miss Fenwick's 'admiration for the personal qualities of the wife' may have been 'more unmixed than her admiration for the personal qualities of the husband,' still, as Henry Taylor said,

> even when she had arrived at the knowledge of all his faults—and no man's were less hidden—she retained a profound sense of what *was* great in his personal character, as well as an undiminished appreciation of his genius and powers.[46]

When the message of Wordsworth's death reached Miss Fenwick, she said: 'He did the work he had to do in this world nobly.' [47] Her next thought was to go to his widow. 'Miss Fenwick's presence,' said Crabb Robinson, 'has been a great consolation to her. . . . She is scarcely able to move—But her mind is admirably qualified to render her a counsellor and friend to all in trouble.' [48] Miss Fenwick remained at Rydal Mount for many months, trying to help Dr Wordsworth with the *Memoirs*. She was proud that Wordsworth had referred his nephew to her as 'one who could give him information and who knew him well.' [49]

But her idea was not followed. Though her opinion and that of Mrs Wordsworth were that the *Memoirs* should be short, a mere factual chronicle, the book was extended to two volumes. She considered Dr Wordsworth 'without much knowledge of his uncle, or indeed of his poetry,' though 'a very able man and good.' Of the finished *Memoirs* she said: 'It was written in far too great a hurry. The original idea of it was good; but time was wanting to select his materials and condense. A few years hence a better life may be written.' [50]

Miss Fenwick outlived Wordsworth by six years. When Professor Reed wrote in 1853 that her stock in the Bank of the United States was at last marketable, her gratification was less for the financial advantage than for the fact that she owed Reed's kindness to his 'remembrance of the friend whom we both look back upon with unabated love and respect.' [51]

Wordsworth was afraid that Isabella Fenwick would be forgotten. His contemporaries and younger friends knew what the friendship meant to him, for they knew Miss Fenwick. Sara Coleridge said:

I take great delight in Miss Fenwick and in her conversation . . . her mind is such a noble compound of heart and intelligence, of spiritual feeling and moral strength, and the most perfect feminineness. She is intellectual, but . . . never talks for effect, never *keeps possession of the floor*, as clever women are so apt to do. She converses for the interchange of thought and feeling, no matter *how*, so she gets at your mind, and lets you into hers. A more generous and a tenderer heart I never knew.[52]

And later, suffering intensely, Sara received great solace from Wordsworth's friend.[53] Aubrey de Vere said of Miss Fenwick:

She was so much not only to me, but to many others who are also much to me . . . and I shall ever remember her as one of the

noblest and most great-hearted beings I have been permitted to know.
. . . In some things how much she resembled Wordsworth; but
then how free she was from that alloy of egotism which commonly
clings to the largest masculine nature!

Whereas Wordsworth's life was pre-eminently happy, Miss
Fenwick's, he said, was not:

Even had she been well and strong all her life, though she would
have had soaring hours in larger abundance, there would have remained a craving not to be satisfied. . . . Her heart was as tender
as her aspirations were elevated and unremitting; and such a being
. . . must ever be condemned . . . to 'draw nectar in a sieve. . . .'
Great love, great aspiration, great suffering: these are the recollections which will, perhaps, remain longest with me as representing
the earthly life of Miss Fenwick.[54]

Henry Taylor appreciated Miss Fenwick; Crabb Robinson and
Carlyle in a less degree.

But Wordsworth wanted those who were to know him in
later generations to know, also, Isabella Fenwick. To her he
wrote two sonnets, one on New Year's Day, 1840, the other
in February.[55]   In the second he referred to friendship as

> The star which comes at close of day to shine
> More heavenly bright than when it leads the morn,

and called Miss Fenwick,

> though known but for a few fleet years,
> The heart-affianced sister of our love!

In the first, *On a Portrait of I. F.*, he expressed the fear that his
love for her would be forgotten after his death,

> And not by strangers to our blood alone,
> But by our best descendants be unknown.

The portrait has kept alive, as the poet hoped it would,

> Some lingering fragrance of the pure affection.

It was this portrait of Isabella Fenwick which the writer saw
in the late Mr Gordon Wordsworth's living-room—hanging
opposite that of the poet.

Wordsworth's affection for Crabb Robinson was not so
intense as that for Miss Fenwick, but there was probably a

greater intimacy than the latter recognized when she wrote,
early in 1839:

The Crabb seems to study him, but he can only know him very
superficially; he sees but the man of genius, or the simple, kind-
hearted, oddest, irritable man in his own family; but the *inner man*
he cannot know; yet what he does know I dare say the world will
know too some time or other.[56]

Born in 1775, Crabb Robinson had enjoyed every advantage
which schooling, travel, reading, and association with interesting people could give. Educated for the Bar, he had studied
in Germany, had acquired a broad knowledge of the German
language and literature, and had become the friend of Goethe.
As early as 1802 he perceived Wordsworth's greatness,[57] and
by 1812 he and Wordsworth were friends. In 1820 he toured
Switzerland with the poet and Dorothy. In 1822 Dorothy
wrote to him: 'You certainly have the gift of setting him on
fire.'[58] Crabb Robinson visited at Rydal in 1833 and departed 'with encreased love for the excellent friends there
And enhanced admiration of the great man, yet so ill appreciated.' The poet had given him 'some delightful specimens
of his recent compositions,' which Robinson was 'not at
liberty to copy.'[59]

A successful and wealthy lawyer, the writer of at least one
book and innumerable articles, a Liberal in Church and State,
one of the prime movers of the Dissenters' Chapels Act, of the
Flaxman Memorial Gallery, and of University College, a
trustee of the latter and of Doctor Williams's Library, the
friend of literary men and women in London and in Germany
—Crabb Robinson was yet a modest man. He was constantly
surprised at his wide circle of interesting friends.[60] When, in
an article on Goethe, Carlyle made a veiled reference to
Robinson as one of the shallowest men in Europe, the latter
wrote in his diary:

This does not in the least annoy me. I am conscious of being a
shallow man in his eyes and deservedly so.[61]

When Henry Taylor called him 'the friend of Schiller and of

most of the other great men of letters of his times in England and Germany . . . the friend of all men great and small who stand in need of friendship,' Robinson was embarrassed. '*Celui qui exagère diminue . . .*,' he wrote in his diary. 'I must write and remonstrate with him.' [62]

Crabb Robinson was exceptionally ugly. He recognized the fact, and joked about his ugliness. He made fun of his portrait painted by Helios, asking Mrs Wordsworth to prepare and attach to the canvas a signed statement that 'the original of this light begotten portrait' was not so evil as his painted likeness.[63] Miss Fenwick thought that Robinson's ugliness had enriched his personality, that it had preserved for him 'kindliness and courtesy in his bachelor state.' In January 1839 she gave Taylor an amusing picture of the Crabb sleeping—'he always sleeps when he is not talking'—and of little Willy, the poet's three-year-old grandson, fascinated by his ugliness:

> Willy contemplates him with great interest and often enquires 'what kind of a face has Mr Robinson?' 'A very nice face,' is the constant answer; and then a different look comes, and another enquiry of 'what kind of face was that?' 'A *nice face* too.' What an odd idea must he have of nice faces! [64]

Crabb Robinson was cheerful and sociable, and always generous. The severe pain caused by a fall at Rydal he endured with composure; and when he had to forgo his usual Christmas visit in 1849 because of an operation, his only comment was on the beneficent effects of chloroform. Despite the surgeon's order, he slipped off to the home of one of his friends for Christmas dinner. He recorded with joy his great-nephew's fondness for him:

> Perhaps a mere childish caprice—He became excessively fond of me, clinging to me and kissing me and calling me *dear Lion*. . . . I find it gratifying to be loved even by a child.[65]

When he and Wordsworth were planning their Italian journey, he wanted the poet to set the scale of their expenditure.[66] He gave to innumerable public and private charities, to edu-

cational institutions, to art, to philanthropies of every sort;
and he gave largely and intelligently. He did not wish to
hoard, he wrote in his diary for 23rd November 1845: 'But
I have difficulty in spending rightly and agreeably, and even
judiciously to give does not occur every day.' [67] His answer
was typical, when he was asked to contribute to Watson's
statue of Flaxman: 'He asked me to put down my name for
£1—I told him to put me down for £2.' [68]

Crabb Robinson was intellectually honest and usually
tolerant of those with whom he disagreed. He envied his
more orthodox Christian friends, but would not compromise.
Once he wrote: 'I would give all I have in the world to arrive
at a happy conviction on these points.' [69] Numerous entries
in his diary show his honesty with himself.[70] Eventually he
allied himself with the Unitarians.

In the last decade of Wordsworth's life Crabb Robinson
visited him in the Lakes almost every Christmas, having begun
the habit in 1835. He would stay in a cottage at the foot of
Wordsworth's hill, have his simple breakfast and luncheon
alone, go up to Rydal Mount for dinner and the evening until
nine o'clock, and then retire to his cottage and read until very
late. Wordsworth treated him casually, leaving him alone or
dropping in on him for a discussion or a walk. Despite the
younger man's great reverence for the elder, between the two
was a warmth of understanding that made formalities unnecessary. The stream of Robinson's talk, though interesting,
was sometimes overpowering.

He quite out-talks the old poet [said Miss Fenwick]; so in the
mornings he often comes to me as a good listener. I like the Crabb's
talk very well; he knows a great deal of all the most remarkable
people of the last half-century.[71]

In the evening Robinson would usually read aloud to the
Wordsworth family, and sometimes play a rubber of whist.

On Christmas Day, 1840, the Wordsworths went to church
as a matter of course, and equally as a matter of course they
left Crabb Robinson to himself:

No one luckily seemed to expect that I should go to church. On coming out of church Dr Arnold stepped in for a moment with Wordsworth. I went to an early dinner, after which I took a walk with Wordsw[orth] . . . a very lively talk over our tea to which came Mr and Mrs Hill.[72]

Just before the Christmas guest departed, on 21st January, Wordsworth read him a new poem, *The Norman Boy*.[73]

During the Christmas visit of 1841–2 Wordsworth and Crabb Robinson continued their walks and their talks, dropped in to see the invalid Carr, argued theological questions with Faber, discussed Chatterton, and played whist in the evening. And sometimes there was a party at Rydal Mount. Dora had come up with Robinson, leaving her husband in London. It was during this visit that Wordsworth discussed with his friend his plans for a second tour to Italy, and on the last night of the visit, 17th January, read him the tentative dedication of his *Memorials of a Tour in Italy*.

On Christmas night, 1843, Robinson slipped and fell headlong down the stairs of his little cottage, and though not internally injured was painfully bruised. He suffered a good deal throughout the visit, but was sustained by the affectionate kindness of the Wordsworths. They moved him to Rydal Mount the next morning, where he wrote to his brother: 'Though I am not substantially better yet, the being in this house makes me feel half cured.' 'I am utterly helpless,' he wrote two days later, 'and can with difficulty turn myself. But I . . . am continually relieved and refreshed by calls in addition to the affectionate tenderness of Mrs W. And the constant solicitude of the poet.'[74] After this accident the Wordsworths insisted on Crabb Robinson's staying at Rydal Mount, and not in his little cottage.

A meeting of the trustees of Doctor Williams's Library postponed the 1846 visit. Robinson dined with friends in London on Christmas Day, and went to the Wordsworths' in January.

He went as usual to Rydal Mount the Christmas of 1847,

the first dark Christmas after Dora's death.   He did not enjoy
the visit, and did not feel that he was of much comfort to the
stricken father; but, unlike Miss Fenwick, he took sides with
Wordsworth in the estrangement from Quillinan.   In 1848
he arrived after Christmas Day, and found the old poet more
like himself.   During this visit Hartley Coleridge died, and
Crabb Robinson sat with Mrs Wordsworth while the poet
attended the funeral.   Wordsworth enjoyed these Christmas
visits, and the next year he wrote some time before the holiday
to make sure that Crabb would come as usual.   But Robinson
spent Christmas Day recovering from an operation.

Wordsworth's visits to London were not so frequent as
Robinson's to the Lakes, and he usually stayed with the Hoares
or the Marshalls, but 'the Crabb' went to see him almost
daily, and entertained him usually with a breakfast or a dinner.
After Dora's wedding and the tour with Miss Fenwick in 1841,
the Wordsworths went to London—arriving early in June and
remaining well into July.[75]   The next spring, too, they visited
in London—from the first week in May to the middle of June
—staying partly with their daughter in Upper Spring Street,
partly with Mrs Hoare in Hampstead.   Crabb Robinson entertained the poet with a breakfast on 9th May and a dinner on
21st May.

On the 1845 visit Wordsworth stayed with Moxon until
after the queen's ball, and then joined Mrs Wordsworth and
Dora at Mrs Hoare's.   Crabb Robinson gave a breakfast in
Wordsworth's honour, and the latter failed to appear, because
of inflammation of his eyes.[76]   But when Robinson dined at
Mrs Hoare's the next evening and found the poet unusually
silent, he knew that something more than the inflammation
was making Wordsworth unhappy.   Dora was sailing for
Portugal in four days.

The last time the Wordsworths went to London was in 1847,
just after their visit in Bath.   They went to the Hoares' in
Hampstead, and then to Dr Christopher Wordsworth's in
Westminster.   During this visit Wordsworth was so much

distressed about Dora's illness that he accepted few invitations. But Crabb Robinson dined with him at Mrs Hoare's, and called on him—at Wordsworth's suggestion—in the West-minster cloisters. He was with him when Wordsworth received the distressing news which called him home on 26th April.

Robinson was in the habit of giving presents to Wordsworth through the members of his family. When he heard that the afflicted Dorothy enjoyed oranges, he sent her a chest of them and promised to send more when those were gone. It was a joy to the affluent old bachelor to lavish gifts on his friends, and there is no evidence that Wordsworth was embarrassed.

Usually about February or March Robinson sent Mrs Wordsworth a handsome present after his return to London. In 1842 it was eighteen silver teaspoons; [77] the next year, a lamp. [78] The 1844 gift was more pretentious, this being the Christmas of his accident. 'I went about buying a set of tea and breakfast things for Wordsworth at Daniell's,' he gloated.

I did not attend to Miss Fenwick's injunctions, and bought a set of china with gilt rims for £6/18/–. A full set except that I had only six breakfast cups and saucers and consisting of 80 pieces. They are however neat rather than gaudy and I have no doubt will please. [79]

Mrs Wordsworth, though troubled at the value of the present and amazed at the Crabb's astuteness in divining the needs of Rydal Mount, expressed her sheer delight in the gift:

Never, since we were housekeepers, did we possess a *Company* Tea Service—and you have before provided spoons suitable to the very elegant and *fashionable*-shaped set—so that our table henceforth will vie with, if not take the lead of those of our neighbours. [80]

The china was saved until the poet's birthday, which fell that year on Easter Sunday—a double festival for its 'hanselling.' [81]

Contemplating a dinner service the next year, Robinson asked Miss Fenwick's advice. She answered that they had 'a very handsome dinner and desert [sic] service at Rydal,' and really needed nothing, but that she might suggest a new urn for making tea or a Concordance for Shakespeare which is now in the course of publication but the Poet hardly deserves a book—he so seldom reads one.[82]

She described the urn, and said that it would probably cost about £5. Robinson bought one at Bailey's, and added books and stationery to the package.[83]

One of the handsomest presents recorded in Robinson's diary was the house-warming gift to Dora and Quillinan on their return from Portugal in the summer of 1846, two bookcases specially planned and built for Loughrigg Holme. Early in June Robinson had written to Mrs Wordsworth and asked her to choose something 'handsome and useful,' and to spend at least £20.

The best way to disturb Crabb Robinson's poise was to make derogatory remarks about Wordsworth. His good nature was 'a little tried' by 'the prosaic remarks and soidisant criticisms' of two of his women-friends.[84] He was more annoyed by another woman's 'captious remarks on Wordsworth' which sent him off 'in a tiff.'[85] With this woman, Miss Aikin, he finally had a definite split as the result of an argument about Wordsworth:

Miss A: roused my anger by calling Wordsworth's conformity to the Church base and imputing unworthy motives to him and this provoked me to great and unwarrantable rudeness. I called her language insolence and declared my determination never to enter her doors again. This was very foolish on my part certainly—yet the loss of Miss A:'s society is not to be in itself regretted.[86]

The Crabb's comment was peculiar when he heard that a former acquaintance had been shot in Vienna: 'He was a thoroughly bad fellow—On leaving England many years ago he literally stole from me a copy of Wordsworth's poems.'[87]

Loving and reverencing Wordsworth as he did, Robinson had nothing possessive in his affection, and was confident of Wordsworth's attachment in return. During the later years he enjoyed a growing intimacy. Earlier he had felt that what he had to say was hardly worth the great man's reading. Now, in 1840, he said: 'The feeling is not so strong as it was, because I have for some years been aware of a part of your character which I was at first ignorant of.' Now he knew Wordsworth's interest in people; now he knew how the man loved his friends. And yet he was still unable to write 'mere rattling letters . . . spinning out of one's brain any light thing that one can pick up there.' [88]

Wordsworth's visits to London Robinson anticipated with a kind of elation.[89] And in the Lakes he was conscious of the affection of all the Rydalites. He had long accepted Wordsworth's 'heart-affianced sister,' and he realized in 1843 that she was catching the poet's enthusiasm for him. 'I had a great deal of interesting chat with Miss Fenwick,' he wrote in his diary on 15th January, 'about the Wordsworths and herself—She is I perceive become really a friend—her tone is very cordial. The Ws are most affectionate.' The next day he added: 'I went up the Mount and spent more than an hour with my friends. Their attachment to me is warm and affectionate, and Miss Fenwick seems to have caught the feeling.' [90]

Wordsworth was honest with Crabb Robinson, and their understanding could weather wide disagreement. He knew that the nonconformist had worked hard for the Dissenters' Chapels Bill, and that his own approval would mean much to him. But he could not gloss the truth to his friend. Moreover, when sentiment did not keep him from giving away one of Robinson's gifts, sentimentality did not prevent his telling him. A week after sending the *Glossary of Architecture* to Professor Reed, Wordsworth wrote to Crabb Robinson. He explained the situation, and then suggested a scheme by which he could still have the gift from Robinson:

Now what I have to beg is that you would procure another Copy of this work write your name in it as a present from you to me, have it sent to Moxon to be forwarded by the first convenient opportunity, and request him to put the cost of the Volumes down to me. In this way Miss F. will have attained her wish, and things will stand on the same footing as before.[91]

Henry Crabb Robinson
Drawing by Masquerier

Between the two friends was an interdependence which was more apparent on Robinson's side. When the lawyer wrote for publication, he asked for and obtained the poet's criticism.[92] He sought Wordsworth's advice about a difficult letter he had written from Rydal Mount, and was elated over his friend's approval.[93] He said that part of his philosophy was adopted from Wordsworth.[94] And, years after Wordsworth's death, he said: 'I owe much of the happiness of my life to the effect produced on me first by his works and then by his friendship.'[95]

But Wordsworth was also somewhat dependent on his friend. He counted on the Christmas visits, and would have been sadly disappointed if Crabb had failed to come.[96] He had originally named Crabb Robinson his executor, but when he was seventy-one and the lawyer sixty-six, Wordsworth thought it wiser to choose a younger man. After making the change, he talked it over with Robinson, who could see the wisdom of it, though with a shade of regret. Returning from the usual Christmas walk to old Mary Fisher's, Robinson wrote in his diary:

He was very cordial and communicative. He informed me that he had when last in town altered entirely the arrangements *of his will, he had substituted for executors his son William, Mr Cookson and his bailiff Mr Carter instead of Courtenay* [97] *and myself on account of my age. He thought it would* relieve *me from a* burthen. I told him I entirely approved of this—as I most sincerely do.[98]

His mingled pride and regret Crabb expressed to his brother several years later:

I was Executor to Wordsworth—Now this would have been a higher honour than to be the dedicatee of a poem. Yet I approved of what he had done when he told me he had made a change.[99]

Later still, he referred to the honour in his diary.[100]

Though he did introduce friends of his to the poet, Crabb Robinson was careful not to abuse Wordsworth's confidence. He was on his guard against tuft-hunters when the poet was in London,[101] and he would not make requests of Wordsworth merely to please others.[102] He could even refuse the poet's best friends when he felt that compliance with their wishes would be unworthy of his relationship with Wordsworth.[103] This habitual discretion of Robinson's was amply rewarded by the trust placed in him by Wordsworth.[104]

At the time of their great sorrow, the Wordsworths knew that they had Crabb Robinson's sympathy, and they knew, too, that he would understand if they could not write. Quillinan wrote for Mrs Wordsworth: 'She is sure you understand why you do not hear from them. Writing is painful—and of you and your heart they are sure, silent or not.'[105] And after the poet's death, when Mrs Wordsworth did not invite Robinson for Christmas, she wrote: 'I need not explain why —you would understand the feeling.'[106]

In his last will and testament Robinson expressed the wish that Wordsworth's prose should be collected, and when—eight years later—the Rev. Alexander B. Grosart edited the *Prose Works*, he said that Robinson's wish was partly responsible for the edition.[107] On 13th November 1932 the poet's grandson wrote to me about Crabb:

I was getting on for six and a half when he died, and I must often have been shown to him, but alas! I have no recollection of his being shown to me, which would have been a much more valuable asset.[108]

The friendship between Wordsworth and Henry Crabb Robinson has been crystallized in nine lines dedicating the *Memorials of a Tour in Italy*, 'Companion! by whose buoyant Spirit cheered . . .' The original plan may have been to dedicate the Italian Memorials in prose. At the time of Dora's wedding, Wordsworth wrote to Crabb: 'Some time before Mary and I left home we inscribed your name upon a Batch of Italian Memorials, which you must allow me to dedicate to you when the day of Publication shall come.'[109] The matter of the dedication was brought up again the following Christmas. Wordsworth spoke of it when Robinson arrived on 24th December 1841,[110] and again ten days later. By this time the idea was beginning to take shape in verse.[111]

The lines had not taken their present form by 17th January.

W: read the intended dedication to me [said Robinson]. 'Cheerful companion and experienced guide and long tried friendship' are words of kindness I feel to be honouring—But he is dissatisfied with the word 'chearful' [sic] and 'tried friendship' as too strong, experienced would be better.[112]

To his brother Crabb wrote: 'The dedication will not be precisely what I wished, but it will be very honourable to the dedicatee.'[113]   But when Moxon showed him the proof-sheets on 16th February, Robinson wrote:

I am perfectly satisfied with these lines.   They are neither poetical nor encomiastic—so much the better—They come from the heart and the highest praise after all that I can receive is that I am an object of regard to such a man.[114]

Crabb Robinson was delighted with the dedication. He recited the lines to Samuel Rogers. He wrote gratefully to Mrs Wordsworth, commenting on 'the simple cordial and unadorned style.' Other honours, he said to Mrs Quillinan and to his brother, might make him vain, but this made him proud. Then his wit began to play over his own egotism. 'Here is a poor creature . . . who is delighted that his name will be stamped with that sort of immortality which is given by the writers of books that are to live for ever.'[115]

With the freedom expected of him Crabb criticized even the lines of dedication. He wanted to in the second line changed to in.[116]   Wordsworth objected to having in and ing so close together,

In whose experience trusting day by day,

and Crabb accepted the point—adding that it was 'strengthened by the custom in the North of sinking the g's in the participle present.'[117] But when the poem was published Crabb Robinson's alteration stood.

When the barrister found the 1842 volume in his chambers on 22nd April, he wrote to Mrs Wordsworth of his 'feverish anxiety to begin.' The next day he wrote again:

Reading the Dedication as part of a published book and not by

stealth . . . I am well aware that I have received the highest honour
I ever shall receive in this Life—Being in the King's Commission of
Assize and Nisi Prius is a fool to it! My pride is mixed up with
humility. I feel that I possess—that is, my name possesses a sort of
vicarious immortality   It is well—if a man can *do* nothing to stamp
his name, that the friendship of a great poet should *fix* it.[118]

This same thought was with him when Dr Wordsworth was
collecting material for the *Memoirs*. 'To be known as the friend
of Wordsworth,' Crabb wrote to his brother, 'confers a higher
distinction than a patent of nobility . . . I need not say—
with Cowley—

> I shall like other people dye
> Unless you write my elegy,

for I have got my passport to posterity.' [119]

Crabb Robinson it was who managed to salvage the friendship between Wordsworth and Coleridge when Wordsworth's
own negotiations seemed about to fail.

The rift between Wordsworth and Coleridge does not
properly belong to Wordsworth's later years, but a résumé of
the circumstances may throw light on Wordsworth's feeling
for Coleridge and for the children of Coleridge throughout his
life. The quarrel is commonly said [120] to have come from
Wordsworth's warning Basil Montagu about Coleridge in
October 1810, and Montagu's repeating the words to Coleridge
—probably with exaggerations. But the real cause of the break
was the later inequality of the men who had once been intimate,
and Coleridge's realization of this inequality. Coleridge could
accept hospitality and even money from Wordsworth,[121] but
he could not face the fact that he was weak-willed and Wordsworth self-reliant. It has been easy to blame the stronger
character, but Hartley and Sara Coleridge did not blame
Wordsworth.

Coleridge had sailed for Malta on 9th April 1804. Wordsworth had written to his friend: 'Heaven bless you for ever
and ever. No words can express what I feel at this moment.'

It is true that he had thought first of his own autobiographical poem when he heard of Coleridge's violent attack of illness. He feared he might never get Coleridge's criticism, and told him so.[122]   But Coleridge knew that he was then essential to Wordsworth—that the poetry and the man were inseparable.

For two years Coleridge was gone, and during much of that time Wordsworth was working on what is now called *The Prelude*. He had begun again about the time that Coleridge left Grasmere, in January 1804, and he finished the poem in May 1805.[123]   It was written to Coleridge, and in the early draft Wordsworth referred to him as the friend 'who in my thoughts art ever at my side,' and wrote 'as if to thee alone in private talk.' [124]   When Wordsworth lost his favourite brother, who perished on 11th February 1805, he said: 'He was worthy of his sister . . . and of the friendship of Coleridge.' [125]

The latter was gradually becoming addicted to opium. He accepted little or no personal responsibility, and when he returned to England in August 1806—though he knew that Wordsworth was eagerly waiting for his return to choose a suitable home—he did not even tell the Wordsworths his plans until October. Finally on 26th October they saw him,[126] and how changed he was!

> There is a change—and I am poor;
> Your love hath been, nor long ago,
> A fountain at my fond heart's door,
> Whose only business was to flow;
> And flow it did; not taking heed
> Of its own bounty, or my need.
>
> What happy moments did I count!
> Blest was I then all bliss above!
> Now, for that consecrated fount
> Of murmuring, sparkling, living love,
> What have I? shall I dare to tell?
> A comfortless and hidden well. . . .

Wordsworth wrote these lines about Coleridge at Coleorton before the year was out.[127]   This was four years before the definite quarrel, but the rift was beginning.[128]

I

Coleridge went to Coleorton just before Christmas, taking
ten-year-old Hartley with him, and remaining nearly two
months.[129]   There, Wordsworth read *The Prelude* to him.
There, Coleridge wrote his reply, *To a Gentleman*,[130] in which
he pictured the scene—Wordsworth reading the poem about
his spiritual development—

> And when—O Friend! my comfortor and guide!
> Strong in thy self, and powerful to give strength!—
> Thy long sustained Song finally closed,
> And thy deep voice had ceased—yet thou thyself
> Wert still before my eyes, and round us both
> That happy vision of beloved Faces.

But Coleridge was aware of the difference between them. After
calling his friend's poem

> An orphic song indeed,
> A song divine of high and passionate thoughts,
> To their own Music chaunted!

Coleridge thought of himself:

> And Fears self-willed, that shunn'd the eye of Hope;
> And Hope that scarce would know itself from Fear,
> Sense of past Youth, and Manhood come in vain,
> And Genius given, and Knowledge won in vain,
> And all which I had cull'd in Wood-walks wild,
> And all which patient toil had rear'd, and all
> Commune with *thee* had open'd out—but Flowers
> Strew'd on my corse . . .

In his bitterness he became jealous of Wordsworth. Professor de Selincourt says that he wrote his fears and suspicions
down in notebooks and brooded over them:

> He knew them to be unworthy alike of his friends and of himself
> even as he wrote them down; but by committing them to paper and
> brooding over them he gave them a stronger hold upon him. . . .[131]

Coleridge stayed at Coleorton until February, and Wordsworth spent April with him in London. Then for months
the Wordsworths heard nothing of him, and they believed
that he did not even open their letters. But when Wordsworth

heard in February 1808 that Coleridge was ill again, he went to London immediately and spent a month with him.

His illness [says Mr de Selincourt] was rather of the mind than of the body. William had often to wait till four o'clock in the afternoon to gain admittance to him, and then saw no appearance of disease which could not have been cured, or at least prevented by himself.[132]

Under Wordsworth's influence Coleridge seemed to improve, but shortly afterwards began his old suspicions, and—according to Mr de Selincourt—'he now persuaded himself that he was the object of a most cruel, and wellnigh universal, persecution.' In his morbidness he wrote Wordsworth a passionate letter 'accusing him of petty jealousy, and of lukewarm friendship even when he was not actually siding with his enemies against him,' and accusing Mrs Wordsworth and Dorothy of reading his letters to Sara Hutchinson and infusing into her mind the notion that Coleridge's attachment to her had been the curse of all his happiness.[133] Incapable now of generous friendship, Coleridge had to blame someone else for his own failure.

But the Wordsworths welcomed him to their home, and he lived with them at Allan Bank from September 1808 to May 1810. Hartley and Derwent came over from school at Ambleside to spend their week-ends with him, and little Sara visited now and then from Keswick. When Mrs Wordsworth's fifth baby was about to be born, Coleridge went to Keswick, supposedly for ten days. He stayed there five months, and at the end of October went to London with the Montagus, the party stopping overnight at Allan Bank.[134]

It cannot be denied that Wordsworth gave Basil Montagu a word of caution that Coleridge's habits would make him a difficult guest, and that Montagu in a moment of exasperation repeated the warning to Coleridge. Just what Wordsworth said is uncertain, and how Montagu repeated it. The latter was inclined to exaggerate, and Coleridge could easily make a mountain out of a molehill. But Wordsworth may have been patronizing, and Coleridge—almost four years before—had expressed his dread of being pitied by Wordsworth:

> Nor do thou,
> Sage Bard! impair the memory of that hour
> Of thy communion with my nobler mind
> By Pity or Grief, already felt too long! [135]

Wordsworth did not know until May how seriously Coleridge was offended. He heard later, in February 1812, that Coleridge had stopped at Ambleside for Hartley and Derwent and gone on to Keswick, without pausing at Grasmere to speak to him.[136] Coleridge had at last found something to fix his morbid fancies upon.

Mrs Thomas Clarkson, a friend of both poets, wrote of Coleridge:

> He is apt to make any one who listens to him the confident of his gloomy fancies or wild dreams of injuries—his best friends are not exempted from his accusations upon these occasions—let me caution you therefore against believing any thing to the prejudice of W. W. I mean with regard to his conduct as a friend of C. It has been affectionate and forbearing throughout.

'It is possible,' she said later, 'that there might be something stern in W—s manner but he has done so much for C— born [sic] so much from him that C. ought to forget it.' And when Crabb Robinson had accomplished what he did of reconciliation, she said:

> I knew before that C. was worthless as a friend—but nothing would have made me believe that he, who knew W. so thoroughly—and who must know himself—could have acted as he has by W—[137]

The reconciliation is treated in detail in Crabb Robinson's diary, extracts from which have been published by Miss Edith J. Morley in 'The Estrangement between Coleridge and Wordsworth.'[138] On 3rd May 1812 Coleridge told Crabb Robinson the whole bitter story, with permission to repeat to Wordsworth all that he said. Five days later Robinson did so, and Wordsworth denied much that he was charged with, but blamed himself for forgetting 'that M. was not a man whose discretion could be trusted with even so much as he did say to him.' Wordsworth preferred not to see Coleridge alone, because of the latter's 'bursts of passion or rather weakness.'

Coleridge apparently believed Basil Montagu implicitly, 'notwithstanding his own bad opinion of his veracity.' This Robinson intimated to him, 'and this he justified.'

Finally on Sunday, 10th May, Robinson got from Coleridge a plain statement in writing of what Montagu had reported Wordsworth to have said. This Wordsworth answered in writing, to Coleridge's satisfaction, or as Mr de Selincourt says:

Wordsworth, waiving all inquiry as to whether the initial error lay with Coleridge or Montagu, expressed his belief in Coleridge's sincerity, and convinced Coleridge that the 'monstrous words' attributed to him had never been spoken.[139]

Talking with Crabb Robinson while composing the letter, Wordsworth discussed Basil Montagu unfavourably: 'Of his veracity he has a very bad opinion indeed!'[140]

Basil Montagu's reputation as a gossip is fairly well established, but his reliability is further weakened by a hitherto unpublished entry in Crabb Robinson's diary thirty-three years later. Barry Cornwall and Crabb Robinson were breakfasting with Kenyon, eleven years after Coleridge's death. The former had married the stepdaughter of Basil Montagu, and he now told the Crabb about his father-in-law:

We talked of Coleridge, Bas[il] Montagu etc. freely. *He said of the latter that he seldom sees him, and intimated that though a man of good impulses . . . he wants principles so that there is no reliance upon him.*[141]

The reconciliation was supposedly accomplished, but the inequality remained and Coleridge could not entirely forget his bitterness. Just as he had apparently exaggerated his admiration for Wordsworth when the two were in complete accord,[142] he now seemed to exaggerate the hurt. Ten years after the supposed healing of the wound, Coleridge was dramatically telling Thomas Allsop of the 'four griping and grasping sorrows' of his life:

The second commenced on the night of my arrival (from Grasmere) in town with Mr and Mrs Montagu, when all the superstructure raised by my idolatrous Fancy during an enthusiastic and self-sacrificing Friendship of fifteen years—the fifteen bright and ripe years—the strong summer of my Life—burst like a Bubble![143]

Difficult though Coleridge was as a friend, Wordsworth never ceased to love him. He and Dora made a tour of the Rhine with him in 1828.[144] A few years later, after seeing Coleridge in London, he wrote to the brilliant young Irishman whom he considered like Coleridge, Sir William Rowan Hamilton:

I saw him several times lately, and had long conversations with him. It grieves me to say that his constitution seems much broken up. . . . His mind has lost none of its vigour.[145]

Wordsworth had hoped that Hamilton might meet Coleridge: 'You may pass your life without meeting a man of such commanding faculties.' But his affection for new friends was as nothing compared with his thoughtfulness of Coleridge. And when he heard that Hamilton's prospective trip to London had been given up, he was almost glad.

It would have grieved me [he wrote to him] had you been unfurnished with an introduction from me to Mr Coleridge, yet I know not how I could have given you one—he is often so very unwell . . . unless I were assured he was something in his better way, I could not disturb him by the introduction of anyone.[146]

And when Coleridge died, Wordsworth was even more aware of his lasting affection for him. Robert Perceval Graves, the clergyman at Windermere, called at Rydal Mount the Sunday after and was immediately told of the death of Coleridge—'one who had been, he said, his friend for more than thirty years.' Wordsworth talked a good deal about him,

called him the most *wonderful* man that he had ever known—wonderful for the originality of his mind, and the power he possessed of throwing out in profusion grand central truths from which might be evolved the most comprehensive systems.

He regretted the captivation of his taste by German meta-physics, for he thought Coleridge

might have done more permanently to enrich the literature, and to influence the thought of the nation, than any man of the age. As it was, however, he said he believed Coleridge's mind to have been a widely fertilising one. . . .

And when he read the clergyman the letter about Coleridge's death, Wordsworth was deeply moved.[147]

When *Blackwood's* published an article on 'The Plagiarisms of S. T. Coleridge' in March 1840, accusing Coleridge of thefts from Schelling and Schiller, Wordsworth was provoked to say: 'It is beyond measure absurd, to talk of this paltry stuff as the Magazinist has ventured to do.' Admitting his friend's slight debt to Schiller, he said: 'He gave to Schiller 50 times more than he took without thinking worth while to let the world know what he had done.'[148]

In conversation Wordsworth often got on the subject of Coleridge. At a neighbourhood tea-party in Mrs Davy's little parlour in July 1844, he was asked about Coleridge's discourse, and he said that it was like a 'majestic river,' which, though you sometimes could not see it for the bushes and sand, yet had a continuous stream. Again he said that 'Coleridge had been spoilt as a poet by going to Germany,' and that 'he would have been the greatest, the most abiding poet of his age.'[149] To Aubrey de Vere the next spring,[150] Wordsworth said that he had known many *clever* men, and many of real ability, 'but few of genius: and only one whom I should call "wonderful." That one was Coleridge.'[151]

David Hartley Coleridge, called 'Moses' in his childhood,[152] inherited something of his father's genius and much of his erratic nature. His love and veneration for his father were unbounded, and to him he dedicated his first volume of poems.[153] But Hartley did not fulfil his brilliant promise. Though many were fond of him, few, if any, respected him. 'I cannot help loving him,' wrote Wordsworth's grandson to me on 17th August 1933, 'everyone who knew him in the flesh loved him dearly, even the most straight-laced. Admiration of course is out of the question, but his humility and tenderness of affection win him *lovers* to this day.' [154]

Some of Wordsworth's friends disapproved of Hartley, for they saw only the drunkenness and the weakness of will.

> In no aspect [said Miss Martineau, after moving to the Lakes] did Wordsworth appear to more advantage than in his conduct to Hartley Coleridge . . . as long as there was any chance of good from remonstrance and rebuke, Wordsworth administered both, sternly and faithfully: but, when nothing more than pity and help was possible, Wordsworth treated him gently as if he had been—(what indeed he was in our eyes)—a sick child. [155]

She said of Hartley: 'The simple fact is that I was in company with him five times; and all those times he was drunk.' But Aubrey de Vere mentions one occasion in October 1845 when Coleridge's son and the rigid feminist were dining at Miss Fenwick's, and Hartley 'never exchanged a word with Miss Martineau . . . but read his father's poetry as well as his own drama of *Prometheus*.' [156] In 1849 Crabb Robinson was disgusted with Hartley's drunkenness:

> Poor Hartley ruined his intellects by a life of intense sottishness. . . . The best that can be said of him is that he was a kind-hearted man—Nobodys enemy but his own—He had considerable powers of conversation—The farmers and even gentry of the neighbourhood delighted in supplying him with drink—he made fun for them!!! [157]

Thomas Arnold saw both the lack of discipline and the colourful imagination. 'It is better not to probe one's reminiscences too far,' he said of Hartley. 'He was a melancholy ruin; when he was in the vein he would talk in an eloquent and richly imaginative strain, walking about the room all the time.' Once Hartley attended family prayers at Fox How, and seeing a jug of water brought in for Doctor Arnold, said 'in his deep emphatic tones, "Might I ask for a glass of *beer*?"' He had his beer, and departed. [158]

But Miss Fenwick liked Hartley Coleridge; for she cared little for 'worldly respectability,' [159] and—as Aubrey de Vere said—Hartley was not 'one of the smooth plausibilities of modern society.' [160] De Vere liked him, too. 'I have made acquaintance with Hartley Coleridge,' he wrote to Henry Taylor, in March 1845, 'whom I was anxious to know. It was a strange feeling to look at him and see his father in him. . . . If I were staying here I could wish to see a great deal of him.' [161] And Tennyson said: 'I liked Hartley Coleridge, "Massa Hartley" as the rustics called him. He was a loveable little fellow.' [162] Hartley was 'mightily taken' with Tennyson. He wrote a sonnet to him, and thanked Spedding for introducing them, or as Spedding wrote: '. . . after the fourth bottom of gin, deliberately thanked Heaven (under me, I believe, or me under Heaven, I forget which) for having brought them acquainted.' [163]

In the autumn of 1837, when Hartley was in his early forties, Caroline Fox met him. 'In person and dress,' she wrote in her diary, 'he was much brushed up; his vivid face sparkled in the shadow of a large straw hat.' She described him as

a little, round, high-shouldered man, shrunk into a little black coat, the features of his face moulded by habit into an expression of pleasantry and an appreciation of the exquisitely ludicrous. Such as one could fancy Charles Lamb's. Little black eyes twinkling intensely, as if every sense were called on to taste every idea. He is very anxious to establish an Ugly Club and to be its chairman; but really he is quite unworthy of the station, for odd enough he is, but never ugly, there is such a radiant light of genius over all.[164]

Hartley took Caroline and her sister up to the Mount, where Mrs Wordsworth gave them 'ginger-wine and gingerbread,' and congratulated them in an undertone on their 'rare good fortune in having Hartley Coleridge as a guide.' He drove with them to Ambleside, and then did not leave them: 'At dinner, he had a sad choking-fit, so queerly conducted as to try our propriety sadly. Then when he had anything especially pointed to say, he would stand up or even walk round the dining-table.' [165]

This strange method of emphasizing his remarks Caroline

Fox noted again, seven years later. Hartley had told her that the Arnolds were 'a most gifted family,' and she had asked him to be more specific. 'He rose from the dinner-table, as his manner is, and answered, "Why, they were suckled on Latin and weaned upon Greek."' [166] It was not only at dinner that Hartley surprised his companions by suddenly rising. Sometimes, at church, he 'assumed the attitude of an approving beneficent spirit, and to the surprise of the congregation would rise from his knees whilst they were still engaged in prayer, spreading out his hands above their heads in a gesture of benediction, and with a gentle, benevolent smile.' [167]

Hartley's eccentricity is further illustrated by two stories of Tennyson's. Hartley was invited to dine with 'a stiff Presbyterian clergyman' and his family:

The party sat a long time in the drawing-room waiting for dinner. Nobody talked. At last Hartley could stand it no longer, he jumped up from the sofa, kissed the clergyman's daughter, and bolted out of the house.

In the other story Hartley started on a walking tour with some friends. 'They suddenly missed him, and could not find him anywhere, and did not see him again for six weeks, when he emerged from some inn.' [168]

His walk was peculiar. 'He wandered about the room,' said de Vere in 1845, 'having as it were no hold of the ground, and supporting himself like a swimmer on extended arms. Every moment he laid his hand on his round grey head—a strange, interesting, forlorn being.' [169]

Hartley lived at Nab Cottage, between Grasmere and Rydal, which he tried to get people to spell 'the Knbbe.' Caroline and Anna Maria Fox once took refuge from a shower in Hartley's cottage, and found it 'a snug little *room*, well furnished with books, writing affairs, and MSS. . . .' [170] When one of them suggested that a person could be very happy there, '"*Or very miserable*," he answered, with such a sad and terrible emphasis.' [170]

Wordsworth loved Hartley Coleridge as a son. In 1840

Hartley was forty-four years old—and still childlike. Forty years earlier, when the child's father had proudly written:

Hartley is a spirit that dances on an aspen leaf. . . . Never was more joyous creature born. Pain with him is . . . wholly transubstantiated by the joys that had rolled on before, and rushed on after,[171]

Wordsworth had feared for the 'faery voyager.' His poem to Coleridge's little six-year-old boy seems prophetic of Hartley's later years.[172] In 1814, when Joseph Cottle urged Coleridge to throw off the opium habit and try to develop the brilliant possibilities of his children—especially Hartley [173]—it was Wordsworth and Dorothy, not Coleridge, who were taking thought for the boys' schooling. It was Wordsworth who assisted Hartley's uncles and Thomas Poole in raising the money for college expenses. It was Wordsworth who gave him paternal counsel when Hartley went up to Oxford as a postmaster of Merton.[174] When the latter took his degree and won the Oriel Fellowship in 1819, his honours rejoiced Wordsworth. But Coleridge's son was not happy in his triumph, and the Fellowship was forfeited at the end of a year, 'mainly on the grounds of intemperance.'[175] It was Wordsworth, too, who 'was with him when he received the tidings of his father's death, and found him calm but much dejected, deeply lamenting that he had seen so little of him during the course of their lives.'[176]

During most of Wordsworth's last decade Hartley was in the Lake District, and the poet was delighted when he moved to Nab Cottage, closer to Rydal Mount. 'Of Genius,' wrote the poet to Crabb Robinson, 'he has not a little, and talent enough for fifty.'[177] Hartley's will-power, however, was nothing, and Wordsworth could not fail to recognize the fact. When Moxon asked him to spur the younger man on, Wordsworth replied that he had done all he could, and that Hartley now avoided him—'tells every one . . . that he is going to send off the last remainder of the copy next day, and this has been the case for the last month or six weeks.' The old friend added sadly: 'It is, therefore, evident that you must trust

nothing to him in future.'[178]   He had told Caroline Fox the
summer before that Hartley was like his father in 'the want
of will which characterized both,' and that in the father 'the
amazing effort which it was to him to will anything was
indescribable.'[179]

Wordsworth's affection for Hartley was probably greater
than that which the latter felt for him. Having known his
father's friend as long as he could remember, Hartley took the
stronger side of the old man's character for granted. 'He is
a most unpleasant companion in a tour,' he told Caroline Fox,
'from his terrible fear of being cheated; neither is he very
popular as a neighbour.'[180]   Of Wordsworth's genius, he told
her: 'Whilst the fit of inspiration lasts he is every inch a poet;
when he tries to write without it he is very dragging.' On
another occasion

He talked of Wordsworth with high respect, but no enthusiasm.
. . . The reason for his not permitting the prologue to the 'Excursion' to be published till after his death is, he believes, that the
benefit of copyright may be enjoyed longer.[181]

Aubrey de Vere, however, said in 1845 that Hartley read
Wordsworth's poems with enthusiasm.

Though Hartley took his old friend so much for granted, he
did feel close to him, and he understood Wordsworth's intense
affection for his only daughter. From childhood, Hartley had
teased Dora Wordsworth, eight years his junior, and she had
parried his thrusts. When she had tried to palm off some
of Quillinan's verses as written by one of the Westmorland
rustics, Hartley's repartee was quick enough.[182]   Underneath
their merry banter Dora and Hartley understood each other,
and Hartley's sympathy for the Wordsworths during their
daughter's lingering illness in 1847 shows the strength of the
bond between Wordsworth and the son of Coleridge. To a
contemporary friend Hartley wrote:

If you had seen how by the secret strength of affection she entered
into the recesses of her Father's mind, and drew him out to gambol
with her in the childishness that always hung upon her womanhood,

you would feel as we do, what earth is about to lose and Heaven to gain. May God support her Father and Mother under the loss—and to that end join your prayers to mine.[183]

Hartley Coleridge fell ill in December 1848, after spending five hours, drunk, in the open air on a rainy night. Diarrhoea developed, and his condition rapidly became worse. Four medical men attended him voluntarily, and the whole country-side was distressed. Wordsworth was 'deeply excited,' and walked every day or oftener to Nab Cottage. Mrs Words-worth wrote to Sara Coleridge of her brother's alarming con-dition, the letter arriving on Christmas Day. The Rev. Derwent Coleridge, now Principal of St Mark's College, Chelsea,[184] and Prebendary of St Paul's,[185] hurried to his brother and attended him to the end, and 'the old poet who had so often held him in his arms . . . knelt at his side to receive his last Communion with him.'[186] Derwent was impressed by the simple piety of his brother, and by the devotion of Wordsworth. 'Mr W— has seen him,' he wrote to Sara, 'and was much affected. His own appearance was very striking, and his countenance beautiful, as he sat by the bedside.'[187]

On Saturday, 6th January 1849, Hartley Coleridge died.[188] Afterwards, Derwent wrote to his sister:

Mr and Mrs W— had been at the cottage during my absence. Mrs W— kissed the cold face thrice, said it was beautiful, and decked the body with flowers. . . . Mr W— was dreadfully affected, and could not go in.[189]

Wordsworth went with Derwent to Grasmere churchyard the following Tuesday to pick the place for Hartley's grave. They decided on a spot just behind the Wordsworth graves, the old poet saying: 'Let him lie as near to us as possible, leaving room for Mrs Wordsworth and myself. It would have been his wish.'[190]

The funeral took place on Thursday, 11th January, at noon. It was a bitter day, raining during the actual service, but Wordsworth and Quillinan attended—along with Derwent, Angus Fletcher, and the medical men.[191] After the funeral

Wordsworth walked over to Loughrigg Holme and sat with his son-in-law: 'He talked . . . a good deal about the Coleridges, especially *the* S. T. C.' [192]

That her brother was buried near the Wordsworths, and that the poet was present at the ceremony, was a consolation to Sara Coleridge. 'It soothes me,' she wrote to her brother-in-law, 'to think that my dear brother, the greater part of whose life has been spent in our dear friend's daily sight, should in death not be parted from them.' [193]   She derived great comfort from remembering what Wordsworth had said about Hartley two years before:

Tributes of admiration to his intellectual endowments, his winning, though eccentric manners, were plentiful as flowers in summer. This was *more*. It showed me that he was esteemed in heart by one who knew him well, if ever one man could know another—one not too lenient in his moral judgments.[194]

The old poet's love for the son of his friend impressed Ellis Yarnall the next summer: 'Of Hartley Coleridge he spoke with much affection: he was much beloved by all who knew him, notwithstanding his wayward and careless life.' [195]

Only less than Hartley Coleridge did Wordsworth love the sister—unlike her irresponsible brother and father in many ways, and yet something akin to both.   'Sarah [*sic*] Coleridge . . .,' said Crabb Robinson in 1849, 'has as much industry as Derwent and as much genius as Hartley.' [196]   Aubrey de Vere said of her: 'To those who knew her she remains an image of grace and intellectual beauty that time can never tarnish.' [197]   And one friend wrote to another: 'She justifies her father's existence, if it needed it.' [198]   The late Gordon Wordsworth wrote in August 1933:

I share your admiration for Sara Coleridge.   Neither her extraordinary keenness of critical insight, nor the beauty of much of Hartley's verse has ever met its due appreciation. . . . But for being their father's children both would be larger figures in English Literature.[199]

Born on Christmas Eve, 1802, Sara Coleridge saw comparatively little of her brilliant father. She grew up at Greta Hall, Keswick, where her Uncle Southey, as a consequence of the Pantisocracy scheme, made a home for three of the Fricker sisters—Mrs Southey, Mrs Coleridge, and Mrs Lovell—and all the children.

When little Sara—not quite six years old—visited her father at Allan Bank, she felt the emotional strain between her father and her absent mother, and the unreasonable demands made by her father on her own affection. She felt, too, the ease with which Dora Wordsworth and her brothers romped over Coleridge, whereas she was almost a stranger. In later life she recorded the visit for her own daughter.

. . . I think my dear father was anxious that I should learn to love him and the Wordsworths and their children, and not cling so exclusively to my mother, and all around me at home. He was therefore much annoyed when, on my mother's coming to Allan Bank, I flew to her, and wished not to be separated from her any more. I remember his showing displeasure to me, and accusing me of want of affection. I could not understand why. . . . I sat benumbed; for truly nothing does so freeze affection as the breath of jealousy. . . . My father reproached me, and contrasted my coldness with the childish caresses of the little Wordsworths. I slunk away, and hid myself in the wood behind the house. . . .[200]

In some ways, however, her father understood her, where her mother and her Uncle Southey completely failed. Sara was terrified of the dark, which she peopled with lions, with the ghost in *Hamlet*, with Death at Hell-Gate (from an old copy of *Paradise Lost*), and with horrors from Southey's own ballads, especially 'the horse with eyes of flame.' Her uncle 'laughed heartily' at her agonies. Her mother scolded her 'for creeping out of bed after an hour's torture, and stealing down to her in the parlour.' But Coleridge understood. 'He insisted,' wrote Sara, grateful even after forty years, 'that a lighted candle should be left in my room, in the interval between my retiring to bed and mamma's joining me. From that time forth my sufferings ceased.' [201]

Sara did not play much with the boisterous Dora Wordsworth. She was delicate in childhood, and preferred her quiet
cousin, Edith Southey. Though only eleven when Cottle
urged Coleridge for the sake of his children to throw off the
opium habit, Sara was already a student. With her indefati-
gable uncle as model and occasional tutor, she was largely
teaching herself, and poring over the volumes of Southey's
immense library.

When she was twenty Sara went with her mother to visit
Coleridge at Highgate. Of her appearance about that time
Henry Taylor said:

I have always been glad that I did see her in her girlhood, because
I then saw her beauty untouched by time, and it was a beauty which
could not but remain in one's memory for life, and which is now
distinctly before me as I write. The features were perfectly shaped,
and almost minutely delicate, and the complexion delicate too, but
not wanting in colour, and the general effect was that of gentleness,
indeed I may say of composure, even to stillness. Her eyes were
large, and they had the sort of serene lustre which I remember in
her father's.[202]

Mrs Towle writes that Sara's beauty was at this time 'so
remarkable that once, upon her entering a theatre, the audience,
as she went to her place, stood up simultaneously to see her
pass.' [203]

Among the young disciples of Coleridge at Highgate that
winter of 1822 was his nephew, Henry Nelson Coleridge,
'a younger son of James Coleridge, Esq., of Heath's Court,
Ottery St Mary,' formerly of Eton and Cambridge, and now
a Chancery barrister living in Lincoln's Inn. [204]   As an
undergraduate, Henry Nelson had been a serious student,
winning the Browne medal for Greek and Latin Odes and a
Fellowship at King's College. He was also an ardent Wordsworthian.[205] It is no wonder, therefore, that when he fell
under his uncle's spell he should be drawn to his brilliant
and beautiful cousin whom he now met for the first time.

When Sara returned to Keswick she applied herself even
more to the Greek and Latin classics, and studied French,

Sara Coleridge
Miniature by Miss Jones

Italian, German, and Spanish.[206] She translated from the French and published, in 1825, the *Memoirs of the Chevalier Bayard, by the Loyal Servant.*[207] In 1826 she went again to London.[208]

Meanwhile, she had become intimate with Dora Wordsworth, and in April 1829, she and her mother visited at Rydal Mount. Wordsworth enjoyed the daughter more than the complaining mother, for he wrote to Crabb Robinson:

> Sara Coleridge, one of the loveliest and best of Creatures, is with me so that I am an enviable person notwithstanding our domestic impoverishment. Mrs Coleridge is here also—and if pity and compassion for others anxieties were a sweet sensation I might be envied on that account also for I have enough of it.[209]

To Sara, to Dora, and to Edith Southey he had written *The Triad* the year before, and published it in the *Keepsake* for 1829.[210] He was probably influenced to write this poem by Sara's long engagement and approaching marriage, for on 3rd September 1829 Sara Coleridge was married at Crosthwaite church, Keswick, to Henry Nelson Coleridge.[211]

Her early married life was marred by ill-health. Never robust, she bore five children, of whom only two survived. For much of the time that she lived in the 'tiny cottage' in Hampstead, she was confined to her bed,[212] and during this time of prolonged ill-health she wrote the fairy tale, *Phantasmion*, for the amusement of her children. By 1837, however, when the family moved to a more commodious home at 10 Chester Place, Regent's Park, Sara Coleridge's health had improved a little, her two children were well, and she made her presence felt in intellectual circles of London society.

An intensely genuine person, Sara Coleridge presented many facets to her various friends. Though serious by nature, she was able to enter into the lighter moods of others. Aubrey de Vere was impressed by her many 'friendships so faithful and unexacting.'[213] She wrote verse, too, but not such original verse as Hartley's. Her literary gift was rather that of appreciation and criticism. 'Few have possessed such learning,'

K

said Aubrey de Vere; and then, rejoicing at her unconsciousness of it, he added: 'Her great characteristic was the radiant spirituality of her intellectual and imaginative being.' [214]

In January 1843 came to Sara Coleridge the great sorrow of her life. She had already lost her father and three of her children. Her Uncle Southey was now in a state worse than death. She was later to lose her mother, her friend Dora Wordsworth, and her strange, lovable brother, Hartley. But in 1842 Henry Nelson Coleridge was stricken with spinal paralysis. Wordsworth's son went with Robinson to inquire after his health.[215] The poet wrote in November to Henry Nelson's brother: 'Towards Sara I have much of the tenderness of a father, having had her so near us and so long under our eye while she was growing up.' [216] On 17th January Crabb Robinson heard distressing news: 'The old lady ill of the rheumatism. H: N: C: himself in a hopeless state—Sarah [sic], that delicate and tender creature bearing up as bravely as possible against such complicated calamities.' [217] The end came on 26th January. Though naturally restrained, Sara Coleridge probably spoke from the depths of her own suffering when she wrote to Robinson, in June, that most of Wordsworth's poems refer 'not to the heaviest loss of all.' The mother of two half-grown children herself, she wrote: 'Even those who are not childless may be ready to exclaim with Wordsworth's gray-haired man of glee

And many love me, but by none
Am I enough beloved.' [218]

Sara Coleridge's widowhood was enriched by her children, and by her literary and theological interests. Herbert and Edith had good minds, Herbert particularly showing great precocity in early childhood. His mother supervised his education, continuing to read Greek with him in the summers as long as he was at Eton.[219] Herbert went up to Oxford as Newcastle and Balliol scholar, and in 1852 took a double first. He became, also, an Icelandic scholar, and was one of the first instigators of the *New English Dictionary*.[220] Edith was a companionable girl,[221] and went with her mother to visit the Wordsworths and Miss Fenwick at Bath. She used to read aloud to Sara 'the Bible in the afternoon and in the evening Wordsworth.' [222]   It was Edith who later edited her mother's *Memoir and Letters*.

Sara Coleridge's affection for her father was partly responsible for her literary interests, and these in turn led her into metaphysical and theological inquiries. Attempting to understand and explain her father's writings, Sara edited several of his works, and studying him, became involved in the theological battles of the mid-nineteenth century.

Shortly after her husband's death Sara Coleridge was 'writing on her father's religious opinions.' [223]   She took up, also, her husband's unfinished task of editing the *Biographia Literaria*, and spent years on it, bringing it to completion in March or April 1847.   Two years later she edited two volumes of Coleridge's lectures on Shakespeare. And just before her death she edited his poetry, 'the last monument of her highly gifted mind.'   The edition purports to be by Sara and Derwent, but the latter says: 'At her earnest request, my name appears with hers on the title-page, but the assistance rendered by me has been, in fact, little more than mechanical.' [224]

Always on the defensive about her father, Sara resented Cottle's publishing the letters about Coleridge's opium-taking. Toward Wordsworth, too, she seemed to feel some bitterness for a while.[225]   And yet when she wrote the memoir for her father's poetry, she quoted the letters from Cottle's *Reminiscences*, and spoke of her father's weakness as frankly as his worst detractors.   She always presented the truth as she saw it, both the 'splendid spacious halls' and the 'dark narrow chambers' of her father's mind, the 'tawdry imitations' as well as the 'real glories.' [226]

Sara Coleridge was intensely interested in the great religious upheaval of her day, the Oxford Movement. Aware that theological discussion was now the fashion,[227] she was not blinded by terms or by great names.   Partly in sympathy with the High Church party, she was against Puseyism.[228] She corresponded with Frederick Maurice, but unlike him, did not believe in 'baptismal regeneration considering regeneration as a state of certain salvation.'[229] Stirred by the spiritual revival in the Church of England, she went only half-way with Newman.[230]

Crabb Robinson, himself a Unitarian, was impressed by the essential liberality of young Mrs Coleridge.[231] And when Harriet Martineau began to be ostracized for her anti-theological opinions,[232] Sara Coleridge was tolerant.[233] Her own ideas were the result of honest conviction, and she accorded others the same liberty of thought.

Sara Coleridge lost her mother on 24th September 1845, and Hartley on 6th January 1849. In both sorrows the Wordsworths expressed their sympathy. The poet wrote to Derwent when Mrs Coleridge died, and sent his 'kindest and most earnest and affectionate wishes' to Sara.[234] The latter had made a home for her mother, had thought of her 'every minute of the day'; and now, when the old lady suddenly passed away, Sara felt that the loss was almost insupportable.[235] Between Hartley and Sara there had been no real intimacy, but her love reached out to him, and his death left a gap which Crabb Robinson could not understand.[236]

Sara Coleridge felt for Wordsworth, poet and man, the kind of debt one cannot pay. 'To Mr W. and my father,' she wrote to Miss Fenwick in July 1847, 'I owe my *thoughts* more than to all other men put together.'[237] Before she had any notion what the abstract discussions meant, she used to like to listen to Wordsworth's talk.

I knew dear Mr Wordsworth [she wrote to Professor Reed in 1851] perhaps as well as I have ever known any one in the world—more intimately than I knew my father, and as intimately as I knew my Uncle Southey. There was much in him to know, and the lines of his character were deep and strong—the whole they formed, simple and impressive. . . . I used to take long walks with Mr Wordsworth about Rydal and Grasmere, and sometimes, though seldom, at Keswick, to his Applethwaite cottage, listening to his talk all the way;

and for hours have I often listened when he conversed with my
uncle, or, indoors at Rydal Mount, when he chatted or harangued
to the inmates of his household or the neighbours.[238]

When the Wordsworths were old, she loved them for what
they were then, but more for the past. In the latter part of
March 1847 she and her daughter journeyed to Bath, and
visited Miss Fenwick at 8 Queen Square, to be with her 'dear
old friends, Mr and Mrs Wordsworth.' The old couple were
waiting at the station, 'and most affectionate was their greet-
ing.' To her brother-in-law Sara wrote: 'Mr Wordsworth has
always called me his child, and he seems to feel as if I were
such indeed.'[239]   A week later she wrote to Crabb Robinson:
'It is quite a happiness to me to be with my dear old friends
here. The remembrance of their affectionate behaviour to me
will remain with me a lasting possession. I am glad also for
my Edith to know them.'[240]   She could not help comparing
the later Wordsworth with the earlier—just as she was in the
habit of comparing his later poetry with his earlier—and a man
of seventy-seven is likely to suffer by such comparison. She
wrote to Aubrey de Vere in April 1847:

Mr Wordsworth can walk seven or eight miles very well, and he
talks a good deal in the course of the day; but his talk is, at the best,
but the faintest possible image of his pristine mind as shown in conversation; he is dozy and dull during a great part of the day. . . .
He seems rather to recontinue his former self, and repeat by habit
what he used to think and feel, than to think any thing new. To
me he is deeply interesting, even in his present state, for the sake
of the past.[241]

But on Milton Wordsworth spoke in a manner satisfactory even
to Sara Coleridge. 'They are aged since I saw them last,' she
wrote to one friend, 'but still wonderful people of their age,
very active in body, and in mind to me most interesting. We
have many, many mutual recollections and interests and
acquaintanceships.'[242]

In London, too, she saw Wordsworth—looking 'remarkably
well,' and with a 'rosy hue over his face.' Her husband's
nephew, John Duke Coleridge, had met him at Paddington

station and found him 'wondrously full of vigour, quite a grand
old man, and as one might expect the poet Wordsworth to
be.' [243] During that last visit to London, or before, the
Laureate began his one laureate poem, *Ode on the Installation of
His Royal Highness Prince Albert as Chancellor of the University of
Cambridge, July 1847*. Sara wrote to Miss Fenwick on
26th April:

> You have heard, no doubt, that he has written part of the Instal-
> lation Ode; Miss F. says that there is a great deal of thought in it;
> but he says himself that it is but superficial thought, and that it is
> not worth much. However, I am glad that his mind is still lithe
> enough to perform such tasks, even in an ordinary manner, if
> ordinary it be.[244]

But the visit and the ode were cut short that very day by news
from the north that his beloved daughter was in imminent
danger.

Sara Coleridge's letters for the next few months are full
of Dora Quillinan, her 'earliest companion-friend,' of Dora's
heavenly composure in the knowledge of her approaching death,
of reminiscences of Dora's bursting into tears in the midst
of childish games in Grasmere churchyard when the other
children thoughtlessly 'read aloud the names of her little
departed sister and brother.' And then, when the bright-
hearted Dora was laid beside Catharine and Thomas, Sara
Coleridge went to Westmorland to accompany the body to
its last resting-place and to comfort the parents.

Wordsworth's own death she bore serenely, for the aged poet
had been 'no longer glad as of yore.' [245] But his death removed
almost the last prop of Sara's girlhood, and brought back to
her the loss of those others whom she greatly loved.[246] 'Hartley and Mr Wordsworth,' she wrote, 'were great figures in my
circle of early friends, and leave a large blank to my mind's
eye.' [247] Later in the year Sara Coleridge wrote the last entry
in Dora's album, fourteen lines in octosyllabic couplets
entitled *Prayer for Tranquillity*.[248]

Pickersgill's fashionable portrait of Wordsworth aroused in

Sara Coleridge the same kind of fury that she felt for the detractors of her father:

Pickersgill's portrait of our dear departed great poet is *insufferable* —velvet waist-coat, neat shiny boots—just the sort of dress he would not have worn if you could have hired him—and a sombre senti- mentalism of countenance quite unlike his own look, which was either elevated with high gladness or deep thought, or at times simply and childishly gruff; but never tender after that fashion, so lacka- daisical and mawkishly sentimental.[249]

Sara Coleridge studied Wordsworth throughout her life and regarded his poetry as a sort of norm for that of others. Keats and Shelley she compared with Wordsworth in 1845: 'To be always reading Shelley and Keats would be like living on quince marmalade. Milton and Wordsworth are substantial diet for all times and seasons.'[250] Milton's treatment of nature she contrasted with that of Wordsworth the following year,[251] and said that Crabbe's descriptions bear the same relation to Milton's and Wordsworth's as the expression of Murillo's pictures to that of Raphael's and Leonardo's.[252] She amused herself by re-reading and grouping Wordsworth's sonnets, 'as we play with a wreath of gems, placing them in many different lights and positions for the gratification of the eye.'[253]

When *The Prelude* was posthumously published, she rejoiced in the individual beauties of the poem, in the reflections of Wordsworth's mind, and in the testimony of friendship to her father. Even before she saw the poem, she wrote to Wordsworth's son-in-law:

It is great pride and pleasure indeed to me that it is addressed to my father. They will be ever specially associated in the minds of men in time to come. I think there was never so close a union between two such eminent minds in any age. They were together, and in intimate communion, at the most vigorous, the most inspired period of the lives of both.[254]

After reading the poem she wrote to Professor Reed, the American editor:

It is deeply interesting as the image of a great poetic mind: none but a mind on a great scale could have produced it. As a supplement to the poetic works of the author, it is of the highest value. You may imagine how I was affected and gladdened by the warm tributes which it contains to my father, and the proof it affords of their close intimacy and earnest friendship. I think the history of literature hardly affords a parallel instance of entire union and unreserve between two poets.[255]

With Aubrey de Vere she discussed *The Prelude* in more detail, revealing her happiness that the friendship was not one-sided, her gratitude that Wordsworth recognized his debt to Coleridge:

And, oh, how affectionate is all the concluding portion! I do feel deeply thankful for the revelation of Wordsworth's *heart* in this poem. Whatever sterner feelings may have succeeded at times to this tenderness and these outpourings of love, it raises him greatly in my mind to find that he was able to give himself thus out to another, during one period of his life—not to absorb all my father's affectionate homage, and to respond no otherwise than by a gracious reception of it. There are many touches, too, of something like softness and modesty and humbleness, which, taken in conjunction with those virtues of his character which are allied to confidence and dignified self-assertion, add much to his character of amiability. To be humble, in *him* was a merit indeed; and this merit did not appear so evidently in his later life as in these earlier manifestations of his mind.[256]

She blurted out at the end: 'I believe W— took quite as much as he gave in this exchange.'

The 1847 edition of the *Biographia Literaria*, begun by her husband and finished by Sara Coleridge, was a labour of love,[257] and it was fitting that she should dedicate it to her father's old friend. She did not hesitate, moreover, to draw on Wordsworth's poetic lore to identify various quotations.[258] As early as July 1846, Crabb Robinson wrote in his diary that Mrs Coleridge was 'in the Press' with the *Biographia*. She was worried by the charge of plagiarism from Schelling,[259] but Robinson reassured her that in his opinion Coleridge was unaware of the theft.[260] In November, too, she was 'at work on her father's Literary Biogr:.'[261] Correcting proof the first months of 1847, she postponed her trip to Bath until late March.

Meanwhile, she wrote to Crabb Robinson, then on his Christmas visit at Rydal Mount, to ask Wordsworth's permission to dedicate the book to him. 'Soon I had from himself,' she wrote to Miss Fenwick, 'an affectionate and gracious accedence to my wish. He said, what I wished him to say and feel, that no one now had so good a claim.' [262] She wrote the dedication on 30th January 1847, linking her father and Wordsworth:

. . . His name was early associated with your's [sic] from the time when you lived as neighbours, and both together sought the Muse, in the lovely Vale of Stowey. That this association may endure as long as you are both remembered,—that not only as a Poet, but as a Lover and a Teacher of Wisdom, my Father may continue to be spoken of in connection with you, while your writings become more and more fully and widely appreciated, is the dearest and proudest wish that I can form for his memory.

I remain, dear Mr Wordsworth,

With deep affection, admiration, and respect,

Your Child in heart and faithful Friend,

Sara Coleridge.[263]

Not only for the dedication, but for the elaborate preface, 'a dissertation for its depth and clearness unrivalled,' [264] and the illuminating, interpretative footnotes—this second edition of the *Biographia Literaria* is another monument to the friendship between Coleridge and Wordsworth.

Sara Coleridge was never old; she was not quite fifty when she died. Three years before, Ellis Yarnall visited her in London, and found her gracious and stimulating:

I see her now as she entered her pretty drawing-room, her face pale, her complexion almost transparent, her eyes large and of a peculiar lustre. I could well understand that she had been beautiful in youth. She received me with gentle cordiality. . . . Her talk impressed me much; for I felt how rich was her mental endowment, how high and pure her thought.[265]

He spent an hour and a half with her later. This time 'she

talked with peculiar animation; there was the glow of genius
in her face—a radiant expression that put one under a spell.'
Yet even in 1849 Yarnall noticed

a look almost of languor in her eyes, an undefined something showing
that her health might be frail. The hand of death was probably even
then on her, known only to herself. I learned afterward that she
gave no sign to those nearest to her of her dread anticipation.[265]

For years she suffered from cancer. Just how early she suspected the nature of her disease is uncertain. Two years
before the end,

her medical attendant had become aware of its existence and saw how
great was her danger. Hope for her, however, was cherished; but
for the last few months the progress of the disease was rapid. She
bore her sufferings with remarkable fortitude.[266]

In March 1851 she contracted influenza,[267] from which
apparently she never rallied. A few months before the end
she wrote to a friend of Hartley's:

> 'Espouse thy doom at once, and cleave
>   To fortitude without reprieve,

are words that often sound in my ear. Wordsworth was more
to my opening mind in the way of religious consolation than
all books put together, except the Bible.' [268]   On 3rd May
1852 she died.[269]

IV. FRIENDS OF THE LAKE DISTRICT

BESIDES his most intimate friends, Wordsworth was on friendly terms with almost every family in the neighbourhood. From Greta Hall in Keswick to Elleray in Windermere, and from the little rectory at Langdale to Lowther Castle, the poet was welcome; and he liked to wander to Lancrigg, to Dove Cottage, to Nab Cottage, to the Flemings' cottage at the foot of Rydal hill, to Loughrigg Holme, to Fox How, to the Oaks, to the Knoll, and to many homes in Ambleside.

At Greta Hall lived Southey, Coleridge's brother-in-law, and Wordsworth's friend for more than forty years—a changed Southey, married in later life to Caroline Bowles and suffering from a rapidly increasing brain disease, a Southey whose grown children were quarrelling among themselves over their step-mother.

Wordsworth had first met Robert Southey through Coleridge either at Bristol about 1795 or at Keswick on Wordsworth's return from Scotland in 1803.[1] Though there was never between Wordsworth and Southey any great intimacy, they soon became friendly, and Southey felt, as early as 1805, that Wordsworth was the greatest poet of their generation.[2] When Jeffrey boasted in 1814 that he had written a *crushing* review of *The Excursion*, Southey said: 'He might as easily crush Skiddaw.'[3] Wordsworth felt the worth of Southey, too—particularly the moral worth.[4] Despite the rift between Coleridge and Wordsworth and the greater rift between Coleridge and Southey, despite Landor's attacks on Wordsworth for supposed slights to Southey, Wordsworth and the lesser poet at Greta Hall steadily continued their even friendship.

Though Landor's first attack, *A Satire on Satirists and Admonition to Detractors*, claimed that Wordsworth had belittled Southey's poetry to Landor in May 1836, it was at Wordsworth's 'urgent recommendation' that Southey was then

bringing out a complete edition of his poems.[5]   Crabb Robinson
was afraid that Landor's attack might interrupt the friendship
between Wordsworth and Southey; so he made each promise
not to read the attack, and then told Landor what he had done.[6]
The friendship was not broken, even by Landor's dialogue
between *Porson and Southey* six years later.   By this time
Southey was beyond the power of Landor's venom, and
Wordsworth did not even read the dialogue.

In 1834 or 1835 Mrs Southey had lost her mind, and Southey
and the children, especially Kate, had nursed her constantly
until her death, in the autumn of 1837.   In the spring, while
his first wife was still alive, Southey had visited Caroline
Bowles,[7] then over fifty, with whom he had corresponded for
years.   In October 1838, while Bertha and Kate were still in
deep mourning, their father announced to them by letter that
he was to be married again.[8]   They were then on a visit to
Miss Fenwick at Ambleside.

It was naturally a great shock to them both [wrote Wordsworth]
and nothing could have been more fortunate than that the tidings
reached them when they were here; as we all contributed greatly to
reconcile them to the step, much sooner and with less pain, than they
could have effected a thing so difficult, of themselves.[9]

Carlyle describes the elderly bridegroom, calling with Miss
Fenwick at Chelsea:

He was now about sixty-three; his work all done, but his heart
as if broken.   A certain Miss Bowles, given to scribbling, with its
affectations, its sentimentalities, and perhaps twenty years younger
than he,[10] has [*sic*] (as I afterwards understood) heroically volunteered
to marry him, 'for the purpose of consoling,' etc., etc.; to which he
heroically had assented; and was now on the road towards Bristol, or
the western region where Miss Bowles lived, for completing that poor
hope of his and hers.   A second wedlock; in what contrast almost
dismal, almost horrible, with a former one . . . this second one
was to be celebrated under sepulchral lamps, and as if in the fore-
coast of the charnel-house!   Southey's deep misery of aspect I
should have better understood had this been known to me; but it
was known to Taylor alone.[11]

Southey and Miss Bowles were married on 4th June 1839.[12]

Mrs Southey later blamed Cuthbert and Kate for not having informed her of their father's mental condition. But William Jerdan, whose account is otherwise partial to Caroline Bowles, gives an incident at the house of Miss Bowles, two days before the marriage:

Southey, as was his custom in the afternoon, lay down on a sofa for his siesta, Miss B. sitting quietly by. From this he suddenly started, and terrified his poor bride by wild ravings about their wedding day, and incoherent descriptions of what he had been dreaming. The amazed lady was so painfully alarmed, that she deemed it her duty to communicate the circumstances to, and seek the advice of, Sir H. R. Nagle, her neighbour, relative, and friend. There was consequently considerable discussion; but matters had been carried so far that the die was cast, and it was decided to abide the result. On the following Monday, the Admiral gave her away. . . . They returned to Keswick by way of London, where his son says that the debility of his mind (I think, from my own recollection, rather exaggerated) excited great commiseration. At Keswick the confusion of his intellect increased.[13]

The mental decline manifested before the marriage increased rapidly afterwards. That summer in London, Southey acted so strangely that people began to whisper. Immediately anxious, Wordsworth inquired about the rumours, but received little reassurance from Crabb Robinson.[14] Later he tried to represent Southey to his publisher.[15] Thomas Arnold speaks of Wordsworth's affection for Southey, and of his bringing the latter to call. During the visit Southey 'looked down and scarcely opened his lips . . . his mind was already failing.'[16]

Wordsworth's letters throughout 1840 continue to refer to Southey's gradual decay. And yet he urged Crabb Robinson, in a manuscript submitted for his criticism, to soften the references to Southey's 'lamentable' condition.[17] He called at Greta Hall in July, and found Southey

past taking pleasure in the presence of any of his friends. He did not recognise me till he was told. Then his eyes flashed for a moment with their former brightness, but he sank into the state in which I had found him, patting with both hands his books affectionately, like a child. Having attempted in vain to interest him by a few observations, I took my leave, after five minutes or so. It was, for me, a mournful visit, and for his poor wife also. His health is good, and he may live many years; though the body is much enfeebled.[18]

The image of this visit was still painfully present to Wordsworth a year later, when in the summer of 1841 he dined with Joseph Cottle and told him of the pitiable state of their old friend.[19]

Meanwhile friction arose between Mrs Southey and the Southey children. Edith and her husband, the Rev. Mr Warter, took sides with the stepmother; Cuthbert, Bertha, and Kate were against her. Crabb Robinson was at first predisposed in Mrs Southey's favour,[20] and he never liked Cuthbert; but he soon felt that Mrs Southey was indelicate, dishonest, and unreasonable.[21]

Kate was most actively resented by the new wife. After leaving her father's home she went to her sister, Mrs Hill, in the Flemings' cottage toward the end of 1840,[22] and then stayed with the Wordsworths for three weeks.[23] By the middle of February she and her aunt, Mrs Lovell, were planning to take Crabb Robinson's cottage at Rydal,[24] but, instead, she took a house in Keswick, doubtless to be near her father. She was not allowed, however, to visit him oftener than once a week, because of Mrs Southey's jealousy.[25] Bertha was welcome at Greta Hall, though her husband was not permitted to visit Southey.[26]

Investigating both sides of the quarrel with the carefulness of legal procedure, Crabb Robinson was soon irrevocably on the side of Kate. Wordsworth, also, sympathized with Kate, and while she was staying at Rydal Mount wrote a long letter explaining the part he had taken in the affair.[27] It speaks well for Kate that Sara Coleridge took her side against Edith, her childhood playmate and favourite cousin. Indeed, she thought the letters of Edith and her husband—sent her by

Dora Wordsworth—'so disgraceful that she would not part with them without Dora's express permission.'[28]

But he who was the cause of this dissension was mercifully unaware of it. Robert Southey had a stroke of apoplexy in February 1843[29]—the beginning of the end. Seized later with typhus fever, he died on 21st March about nine o'clock in the morning, apparently without pain. Kate sent a message to Wordsworth immediately, and he decided to attend the funeral, 'invited or not.'[30] The service took place on 23rd March at Crosthwaite church. Quillinan drove Wordsworth over to Keswick, and there they found John Wordsworth and his son, William, Southey's godson.[31]

It was a dark and stormy morning [wrote Cuthbert] when he was borne to his last resting-place, at the western end of the beautiful church-yard of Crosthwaite. . . . But few besides his own family and immediate neighbours followed his remains. His only intimate friend within reach, Mr Wordsworth, crossed the hills that wild morning to be present.[32]

Wordsworth was saddened by the death of his old friend. 'Of the poets, my contemporaries, who are no more,' he wrote to Professor Reed, 'dear Southey, one of the most eminent, is just added to the list. . . .'[33] Wordsworth felt that Southey's greatest literary remains were his letters: 'He had a fine talent for that species of composition, and took much delight in throwing off his mind in that way.'[34] Henry Taylor was his literary executor.

In public and private matters Wordsworth defended Robert Southey. When the story grew and even got into the papers, that Caroline Bowles had lost money by her marriage, Wordsworth definitely contradicted it through his son-in-law, stating that Southey had settled on her for life the income from £2,000.[35] In September 1846, when Thomas Cooper mentioned James Montgomery's admiration of Southey, Wordsworth replied: '"Well, that is pleasing to hear, for Mr Montgomery's political opinions have never resembled Southey's."' And when Cooper added that they wronged

Southey who attributed his political change to bad motives,

'And, depend upon it, they did,' Wordsworth answered, with great dignity: 'it was the foulest libel to attribute bad motives to Mr Southey. No man's change was ever more sincere.'[36]

Wordsworth continued his friendship with the Southey children, especially with Kate, who often visited at Rydal Mount. Shortly after the funeral Miss Fenwick went over to Keswick for ten or twelve days to try to reconcile Kate and Edith. And while she was there Quillinan visited her, and described Miss Southey in a letter to Robinson:

Kate came for the rest of the evening. She looks very lovely and interesting, but she is a faded or rather a blighted flower, and the traces of severe suffering are but too apparent in her feeble frame and delicate countenance. She however seems happier than when her dear Father was alive.[37]

Kate Southey visited the Wordsworths in August 1845,[38] and after Dora's death she stayed at Rydal Mount a good deal, to keep the old poet from brooding. In June 1848 Harriet Martineau said: 'I was glad to see that the amiable Miss Southey is staying with them.'[39]

Cuthbert was meanwhile getting on with his father's life, and Henry Taylor was collecting the letters. Both, however, had Warter to reckon with, who apparently regarded himself as head of the family. Edith's husband was so rude and aggressive that he antagonized not only Cuthbert and Mr Hill, not only Henry Taylor and Quillinan, but Sara Coleridge and Miss Fenwick too. At the sale of Southey's effects he incurred the disdain even of strangers.[40] He consented to Cuthbert's writing the life, 'but subject to a vote by Warters [sic] and on condition that Mr Hill should not interfere.'[41] He threatened Henry Taylor with a Chancery suit if he published Southey's letters.[42]

These limitations on the representatives of Southey made the aged Wordsworth unhappy.

Never a day passes [wrote Mrs Wordsworth to Kate] that my

Mrs Fletcher

Engraving by Saed, from a portrait by Richmond

husband does not mourn over the injustice that has been done to your father's memory by the suppression of his invaluable works, not to speak of the injury that bad passions have caused to the fortunes of you all.[43]

At Grasmere in 1840 were two homes (besides that of his old servant, Mary Fisher) where the poet was always welcome: Lancrigg, just north of the village, and Dove Cottage, Town End, his own former home. At Lancrigg lived his comparatively new friends, the Fletchers; at Dove Cottage, probably his oldest, the Cooksons.

The beautiful old widow, Mrs Fletcher, long a social power in Edinburgh—especially among Whig reformers—moved to the Lakes with her daughter, Mary Fletcher, on 1st June 1840. Her son, Angus, and her daughter, Mrs Taylor, and Mary Grace Taylor had preceded her. Mrs Fletcher had bought the farm below Easedale, but as the farm-house was not yet ready, the family settled themselves for the time being at Thorney How, adjoining Lancrigg.[44]

Mrs Fletcher was born the same year as the poet and Mrs Wordsworth. She had first met them in the summer of 1833 when visiting the Arnolds at Allan Bank, while Fox How was building. The following Christmas she and Mary had visited at Fox How for a week, and had enjoyed the Wordsworths: 'The home life at Rydal Mount was a great attraction to us, as well as the kindness we always received there.'[45] Wordsworth and Dora, returning from the Italian tour on 19th August 1837, had surprised Mrs Fletcher and her daughter at Darland, in Kent.[46]

By the summer of 1839, when Mary Fletcher was again visiting the Arnolds, and old Rowlandson came to tell her that he must sell his little Lancrigg farm, the Wordsworths and the Fletchers were such friends that Mary turned naturally to the poet for advice. 'He entered into the subject most kindly,' she wrote in her note-book, 'and offered to find out for us its real value. He described the tangled copse and a

L

natural terrace under the crag as a very favourite resort of his
and his sisters [sic] in bygone days.' 47   And then he turned to
Mrs Wordsworth and asked her to read his sonnet on the
subject.   Mrs Fletcher authorized the poet to act as her agent,
and by October he had made the final arrangements.

Mrs Fletcher was an interesting old lady, with great force
of personality.   She was a good friend of the poet Campbell
and of the critic Jeffrey, and was most enthusiastic about
Mazzini, whom she had met in London.

In 1840 Mrs Fletcher had been twelve years a widow and
was the mother of four living children: Elizabeth, Margaret,
Angus, and Mary.   Margaret had married, in 1830, Dr John
Davy, brother of Sir Humphry, and they now had five
children.   Mary Fletcher, the youngest, born in 1802, remained
for years her mother's 'inseparable companion.'

When the Fletchers came to the Lakes, in the summer of
1840, they depended a good deal on Wordsworth.   He and
Mrs Wordsworth called the day after their arrival, and between
the two families was much tea-drinking and dining.

After this [wrote Mary Fletcher] we had many meetings of real
business with several neighbours Wordsworth consulted, because,
as he said, 'They understand these things much better than I do.'
When we attempted to thank him for the trouble he was taking for
us, he took leave, saying 'I always feel that those who receive a
benefit kindly also confer a favour.' 48

The Fletchers spent the summer at Thorney How, returning
to Edinburgh in the autumn.

The next April they came again to Thorney How, moving
into their own little home at Lancrigg on 16th July 1841.49
The Wordsworths were away at the time, and in the poet's
absence the workmen had been careless, saying: 'They 're
nobbut women, they 'll niver find it out.' 49   At the end of the
next April Mrs Fletcher and Mary returned to Lancrigg; and
soon after their arrival Mrs Fletcher was seized with a sudden
giddiness, which recurred frequently.   Her son-in-law, Dr
Davy, came down from Edinburgh, and attended her for a

month.[50] It must have been shortly before this attack that Wordsworth and Miss Fenwick called, when Wordsworth gaily planted the holly berries, chanting Burns's poetry while he did so.[51]

Another April brought the Fletchers again to Lancrigg, this time to make it their permanent home. The Davys, also, decided to move to the Lakes, having lost two of their sons in Edinburgh. They bought land near Ambleside, on the way to Rydal, and built a handsome home. Just as it was finished Dr Davy received an appointment to the West Indies, but Mrs Davy settled with the children at the Oaks, not many miles from her mother and sister.

Mrs Fletcher's first winter at Lancrigg was enlivened by the Davy children, who spent Christmas week at Lancrigg, and by Henry Fletcher, the grandson just ready for Oxford.[52] On the 'shortest day' Wordsworth and Miss Fenwick came, self-invited, to spend the day. It was the anniversary of the poet's arrival at Grasmere,[53] and he liked to spend it near Easedale. Henry Fletcher got his summons for Balliol College on 22nd January. He ran in to tell his aunt, Mrs Davy, whom Dora Quillinan was at the time visiting. Mrs Davy and her children went down to the market-place with Henry to see him off, and there they found

Mr Wordsworth walking about before the post-office door, in very charming mood. His spirits were excited by the bright morning sunshine, and he entered at once on a full flow of discourse. He looked very benevolently on Henry as he mounted on the top of the coach, and he seemed quite disposed to give an old man's blessing to the young man entering on an untried field.[54]

The Fletchers and Mrs Davy often met the poet casually. Early in March 1844 Mrs Davy stopped at Fox How on her way to Lancrigg, and finding Wordsworth there, invited him to join her. They walked to Pelter Bridge, where the carriage met them. Just after Easter Mrs Fletcher and Mary left home for a journey to Yorkshire. When they reached Rydal Mount and found the poet's birthday party about to begin, they

remained for the afternoon, spent the night with Mrs Davy, and
started for Yorkshire the next day. In July the Wordsworths
were drinking tea at Lancrigg and dining at the Oaks. It was
on the eleventh that the large party took place, where Mr
Price of Rugby drew Wordsworth out on literary subjects.
After the Wordsworths returned from a trip, the Fletchers
called immediately. 'We found him only at home,' wrote
Mary Fletcher, 'looking in great vigour and much the better
for this little change of scene and circumstance.' [55]

Christmas brought its guests and its round of parties. Crabb
Robinson, as usual, returned to Rydal Mount. Henry Fletcher came from Oxford to spend the holidays with his grandmother, and his brother, Archibald—just promoted to lieutenant
in the Navy—joined him at Lancrigg. Mrs Fletcher gave a
dinner for eight the day after Christmas: Crabb Robinson,
Hartley Coleridge, 'young Fletcher, the Oxonian, and future
head of the house . . . a genteel youth, with a Puseyite tendency.' [56]   The parties continued into January, when the old
lady's birthday was celebrated. She wrote of them:

We had some pleasant neighbourly gatherings at Christmas, and
to keep my birthday in January, when games and charades were performed by young and old with great effect. Our pleasant neighbours,
Mrs Cookson and her daughters, assisted and enjoyed the fun, and
I was glad to feel a growing intimacy and regard between Mrs Cookson and myself. . . .[57]

Crabb Robinson particularly enjoyed Mrs Fletcher that
Christmas. 'She retains all her free opinions,' he wrote;
'and as she lives three miles from Wordsworth's, I go and see
her alone, that we may talk at our ease on topics not gladly
listened to at Rydal Mount.' [58]   He liked to twit the Wordsworths on their conservatism; therefore, when he enclosed in
his present to Mrs Wordsworth a small parcel for Mrs
Fletcher—the *Prospective Review* and an article by James Martineau—he wrote that it 'should have been marked Poison.' [59]

In September 1846 Sir John Richardson, a widower, visited
at Lancrigg. The Fletchers had known him before and had

known his wife and children. Now he spoke a great deal of the children.[60] The following summer, on 4th August 1847, Mary Fletcher became Lady Richardson.[61]

After this, Mrs Fletcher's stay in Westmorland was not so continuous as before. It was planned that she should divide her winters between the Richardsons and the Davys and spend her summers at Lancrigg. She did spend part of the next winter in London,[62] but when Sir John Richardson undertook the perilous search for the Franklin expedition, he arranged for his family to remain in Westmorland. He rented Thorney How for his children and their governess, so that Lady Richardson could be with her mother at Lancrigg as before, and the old lady's summer entertaining might not be curtailed.[63] Mrs Fletcher and Mrs Davy went to the Lakes in April, and were followed by Lady Richardson and her step-children.[64]

Mrs Fletcher could not remain long away from Lancrigg. Of her Mrs Wordsworth wrote, in February 1849: 'The dear old Lady is well and visiting her friends and dispensing hospitality as usual.' [65] Mrs Wordsworth and her sister-in-law, Mrs Thomas Hutchinson, dined at Lancrigg, where they found Harriet Martineau. Dr Davy had returned from Barbados, and Mary Grace Taylor, a granddaughter of Mrs Fletcher's, was in Westmorland during the summer. A lock of hair in Dove Cottage is labelled: 'Wordsworth's hair, cut off and given to me by Mrs Wordsworth at Lesketh How in the summer of 1849.—Mary Grace Taylor.'

April 1850 brought Mrs Fletcher to the Lakes as usual. She reached Lesketh How on 8th April, when her old friend was already in his last illness. Of Wordsworth's death she said: 'It was a personal loss; every one who had enjoyed his society and friendship felt there was much taken out of life that was most worth living for.' [66] To Lady Richardson she wrote:

It has . . . been a great privilege to have seen this great and good man so nearly. I think it may be said of him 'that he did justly, loved mercy, and walked humbly with his God.' [67]

The funeral affected her so deeply that she was unable to sleep afterwards, and the next morning she put into twenty-five lines of blank verse her *Thoughts on Leaving Grasmere Churchyard, April 27, 1850, after the Funeral of William Wordsworth*.[68]   Mrs Fletcher outlived her revered friend eight years.

Old Mrs Cookson and her two spinster daughters, Miss Cookson and Miss Hannah Cookson, were unpretentious folk; but the Wordsworths had known the family some sixty or seventy years, and they valued the friendship.   Mrs Cookson had been a schoolmate of Sara Hutchinson's, and the Cooksons always dined with the Wordsworths on Miss Hutchinson's birthday, New Year's Day.   Strickland Cookson, brother of the Misses Cookson, lived in London.   It was he who had invested Sarah Hutchinson's money in Mississippi bonds on 9th February 1835,[69] and he who succeeded Crabb Robinson in 1841 as executor for the poet.

The Cooksons do not appear often in letters or journals, for the Wordsworths took them for granted.   Crabb Robinson wrote, on New Year's Day, 1842: 'We dined at 1—a family custom and the Cooksons with us—They are excellent women but still not easy to keep up a conversation with.'[70]   As late as January 1858 the poet's grandson, William, wrote of his grandmother and her old friends: 'Mrs Cookson and her daughters are with her now, for the first six days of the New Year according to a long established custom.'[71]

Between Grasmere and Rydal stood Nab Cottage, or the Knbbe, where De Quincey had once lived, and where Hartley Coleridge lived in Wordsworth's last decade.

The Flemings' cottage, at the foot of Rydal hill, was the home of Bertha Southey and her husband, the Rev. Edward Hill, and after 1841 of little Herbert Southey Hill.   Mr Hill was the curate of Rydal chapel, but not a brilliant preacher.   It was apparently the habit of the Wordsworths and sometimes of their Christmas guest to attend service here on Sunday morning, and the entries in Robinson's diary probably measure Mr Hill's best and worst:

January 3, 1841. Heard Mr Hill preach a good practical discourse.

January 1, 1843. I could not well avoid going to church to-day and I heard from Mr Hill, delivered in a feeling tone, one of those unimpressive discourses which leave not the slightest impression on the memory. The day was fine and I grudged the lost morning.

January 8, 1843. I read early as usual and heard Mr Edward Hill preach—A poorer discourse I never heard—the veriest commonplace in the most ordinary language.[72]

It must have been a welcome change when, in November 1842, Mr Hill was absent and Faber filled his pulpit.

From Rydal Wordsworth could go to Ambleside along the regular coach road, passing the Knoll, where Harriet Martineau did her farming; or he could go to the right, across Pelter Bridge, and take the road across the meadows through which flows the Rothay, by Loughrigg Holme and Fox How, the holiday home of Dr Arnold.

Dr Arnold and Wordsworth were 'ter'ble friends,' according to an old servant at Rydal Mount. Unlike in politics, unlike in churchmanship, widely apart in age, they had for each other a profound respect and a great warmth of affection.

Before the Arnolds moved to Fox How they were in the habit of going often to Westmorland.[73] Sometimes they stayed at Kendal, sometimes at Ambleside; the last summer before they settled in their own home they were at Allan Bank.

The younger Thomas Arnold says of the rapidly forming friendship between Wordsworth and Arnold:

Wordsworth assisted my father in finding out the small property of Fox How under Loughrigg. . . . While the house was being built, the poet—since my father, most part of the time, was obliged to be absent at Rugby—was frequently on the spot, and watched the proceedings of the contractor. A close intimacy sprang up between Fox How and Rydal Mount. Not that Wordsworth, sturdy Conservative as he was in those years, could ever have relished my father's

Whiggism; indeed, I remember hearing that once after a sermon in Rydal Chapel, in which my father had made unflattering allusion to the law of primogeniture and the custom of entail, the old man grumbled a good deal on his way home, and showed considerable displeasure.   But they never ceased to be excellent friends.[74]

Mrs Humphry Ward tells an anecdote of a little girl who once accompanied the two friends from Fox How to Pelter Bridge. Something in the conversation stirred Wordsworth, 'and he broke out in indignant denunciation of some views expressed by Arnold.' The little girl was alarmed. At Pelter Bridge they parted, the child going back with Arnold. 'Arnold paced along, his hands behind his back, his eyes on the ground, and his companion watched him, till he suddenly threw back his head with a laugh of enjoyment—"What beautiful English the old man talks!"' [75]

Dr Thomas Arnold, head master of Rugby, famous disciplinarian, keen theologian, and ardent opponent of the Oxford Movement, was a man of youthful spirit and happy temperament. With his own boys and girls, and even with his pupils, he was able to romp and play. 'I knew him well,' one of Miss Mitford's friends wrote to her after Arnold's death: 'he was the finest great boy in the world; and the fault of the life is that it does not show him half young enough.' [76]   Crabb Robinson said of him:

He was a delightful man to walk with, and especially in a mountainous country. He was physically strong, had excellent spirits, and was joyous and boyish in his intercourse with his children and his pupils.[77]

Arnold's popularity with boys sometimes annoyed his adult friends.

The poet complained sometimes [said Mrs Humphry Ward] . . . that he could not see enough of his neighbour, the Doctor, on a mountain walk, because Arnold was always so surrounded with children and pupils, 'like little dogs' running round and after him.[78]

Arnold's spirituality was apparent to all who knew him well.[79]   But the doctor's theological ideas sometimes came in conflict with those of the High-Church Wordsworth, who once said 'very emphatically' to Mrs Arnold: 'I *love* Dr Arnold—he was a *good* man, and an admirable schoolmaster, but he would make a desperate bad bishop!' [80]

By Christmas 1833 the Arnolds were settled at Fox How, and from then on they spent winter and summer holidays there, returning to Rugby usually about the end of August. The Arnold family in 1840 consisted of nine children.

As for the regattas on Lake Windermere, the sailing and rowing just for the amusement's sake, the picnics, the building up of fires on lonely shores where dead wood was abundant, the fishing for perch, pike, and eels—all these things found the day too short to exploit them fully.[81]

Dr Arnold took his two eldest sons to the Continent for part of the summer of 1840, returning to Fox How on 9th August. Though they reached home at nine twenty-five on Sunday morning, they still took the walk along the Rothay and across Pelter Bridge to the morning service at Rydal Chapel.

The winter of 1840–1 was unusually cold, and Rydal Water was frozen over. In January Dr Arnold wrote: 'Rydal Lake is frozen as hard as a rock, and my nine children, and I with them, were all over it to-day; to our great delight.' [82]   Wordsworth was a good skater, and so were the older Arnold boys; but the doctor and his daughters had to content themselves with merely sliding across the ice, dragging the baby on a sled.   Crabb Robinson delighted in Arnold's society during the Christmas holiday.   He went to dinner at Fox How on 16th January, trudging through the slush of melting snow.

All the way [he said] I was nearly ankle deep in the snow & water. It was quite folly going on, but I had provided myself with change of stockings so that I took no harm. . . . I had a very agreeable afternoon and would not yield to the pressing invitation to take a bed at the Doctor's.[83]

When the weather cleared, three days later, Robinson and

Arnold walked to Stock Ghyll Force, discussing politics and the Church as usual.[84]

The Arnolds remained in Westmorland longer than usual, the summer of 1841. A fever epidemic had sent some of the Rugby boys and masters to Fox How; this was probably the real cause of the delay. But Dr Arnold loved his mountain home, and was not eager to depart from it. Perhaps, too, he had a premonition that he would never spend another summer at Fox How. At any rate, he remained through most of September, writing on the 22nd:

> There will be a sad wrench in leaving Fox How. It is not the mere outward beauty, but the friendliness and agreeableness of the neighbourhood in which we mix, simply as inhabitants of the country, and not as at Rugby, in an official relation.[85]

After the Rugby group had departed, Mrs Wordsworth wrote that 'that nice creature Jane Arnold' was soon to be married to one of the masters, and in less than a year 'to be converted into the *Matron of a boarding house*[86]'! Dora Wordsworth had recently been married at the age of thirty-seven, and Mary Fletcher was still single at thirty-nine; and Mrs Wordsworth regarded Jane Arnold as a mere child. 'The connection seems to be highly approved by the family—but we think it a pity so early that her youthful freedom should be interrupted.'[86]

At Christmas time the Arnolds returned to Fox How, and Crabb Robinson and Dora Quillinan to Rydal. Dr Arnold had accepted the Regius Professorship of Modern History and was working hard on the lectures, finishing the first seven during the holiday. 'The last vacation at Fox How,' writes one biographer, 'was a season of mingled labour, enjoyment, and the most delightful anticipation.'[87]

Crabb Robinson apparently saw less of Arnold this Christmas. Perhaps the latter was too busy with his writing; perhaps he found Robinson's agnosticism and theological questioning a bit tiresome. On the afternoon of 12th January, the last bright day before a new fall of snow, Dr Arnold took a walk with Crabb Robinson, who began as usual a theological discussion. Along the Rydal beck they walked, across the mountain, and back by the Scandel beck. Arnold helped the older, stockier man over the harder places. 'I was not quite satisfied with myself,' Robinson wrote in his diary, 'for my conversation with Dr Arnold. . . . He shirked discussion even when I spoke like a seeker—Was it dislike or apprehension?' [88]

Arnold was not robust, but his spirit was so youthful and his industry so great that his family and friends little realized that before the next vacation he would

> tread,
> In the summer morning, the road
> Of death, at a call unforeseen,
> Sudden.[89]

Five months later, early on Sunday morning, 12th June 1842, the day he was to have preached the Commencement sermon, the head master of Rugby was stricken with angina pectoris. After two hours of acute suffering all was over. Matthew was at Oxford, Thomas at Rugby; some of the younger children had gone on to Fox How. The news of their father's death reached those at Fox How early on Monday morning. A neighbour walked over to Lancrigg before seven o'clock in the morning so that Mary Fletcher could break the news to her mother before the old lady heard it by chance in her daily drive.[90]

Wordsworth was in London at the time, having been there about six weeks. He and Crabb Robinson, on 13th June, were attending the 'splendid affair' of the fashionable Miss Burdett-Coutts, along with 'two hundred and fifty of the *Haut Ton*'—according to the *Post* [91]—when Monckton Milnes told them of Dr Arnold's death. 'The sad information of the evening rendered everything else uninteresting'; and when Robinson went to see the Wordsworths the next morning he found them 'all in affliction at the death of the Dr.'

Chevalier Bunsen, also at Miss Burdett-Coutts's party, said:

'The History of Rome is never to be finished.' [92]   Harriet Martineau wrote Crabb Robinson such a beautiful letter about Dr Arnold that he sent it on to the widow.[93]   And the usually harsh Francis Jeffrey wrote to Mrs Fletcher:

> It is long since I have met with anything at once so loveable and so exalted . . . with the firmness of a hero, he had the softness of a woman, the devotedness and zeal of an apostle or a martyr, and the gentleness and lowliness of a bashful child.[94]

Wordsworth's love and admiration of Thomas Arnold more than blotted out his distrust of the doctor's theology.   After Mrs Wordsworth had read him the *Life of Arnold* Wordsworth wrote:

> . . . His benevolence was so earnest, his life so industrious, his affections domestic and social so intense, his faith so warm and firm, and his endeavour to regulate his life by it so constant, that his example cannot but be beneficial even in quarters where his opinions may be disliked.[95]

With the younger Arnolds, as with the second generation of Coleridges and Southeys, Wordsworth kept up the friendship begun with their father, and with Mrs Arnold, more than with Mrs Coleridge or Mrs Southey, the Wordsworths were friends in their later years.

Mrs Arnold loved the Wordsworths and missed them when they went away even for a short visit.   She wrote to Crabb Robinson in the autumn of 1844 of 'our dear friends at Rydal Mount whose honoured age it is such a privilege to see, and to experience as we do their constant loving kindness.   Next week,' she said, 'they go to Leamington to meet Miss Fenwick, and though dear Fairfield keeps its place and the Rotha flows on, the valley never seems like itself without them.' [96]   In Mrs Wordsworth's extreme old age Mrs Arnold often went to sit with her, and said she felt almost like a daughter.   Susan Arnold was apparently an invalid for years, but survived her healthier brothers and sisters.   'Susy Arnold is *much* better,' wrote Quillinan in March 1844, 'able to walk to Ambleside and back.' [97]   She lived to be an old, old lady, and to tell later generations her reminiscences of the poet. From Miss Arnold herself Professor Harper heard the story, how she and her younger sister watched Rydal Mount from Loughrigg terrace when Wordsworth was dying.[98] Miss Arnold had told the story, also, to Ellis Yarnall in 1855.

Most interesting, of course, is the relationship between Wordsworth and Dr Arnold's eldest son, the poet. When Matthew Arnold was elected Fellow of Oriel College, Oxford, Wordsworth rejoiced in the young man's triumph. Clough, who had been at Fox How that spring, wrote to a friend:

First of all, you will be glad to hear that Matt Arnold is elected Fellow of Oriel. This was done on Friday last, March 28, just thirty years after his father's election. Mrs Arnold is of course well pleased, as also the venerable poet at Rydal, who had taken M. under his special protection.[99]

And Matthew Arnold felt indebted to Wordsworth. It was partly to pay this debt that he made his selection of Wordsworth's poems. In the preface he says: 'It is not for nothing that one has been brought up in the veneration of a man so truly worthy of homage; that one has seen him and heard him, lived in his neighbourhood, and been familiar with his country.'[100]

When Arnold's first volume of poems came out in 1849, *The Strayed Reveller and Other Poems*, we can well imagine the excitement at Fox How and at Rydal Mount. By June the volume had found its way to Loughrigg Holme; Quillinan was reading the poems and asking Crabb Robinson his opinion of them.[101] Unfortunately we do not know what Wordsworth thought of these early verses.

When Wordsworth died, Matthew Arnold paid his tribute, and Wordsworth's son-in-law was impressed by the poem— not as the debt of one great poet to another, but as lines written by one of the Westmorland boys to Mr Wordsworth.[102]

Dr Arnold was not the only theologian in Westmorland in the late thirties and early forties. Frederick William Faber came to Ambleside in the summer of 1837, and continued to come periodically until January 1843. He met Wordsworth during the summer of his arrival, and 'in after years he used to describe the long rambles which they took together over the neighbouring mountains, the poet muttering verses to himself in the intervals of conversation.'[103]

Not unlike Dr Arnold in the ardour of his faith, Faber was diametrically opposed to him in Church doctrine. Both were clergymen in the Church of England, Faber only a deacon at this time, but they were on opposite sides of the Oxford Movement. Faber was a 'flaming zealot' of the new 'reform,' preaching catholicity and harking back to the thirteenth century as the time of the purity of the Church. Against such theologians as Faber Arnold preached his sermons and wrote his pamphlets. With Faber's theories Wordsworth was much more in sympathy than with Arnold's.

At first Faber came in the summer, returning to Oxford in the autumn, and he usually came again at Christmas. He preached and acted as tutor to the son of the Benson Harrisons. In the winter of 1840–1 Faber was taken ill in church, and the Harrisons planned a tour for him and their son. Meanwhile, he spent the Christmas holiday at Ambleside. Crabb Robinson became interested in the ardent young deacon, chatted with him at the Harrisons', and read his sermon on education; but Faber was too much the religious enthusiast for the canny barrister. Robinson was particularly disturbed by Faber's

sundry little ways and means of remembering God's presence and sundry little sacred habits of keeping impure habits [thoughts] out of his head, such as the retracing on himself the sign of the Baptism.[104]

He feared the theological influence of 'the high flying Oxonian.'[105]

Faber and young Harrison went to the Continent, remaining abroad from February to August or September. The former kept a journal, which was published early in 1842 as *Sights and Thoughts in Foreign Churches and among Foreign Peoples.* The book was dedicated 'to William Wordsworth, Esquire, in affectionate remembrance of much personal kindness, and many thoughtful conversations on the rites, prerogatives, and doctrines of the Holy Church.' [106] Wordsworth liked Faber and considered him a promising poet, and was partly in sympathy with his religious views.

Wordsworth and Robinson saw more of Faber during the Christmas holiday of 1841–2, and Robinson began to like him better. The Wordsworths gave a dinner party on 27th December, and invited among others the Harrisons and Faber.[107] The next day the Puseyite, the poet, and the Unitarian went for a walk, Faber still talking about his travels. He told shocking stories of immorality in Berlin, strange stories to be telling the septuagenarian Wordsworth. Robinson was amazed, and when Faber left them said: 'I have enjoyed your company but I hold some of your doctrines in only less abhorrence than those of your German friend.' [108] Robinson and Wordsworth then went over to Fox How, and took a walk with Dr Arnold.

Robinson re-read Faber's sermon on education, and disliked it less. He foresaw, however, that such philosophy led inevitably to Roman Catholicism.[109] And he still objected to the '"little ways that devoutness invents" retracing on himself the sign of his baptism,' and was perplexed over Faber's placing Milton 'among objectionable books.'

Faber remained at Ambleside through much of 1842. On 3rd April Wordsworth defended his own objection to sending his poems to reviewers by saying that his 'friend and present neighbour, Mr Faber,' felt the same way. The young clergyman went to Oxford in the summer, to be with his sick brother, the Rev. F. A. Faber. In the autumn he accepted a living at Elton, in Huntingdonshire, his duties to begin in January.[110] When he told Wordsworth that he was leaving Westmorland for parochial work, the latter replied: 'I do not say you are wrong; but England loses a poet.' [111]

Faber's last Christmas at Ambleside was the time of greatest intimacy with Wordsworth.

The poet is a *high* churchman [wrote Crabb Robinson to his brother] but luckily does not go all lengths with the Oxford School—He praises the *reformers* (for they assume to be such) for inspiring the age with deeper reverence for antiquity And a more cordial conformity with ritual observances—As well as a warmer piety—But he goes no further—Nevertheless he is claimed by them as *their* poet. And they have published a selection from his works with a dishonest preface from which one might infer he went all lengths with them.[112]

Regretting the loss of Dr Arnold, who had been with them the Christmas before, Robinson said:

Instead of him we have this year a sad fanatic of an opposite character. . . . This is *Faber*. . . . He is a flaming zealot for the new doctrines And like Froud [*sic*] does not conceal his predilection for the Church—in Rome—(not *of* Rome *yet*) And his dislike to Protestantism. . . . This Faber is an agreeable man, All the young ladies are in love with him And he has high spirits conversational talent and great facility in writing both polemics and poetry.[112]

On Christmas morning, which was Sunday, Robinson read an article by Dr Wiseman in the *Dublin Review* on Faber's book. Though Faber had said the year before that Dr Wiseman was not an honest man, the Catholic writer now liked the Puseyite's book. 'F: is warmly praised,' wrote Robinson, 'for his strong propensities in favour of Romanism but of course blamed for not going the whole hog.'[113] That evening Crabb Robinson went to hear Faber preach, and found in the sermon 'a sentimentality approaching to eloquence which pleased the ladies,' but which he himself 'could not relish.'

The next day Robinson walked back from Fox How with Faber and the poet, and dined at Rydal Mount with the Harrisons and their protégé. Whist following dinner, he had little opportunity to discuss theology. 'Only a slight allusion on my part to Faber's intolerance,' he said—'But I hope before I go to have some talk on the subject.'[114] Again on Thursday the young clergyman dined at Rydal Mount.

On Friday morning, when Crabb Robinson was reading the
work of Dr Arnold, Faber came for a walk and Robinson was
delighted.   They walked and talked for more than three hours
and a half, and even then did not part, but made a call together
on one of the neighbours.   It was 'a very interesting walk to
Easedale Tarn—the wind high, the sky overcast, but no actual
rain, ground wet—the tarn more grand from the gloom of the
day.' [115]   Faber's ecclesiastical position greatly interested his
legal companion, who wrote in his diary:

> He is certain he will never go over to Rome, tho' he rather regrets
> not being born in that communion.   He believes both the Romish
> and Anglican churches to be portions of the Catholic Church.   On
> my objecting to the manifold corruptions of the Romish Church,
> he admitted these but held that they do not invalid its authority—
> They are trials of the faith of the believer. [116]

Like Newman, Faber was irresistibly drawn to Rome; like
Newman, he kept reassuring himself that this was not the case.
The more irrational a doctrine seemed, the greater the virtue
in accepting it.   'A revelation ought to have difficulties,' he
said, 'it is one of the signs of its divine origin that it seems
incredible to the natural man.'

Crabb Robinson walked with Faber and Wordsworth on
Saturday, and again on Wednesday, and on Thursday.   He
listened while the other two discussed Transubstantiation,
Consubstantiation, and the Real Presence.   'They [sic] conversation,' he said, 'I was not competent altogether to follow
but certainly W's tone was that of deference towards his
younger and more consistent friend.'   On occasion, however, the old poet spoke up—and spoke up vigorously: 'W:
denied Transubstantiation on grounds on which says Faber—
"I should deny the Trinity"— . . . W: declared in strong
terms his disbelief of eternal punishment which Faber did
not attempt to defend.' [117]

On Saturday, 7th January, two days before his departure
from Ambleside, Faber dined for the last time with the
Wordsworths, playing whist in the evening as usual. [118]   He

M

preached his farewell sermon on Sunday afternoon, and departed on Monday.

F[aber] is a man whom one must love [Crabb Robinson wrote in his diary]—he is a generous enthusiast—He did all his duty at Ambleside gratuitously and was very charitable to the poor—But his opinions are very dangerous so that I fear he may perform a mischievous part in the world.[119]

Robinson wrote in the same vein to his brother, adding: 'He has, as W. Wordsworth thinks, considerable talent even as a poet.'[120]

Faber's last officiation in the Church of England was on Sunday, 16th November 1845. Immediately thereafter, following Newman, he became a Roman Catholic.[121] In September Clough had written that Ward had gone over to Rome, and that Newman would probably go at Christmas.[122] On 23rd November, one week after the last officiation, Clough wrote to his sister:

Another convert is gone over to Rome—Faber, the poet, who used to excite admiration when preaching some seven years ago at Ambleside; and at Cambridge a flitting from the Camden is expected.[123]

Wordsworth must have been disappointed, but even from Robinson's letter we can see that the old man's attitude toward Faber was substantially unchanged. 'W: respects F's poetic abilities,' Crabb wrote his brother; then—slightly modifying his own disapproval—he added: 'He is a superior man; but rationation [sic] is not his forte as you may suppose.'[124]

Faber is better known, now, for his hymns[125] than for his sonnets, but in both can be traced the possible influence of the greater poet. With Wordsworth, too, there probably remained a lasting impression of the young religious enthusiast who preached at Ambleside and walked about the Lakes.

And to the Lakes came, in January 1845, one whom no one could fail to notice, whether one liked her or not—Harriet Martineau. Coming first to visit W. R. Greg, she liked Westmorland so well that she took lodgings, and later bought two acres of land and built herself a cottage near Ambleside, on the main road from Rydal.

Harriet Martineau was a woman of immense vitality, who inspired persons of her own day with contradictory emotions. Much lauded by some, she was laughed at by others. Her admirers regarded her as strong and independent; her scoffers, a fanatic or worse. Shrewd in some ways, she had the *naïveté* of a child. David Watson Rannie says:

> Between her and Wordsworth there was indeed a potential antagonism which it would have been hard to transcend. Logical, materialistic, utilitarian, she gave her talents to causes which were far removed from Wordsworth's ideals. Moreover, she had an acrid tongue, and an eye quick to see weaknesses and blemishes. . . . She came with the defiant self-consciousness of heterodoxy, foreseeing that provincial respectability would frown upon her, and resolved to have as few dealings with it as possible.[126]

Mary Russell Mitford wrote to Elizabeth Barrett:

> Miss Martineau is a person of great singleness of mind, sincere and truthful; but I have always thought that she did not very well know her own mind. She is so one-sided that I never should be astonished to find her turn short round and change her opinions plump.[127]

Crabb Robinson was disappointed when Miss Martineau expatiated severely on what she called Dr Arnold's illiberality.[128] He had previously said:

> The fact is that H M: with all her mistakes is one of the purest and most high minded persons I ever knew. In spight [*sic*] of her speculative errors a most Christian-hearted creature.[129]

Sydney Smith, the witty divine, regarded Miss Martineau's agnosticisms and fanaticisms as amusing, even in his last illness. Though the jolly canon of St Paul's died in February 1845,[130] he declared in January 'that he had dreamed he was in a madhouse and that there was shut up with him Harriet Martineau and the Bishop of Exeter.'[131] And Samuel Rogers wrote to his sister, when Miss Martineau was visiting at Greg's: 'All of the Rydal party was incredulous and sarcastic. She comes to town, and in her way means to show herself only in the larger towns. If she was Tom Thumb or the Lion Tamer she could not use grander language.' [132]

Harriet Martineau had had unusual experiences. For years she had been an invalid, incurably she thought. When the Government offered her a pension, she scorned it because she felt 'that there can be no peace in benefiting by the proceeds of an unjust system of taxation.' [133]   And yet she was willing to accept a similar endowment raised by private subscription. From January to August 1843 contributions were solicited for her. By 23rd August an adequate fund had been subscribed, £1,100; invested in long annuities, this brought her an income of £240—'an ample competence with her habits.' [134]

Meanwhile she managed to turn her illness to account in 1843, publishing *Life in a Sick Room* anonymously toward the end of the year. Crabb Robinson lent a copy to the Wordsworths, who were high in their praise of the book. [135]

About a year later she cast off her illness! Against the wishes of her mother and elder sister, but on the advice of her physician, Harriet Martineau took up mesmerism in June 1844. With her usual enthusiasm she became an ardent convert to the system, and apparently was cured by it. 'I was first mesmerised on the 22nd of June 1844,' she writes; 'I was well in the following November.' [136]   Her relatives and friends were incredulous, and her mesmeric gospel became dogmatic. Crabb Robinson, usually so cautious, began to come under the spell of her belief, and defended her claims. At Kenyon's, when the cure by mesmerism was discussed, Robinson could not convince his friends. 'It disgusts me the remarking how bigotted [sic] my Unitarian and Rationalist friends are. Harr: Martineau is declared to be in her dotage.' [137]

It was thought that Miss Martineau's recovery would be better established by a complete change, and the Gregs invited her to visit them at Waterhead on Windermere. 'So, early in January 1845,' she said, 'my mesmeriser and I left Tynemouth, little thinking that I should never return to it.' [138] They arrived at Windermere on 14th January.

Greg was an ultra-Radical, a Unitarian, and a factory master, and the Wordsworths had not called at Wansfell Holme.[139] Wordsworth and Miss Martineau met at a party of Dr Davy's the day after her arrival. They sat next each other. 'They chatted very freely on indifferent subjects—but Mesmerism was not once alluded to—This was judicious, . . .' said Robinson. 'Any thing like a dispassionate discussion was out of the question.' [140] Two days later Crabb Robinson attended a séance,[141] but the Wordsworths, Mrs Fletcher, and Dr Davy continued to scorn the whole matter.

The Wordsworths were ready, however, to accept the friend of Crabb Robinson. They invited Miss Martineau to Rydal Mount, and promised Robinson to call on her. Wordsworth even sent a message to Greg that his not having called 'was not from disrespect but from mere old age on his part and *distance*, etc.' [142]

Miss Martineau has described her first visit to Rydal Mount:

They invited me to Rydal Mount to see the terrace where he had meditated his poems; and I went accordingly, one winter noon. On that occasion, I remember, he said many characteristic things, beginning with complaints of Jeffrey and other reviewers, who had prevented his poems bringing him more than £100, for a long course of years.[143]

When Miss Martineau told him that *The Happy Warrior* was Dr Channing's favourite poem, '"Ay," said Wordsworth, "that was not on account of the *poetic conditions* being best fulfilled in that poem; but because it is (solemnly) a chain of extremely *valooable* thoughts."'

The Wordsworths kept their promise to Crabb Robinson, and called on Harriet Martineau on 1st February. The poet's impression was one of amazement rather than pleasure:

We called on Miss Martineau yesterday. We found her alone, the Greggs [sic] being from home—She relates strong things of cures by Mesmerism, which would be entitled as far as they depend upon her own testimony to more respect, if she were not really of *unsound mind* upon the subject of claire-voyance [sic]. Besides, I hardly think it safe for any one's Wits to be possessed on the manner this extraordinary person is by one subject be it what it may.[144]

Miss Martineau remained in the Lake District until about the middle of February, departing then to visit her brother and his family.   Before she went away she had grown so strong that she could walk about the hills even in a snowstorm, and had found a lodging in order that she might return and become a regular 'Laker.'[145]

At the end of May she returned.   She had many visitors that summer, and her friends in Westmorland welcomed her cordially.

It was all very gay and charming [she wrote], and if I found the bustle of society a little too much—if I felt myself somewhat disappointed in regard to the repose which I had reckoned on, that blessing was, as I knew, only deferred. . . . There is a perpetual change going on in such neighbourhoods . . . as that of Ambleside. Retired merchants and professional men fall in love with the region, buy or build a house, are in a transport with what they have done, and, after a time, go away. . . . When I made up my mind to live there, I declined the dinner and evening engagements offered to me, and visited at only three or four houses, and very sparingly at those. It did not suit me to give parties, otherwise than in the plainest and most familiar way. . . . I had not time to waste in meeting the same people—not chosen as in London, but such as chanced to be thrown together in a very small country town—night after night.[146]

Wordsworth still considered her more a curiosity than a prospective friend, for he wrote to Robinson in August:

You ask me how we get on with Miss Martineau.   She has had with her 4 Aunts and 9 Cousins, and innumerable acquaintances occasionally, so that it has been utterly impossible for us to have more than two or three interviews with her, one of which was at our own house, where she was kind enough to drink tea with us.   I have however heard from others that she is as entêtée as ever upon the ground of mesmerism, and will only see and hear as suits her passionate credulity . . . her quickness of mind, in leaping to conclusions, in conjunction with her imperfect hearing, has much to do in misleading her, and makes her in many respects ever a dangerous companion.[147]

When it was known that Miss Martineau was considering buying property in Westmorland, Mrs Arnold consulted the Wordsworths, and they all urged the newcomer to get the small property on the outskirts of Ambleside, the Knoll. Harriet Martineau was repeatedly surprised at the practical streak in the poet:

'It is,' said Wordsworth, 'the wisest step in her life; for' . . . and we supposed he was going to speak of the respectability, comfort and charm of such a retreat for an elderly woman . . . 'for the value of the property will be doubled in ten years.' [148]

By September 1845 Miss Martineau was building, and gentle Mrs Wordsworth considered her personal energy and dynamic power over the workmen little short of miraculous:

Yesterday week my husband and I as we passed the 'Descenting Shop' [sic] saw your friend as we thought behind that building staking out the foundation for her house, on our return yesterday to our surprize [sic] the walls had risen half-roof high—Surely she must have mesmerized her workmen. [149]

Passing along the road to Ambleside, the poet would twit the newcomer, facetiously quoting his own verses. [150] Harriet Martineau went again to Rydal Mount on 25th November, and the poet wrote to Moxon: 'Miss Martineau called here to-day. She is in excellent health and spirits, very busy with house-building and book-writing, by which latter I hope you will profit.' [151]

It was not long before a friendly feeling grew up between the Wordsworths and Harriet Martineau, though she still continued to talk mesmerism, and they still found the subject distasteful. She attended a dinner-party at Rydal Mount on 22nd December. Miss Fenwick and Mrs Arnold were soon quickening to her enthusiasm, but Mrs Fletcher was 'scarcely tolerant.' [152] Miss Martineau dined at Rydal Mount again, on the 31st, this time to meet Moxon. She talked about mesmerism, 'went on by the hour without intermission.' The group were not in sympathy with her, and afterwards Mrs Wordsworth 'said in a tone of vexation: "According to Miss

M: these Mesmerisers can work miracles just as great as Christ and the Apostles.'''[153]

Harriet Martineau realized, however, that Wordsworth liked her better than at first, and she felt a growing affection for him. As a child she had been a Wordsworth devotee, had pinned up his picture in her room, and 'could repeat his poetry by the hour.'[154] When her adolescent devotion waned, she was still grateful to Wordsworth; but her gratitude was not unmixed with egotism.[155] In February 1846, when she had known Wordsworth personally for about a year, and had been to Rydal Mount five times at least, she was glad that the old man liked her, and she felt that the longer she knew him, the more she would find him worthy of his poetry.

He does me the honour . . . to be fond of me [she wrote], but I see less of them than I shall do when I get to the Knoll—I do not ask him to come so far as my lodgings and so only meet him in company or when I call at the Mount and then only *hear* him when he talks expressly to me—So I miss a good deal—I feel a growing love and tenderness for him but cannot yet thoroughly connect . . . him with his works. Cannot yet feel him to be so great as they. . . .[156]

She moved into the Knoll in April. To Elizabeth Barrett she had described enthusiastically her terrace and her terrace wall, which she intended 'to hang with ivies and honeysuckles, and tuft with foxgloves and ferns.'[157] Many friends in the Lake District had planted trees on her place, and Wordsworth had planted a stone pine. He had taken her hand in both his and wished her many happy years in her new abode, and then he had given her a piece of advice. He told her that she would find visitors a great expense, and that she must promise him —and he laid his hand on her arm to enforce the point—to do as he and Dorothy had done in the early days at Dove Cottage:

You must say, 'If you like to have a cup of tea with us, you are very welcome: but if you want any meat—you must pay for your board.' Now, promise me that you will do this.[158]

Harriet Martineau, with her pension raised by private subscription, could be amused at Wordsworth's parsimony!

At tea there [she said] one could hardly get a drop of cream with any ease of mind, while he was giving away all the milk that the household did not want to neighbouring cottagers, who were perfectly well able to buy it, and would have been all the better for being allowed to do so. [158]

William Howitt tells of asking the peasant woman who owned Dove Nest whether Miss Martineau was a poet. 'Nay,' she said, 'nothing of the sort; another guess sort of person, I can tell you.' Inquiring further, Howitt was told:

They tell me she wrote up the Reform Bill for Lord Brougham . . . and that she's writing now about the taxes. Can she stop the steam, eh? can she, think you? Nay, nay, I warrant, big and strong as she is. Ha! ha! good lauk! as I met her the other day walking along the muddy road below here—'Is it a woman, or a man, or what sort of an animal is it?' said I to myself. There she came stride, stride,—great heavy shoes,—stout leather leggins on,—and a knapsack on her back! Ha! ha! that's a *political comicalist*, they say. . . . But I said to my husband—goodness! but that *would* have been a wife for you. Why she'd ha' ploughed! and they say she mows her own grass, and digs her own cabbage and potatoes! Ha! ha! well, we see some queer 'uns here. Wordsworth should write a poem on her. What was Peter Bell to a comicalist? [159]

Miss Martineau left Westmorland and went on a journey to Egypt.[160] She returned to the Knoll in 1847 or 1848, this time with a pipe. 'All I know about her,' wrote one of her friends to Miss Mitford, 'is that she has brought a pipe from the East, and smokes it every day. Perhaps that may be to subdue pain or deaden irritation.' [161] It is more likely that the pipe was to astonish the other 'Lakers,' for Miss Martineau did like to defy Westmorland convention.

Harriet Martineau was very much alive, and enjoyed her vitality with the ecstasy of one who has not always been well. Over the hills she tramped. Wordsworth, she said, and Mrs Wordsworth cautioned her against over-exertion, but she knew her strength and merely laughed at warnings. One Sunday she took Ewart, her companion on the eastern travels, to Rydal Mount, walked with him through the garden until the Wordsworths returned from church, and then presented him to the poet and Mrs Wordsworth. 'She is the briskest and most active person in the vale,'[162] wrote Mrs Wordsworth; and Quillinan wrote: 'Miss Martineau's intellectual activity shames all idlers.'[163] Though unable to take her political theories seriously, Quillinan liked the vigorous woman. Miss Martineau gave him a hundred cabbage plants for his cow and pigs, and the cabbages flourished in his kitchen garden.[164] Even Crabb Robinson preferred the woman farmer to the writer.[165]

Harriet Martineau outlived the poet, outlived Dorothy, outlived Mrs Wordsworth. Toward them all she felt not entire approval, but a great friendliness. Writing the obituary notice for the last of the generation, Miss Martineau showed that she considered the Wordsworth family an institution in Westmorland. Through their common humanity Harriet Martineau and William Wordsworth had transcended the 'potential antagonism.'

Wordsworth's peregrinations in his later years most often led to Grasmere, to Fox How, or to Ambleside, and to homes between; but now and then he went as far north as Keswick or as far south as Windermere. Through Mrs Hemans, Wordsworth had come to know Robert Perceval Graves, curate later at Bowness on Windermere.[166] It was Graves who called on Wordsworth the Sunday after Coleridge's death; it was Graves who communicated with Sir William Rowan Hamilton about honorary membership for Wordsworth in the Royal Irish Academy.

On Windermere between Waterhead and Bowness stood Elleray, the home of Professor John Wilson, the 'Christopher North' of *Blackwood's Magazine*. The tawny-haired Wilson was a man of great physical strength, and won the esteem of the dalesmen by his wrestling and cock-fighting.[167] He liked to play pranks, to fool his friends by many practical jokes.

But with all his animal spirits and the brilliance which later made him such a scathing critic, Wilson was hampered by 'an imaginative morbidity . . . a downright weakness of will.' [168]

Wordsworth did not see a great deal of Wilson in his later years, but they had been friends in the past, the time of greatest intimacy being from the winter of 1807–8, when Wilson came to Westmorland, until 1811, when he married and began to study for the Bar in Edinburgh.[169]   On 14th December 1809, Wilson's anonymous letter, signed 'Mathetes,' [170] appeared in the *Friend*, recording 'the heights to which the friendship and inspiration of Wordsworth' had raised him.   When Wordsworth's youngest child, William, was christened, in the summer of 1810, Wilson stood godfather, Wilson and De Quincey.[171] John Wilson left Westmorland and settled in Edinburgh, but he did not give up his home on Windermere.[172]

There was certainly between Wordsworth and Wilson, for a time at least, an estrangement—possibly a mutual resentment. Alan Lang Strout makes De Quincey partly responsible:

As the ties between Wilson and De Quincey were tightening, a gradual change appears about this time to have crept into the friendship of Wilson and Wordsworth.[173]

John Wilson also owed a poetic debt to Wordsworth, and the sense of obligation was irksome to him.   When *The Isle of Palms* was published in 1812, and the Edinburgh reviewers put Wilson above his master, Wordsworth said to Crabb Robinson:

Wilson's poems are an attenuation of mine.   He owes everythg. to me & this he acknowledges to me in private, but he ought to have said it to the public also.[174]

Nathaniel Parker Willis reports a breakfast with Wilson, when the latter offered him an introduction to Wordsworth.

I lived a long time in that neighbourhood [said Wilson] and know Wordsworth perhaps as well as any one.   Many a day I have walked over the hills with him, and listened to his repetition of his own poetry, which of course filled my mind completely at the time, and perhaps started the poetical vein in me, though I cannot agree with the critics that my poetry is an imitation of Wordsworth's.[175]

The Edinburgh professor told Willis that the story was true that Wordsworth kept a group waiting to hear Scott's novel while he read aloud his own poem quoted by Scott; Wilson said it happened in his own home, and that Wordsworth accused him of giving the story to the world. When the gossipy American asked if he had recently written any long poem, Wilson answered, after numerous excuses:

I have been discouraged in various ways by criticism. It used to gall me to have my poems called imitations of Wordsworth and his school; a thing I could not see myself, but which was asserted even by those who praised me, and which modesty forbade I should disavow. I really can see no resemblance between the Isle of Palms and anything of Wordsworth's. I *think* I have a style of my own . . . and so pride prevents my writing.[176]

Though N. P. Willis's stories must often be discounted, in each there is probably a grain of truth.

In 1815 Wordsworth felt Wilson's growing indifference. In June 1817 appeared the first of Wilson's published attacks: 'Observations on Mr Wordsworth's Letter relative to a new Edition of Burns's Works.' [177] Usually Wordsworth did not read Wilson's articles, but in January 1829 he wrote to Crabb Robinson:

I have seen the Article in Blackwood alluded to in your last—it is undoubtedly from the pen of Mr Wilson himself. He is a perverse Mortal,—not to say worse of him. Have you peeped into his Trials of Margaret Lyndsay—you will there see to what an extent he has played the Plagiarist—with the very tale of Margaret in the Excursion, which he abuses—and you will also, with a glance learn, what passes with him for poetical Christianity—more mawkish stuff I never encountered. I certainly should think it beneath me to notice that Article in any way—my Friends and admirers I hope will take the same view of it. Mr W's pen must be kept going at any rate— I am at a loss to know why—but so it is—he is well paid twice as much, I am told as any other Contributor.[178]

And yet the friendship never quite died. In 1820, when Wilson became Professor of Moral Philosophy at the University of Edinburgh, Wordsworth wrote a letter of recommendation for him.[179] In the later years the old friendship seemed to revive, the friendship of thirty years before. The professor and his daughter returned to Westmorland, and dined with the Wordsworths and the Quillinans late in August 1843.

We found them very agreeable company [wrote Quillinan] but the cheerfulness of the Professor, I fear, is rather assumed. I understand that he has never recovered the shock of his wife's death. He was in this country a few days only. He is no Bacchanalian now, if he ever were so. . . . Both Mr and Mrs Wordsworth were very glad to meet so old a friend. Mrs Wordsworth has always been admirer and lover of Wilson. Don't be jealous: her husband is not.[180]

Wilson resented De Quincey's including his name in slurs on Wordsworth.

From this [said Wilson, in September 1843] it has been said that I quarrelled with Wordsworth, whom, God knows, I love and revere as I have always done, and am as far from envy or jealousy of him as man can be. I had too much pride to enter into any explanation to Wordsworth, but I have never ceased to love him, and his warmth and cordiality to me and my daughter when we lately met quite affected me.[181]

The Professor of Moral Philosophy—cock-fighter, godfather, poet, critic, humorist—the tawny-haired 'Christopher North' of *Blackwood's*—was uneven in his attitude toward Wordsworth. Now he regarded him with reverence; now he resented the acknowledged superiority of the less versatile man.

Owen Lloyd and the Earl of Lonsdale were other friends of Wordsworth's who lived within the borders of the Lake District. Owen Lloyd was the delicate son of Charles Lloyd, to whom Wordsworth was linked by two bonds. Charles had lived with Coleridge at Nether Stowey,[182] and his sister, Priscilla Lloyd, had married Wordsworth's youngest brother. After his own marriage Charles Lloyd had moved to Old Brathay, near Ambleside. Here Owen Lloyd was born— 'Owen Lloyd of the beautiful face, and "the sanguine complexion and light yellow hair"'; Owen Lloyd, the delighter in music and maker of melody, who loved the dalesmen and the dales.' [183]   He was a friend of Faber and of Hartley Coleridge. He had gone to school in Ambleside to the Rev. John Dawes, who had taught Hartley and Derwent. Wordsworth said of him:

He would have been greatly distinguished as a scholar but for inherited infirmities of bodily constitution, which, from early childhood, affected his mind. His love for the neighbourhood in which he was born, and his sympathy with the habits and characters of the mountain yeomanry, in conjunction with irregular spirits . . . induced him to accept the retired curacy of Langdale.[184]

In 1840 Owen Lloyd's malady became worse. Wordsworth wrote of him on 3rd June: 'Poor Owen Lloyd is in confinement—and our best hope is that he will not live long, as he has lately had frequent shocks of epilepsy—that has made grievous havoc both in his bodily health, and faculties of mind.' [185]   He died in Manchester on 18th April 1841, and Wordsworth wrote his epitaph. The poem was written late in July or early in August, *Epitaph in the Chapel-yard of Langdale, Westmoreland*.[186]   Of it Wordsworth wrote to his brother: 'I find no fault with it myself . . . except that it is too long for an Epitaph.'

It is a far cry from the young, afflicted clergyman at Langdale to the 'good old Earl' of Lonsdale on his estate at Lowther. Having early befriended the poet, the Earl of Lonsdale never ceased to do what he could to look after Wordsworth's interests. On his investiture, he had paid with interest the debt owed by his father to the late John Wordsworth. He had obtained for Wordsworth, in 1813, the Distributorship of Stamps for Westmorland. He was one of those interested in securing the Government pension in 1842.

Wordsworth was fond of the old earl, of his daughter, the Lady Frederick Bentinck, and of the grandson.[187]   In the latter part of September 1840 Wordsworth, Rogers, and many other guests made a ten-day visit at Lowther, Lady Frederick being the hostess. Lord Lonsdale's death in 1844 Wordsworth felt as a personal loss. To the earl's daughter he wrote: 'As long as I retain consciousness I shall cherish the memory of your father, for his inestimable worth, and as one who honoured me with his friendship, and who was to myself and my children the best benefactor.' [188]

Wordsworth liked people; he liked those who lived about him. Partly a recluse from the hubbub of cities, he was no recluse from men and women. His friendships were lasting, and yet he was always ready for a new friend. One of the oldest residents in the Lake District, he welcomed the new-comers: the Arnolds, the Fletchers, and Harriet Martineau. He helped them in their business negotiations, in planning their homes, and in their landscape-gardening. His mind was alert to all that was going on in Westmorland. He enjoyed the sermons of Faber and of Arnold. He dined at many homes, and liked a rubber of whist in the evening. He was loyal to his friends beyond death and even beyond a failure in their mental capacities; he was a friend to their children and their children's children. Estranged friends he received again, and he was tolerant of those with a point of view different from his own. He had settled in Westmorland because of the beauty of its scenery, and he never failed to enjoy the variations of light and shade, the subtle nuances of colour, the sudden ecstasy of spring, or the dazzling radiance of autumn; but his happiness at Rydal Mount, especially as he grew older, was greatly enhanced by the warmth of affection received and bestowed.

V. LONDON FRIENDS

WORDSWORTH's friends were not confined to the region in which he was born and in which he had spent the greater part of his life. After the Lake District he had more close friends in London than in any other one place, but all over England there were people whom he liked and visited, and with some of his admirers in foreign countries he was on terms of great intimacy.

That Rogers and Wordsworth enjoyed each other speaks well for both, for two men could hardly be found who were more different in their circumstances and habits of life; and yet between the two old poets was a friendship of forty years, a friendship that grew warmer toward the end.

Samuel Rogers was a rich old bachelor, and lived in a handsome home in St James's Place. The house was 'a perfect bijou of curiosities, fine paintings, and objects of virtu.'[1] There were so many works of art and valuable books that people often wondered what would happen to them after Rogers's death. No large share would go to nieces and nephews. 'I do not acknowledge nephews and nieces as relations,' he told Crabb Robinson, one Sunday morning in June 1840— 'I had nothing to do with begetting either bodies or minds. They are nothing to me and I am nothing to them except as I may cut up. But they have no claim on me for that,'[2] he said as he slapped his breeches pocket.

Crabb Robinson was concerned that the beautiful collection should be dissipated after the death of his old friend.

I went out early to breakfast with Rogers [he wrote in his diary] . . . he pointed out to us his beautiful works of art and curious books. I could not help asking what is to become of them. 'The auctioneer,' he said, 'will find out the fittest possessor hereafter— he who gives money for things values them.[3]

Wordsworth, too, felt that the scattering of the collection would be a pity, and once became inopportunely philosophical at a breakfast of Rogers's. Admiring the house, he said it reminded him of Horace, 'Linquenda est domus.' The deaf host asked him two or three times what he had said; finally, Wordsworth replied that since ladies were present he would translate. The urbane Rogers was not pleased that death should be mentioned at his table; so he made a face at Wordsworth and said: 'Don't talk Latin in the society of ladies.'[4]

Rogers had early won reputation as a poet, and in the eighteen - forties was a figure long established in London society. With those before whom he was natural his disposition was variable—now charming, now rasping, now merely the old man.[5] The changeable Rogers suited Crabb Robinson better than the smooth host. In March 1840 Robinson said: 'But with all his worth R: does compliment,[6] and on another occasion: 'He was full of praise but it was not precisely what I liked.'[7]

Rogers was known for his breakfasts. He invited most of the literary people in London and an occasional traveller from America, and his intimates understood that they were to drop in whenever they liked. He was witty and urbane, able to draw out his varied guests—except that now and then his wit became too sharp.

Aubrey de Vere says that because the host had a weak voice everything was kept subdued at Rogers's parties: 'No candles were put on his dinner table.'[8]

Perhaps it was the very difference between Rogers and Wordsworth that made them friends. They met in 1803, and remained friends throughout Wordsworth's life. Rogers sometimes visited in Westmorland, and Wordsworth often went to St James's Place. Rogers was the business man, the Londoner; whereas Wordsworth, despite his trips to London and his tours in England and in other countries, was primarily the mountaineer. Roberts says of this difference:

Rogers, like so many kind-hearted people, was fond of 'managing':

N

he loved to have control of people's affairs. And Wordsworth not
only liked, but had a respect for Rogers, not unmingled with that
simple awe which so many country-folk feel to the townsman, who
moves at ease in circumstances that abash and baffle the unaccustomed
visitor.[9]

Besides this, Rogers had been a famous poet when Wordsworth
was still an undergraduate.

His *Yarrow Revisited, and Other Poems*, late in 1834, Wordsworth had 'affectionately inscribed to Samuel Rogers, Esq., as
a testimony of friendship and an acknowledgment of intellectual obligations.'[10] He once said of him: 'Rogers is a
wonderful Man—his life is worthy of being written with care,
and *copiously*—but I fear so valuable a work as that would be,
will never be produced.'[11]

The Londoner joined Wordsworth at Rydal, in September
1840, went with him to Lowther, and later returned for a
short visit at the Mount. Miss Fenwick found him 'somewhat dwarfed by what surrounded him,'[12] but Wordsworth
could not understand his friend's going back to London when
the country was bright with autumn colours.

Wordsworth probably saw much of Rogers during his 1841
visit to London. He was there in June and through most of
July. Dean Stanley describes one of Rogers's breakfasts,
where he found Wordsworth, 'Philip van Artevelde,'[13] Spedding, and 'three mutes':

> The great feature of the breakfast was the lively and protracted
> dialogue of the two poets. Whenever I had seen Wordsworth
> before, he was stiff or prosy; but on this occasion he not only gave
> birth to several wise remarks on words and metre, but it was beautiful
> to see the playful way in which he and his brother-poet sported
> together, and bantered each other on their respective habits. It was
> exactly the *town* and *country* mouse: the town-mouse a sleek, well-fed,
> sly, *white* mouse, and the country-mouse with its rough, weather-
> worn face and grey hairs; the town-mouse displaying its delicate
> little rolls and pyramids of glistening strawberries, the country-
> mouse exulting in its hollow tree, its crust of bread and liberty, and
> rallying its brother, on his late hours and frequent dinners. . . .[14]

The next spring, too, Wordsworth went to London. Before the visit, Crabb Robinson and the sophisticated little host chatted often about the forthcoming 1842 volume, especially about the dedication of the Italian poems. On 8th February Robinson dropped in for breakfast, and found Rogers 'alone and very amiable. Talked with great kindness of Wordsworth and everybody else.'[15] About a fortnight later, when he had an early draft of the dedication of the *Memorials of a Tour in Italy*, Robinson went proudly to Rogers and recited the lines.

I had a very agreeable several hours' chat with him [he wrote] . . . I repeated to him the seven lines which he expressed heartily his approbation of—He called them very beautiful and even poetical, which I should not, on account of the simple style and the warmth of the feeling. He told good stories and was in capital humour.[16]

The amended form, also, Robinson took to St James's Place, and then wrote happily to Rydal Mount: 'I breakfasted lately with Rogers—I could not resist the temptation to repeat the *nine* lines. . . . He praised them with great warmth and intimated how PROUD I might well be etc. etc. etc.'[17]

In April, when the new volume was out, Robinson found the banker-poet's enthusiasm almost enough to satisfy even himself.

I staid till 12 with him [he wrote]. He was as amiable as ever and he spoke with great warmth of the new volume of Wordsworth's— 'It is all gold—the least precious is still gold.' He said this accompanying a remark on one little epitaph which he said would have been better in prose.[18]

Not willing to believe that any poem of Wordsworth's would be better in prose, the Crabb added: 'This is not the first time of his preferring prose to verse.'

Wordsworth came in May. He enjoyed being fêted, but said that he had several grudges against London. One was that he pretended to have heard of people because he thought he should have. 'It is too bad,' he said, 'that, when more than seventy years old, I should be drawn from the mountains in order to tell a lie.' He grumbled, too, because he was invited out so much that once he had to eat three breakfasts in one morning—the first at seven.[19]

Charles Robert Leslie tells a story of the playful antagonism between Wordsworth and Rogers. The two poets, Leslie, and Washington Irving had breakfasted with Rogers's sister. When the party broke up, Rogers walked home with Leslie, 'and Wordsworth and Irving, promising to come, took a cab. As they got into it Rogers said: "They are a couple of humbugs, I believe, we shall see no more of them." ' [20] But he was wrong; the party was soon reunited.

Wordsworth was quick to resent a slur on his friends. In the newspapers appeared a cartoon, representing old crones attacking Rogers and his beating them off with a green umbrella. The picture was allegedly based on fact, but the old women were supposed to stand for the muses and—possibly—for former sweethearts of the old bachelor. Wordsworth was disgusted.[21]

The writer has in her possession a manuscript letter by Wordsworth which may refer to the incident. It is dated more than two years later; but Wordsworth was a notoriously poor correspondent. The letter follows:

Rydal Mount

Dec. 21st 1844

Dear Sir,

Absence from home and much occupation partly consequent upon it have prevented the expression of sympathy with you upon the occasion of the brutal assault to which you have been subjected. I say the *expression* to you of sympathy, for I assure you I resented it most deeply when I first heard of it. I presume it is yourself whom I have to thank for two Copies of your Journal giving an account of the case.

I hope you were not much injured, and that the effe[c]ts of the ferocious violence are entirely gone off. Pray let me know of this better.

This detestable action will at all events have called out the Sound feelings of your friends and supporters towards you in a way which must have been highly gratifying.

Believe me with every good wish

dear Sir

sincerely your obliged

Wm Wordsworth [22]

In 1843 and 1844 Wordsworth did not go to London, and he intended not to go in 1845.[23] But when he received from the Lord Chamberlain an invitation to attend the queen's ball, he changed his plans and turned to Rogers as the authority on court etiquette. Rogers supplied not only the necessary information, but the court dress as well. The ball took place on 25th April. Aubrey de Vere went to Moxon's the day before, and had tea with Wordsworth, who was 'in great force —had borrowed Mr Rogers's court dress, and Dr Lang's sword for the Queen's Ball.'[24] Crabb Robinson called on the 25th:

The Poet Laureate is come on purpose to attend the Queen's Ball, to which he has a special invitation, and for which he has come up 300 miles. He goes from Rogers's this evening with a sword, bag-wig, and court-dress.[25]

And the next evening de Vere found him 'but indifferently pleased with the Queen's Ball.'

Many have told the story of Wordsworth at Queen Victoria's ball, but his friends in London were amused at the trouble they had squeezing the gaunt, stately Wordsworth into the suit of the dapper little Rogers. Serjeant Talfourd told Haydon:

Moxon had hard work to make the dress fit. It was a squeeze, but by pulling and hauling they got him in. Fancy the high priest of mountain and of flood on his knees in a court, the quiz of courtiers, in a dress that did not belong to him, with a sword that was not his own, and a coat that he had borrowed.[26]

Wordsworth enjoyed the companionship of Samuel Rogers particularly on this visit to London.[27] Many of his friends looked up to him, and the adulation must sometimes have grown tiresome. With Rogers he was on terms of equality, and to Rogers he often exhibited the lighter side of his nature. Aubrey de Vere, having brought Tennyson out to Hampstead to meet Wordsworth, witnessed a minor contest between Laker and Londoner:

There was an amusing scene in the garden, Rogers insisting upon Wordsworth's naming a day to dine with him, and Wordsworth stoutly exhibiting his mountain lawlessness, stating that he would dine or not as it happened, or as it suited his convenience, and saying that he was sure he would find the best accommodation of every sort at Mr Rogers', whether Mr Rogers was in the house or not. Mr Rogers at last replied: 'Well, you may as well tell me at once to go to the Devil; I can only say that my house, its master, and everything in it are heartily at your service—come when you will.' [28]

The standing invitation Wordsworth accepted a few days later.

There was no diminution but rather an increase of friendship between Wordsworth and Rogers. Though he wrote few letters after the death of his daughter, Wordsworth did write to Rogers. He called him 'my friend of nearly half a century,' and referred to his own grief and the bond between the two families.[29] Rogers replied in the same vein, speaking of 'a friendship so long and so uninterrupted as ours.'

Edward Moxon, John Kenyon, and Basil Montagu were part of the circle in which Wordsworth moved when in London. Moxon was Wordsworth's publisher in the later years. Through Crabb Robinson Wordsworth had met him in 1834. When Wordsworth came to London in 1836 to see the *première* of Talfourd's *Ion*, Moxon contended with Talfourd for him.[30] That time Talfourd won, but Moxon was the host in 1845, when the Poet Laureate attended the queen's ball. In 1837 Moxon went to Paris with Wordsworth and Crabb Robinson; he visited at Rydal with Robinson in December 1845; he went to Great Malvern in June 1849, to be with Wordsworth. He was invited by Mrs Wordsworth to accompany Robinson that year on his Christmas visit: 'Cannot you make a Christmas holiday also . . .? You know we should be glad to see you, and a little of your company would be salutary to my husband.' [31]

Moxon fancied himself a poet, and 'published two volumes of rather poor sonnets, one of which he dedicated to Wordsworth.' [32] Thomas Powell quotes a review of the sonnets: 'What might be a scanty plot of ground for an elephant like

Wordsworth, would be a boundless wilderness for a flea, like Edward Moxon.' [33]   Mrs Moxon was the granddaughter of Agostino Isola,[34] and the adopted daughter of Charles and Mary Lamb.[35]   Moxon wrote some verses *To the Memory of Charles Lamb*.

Wordsworth corresponded a good deal with Moxon, and usually when he was in London he was given a party by his publisher.   On 10th June 1842 Crabb Robinson wrote: 'I went early to Moxon's Wordsworth being there.   A large party of authors. . . . It was not till past one that I could get Wordsworth away.' [36]

If Mary Russell Mitford's remark be literally true, Moxon lost money when he published Wordsworth's poems.[37]   Perhaps it was an exaggeration; perhaps it was true only at the beginning of their relationship.   Whether he lost or made money on the Poet Laureate, Edward Moxon enjoyed William Wordsworth.

John Kenyon and Wordsworth were old friends.[38]   In May 1838 Kenyon sent Wordsworth a volume of his poems.[39]   To accommodate Kenyon, who wanted to give him a dinner, Wordsworth extended his 1842 visit in London a week. During this visit Wordsworth asked Kenyon if he might call on Elizabeth Barrett, but 'that jealous guardian refused his permission.' [40]   At least once in Wordsworth's last decade John Kenyon went to Rydal.

The last I heard of poor Dr Arnold's family [wrote Miss Mitford] was from a dear friend (John Kenyon) who was visiting Mr Wordsworth, and he said that he met Mrs Arnold and her children crossing a field by a country pathway in their deep mourning, and that it impressed him like a village funeral.[41]

Basil Montagu was the man whose little boy Wordsworth and Dorothy had taken to eke out their early housekeeping expenses.[42]   It is hard to forgive Basil Montagu for betraying Wordsworth to Coleridge, but Wordsworth forgave him. When Montagu asked him in 1844 for a lock of his hair, the old poet not only sent the desired lock, 'white as snow, and taken from a residue which is thinning rapidly,' but wrote a long, affectionate letter, full of reminiscences of friends long dead.[43]

By 1840 the gentle Charles was no more, but his afflicted sister had outlived him. Mary Lamb was almost eighty and in an institution now, but her friends did not lag in their interest. The life of Charles Lamb could not be fully written because it must not be told that Mary, in a fit of temporary insanity, had stabbed her mother to death. Wordsworth often sent affectionate messages to the old lady: 'Tell us something about dear Mary Lamb—and give her our love if she is in a state to receive it.' [44]   In July 1841 her brother's friend, Bryan Waller Procter, who was a Commissioner in Lunacy, had Mary Lamb removed from Edmonton to a private home near Regent's Park. Poor old Miss Lamb rejoiced at 'having escaped from a place far removed from all her friends and where she was not even kindly treated.' [45]

Now her friends could do more for her. Crabb Robinson invited her to dinner, called on her again and again, and often took her presents. The Talfourds entertained her, too, and Mrs Talfourd seemed to act as her sponsor.[46] Miss Lamb's condition was fluctuating, and though she continued to go in company, she could hardly have done so but for the understanding of those whom she visited.

It is pleasant to think of Wordsworth, lionized as he was in 1842, slipping away from a party where Samuel Rogers and Washington Irving were guests, to call on his old friend Mary Lamb. Though Crabb Robinson's version is a little different from that of Charles Robert Leslie,[47] it is apparently the same occasion. There had been a breakfast at Miss Rogers's on 11th May, and the group was to reassemble at Leslie's home. After describing Washington Irving, Robinson said: 'W: called with me on Mary Lamb. She received us with composure and then W: and I followed Rogers and Washington Irving and Mrs Leslie to the painter's house.' [48]

Robinson called in August and found Miss Lamb just starting out to call on Thomas Hood. Though she had 'not been long visible,' she was now 'quite in possession of her faculties and recollecting everything nearly.' Crabb Robinson walked with her to St John's Wood.[49]

Just before the Christmas visit to Rydal Mount in 1844 Crabb Robinson bought and carried to Miss Lamb a handsome shawl. 'She received it with manifest pleasure,' he said, 'and I had a nice chat with her.' [50]

The Wordsworths were always interested in Mary Lamb. 'When you see Miss Lamb, and in pretty good health,' wrote Quillinan, in June 1843, 'pray remember the Rydalites and Dora to her very affectionately.' [51] The poet wrote to Moxon in November 1845: 'Remember me most kindly to Mr Rogers and his sister, and to dear old Miss Lamb.' [52] And Mrs Wordsworth wrote to Robinson a fortnight later: 'Of course you will bring the latest news of Miss Rogers and dear Miss Lamb—to whom when you make your farewell call give our best remembrances.' [53] Crabb Robinson called on Mary Lamb immediately. 'She and Miss Rogers,' he wrote to his brother, 'are among the friends the Wordsworths most love.' [54]

Mary Lamb died on 20th May 1847,[55] during the long period when Dora Quillinan was wasting away. Crabb Robinson attended the funeral, riding in a coach with Talfourd and Forster. 'We chatted about our dear old friends . . .,' he wrote in his diary. 'Talfourd it is understood will now relate the whole history of the death of her mother. The 2nd edition of the Letters will be a very valuable book.' [56]

Two of Wordsworth's friends turned against him in his later years, Walter Savage Landor and Thomas Noon Talfourd.

Until 1836 Walter Savage Landor had been an ardent Wordsworthian. It is amusing to read how much he admired Wordsworth in the early eighteen-thirties. Crabb Robinson said: 'In his admiration and love of Wordsworth he goes

beyond me. . . . L: is the very opposite of a general liker.
. . . And yet he says—Scarcely any thing in Wordsworth is
bad—Almost all is good and first rate!!!' [57]   It was through
Wordsworth that Robinson had met Landor, and he wrote to
Dorothy: 'The bond which united us so cordially was our
common love and admiration of the works of your brother—
I never met with any one who is so warm and eloquent in the
expression of his judgement in favour of Mr Wordsworth's
poetry.' [58]   Then he became unwittingly prophetic. It was
because Landor was usually 'so unsparing in the expression
of his contempt—Indeed towards the really great poets . . .
severe not to say unmerciful in his censures' that Robinson
was surprised. 'From such a *murderous* critic,' he said, 'I
expected of course that he would limit the praise of your
brother to a few favourite works only. . . . I found him an
Admirer en masse—he will scarcely give up a page to the
enemies!!!'

Such a man would make an excellent hater if anything should
distort the conformation of his deity. Meanwhile, he was
reading Cary's Pindar, and finding Pindar inferior to Wordsworth.[59]   He wrote an ode to Wordsworth, and sent a message
that he would try to remain in London until Wordsworth
arrived.[60]

Talfourd's *Ion* was played by Macready on 26th May 1836,
and the performance was the occasion of a great celebration
on Talfourd's part. Mary Russell Mitford and Wordsworth
were house guests, a number of poets dined with Talfourd
that evening, seats at the theatre were reserved for *littérateurs*
and benchers, and after the performance came an elaborate
supper.[61]   Landor and Wordsworth sat in the same box at
the *première*.

It was on this occasion that Landor's love for Wordsworth
turned to hate. Landor claimed that Wordsworth disparaged
Southey's poetry, called Goethe an impostor, and was insensible
to Talfourd's *Ion*. Their common friends did not side with
Landor; his biographers do not defend him. Even Talfourd

—inflated as he was and jealous of any slur on his talent—was not offended at Wordsworth. And yet Landor became more and more atrabilious.

Landor published the same year, *A Satire on Satirists and Admonition to Detractors*, disclosing his bitterness toward his former idol—a small pamphlet, little noticed. Afterwards, people began to wonder at his sudden change. Daniel Macmillan wrote to George Wilson:

Did you ever see his 'satire,' in which he so fiercely attacks Professor Wilson and Mr Wordsworth? He seems to have forgiven the Professor, but he does not seem at all inclined to let the good old poet alone. . . .

I have been told that the origin of his dislike to Wordsworth is some foolish story of this kind. Some one told Wordsworth of the new edition of Southey's works edited by himself. Wordsworth asked the price and the number of the volumes; and when told said he thought it ought to be cheaper. Perhaps he said it in such a way as to show that *he* did not value Southey's poetry very highly. . . . However that may be, it is certain that Landor delights to pull down Wordsworth ever since he heard this story.[62]

Wheeler's version is that 'Wordsworth said, or Landor fancies he said, that he would not give five shillings for all Southey's poetry.' [63] Landor regarded Wordsworth as ungrateful, for he felt that Southey had first called the attention of the public to him.

Crabb Robinson took up the cudgels for Wordsworth. He wrote two letters to Landor in December 1836, wherein he answered in detail Landor's attack.[64] The second letter maintains a tone of pity for Landor, who buffets his antagonist so clumsily that he wounds, also, those whom he attempts to defend. Robinson hopes, therefore — not without malice — that 'as the pamphlet is too small to advertise it may escape notice.' His loyalty to Wordsworth was so great that for a time he gave up Landor's society.[65]

Landor suppressed the *Satire*, but continued his gibes at Wordsworth. Resenting some jocular lines about Southey in the *Globe*, he discharged verses against the writer. This time his bitterness was directed mainly at someone else, but he veiled a slur on Wordsworth:

> No by my Soul tho' greater men
> And nearer the envenomed pen
> In Southey's breast . . .

Crabb Robinson was furious. '*Greater* and *nearer* can mean none but Wordsworth,' he said, 'and this is a monstrous injustice to that great and good man.' [66]

In *Blackwood's Magazine* for December 1842 appeared Landor's famous attack on Wordsworth, the second Imaginary Conversation between Porson and Southey. Wordsworth was not upset by the article; he did not even know about it. But his friends and his son-in-law were. Crabb Robinson was glad to find that Kenyon felt as he did about Landor: 'Like me he has no wish to see him again, there is so much malignity mixed up with his best compositions.' [67] Before the month was out Quillinan was eager to answer the attack. [68]

Living then at Ambleside, Wordsworth's son-in-law wrote an answer to Landor, a 'Dialogue between Walter Savage Landor and the Editor of *Blackwood's Magazine*.' He ridiculed Landor's Imaginary Conversation, quoting from the *Satire on Satirists and Admonition to Detractors*. The *Satire* had attacked *Blackwood's*, and the Imaginary Conversation was printed in *Blackwood's*; Quillinan brought out this inconsistency, and thought the irony would be complete if his own burlesque were printed in the same magazine. [69] Possibly because of the clever irony, possibly, also, because of his friendship for Wordsworth, Christopher North did accept the article, and printed it in *Blackwood's Magazine* for April 1843.

Robinson was delighted. 'You have done the thing capitally,' he wrote to Quillinan. Now he suggested that Quillinan should tell the poet of his article: 'If you do not let him know of it, he is likely to remain as ignorant of the defence as he still is of the attack.' [70] But one of the neighbours had sent in a copy of the *Morning Post*, which mentioned Quillinan's article. Wordsworth was satisfied.

Everybody in London, according to Crabb Robinson, was also satisfied—except Landor, of course:

The *Herald* has *lauded* your article. And your adversary will hardly find anyone to sympathy [*sic*] with him. Or to think you are not warranted in your attack. . . .

That B: [Blackwood] himself should not mind inserting the abuse on B: is an additional proof of the contempt in which L's [Landor's] judgement is held by every one. . . .

I dined yesterday with Rogers I told him of the article—He highly approved of what I reported of it And seemed to think it quite right that 'Execution should be done on' so flagrant an offender. . . .

You need not fear being reproached for cruelty—Nobody mourns when a mad dog is knocked on the head.[71]

Landor, meanwhile, got a mild revenge by going about in literary circles with a little joke which purported to be original: "'I am told a Mr Quillinan has been attacking me — His writings I hear are Quill-inanities.'"[72] But the pun was not Landor's. It was made by one of Quillinan's fellow dragoons and told to Landor, some thirty years earlier, by Quillinan himself.[73]

The attitude of John Forster, Landor's publisher, is significant. He was unwilling to print the attack in 1844,[74] and in 1866 said of Landor:

He is so entirely in the wrong about this Wordsworth matter that it seems needless to revive what is best forgotten—especially where there are so many other disagreeable subjects which cannot be evaded so easily.[75]

Thomas Noon Talfourd turned against Wordsworth only during the last two years of the poet's life.

Talfourd gave himself the credit of being one of the first to discover the greatness of Wordsworth. In 1815, when he was only twenty years old, he had published a paper called *An Estimate of the Poetry of the Age*, in which he called Wordsworth 'the first of the modern poets.' He was making proselytes for Wordsworth in 1817. Mary Russell Mitford describes her efforts at equalling Talfourd's enthusiasm.[76]   And about 1820 Talfourd printed an article, 'On the Genius and Writings of Wordsworth,' in which his raptures rise like incense and he calls himself not a critic but a disciple.[77]   Such a high point of enthusiasm would be hard to maintain, but for twenty-eight years more Talfourd enjoyed the poetry and admired the man.

It was apparently Talfourd's nature to change toward his friends, for Mary Russell Mitford, at the time of the production of *Ion*, was hurt by her host's egotism and jealousy.[78]

Meanwhile, Serjeant Talfourd was a Wordsworthian. He and Wordsworth were working hand in hand for the Copyright Bill. Talfourd made several speeches before the House of Commons, and usually became eloquent on the subject of Wordsworth. On 18th May 1837 the most oratorical part of his speech reached its climax in the name William Wordsworth.[79]

Talfourd sent Wordsworth a petition to sign, but the latter refused for conscientious reasons: he was not sure of the truth of certain allegations, and he considered the wording discourteous to American publishers.[80]   He did, however, write forty letters to support Talfourd's motion,[81] and when the Bill was coming up again sent a personal petition for Talfourd to use in his speech.   He also wrote to Crabb Robinson to get as many friends as possible to attend early, 'as Talfourds bill stands first upon the list for that day.'[82]   Talfourd made the speech on 28th February 1839,[83] but the Bill dragged on until 1842.[84]

Serjeant Talfourd was very prosperous in the eighteen-forties, and was rising professionally. In June 1840 Crabb Robinson dined with him—'a sumptuous dinner but by no means a comfortable one.'[85]   Wordsworth spent a week-end with Talfourd during the London visit of 1841, just after Dora's wedding.[86]

Partly to be near Wordsworth, Talfourd planned a summer in the Lake District, and wrote to the poet about it.   Wordsworth was pleased that the serjeant considered his presence indispensable, and told him of two possible houses. In the summer of 1844 the plan materialized. On 14th July Talfourd wrote to Professor Wilson: 'I hope to take my family to the country you know so well in the neighbourhood of Windermere, where Mr Wordsworth has taken a cottage for us for the holidays.' [87] There, Talfourd wrote his *Vacation Rambles and Thoughts, 1841–3*, which Robinson said 'contains many thoughts concerning the poet.' [88]

Politically and theologically Talfourd was eminently correct; Mrs Talfourd attended divine worship every day as well as three times on Sunday. Crabb Robinson felt that there was a gradual change, and that he and Talfourd now had little in common. On 22nd December 1844 he noted sadly in his diary:

I concluded the evening by a call on the Talfourds. We talked chiefly about the Wordsworths. . . . He could not talk at his ease on any really interesting subject except Miss Lamb and perhaps Wordsworth on which we still feel alike—but in politics and religion he is utterly changed. . . .[89]

It was through Talfourd's interest in the Lambs that he became estranged from Wordsworth. As soon as Mary Lamb was dead, Talfourd began to work on the second edition of the letters of Charles Lamb, supplying tragic letters which could not be published during the sister's life and comic letters which could not be published during George Dyer's life.[90] Crabb Robinson borrowed letters from the Wordsworths and turned them over to Talfourd, possibly without permission; and Talfourd printed all that Robinson gave him. On 6th February Robinson gave him 'all those letters of Lamb to Wordsworth' which he thought 'might without giving offence be printed.' The book was finished by 17th May. 'I wrote a letter to Quillinan . . .' said Robinson. 'I said nothing about the forthcoming vol. of Lamb's letters. . . . I am apprehensive that it may not quite suit Wordsworth.' [91]

The edition came out in the summer of 1848, and was

dedicated to Wordsworth.   Quillinan wrote to Crabb Robinson on 23rd July:

Mr W. will be glad to see Serjt Talfourd's new publication of Mr Charles Lamb's letters and will no doubt acknowledge the dedication, of which you speak so handsomely that I am sure it will give great pleasure to the dedicatee, who is by no means insensible to such attentions.[92]

Robinson still felt a little guilty for having allowed Talfourd to publish Lamb's letters to Wordsworth, for he wrote in his diary in August:

All the reviews express high admiration of Lamb—so T: [Talfourd] on this score will not be blamed—not even Wordsworth will on that ground be dissatisfied and I hope to escape blame even for the insertion of the letters to the Wordsw[orth]s themselves.[93]

Wordsworth failed to acknowledge the dedication, and Talfourd never forgave him.   It is possible that Wordsworth was not pleased at Talfourd's publishing his letters, but more likely that sorrow drove everything else from his thoughts.   Talfourd's book came out about a year after Dora's death,[94] when Wordsworth was completely absorbed in his grief.

It is hardly surprising, when Wordsworth was neglecting his closest friends, that he should have been slow to acknowledge the dedication of a book which was, after all, only a piece of editing.   He received many dedications in his later years, and Serjeant Talfourd's was not exceptional.   The surprising thing is that Talfourd, for this negligence of Wordsworth's, should have let his admiration and friendship of more than thirty years become embittered.

Talfourd was offended and let his hurt be known, and Crabb Robinson thought in December that he was justified.[95]   Perhaps the busy little lawyer, visiting at Rydal Mount before the week was out, told Wordsworth; perhaps the poet asked him to smooth the matter over.   At any rate Quillinan wrote to Robinson soon after the latter had returned to London: 'I hope Serjt Talfourd was satisfied that Mr Wordsworth had

not [could not] intentionally have neglected a timely acknowledgment of the Charles Lamb and the dedication.' [96]

But Talfourd was not satisfied. His prosperity increased;
the next July he was appointed judge.[97] And he talked a great
deal about himself.[98] It was even rumoured, without foundation, that he was Wordsworth's 'Happy Warrior.' [99] And
yet it rankled in his mind that Wordsworth had not written
to him to thank him for the dedication. Even after Wordsworth's death Talfourd did not forget his bitterness.[100]

Landor and Talfourd were unusual among Wordsworth's
friends, for they had known him well, and yet turned irrevocably against him. It was not so with Benjamin Robert Haydon. If he turned from his friend, it was for one decade only,
and afterwards their friendship was stronger than before.

> High is our calling, Friend—Creative Art
>
> .　　　.　　　.　　　.　　　.　　　.　　　.
>
> Demands the service of a mind and heart,
> Though sensitive, yet, in their weakest part,
> Heroically fashioned—to infuse
> Faith in the whispers of the lonely Muse,
> While the whole world seems adverse to desert. . . .

Thus wrote Wordsworth to his new friend in 1815. Haydon
needed this advice then and always; but his career as painter
was harder than Wordsworth's as poet, for Haydon's fame
was the flare of a sky-rocket, whereas Wordsworth's mounted
slowly but steadily.

Haydon suffered from megalomania, overweening vanity
coupled with a lack of self-confidence. He was convinced
that he was a genius, but that the world was unfair in its
recognition of him. His moods shot from high enthusiasm to
black despair. Mary Russell Mitford wrote of him years after
his death:

He was a most brilliant talker—racy, bold, original, and vigorous;
and his early pictures were full of promise; but a vanity, that
amounted to self-idolatry, and a terrible carelessness, unjustifiable

o

in many matters, degraded his mind, and even impaired his talent in art.[101]

She had described his energetic side in earlier letters: 'Haydon himself is a very brilliant person, full of talent and fire and conversational power. His lectures are splendid things.' [102] To Elizabeth Barrett she wrote in October 1836, recommending Haydon not so much to Miss Barrett as to her younger sister: 'Miss Arabel will like his vivacity and good spirits. Those high animal spirits are a gift from heaven, and frequently pass for genius; or rather make talent pass for genius —silver-gilded.' [103]

Haydon reached his zenith about 1820 or 1821, when his 'Christ's Entry into Jerusalem' was exhibited:

It was considered 'a masterpiece,' the greatest historical painting that England had produced, a work that would mark an epoch in art. Charles Lamb wrote a poem in its praise; Wordsworth, referring to the six years Haydon had spent on it, said that it was worth waiting fifty years to get so perfect a picture. Other writers of eminence proclaimed its unsurpassed greatness.[104]

Keats said of it: 'I am nearer myself to hear your "Christ" is being tinted into immortality. Believe me, Haydon, your picture is part of myself.' Mrs Siddons admired it.[104] The ambitious painter had begun in 1814 the tremendous canvas containing portraits of Keats, Wordsworth, Voltaire, Newton, Hazlitt, and probably of John Howard Payne. In 1817 he gave 'the immortal dinner' that brought Wordsworth and Keats together, the unfinished picture hanging in the room. Charles Lamb was there, and many another literary guest. Of the evening, the host wrote in his journal: 'It was a night worthy of the Elizabethan age, and my solemn Jerusalem flashing up by the flame of the fire, with Christ hanging over us like a vision, all made a picture which will long glow upon

> that inward eye
> Which is the bliss of solitude.' [105]

England acclaimed the painting when it was exhibited, and Haydon seemed for a time to realize his ambition.

It was after his triumph, according to Miss Batho, and as a result of Hazlitt's influence, that Haydon became estranged from Wordsworth.[106]   But when Wordsworth called on him in 1831 Haydon said:

Wordsworth called after an absence of several years. I was glad to see him. He spoke of my Napoleon with his usual straight-forward intensity of diction. We shook hands heartily.[107]

Haydon did not scruple to ask favours. 'He [Wordsworth] spoke of Napoleon so highly,' he said, 'that I wrote and asked him to give me a sonnet. If he would or could he 'd make the fortune of the picture.' [107]   The poet complied and wrote to the painter:

You are at liberty to print the sonnet with my name, when and where you think proper. If it does you the least service the end for which it is written will be answered.[108]

Wordsworth had faith in Haydon not only before the latter was recognized, but after his reputation had begun to wane. And Haydon felt a deep sense of gratitude. He had named his son Frederic Wordsworth, and through the last years of his life he shared his joys and his disappointments with his stronger friend.

He lectured by invitation at Oxford in 1840, and in his exuberance he wrote to Wordsworth after his first lecture:

There are four honours in my life—First, the sonnet of Words-worth; second, the freedom of my native town for Solomon [109]; third, the public dinner in Edinburgh; and fourth, my reception at Oxford.

The first and the last are the greatest. But the first is the first, and will ever remain so, whilst a vibration of my heart continues to quiver.[110]

Haydon sent Wordsworth that summer an etching of the Duke of Wellington. On 31st August, while climbing Hel-vellyn with his daughter and her future husband, Wordsworth composed another sonnet to the painter, *On a Portrait of the*

Duke of Wellington upon the Field of Waterloo, by Haydon. He
sent it to Haydon immediately. 'It is warm from the brain,'
he said, 'and may require, in consequence, some little retouch-
ing.'[111] Haydon was overjoyed. 'Heard from dear Wordsworth,' he wrote in his journal, 'with a glorious sonnet on the
Duke and Copenhagen. It is very fine, so I began a new
journal directly, and put in the sonnet. God bless him.'[112]
Haydon soon found how true was the remark about 're-
touching,' for many letters followed in the next week, each
suggesting minute changes in the sonnet.

'The Picture is of great merit,' Wordsworth wrote to Professor Reed in September 1840, 'and is now engraving, so
that perhaps an impression may find its way to America, and
you see it.'[113] He wrote at greater length about his painter
friend a few months later:

Haydon is bent upon coming to Rydal next summer, with a view
to paint a likeness of me—not as a mere matter-of-fact portrait, but
one of a poetical character, in which he will endeavour to place his
friend in some favourite scene of these mountains. I am rather
afraid, I own, of any attempt of this kind, notwithstanding my high
opinion of his ability; but if he keeps in his present mind, which I
doubt, it would be in vain to oppose his inclination—He is a great
enthusiast, possessed also of a most active intellect—but he wants
that submissive and steady good sense, which is absolutely necessary
for the adequate development of power in that art to which he is
attached.[114]

Haydon's desire to paint his friend in a mountain setting
materialized in 'Wordsworth ascending Helvellyn,' painted not
in the Lake District, but in Haydon's studio in London, about
the middle of June 1842. The painter has preserved two
anecdotes of Wordsworth's stay in London. He took him
to church, and since they could not obtain a pew, they 'sat
down among publicans and sinners.' Haydon expected the
old Tory to object, but Wordsworth 'agreed like a Christian.'
Haydon was 'much interested in seeing his venerable white
head close to a servant in livery, and on the same level. The
servant in livery fell asleep, and so did Wordsworth.' The

other story Wordsworth told on himself, walking home with Haydon from one of Samuel Rogers's luncheons:

Once in a wood, Mrs Wordsworth and a lady were walking, when the stock dove was cooing. A farmer's wife coming by said to herself, 'Oh, I do like stock doves.' Mrs Wordsworth, in all her enthusiasm for Wordsworth's poetry, took the old woman to her heart; 'but,' continued the old woman, 'Some like them in a pie; for my part there's nothing like 'em stewed in onions.' [115]

Now and then Wordsworth breakfasted with Haydon and sat for him. Once, Haydon took his measurements, and was surprised to find him '5 ft. 9⅞ in.; and of very fine heroic proportions.' Wordsworth made him write down the measurements so that he could show them to Mrs Wordsworth.[116]

Haydon was happy about his imaginative portrait of Wordsworth ascending Helvellyn, and when it was finished took the canvas to Elizabeth Barrett. Like Charles Lamb, like Keats, like Wordsworth, Elizabeth Barrett regarded Haydon as a great painter. Now she wrote to him:

I have indeed looked at your picture until I lost my obligation to you in my admiration of your work. . . . I have seen the great poet who 'reigns over us' twice, face to face, and by you I see him the third time. You have brought me Wordsworth and Helvellyn into this dark and solitary room.[117]

She also wrote the sonnet, *Wordsworth upon Helvellyn! Let the Cloud* . . . Haydon sent Elizabeth Barrett's sonnet to Wordsworth in October. 'You good-for-nothing old Lake Poet,' he said, in the words of Charles Lamb, 'what has become of you?' [118]

Wordsworth thanked Miss Barrett for the sonnet and for a volume of her poems. 'I have read them with much pleasure,' he said, 'and beg that the thanks which I charged a friend to offer may be repeated to you now.' [119] Two years later Elizabeth Barrett sent her latest volumes, and Wordsworth thanked her at once.

Haydon made a picture of the head of Wordsworth early in 1843, and sent the proof to Francis Jeffrey, to Talfourd, and probably to many others. He also entered two cartoons in a contest, and with his sporadic enthusiasm wrote to Wordsworth: 'Now will come the result, and, if I am successful, and if you do not thunder away a last Sonnet, never look me in the face again.' [120] Wordsworth congratulated him on having finished the cartoons and thanked him warmly, but said:

My verse days are almost over, as they well may be, for to-morrow (God willing) I enter upon my seventy-fourth year, so that I can scarcely entertain the least hope of gratifying you by writing a Sonnet on either of the works which you have just executed.[121]

That Haydon should have sent his proof to the editor of the *Edinburgh Review* is surprising, but Francis Jeffrey no longer scoffed at Wordsworth. At his own request, in 1830 or 1831, Jeffrey had met Wordsworth.[122] Later, when the tide of public opinion had turned and Wordsworth had become Poet Laureate, Lord Jeffrey, reprinting his articles on *The Excursion* and *The White Doe of Rylstone*, inserted a note of apology.[123] Years later, Jeffrey said to Crabb Robinson: 'I was always among Wordsworth's admirers.' Robinson answered him: 'You had an odd way of showing it.' [124]

Now in 1843, when Haydon sent his picture of Wordsworth to him, Jeffrey answered: 'I return your "Proof" . . . though I am very sorry to part with it, and think it very interesting.' [125] And Talfourd, not yet offended, wrote enthusiastically.[126]

A man of Haydon's nature is likely to have disappointments, but the megalomaniac seldom blames himself. When Haydon told Wordsworth in July that he had lost in the contest, he expressed bitterness toward the judges and toward the Royal Academy.[127] This bitterness had been growing since a quarrel with the Academy in 1809, and continued to grow. In 1844 Haydon wrote to Wordsworth that his lectures on art were soon to be printed and were to be dedicated to him.

It would be no bad joke [he added] to dedicate them to the Academy, that respectable institution . . . which in sixty years spent only £4,500 in sending young men to Italy, and £19,000 on 'Dinners.' In commemoration of such distinguished favours to Art, this work is dedicated by their true friend, B. R. Haydon.[128]

Haydon's happiness at seeing Wordsworth when he came to London in 1845, was tinctured with bitterness. 'Dear old Wordsworth called,' he wrote in his journal on 3rd May, 'looking hearty and strong. "I came up to go to the state ball," said he, "and the Lord Chancellor . . . told me at the ball I ought to go to the levee." "And will you put on a court dress?" said I.' [129]   Glad to see his friend, and glad that Wordsworth had been recognized by the queen, Haydon was yet disappointed. 'I wish you had not gone to court,' he wrote to Wordsworth. 'I think of you as Nature's high priest. I can't bear to associate a bag-wig, and sword, ruffles, and buckles, with Helvellyn and the mountain solitudes.' [130]

Haydon's real and imagined disappointments grew. He needed money. He had failed in the cartoon contest. He could not sell his pictures. 'Though I have Wordsworth's and the Duke's head engraving,' he wrote on 6th February, 'I can sell neither.' [131]   He became more and more desperate. It was increasingly difficult to square the person he actually was with his inflated image of himself.

The culminating blow was the failure of his picture, 'The Banishment of Aristides,' and the simultaneous popularity of Tom Thumb, who appeared in the same building. Bayard Taylor describes the situation:

One day a gentleman gave me a ticket of admission to Tom Thumb's show, the entrance to which was on the same landing, and exactly opposite to Haydon's. I lingered about the latter, hoping for a chance to peep in, and was struck by the appearance of a man who was talking to the door-keeper. He was stout, broad-shouldered, about sixty years of age, rather shabbily dressed, and with a general air of dilapidated power. There was something fierce and bitter in the expression of his face, as he glanced across to the groups hurrying in to see Tom Thumb. He made some short remark to the door-keeper, and then entered the room where the paintings were. As the door opened I caught a sight of *two* spectators within. . . .[132]

This was too much for Haydon. On Monday morning, 22nd June 1846, Benjamin Robert Haydon shot himself.

Miss Mitford was convinced that Haydon's devotion to

his wife—a beautiful Jewess—and his three children partly
motivated his act.[133] Elizabeth Barrett said that his death
was not premeditated, and that 'The pecuniary embarrassment was not what sunk him. It was a mind still more
lost. It was the despair of the ambition by which he lived,
and without which he could not live.' Miss Barrett realized
Haydon's fundamental weakness:

In the self-assertion which he had struggled to hold up through
life, he went down into death. He could not bear any longer the
neglect, the disdain, the blur cast on him by the age, so he perished.
The Cartoon disappointment, the grotesque antagonism of Tom
Thumb, to which he recurred most bitterly in one of his last notes
to me—these things were too much for him. The dwarf slew the
giant. His love of reputation, you know, was a disease with him,
and for my part I believe that he died of it.[134]

And Wordsworth's continued affection for Haydon, like
his love for Hartley Coleridge, shows his understanding of a
nature far different from his own. Thirty years before, he
had said to Haydon:

> And oh! when Nature sinks, as oft she may,
> Through long-lived pressure of obscure distress . . .

Wordsworth did not confine his London visits to persons of
literary or artistic reputation. With the Marshalls and the
Hoares he had a warm welcome, and he often accepted the
hospitality of both homes. Mrs Hoare was connected by marriage with the Wordsworths, being a relative of Charles and
Priscilla Lloyd.[135] The late Dame Elizabeth Wordsworth,
great-niece of the poet, gives a vivid picture of old Mrs Hoare,
of Aunt Sally Hoare, and of their home in Hampstead:

Mrs Hoare, known as 'grandmamma' by a large circle of young
people in those days, was a wealthy and generous widow lady, whose
kindness really knew no bounds. Though a Church-woman, she
belonged to the great Quaker and banking connection of which our
great-grandfather Charles Lloyd had been a distinguished member.
. . . We used to make periodical pilgrimages from Westminster

to Hampstead, driving out in a fly . . . and it always seemed as if
her house were the very lap of luxury. I can recall her and her stepdaughter Miss Hoare, usually known as 'Aunt Sally,' when they
came in state to see us in their rich fur tippets. . . .

I hope 'The Heath' is still standing. It was a typical old-fashioned
gentleman's house, with a huge Portugal-laurel bush on the lawn.
Many a man and woman distinguished in literature has sat at that
hospitable table. . . . The Hampstead circle included Coleridge,
Joanna Baillie, Crabbe and William Wordsworth, who frequented
it from time to time; and there seemed to be a shadowy background
of Lloyds, Powells, Pryors and Buxtons hovering round![136]

It was Wordsworth's custom when in London to go to
the Hoares', and from there to visit the Strickland Cooksons,
Moxon, or the Christopher Wordsworths. At Mrs Hoare's
his friends could gather, and young writers could make his
acquaintance. Crabb Robinson describes a family party at old
Mrs Hoare's, in July 1841, typical perhaps of many afternoons
at The Heath:

Found a coach going to Hampstead. . . . At 4 at Mrs Hoare's
—There the Ws, Quillinans and also the D[octo]r Master of Trinity
—He was very lively—decided in politics—The poet quiet—I took
the poet and Quillinan to see Miss Sharpe's garden—A very agreeable
afternoon—Walked back at 10.[137]

Sara Coleridge also lived in Hampstead, with her husband,
Henry Nelson Coleridge, and her mother, and they probably
often joined the group at the Heath when Wordsworth was in
town. One of Mrs Hoare's frequent guests was Joanna Baillie,
eight years older than Wordsworth, and recognized as a poet
sooner than he. The old-fashioned home in Hampstead with
the laurel bush on the lawn was rich in poets that afternoon
in May 1845 when Aubrey de Vere and Tennyson drove out
from London to see Wordsworth, and found Samuel Rogers
already there.[138]

The Wordsworths were visiting the Hoares when Dora sailed
for Portugal, and again in April 1847, when her illness began
to be serious.

Mrs John Marshall was one of the oldest friends the Wordsworths had, having been Dorothy's childhood playmate, Jane
Pollard. She had married and gone to Leeds, but she and
Dorothy had kept up an intense correspondence, and before
1815 the Marshalls had moved to the Lake District and settled
near Ullswater.[139]   Both Dorothy and her brother often visited
at Hallsteads, and it was natural that the Wordsworths should
continue to see a good deal of the Marshalls when the latter
took a house in London. The Marshalls' carriage was at
Wordsworth's service.[140]

In 1842 the poet and Mrs Wordsworth spent less time with
the Marshalls than in the previous summer, for now Dora and
Quillinan were living in Upper Spring Street. But they still
sought the company of Jane Pollard and her husband. 'I went
early to breakfast with Quillinan and the Wordsworths,' wrote
Crabb on 8th June, 'and I accompanied the Ws to the Marshalls on a morning call.' [141]

Aubrey de Vere and Henry Taylor were two of the most
ardent Wordsworthians among the younger literary men in
London, and both visited in the Lake District. They shared
in their letters their admiration and affection for Wordsworth.
It was Henry Taylor who kindled Miss Fenwick's interest
in Wordsworth. Through Southey, Taylor had met Wordsworth in 1823,[142] and had introduced him to his circle of
young Benthamites.[143] He said of Wordsworth in 1831: 'He
is as agreeable in society as he is admirable in the powers of
talking; so perfectly courteous and well-bred and simple in
his manners.' [144]

Coleridge has left a description of Taylor about the time the
latter became acquainted with Wordsworth:

Of *him* personally I know little more than that he is a remarkably
handsome fashionable-looking young man, a little *too deep* or *hollow
mouthed* and important in his enunciation, but clever and well read.[145]

And Aubrey de Vere described him more than a decade later:

He [Taylor] is very (I think remarkably) handsome, and the most

stately person I ever saw. He talks very slowly and in a very mea-
sured manner. There is, I confess, something almost formidable in
the extreme statue-like coldness and serenity of his manner. The
conversation turned a great deal on Wordsworth, his character and
life.[146]

By this time Henry Taylor had achieved and lost popular
favour. *Philip van Artevelde*, published by Moxon in 1834, won
immediate and widespread recognition. Its author was invited everywhere, particularly to Lansdowne House and to Holland House, and was known as Philip van Artevelde.[147] In
another year his popularity waned.

On 17th October 1839, after more than three years of
parental objection, Henry Taylor married Theodosia Alice
Spring-Rice, cousin of Aubrey de Vere. The objection was
mainly a difference in religion, the Spring-Rices being Roman
Catholics. Alice's father, soon to become Lord Monteagle,
admired Wordsworth's poetry. 'He seems to have filled
his daughters,' said the son-in-law, 'as full of Wordsworth
as they could hold, and after coming from church turned
to *The Happy Warrior* and said it was worth a thousand
sermons.' [148]

To interpret Wordsworth to the reading public, Taylor
published two articles in the *Quarterly Review*: 'Wordsworth's
Poetical Works,' in 1834, and 'Wordsworth's Sonnets,' in
1841. According to Taylor, the popularity of Wordsworth's
poetry was increased by these articles, 'one of which, I was told
by the publisher at the time, had doubled the sale of his
works.' [149]

That Wordsworth encouraged Henry Taylor to write the
article on his sonnets is significant, for he had declined similar
articles from Barron Field [150] and Henry Alford [151] the year
before. And yet he gave Henry Taylor, for inclusion in his
article, fourteen unpublished *Sonnets upon the Punishment of
Death*.

While Taylor was preparing the paper, he sometimes had to
defend his position. Caroline Fox tells an anecdote of Taylor's

dining at Holland House, and Lady Holland's asking him what
he was then doing:

'I am writing a review of Wordsworth for the *Quarterly*.' 'What!'
exclaimed her ladyship, 'absolutely busied about the man who writes
of caps and pinafores and that sort of thing?' Taylor replied in the
gravest, quietest way, 'That is a mode of criticizing Wordsworth
which has been obsolete for the last ten years.' And Taylor has
not since been asked to Holland House.[152]

Taylor said that the story, though based on fact, was exaggerated, and that he had received several invitations after the
incident.[153]

Wordsworth valued Taylor's poetic criticism. Citing Milton
as authority for the 'double rhymes' that Taylor objected to
in the Penal Sonnets, Wordsworth nevertheless changed the
rhymes.

You and Mr Lockhart [he wrote to Taylor in November 1841]
have been very kind in taking so much trouble about the sonnets.
I have altered them as well as I could to your wishes, and trust that
you will find them improved, as I am sure they are where I have
adopted your own words.[154]

The article appeared in the *Quarterly Review* for December
1841. Taylor had tried, in conversation, to interest Archbishop Whately in Wordsworth's poetry, and failing, had
written the article. He had developed ideas that were latent
and had added doctrine suggested by the sonnets. But, said
Taylor:

The inexorable Archbishop seized upon these instances of extra-
development, and (in a letter to a friend which reached my hands)
observed with characteristic sharpness that they reminded him of
'pebble soup, which is said to be very savoury and nutritive if you
season it with pepper and salt, a few sweet herbs, and a neck of
mutton.'[155]

Crabb Robinson found the pebbles more palatable than the
sweet herbs and the neck of mutton. 'There came this evening the new Quarterly Review,' he wrote in his diary at Rydal
Mount on the last night of the year—'a very interesting

number—Wordsworth gave Hen: Taylor a set of sonnets on Capital Punishment which he has wrought into a long article on Wordsworth's Sonnets—an article much too preaching and prosy to be suited to the delight[ful] extracts on which he comments.' [156]

Though he was the literary executor of Southey, Taylor was restrained by Southey's son-in-law from publishing the letters. Before he gave up the task, however, he received from Crabb Robinson an interesting letter which proved that Southey had refused to do journalism in London. Robinson had been authorized by John Walter to offer him £2,000 a year, and Southey had declined 'to come to London for any emolument however great.' [157]

Henry Taylor and Mrs Taylor lived for a time at 16 Blandford Square, and later moved to Mortlake on the Richmond Road. Miss Fenwick spent most of her time in London at her cousin's home, having been his housekeeper before his marriage. Taylor was appointed to a post in the Colonial Office.[158]

When Wordsworth was visiting his daughter in Upper Spring Street in May 1842, Taylor enjoyed trudging all over London with him. Indeed, the younger man could barely keep pace with the old poet.[159] And in 1845, when the Laureate came to attend the queen's ball, he probably saw a good deal of Henry Taylor, not so much at Taylor's own home as at Moxon's, at Rogers's, at Mrs Hoare's, and at Lord Monteagle's. Aubrey de Vere gives a glimpse of the Laureate breakfasting with his friends in Grosvenor Street a few days after the queen's ball: [160] 'Wordsworth in great force. . . . Insisted on seeing Henry Taylor's child—took him in his arms and kissed him.' [161]

Wordsworth respected Henry Taylor's mind and valued his friendship. But Taylor knew his own limitations, and realized that he entered only partially into Wordsworth's mind. 'For a composite character,' he wrote to Miss Fenwick, 'will always be inscrutable to the many, very often even to the few.' [162]

More devoted to Wordsworth than the author of *Philip van Artevelde* was the young Irish poet, Aubrey de Vere. Not a Londoner himself, de Vere spent a good deal of his time in London during the eighteen-forties. He was there during at least two of Wordsworth's later visits, and also saw the older poet in the Lake District.

Crabb Robinson, lunching with the Henry Taylors and Miss Fenwick in 1850, saw Aubrey de Vere: 'a very gentlemanly as well as superior young [man] so that the conversation was of a very superior character. De V: is poet and liberal— a thinker and a man of sentiment.' [163]　　Later, Robinson wrote of de Vere:

He is an Irishman but of high Norman family as his name shews —And one of the hopes of the next generation. [164]

Miss Edith Morley says that Aubrey's father, Sir Aubrey de Vere Hunt, [165] 'assumed the name De Vere by letters patent in 1832, but was descended from Aubrey de Vere, second son of the fifteenth Earl of Oxford.' [166]

The younger Aubrey was an intensely spiritual person, a lover of beauty and seeker after truth. Born in Ireland, he had spent most of his youth in his father's country place, Curragh Chase, in County Limerick. Here 'his poetic instincts and religious aspirations had been nurtured and strengthened in a region of meditative peace.' [167]　Steeped in Celtic lore, he was also saturated with the literature of England, and had some acquaintance with that of other countries. At first a member of the Church of England, he was profoundly influenced by the Oxford Movement, especially by Newman. When he was asked: 'Who, among all the great souls he had known, had impressed him the most? He said instantly, "Wordsworth and Newman; they are the two for whom my love has been most like idolatry."' [168]

Sir Aubrey had directed his son's taste from the poetry of Byron to that of Wordsworth. 'I read "Laodamia,"' said young de Vere, 'standing, to the last line, and was converted. I seemed to have got upon a new and larger planet.' [169]　Through the Irish mathematician and poet, William Rowan Hamilton, and through Henry Taylor, both friends of de Vere's, Aubrey had heard much about Wordsworth before he had the privilege of meeting him personally.

When Aubrey de Vere was twenty-seven years old, in 1841, he met both Wordsworth and Sara Coleridge, and the friendship of each meant much to him.

Mrs Henry Nelson Coleridge was twelve years older than de Vere, and was widowed eighteen months after their meeting. She was reserved, rational, balanced; he, an enthusiast. But between them was a spiritual bond which obliterated differences of age and temperament, and even divergence on a matter of the utmost importance to both. Both loved poetry, especially the poetry of Wordsworth. 'How well I remember our discussions about Wordsworth,' Aubrey de Vere wrote later.

She was jealous of my admiration for his poems, because it extended to *too many* of them. No one could be a true Wordsworthian, she maintained, who admired so much some of his later poems. . . . It implied a disparagement of his earlier poems, such as 'Resolution and Independence,' in which the genuine Wordsworthian inspiration, and that alone, uttered itself.[170]

In their letters, too, they discussed literature all the way from Homer to *Evangeline*. The young Irish poet sent volumes of poetry and volumes of criticism to Sara Coleridge. They discussed George Herbert, Crashaw, Tennyson's *In Memoriam*, and Wordsworth's *Prelude*. She commended him for liking Burns, and shared with him her joy in reading Pindar.[171] Homer and Virgil she casually quoted to express to young de Vere the brightness of a blue and white day at the shore or 'foam-white convolvulus' gleaming against nettles. Milton she admired greatly, but would not go so far as Landor, who had just pronounced him greater than Homer and Dante together. 'Mr Wordsworth,' she said, 'considers Homer second only to Shakespeare, deeply as he venerates Milton.'[172]

Sara Coleridge advised de Vere, in 1846, about his contemplated critique of Wordsworth, and made a classification of

the poems for him.[173]   Now and then she would prod him to
go on with poetry and not fritter his time away on politics
and agriculture.[174]   After the publication of de Vere's 'Nine
Letters' on Irish affairs in the *Morning Chronicle*, she wrote:

> Your preaching away about agriculture, while poetry seems your
> vocation, is so like my father at your age, who would turn away from
> 'Christabel' or the 'Ode to Dejection' to give Mr Poole his ideas
> about fattening pigs with acorns![175]

Sara Coleridge and Aubrey de Vere were deeply concerned
with matters of religion and theological dogma.   They did not
think alike, de Vere being always more concrete.   He thought
of the future life as a glorified form of the life on this earth,[176]
whereas Sara Coleridge anticipated a future existence that
would be entirely spiritual.   Though her mind would not
compromise with de Vere's argument, Sara's affection for him
almost won her over to his point of view.   When he fixed his
earnest eyes upon her, she almost felt that the eyes themselves
and the serious young face would survive the grave:

> Keep, oh! keep those eyes on me,
>   If thou wouldst my soul persuade,
> Soul of reasoner, bold and free,
>   Who with pinions undismayed
> Soars to realms of higher worth
> Than aught like these poor heavens and earth.
>
>   .   .   .   .   .
>
> Who that sees the radiant smile
>   Dawn upon thy features bright,
> And thy soft, full eyes the while
>   Spreading beams of tender light,
> But must long those looks to greet,
> When perfect souls in joyance meet? . . .[177]

Sara Coleridge's letters to de Vere were filled with abstract
theological discussions, with many controversial questions on
which she and de Vere were not in accord.   Both were members of the Church of England, and both were in sympathy
with the general claims of the Tractarians, though Sara Cole-

ridge did not go the whole way with any party,[178] and Aubrey de Vere eventually went farther than Pusey and Keble.

Aubrey de Vere was received into the Roman Catholic Communion on 15th November 1851. Wordsworth had influenced his poetry; Newman, his religion.

For a time before the reception Sara Coleridge felt that she must give him up,[179] but their affection was built on mutual respect, and they found that they still had much in common. Sara's letters in 1851 seldom touch on controversial matters, but they show a great tenderness for de Vere. She told him of her malady in October, and he suggested putting off his trip to Rome in order to accompany her to the south of France. Though unable to make the journey, she was touched by his unselfishness, and began even to talk a little of the old subjects. On 26th October de Vere called and left her *The Valley of Lilies*, by Thomas à Kempis. Though Aubrey de Vere may have admired Sara Coleridge even more than she admired him, it is unlikely that he felt the friendship more intensely.

The ardent young Irishman met Wordsworth the same summer that he met Sara Coleridge, in June 1841, when 'the old Druid' was visiting the Marshalls.[180] Aubrey had long admired the poetry and anticipated knowing Wordsworth himself, and still he was not disappointed. He wrote to his sister on 25th June:

It is true I have discovered that he wears a coat and not singing robes—that he gets hot and dusty like other people, . . . but beyond this, Wordsworth is all that an admirer of his writings should expect. He strikes me as the kindest and most simple-hearted old man I know. . . . He talks in a manner very peculiar. As for duration, it is from the rising of the sun to the going down of the same. As for quality, a sort of thinking aloud, a perpetual purring of satisfaction. He murmurs like a tree in the breeze; as softly and as incessantly; it seems as natural to him to talk as to breathe. He is by nature audible, as well as visible, and goes on thus uttering his being just as a fountain continues to flow, or a star to shine.[181]

He told his sister, also, of Wordsworth's 'extraordinary

P

purity of . . . language,' 'the absolute perfection of his sentences,' and 'the exquisite balance of his mind.'

De Vere met Mrs Wordsworth and Dora, recently married to Quillinan. He found Mrs Wordsworth 'as sweet-tempered as possible—single-hearted and full of a spirit of enjoyment and desire to make others enjoy themselves.'

Discussing theology, the young Irishman found that Wordsworth was largely in sympathy with the Oxford Movement, though he had not studied the matter and did not go the whole way. The two went to Windsor together and attended service in St George's Chapel, where there was 'an anthem unusually fine, in compliment to Wordsworth.' [182]

To his new friend Wordsworth talked about his poetry—the volume to be brought out the next year, *The Recluse*, which 'has never been written except a few passages—and probably never will,' and the unpublished but finished *Prelude*. 'The poem on the "Individual Mind,"' said Wordsworth, 'consists of fifteen books, having been lately added to and quite perfected.' [183]

Some time in the late summer or early autumn Aubrey de Vere visited Miss Fenwick at the Lakes. He spent several days at Rydal Mount, which he called 'the greatest honour of my life.' 'We rose early,' he said, 'and went to bed early. Each night prayers were read by Mrs Wordsworth in a voice full of reverence and sweetness. He knelt near her with his face hidden in his hands.' [184]

Aubrey de Vere visited in Westmorland at other times, for he said: 'During the next four years I saw a great deal of him, chiefly among his own mountains.' [185] He mentioned 'many delightful walks with him.' Wordsworth was stubborn, said de Vere, about walking in all sorts of weather: 'One of his dearest friends [186] said to me, with a smile of the most affectionate humour: "He wrote his 'Ode to Duty,' and then he had done with that matter."' [187]

Wordsworth talked about poetry to de Vere, apparently without restraint. Frankly he talked, comparing the poetry of others with his own. 'Indeed, I have hardly ever known any one but myself,' he said, 'who had a true eye for Nature —one that thoroughly understood her meanings and her teachings'; then he made one exception, Frederick W. Faber: 'He had not only as good an eye for Nature as I have, but even a better one.' [188] Wordsworth told de Vere that he regarded his father's sonnets as the best of the time—qualifying with: 'Of course I am not including my own in any comparison with those of others.' [189] Coleridge was the only man whom he would call 'wonderful.'

It may have been on one of these walks that Wordsworth told the young Irish poet how he happened to start writing poetry. Afterwards Aubrey de Vere wrote to his friend, William Rowan Hamilton:

Did Wordsworth ever tell you, as he did me, that the accident of his being given a manuscript book was the first *occasion* (I do not say cause) of his writing poetry? He thought it a pity, after filling up a few pages, to leave the remainder 'white and unwritten still,' and so got into the habit of reducing to shape the thoughts which before had been vaguely haunting his brain, like the body-waiting soul, which wandered by the Lethean pools.[190]

Wordsworth discussed religion, too, with Aubrey de Vere. He told him 'that on religious matters he ever wrote with great diffidence, remembering that if there were many subjects too low for song, there were some too high. Wordsworth's general confidence in his own powers,' said de Vere, 'which was strong, though far from exaggerated, rendered more striking and more touching his humility in all that concerned religion.'[191] The poet's High Churchmanship probably pleased de Vere, and his anti-Roman feeling would not at this time greatly disturb the younger man, especially as Wordsworth's antipathy was largely political.

In March 1845 de Vere visited Miss Fenwick for almost a week. He arrived on Tuesday, 4th March, and called the next day on Robert Perceval Graves, curate at Windermere. There he found Wordsworth, much upset over the Kendal

railway. Wordsworth walked with de Vere, and they called
in the evening on Mrs Davy, where every one discussed Harriet
Martineau and mesmerism.[192]

 On Thursday Mrs Arnold and the Wordsworths took dinner
at Miss Fenwick's. This was the occasion [193] of de Vere's
trying to interest Wordsworth in Tennyson:

I told him that a young poet had lately risen up. Wordsworth
answered that he feared from the little he had heard that if Crabbe
was the driest of poets, the young aspirant must have the opposite
fault. I replied that he should judge for himself, and without leave
given, recited to him two poems by Tennyson: viz. 'You ask me,
why, tho' ill at ease,' and 'Of old sat Freedom on the heights.'
Wordsworth listened with a gradually deepening attention. After a
pause he answered, 'I must acknowledge that these two poems are
very solid and noble in thought. Their diction also seems singularly
stately.' [194]

One night, when the poet and Mrs Wordsworth were staying
at Miss Fenwick's cottage, Quillinan and Hartley Coleridge
came to dine. Hartley 'read some poems of Wordsworth's
aloud with enthusiasm.' [195] He tried to quote one of his own
sonnets, and could not; whereupon de Vere quoted it, to
Hartley's delight.[196]

 De Vere admired Wordsworth and Miss Fenwick intensely.
Though 'his loyalty to Wordsworth was a passion,' he told
Henry Taylor that no man was as great as some women. He
considered Miss Fenwick's a finer nature.[197] Both he and Miss
Fenwick had a 'great desire to see Mr Wordsworth a Catholic-
minded man, and pass his evening of life under the shadow of
some cathedral.' Wordsworth did not share this opinion,
but he did wish to free himself from the charge of paganism,
and therefore tried to revise the *Ode on Intimations of Immortality*. Not being able to suit his friends or himself with
any of the alterations, he abandoned the idea.[198]

 On Sunday, 9th March, Aubrey de Vere went to church at
Ambleside, where he met Wordsworth and went home with
him to dinner. They discussed poetry. Again in the after-

noon de Vere went to the service, and after calling on Hartley Coleridge, walked over and had tea with Wordsworth.

> The days I have passed here [de Vere wrote to Henry Taylor, that same Sunday] will be long remembered with deep interest and affection. The old Man of the Mountains is as strong as ever in body and in soul. I have seen a great deal of him, and listened to more wisdom than could be extracted from all the conversation going on in London for a week together. We have toiled up the mountain sides, and he has murmured like a young pine-grove for hours together, and has not been the least tired.[199]

The next day Aubrey de Vere departed.

Then the Laureate went to London in April, to attend the queen's ball. There he saw much of de Vere, who was visiting his uncle, Lord Monteagle, in Brook Street. Two days after the ball Wordsworth, de Vere, his cousin, and Moxon went to a magnificent cathedral service. The young Irishman called almost daily, and took tea or dined with Wordsworth.

Aubrey de Vere was fraternizing with Tennyson, Fitzgerald, Spedding, Whewell, and Moxon. It was a common occurrence, he said, when Tennyson '"crooned" out his magnificent Elegies till one in the morning.'[200]

Tennyson was interested in Wordsworth. He had barely missed his visit to Trinity College, Cambridge, in 1831, when James Spedding had entertained Wordsworth in his rooms.[201] Though Tennyson had refused to call on Wordsworth when he was visiting Spedding in the Lakes—'his invincible shyness stood in the way'[202]—he read Wordsworth's poetry and even read his notes. He had journeyed to Bolton Priory in 1841, merely because Wordsworth had said in a note that 'everything which the eyes of man could desire in a landskip was to be found at and about the Abbey.'[203]

When Wordsworth had visited his brother, the Master of Trinity, while Tennyson was an undergraduate in the same college, the older poet had said: 'We have a respectable show of blossom in poetry . . . two brothers of the name of Tennyson, one in particular not a little interesting.'[204]   And he had heard de Vere recite Tennyson's lyrics just two months before.

The introduction took place on 4th May in Mrs Hoare's home.[205] 'Wordsworth,' said Tennyson to Aubrey de Vere, 'is staying at Hampstead in the house of his friend Mr Hoare; I must go and see him; and you must come with me; mind you do not tell Rogers, or he will be displeased at my being in London and not going to see him.' They drove out to the Heath, and knocked on the door. When it was opened, there stood Wordsworth and Rogers. Rogers and de Vere paired off; Tennyson and Wordsworth. Afterwards, when the two young men walked home together, Tennyson complained of Wordsworth's coldness.[206]

Tennyson dined with Wordsworth at Moxon's, and this time the Laureate was more informal. He took the young man by the arm and said: 'Come, brother bard, to dinner.' Tennyson was amused and pleased.[207] After the ladies had withdrawn, and Wordsworth had followed them, Tennyson kept saying under his breath to Aubrey de Vere: '"I must go: I cannot wait any longer."' Finally, de Vere discovered the cause of his disquiet:

It was painful to him to leave the house without expressing to the old Bard his sense of the obligation which all Englishmen owed to him, and yet he was averse to speak his thanks before a large company. Our host brought Wordsworth back to the dining-room; and Tennyson moved up to him. He spoke in a low voice, and with a perceptible emotion. . . . The old man looked very much pleased, more so indeed than I ever saw him look on any other occasion; shook hands with him heartily, and thanked him affectionately.[208]

Later, Tennyson told de Vere more about it:

Alfred Tennyson came in and smoked his pipe. He told us with pleasure of his dinner with Wordsworth . . .; said he was ashamed of paying Mr Wordsworth compliments, but that he had at last, in the dark, said something about the pleasure he had had from Mr Wordsworth's writings, and that the old bard had taken his hand, and replied with some expressions equally kind and complimentary. Tennyson was evidently much pleased with the old man, and glad of having learned to know him.[209]

Perhaps it was on this occasion, quietly after dinner in Moxon's dining-room, that Wordsworth said to the rising young poet: 'Mr Tennyson, I have been endeavouring all my life to write a pastoral like your "Dora" and have not succeeded.' [210]   Tennyson's brother-in-law said: 'This was great praise from one who honestly weighed his words and was by no means lavish of his praise.'

Wordsworth had Dora's album with him—given her many years before by Felicia Hemans, and containing, now, autographs and poems from personal friends and famous writers. Tennyson wrote in it *The Eagle*, slightly different from the published version, and an extra stanza, his 'carefully executed monogram' after each. 'The second contribution,' says F. V. Morley, 'a verse far better than the preceding—I do not find elsewhere. It was perhaps written on a different occasion.' [211] The extra stanza follows:

> Like an Aeolian harp that wakes
> No certain air, but overtakes
> Far thought with music that it makes.

After Wordsworth returned to Rydal Mount he wrote to Professor Reed:

I saw Tennyson when I was in London, several times. He is decidedly the first of our living Poets, and I hope will live to give the world still better things. You will be pleased to hear that he expressed in the strongest terms his gratitude to my writings. To this I was far from indifferent though persuaded that he is not much in sympathy with what I should myself most value in my attempts. . . .[212]

Wordsworth expressed a similar belief in Tennyson the following summer. When Thomas Cooper asked his opinion of contemporary poetry, the old man answered:

There is little that can be called high poetry. . . . Mr Tennyson affords the richest promise. He will do great things yet; and ought to have done greater things by this time.[213]

Cooper commented on Tennyson's 'sense of music.' 'Yes,' replied Wordsworth, 'the perception of harmony lies in the very essence of the poet's nature; and Mr Tennyson gives magnificent proofs that he is endowed with it.'

Aubrey de Vere visited Miss Fenwick in Westmorland again in the winter, this time in a tiny house next to the church. He arrived on Christmas Eve, and stayed four or five days. Wordsworth called frequently, sometimes for breakfast, sometimes merely to chat. 'Mr Wordsworth came in,' said de Vere, the day after Christmas, 'and passed some hours with us. He was looking well and hale, and spoke with animation of Burns's poetry, but with qualified approval—of Scott's with contempt.' [214] Miss Fenwick and her guest dined the next evening with Crabb Robinson and Moxon at Rydal Mount.

Through many of their common friends, but especially through Sara Coleridge, Henry Taylor, and Miss Fenwick, Aubrey de Vere kept in touch with Wordsworth. When the old man lay ill, in April 1850, de Vere wrote to Miss Fenwick:

May it be long before this country has to mourn the loss of perhaps the greatest man that now remains to her, and may his removal, whether it be soon or late, be in peace. . . . He has had but few illnesses. . . . [215]

Afterwards, de Vere wrote that 'England had lost her greatest man. He had done his work, however.'

Aubrey de Vere was a worshipper, and Wordsworth was one of his gods. He had known him in London and in Westmorland; he had known him under his own roof. And yet his love and veneration for the old poet never wavered. He made an annual pilgrimage to Wordsworth's grave, [216] and years afterwards, said that any one who knew Wordsworth would realize his greatness, not only 'because he had been endowed with a great imagination, but because he had been a good man, a great man, and a man whose poetry had, in an especial sense, been the expression of a healthily happy moral being.' [217]

VI. OTHER FRIENDS

WORDSWORTH'S journeyings in the last decade were not confined to the four trips to London. Naturally, he had more friends in the Lake District and in London than in any other one place, but he kept up with his old friends and with those of Dorothy and Coleridge in different parts of England, and he continued to make new friends both at home and in other countries.

In the east lived Mrs Clarkson, Dorothy's most intimate friend of the Dove Cottage days; in the west, old friends of Coleridge's. The younger Sir George Beaumont lived in Leicestershire, and a little farther south, at Cambridge and at Oxford, a new generation of Wordsworth devotees had sprung up: Whewell, the Hares, Keble, Clough, John Taylor Coleridge, Shairp, and others. And in Ireland and America more recent disciples became friends.

The friendship between the Clarksons and the Wordsworths had been closer in the earlier days than it was in the forties, for the intimacy was mainly between Dorothy and Mrs Clarkson. But the families were friends, and friends they remained.

They had met about 1800, when the Clarksons were living near Ullswater, and Wordsworth and Dorothy had been at Dove Cottage almost a year. In the spring of 1802, when Wordsworth went to see Mary Hutchinson, Dorothy visited Mrs Clarkson, and it was just after leaving her that the brother and sister saw the host of golden daffodils.[1] On the way to Calais three months later, to visit Annette and Caroline, Wordsworth and Dorothy spent two days with the Clarksons.[2] Mrs Clarkson knew about Annette and Caroline, and Dorothy wrote her the details of Caroline's wedding.[3]

By 1840 Dorothy was unable to enjoy her friend, and

Thomas Clarkson was merely the wreck of his former self. But Mrs Clarkson continued to value her friendship with the Wordsworths and to keep in touch with them through her cousin, Crabb Robinson. Differing with the poet on politics and religion, she was tolerant of his opinions.[4] And Wordsworth, though an infrequent correspondent, wrote a note of sympathy to the widow when Thomas Clarkson died on 26th September 1846.[5]

Mrs Clarkson realized the greatness of Wordsworth as poet and man. When Crabb Robinson, in his pride at Wordsworth's dedicating the Italian Tour to him, sent Mrs Clarkson a copy of the lines, her joy overflowed.[6] She rejoiced also in the recognition finally accorded Wordsworth in his later years, but was a little condescending to those who began to admire his poetry 'only when they would have been mobbed for not doing it.'[7] Like Sara Coleridge, she realized that Wordsworth's later poems did not add to his enduring fame.

Mrs Clarkson knew that Wordsworth had a long, unpublished poem on the development of his mind. It is likely that Wordsworth had read the whole poem or part of it to her in 1805, when she visited them late in the summer and copied Dorothy's journal, for the poem was finished in May of that year.[8] She knew, too, that this autobiographical poem was intended as the prelude of a tremendous opus, of which the already published *Excursion* was to be one section. She shared with Mrs Wordsworth the hope that Wordsworth would yet finish this work.

And after the poet's death, though the solemnity of his passing weighed upon her, Mrs Clarkson thought immediately of the unpublished poem. 'I hope that the Poem on his own Life will be got out as soon as possible,' she wrote, 'lest I should not live to see it. There are parts of it which I remember as well (not the order of words but the meaning and feeling) as any that are printed.'[9] It was published on 20th July 1850,[10] and Mrs Clarkson lived until 1856.[11]

On the opposite side of England, at Bristol, lived Joseph

Cottle and John Peace. Through Southey and Coleridge Wordsworth had met Cottle, the Bristol bookseller who was later to print the *Lyrical Ballads*. By 12th April 1798 Wordsworth was telling him enthusiastically of the poetry he was writing, and urging him: 'Do come and let me read it to you under the old trees in the park.' [12] Cottle came in May and stayed a week. [13] When Wordsworth and Dorothy left Alfoxden, near the end of June, they visited Coleridge at Nether Stowey, and then walked on to Bristol, arriving at Cottle's house in Wine Street [14] about 3rd July. 'We were at Cottle's for a week,' wrote the poet, 'and thence we went towards the banks of the Wye. We crossed the Severn Ferry, and walked ten miles further to Tintern Abbey, a very beautiful ruin on the Wye.' [15]

The poem, composed on 13th July, was probably written down under Cottle's roof. [16]

Wordsworth was in close touch with Cottle for about a month, while the *Lyrical Ballads* were going through the press, [17] and on his return from Germany in 1799 wrote him of his happiness at being once more in England. [18]

In later life Joseph Cottle was not a winsome man. He it was who had written Coleridge the severely moral letter in 1814, urging him for the sake of his children to throw off the opium habit. [19] He had preserved letters and portraits of the important friends of his youth, and in his old age enjoyed showing these valuable mementoes. [20] In 1847 he published his *Early Recollections of S. T. Coleridge*.

Wordsworth dined with Cottle on 30th April 1841, when he was visiting Miss Fenwick at Bath, shortly before the marriage of his daughter. The meeting was arranged by Crabb Robinson, and the poet was accompanied by Mrs Wordsworth, Dora, and Miss Fenwick. [21] On this occasion Wordsworth told Cottle of the failing of their mutual friend, Southey.

But the friendship with Cottle was more of the past than of the present. In the autumn of 1843 Wordsworth wrote to Basil Montagu in a melancholy vein that Joseph Cottle was the only one left of the many friends he had made in Bristol and Somersetshire. And to Cottle he wrote in 1845: 'I do and shall retain to the last a remembrance of your kindness, and of the many pleasant and happy hours which, at one of the most interesting periods of my life, I passed in your neighbourhood, and in your company.' [22]

John Peace, in the City Library at Bristol, was probably not a friend of such long standing as Cottle, but he was an enthusiastic Wordsworthian, and Wordsworth found in him many pleasant points of contact. Peace had walked to Oxford to see the honorary degree conferred on Wordsworth in 1839, and the poet wrote afterwards that he was sorry not to have had the pleasure of shaking him by the hand.[23]

Wordsworth liked to talk about poetry with John Peace. He discussed passages in Cowper's *Task* and Shenstone's ode, *Rural Elegance*, quoting from Horace's Tenth Epistle, which he said contained the germ of the main thought in the other two. 'Knowing how comprehensive your acquaintance with poetry is,' he wrote, 'I was rather surprised that you did not notice the identity of the thought, and accompanying illustrations of it.' [24] Thomson's blank verse and *The Castle of Indolence* Wordsworth discussed the next year with Peace, and he was grateful for Peace's admiration of his own Penal Sonnets.[25]

To Peace he wrote about Alston's portrait of Coleridge, when he was afraid the picture would be sent to America.[26] He said of Sir Thomas Browne:

You have gratified me by what you say of Sir Thomas Browne. I possess his *Religio Medici*, *Christian Morals*, *Vulgar Errors*, etc., in separate publications, and value him highly as a most original author. I almost regret that you did not add his Treatise upon *Urn Burial* to your publication; it is not long, and very remarkable for the vigour of mind that it displays.[27]

When Wordsworth arrived at Miss Fenwick's in Bath he wrote to John Peace, regretting that he had missed him in Bristol, and inviting him to call. The meeting took place at

Cottle's. On the very day of Dora's wedding the poet wrote to John Peace, and in the autumn, after returning to Rydal, he wrote him of his three months' journeying. Early in 1842 he sent him a walking-stick 'cut from a holly-tree,' he wrote, 'planted in our garden by my own hand.'[28]

Peace was one of the few who were able to give Wordsworth any comfort after Dora's death. The poet had previously quoted as his favourite text: 'Thy kingdom come. Thy will be done.' Afterwards Peace reminded him of it, and Wordsworth felt his sympathy. 'I can judge of the depth of your fellow-feeling for us,' he wrote.[29]

While at Bath for Dora's wedding Wordsworth called also on Dr Parry,[30] one of Coleridge's fellow-students at Göttingen more than forty years before.[31] For Dr Parry, Wordsworth felt a great sympathy. The year before, in April, he had known little Ellen Parry, and had been impressed by the unusual intelligence of her face. He had noticed, also, indications of an alarming state of health, and had mentioned his fears to the child's father. The latter was optimistic, but Wordsworth continued to be alarmed about the little girl. Then, on 28th April, she had died. Wordsworth had lost little Catharine very suddenly too; and though his own grief was now almost thirty years old, he felt keenly that of Dr Parry.[32]

Returning from London in 1841, Wordsworth and Mrs Wordsworth visited Sir George and Lady Beaumont at Coleorton, near Ashby-de-la-Zouch in Leicestershire. The present Sir George was a cousin of the poet's special friend—the descendant of Francis Beaumont, painter and patron of the arts, founder of the National Gallery. With the younger Sir George, for more than a decade now, Wordsworth had continued the friendship begun with the elder.

The elder Sir George Beaumont had become interested in Wordsworth through Coleridge, whom he first met in the summer of 1803 at Keswick.[33] Early in August Sir George had bought a piece of property with a small cottage on it at

Applethwaite, under Skiddaw, and presented it to Wordsworth so that he and Coleridge might renew the close companionship enjoyed at Alfoxden and Nether Stowey.

The friendship between the Beaumonts and the Wordsworths was of rapid growth, Sir George and Lady Beaumont catching the infection of Coleridge's enthusiasm, and Dorothy Wordsworth feeling drawn to those who appreciated Coleridge and her brother. Little Dorothy was born on 16th August 1804, and Lady Beaumont at her own request became godmother.[34] When John Wordsworth was drowned in 1805, both the poet and his sister wrote to the Beaumonts, and one of the poems expressing this grief was directly inspired by a painting of Sir George Beaumont's, *Elegiac Stanzas, Suggested by a Picture of Peele Castle in a Storm.*

Wordsworth visited the Beaumonts in Grosvenor Square, London, and Sir George and Lady Beaumont visited at Rydal Mount, but the closest association between the two families was at Coleorton, Sir George's Leicestershire estate. There Wordsworth took his family in October 1806, and spent the winter, remaining until the following June.[35] He helped Sir George to landscape the estate, fashioning a winter garden out of an old sandstone quarry.[36] The Wordsworths lived in a farmhouse while the hall was being rebuilt, and the Beaumonts returned to London, leaving the supervision of building and gardening in their hands. Wordsworth used to pace up and down between farmhouse and hall, composing poetry,[37] and one of the labourers used to pace behind him, trying to catch some of the words. Wordsworth did not know this at the time, but when he heard of it in 1841, he sent the old man some volumes of his poetry, and regretted that he had not known him.[38]

Several poems were written at Coleorton, notably the sonnet, *Thought of a Briton on the Subjugation of Switzerland,* beginning 'Two voices are there; one is of the sea,' and the *Song at the Feast of Brougham Castle.*[39] Some of the other poems written at Coleorton that winter and spring are: *A Complaint,* lamenting the change in Coleridge; *The Nightingale*; the sonnet to Lady Beaumont, *Lady! the songs of Spring were in the grove*; *Gipsies*; and the sonnet, *Though narrow be that old Man's cares, and near.*[40] Other poems probably written at Coleorton, from chronological evidence, are: *Another year!—another deadly blow*, *A Prophecy*, and *To Thomas Clarkson*.

In subsequent years Wordsworth wrote numerous poems about Coleorton and its owner, including four inscriptions for the grounds. The *Epistle to Sir George Howland Beaumont, Bart.* was written in 1811, but was never shown to him for whom it was written because of Wordsworth's modesty: 'So sensible am I of the deficiencies in all that I write, and so far does every thing that I attempt fall short of what I wish it to be.'[41] The inception of the *Ecclesiastical Sonnets* came as the result of a walk with Sir George Beaumont on Coleorton Moor, in December 1820, 'with a view to fix upon the site of a new Church which he intended to erect.'[42]

When Lady Beaumont's sister, Mrs Frances Fermor, died, she surprised the poet with a legacy of £100.[43] Sir George Beaumont died in 1827, bequeathing to the poet, according to Edwin Paxton Hood, 'the sum of £100 annually for the express purpose of a yearly tour.'[44] Lady Beaumont survived her husband only two years.

In 1830 Wordsworth visited Coleorton again, and the younger Sir George took him over the grounds. 'When I sat down in Lady Beaumont's grotto, near the fountain,' he wrote to his sister, 'I was suddenly overcome, and could not speak for tears.'[45] Afterwards he wrote *Elegiac Musings in the Grounds of Coleorton Hall*.[46] And in the summer of 1841, when he visited once more at Coleorton, the poet was delighted to find still flourishing the cedar 'Planted by Beaumont's and by Wordsworth's hands.'[47] Revising the *Epistle to Sir George Beaumont* for publication in the 1842 edition, Wordsworth wrote another poem on this friendship of his youth.

Charles Robert Leslie tells of Wordsworth's joy at discovering pictures of his old friends in London, probably in

the summer of 1842.[48]   Samuel Rogers and Washington Irving
were both present.   'Wordsworth's eye on entering my paint-
ing-room,' said Leslie, 'was caught by copies by Jackson of
Reynolds's portraits of Sir George and Lady Beaumont. . . .
"Ah!" said Wordsworth, "there are my old friends Sir
George and Lady Beaumont."' [49]

Mrs Clarkson and Joseph Cottle were friends of long ago.
Sir George and Lady Beaumont, though comparatively recent
friends, were links with the past.   But at Oxford and Cambridge
were men of a new generation of Wordsworth admirers, and
the poet was not insensitive to their appreciation.   His great-
niece, the late Dame Elizabeth Wordsworth, said that Wordsworth's influence was felt 'at Oxford, where Keble, Arnold,
James Mozley, and others of the rising generation, found in his
religious and reverent nature a spirit akin to that which was
working in their own bosoms and of which the great "Tractarian" movement was one result,' and 'at Cambridge on
men like Whewell, Sedgwick, Tennyson, Hallam, Trench, the
Hares, and others.' [50]

Dr William Whewell (called 'Billy Whistle' by the undergraduates of Tennyson's day) succeeded Christopher Wordsworth, in 1841, as Master of Trinity College, Cambridge.
Wordsworth saw Whewell at the Marshalls' in June 1841,[51]
and in November 1844 he and Mrs Wordsworth visited him
at Cambridge.[52]   Here the poet attended a meeting of the
Camden Society, of which he had been a member for four or
five years.[53]   Founded for the study of ecclesiology, the Camden
Society was linked with the historical interest in the Church
of England, and therefore with the High Church party.   'I
was much interested in the account of dear Mr Wordsworths
reception at the meeting of the Camden Society in Cambridge,'
wrote Mrs Clarkson to her cousin, 'though as you will know I
am no advocate for making protestant worship as like popish
as it can.' [54]

At Cambridge, too, Wordsworth met Daniel Macmillan,
for many years an admirer of his poetry.   'I wish Wordsworth

were here,' Macmillan had said in 1833, when he had gone
home to recover from a severe illness. 'I should like to see
him and hear him speak.' Now, on the poet's visit to
Cambridge, in 1844,

Archdeacon Hare asked him to call on Daniel and he paid several
visits to the shop, especially one long one in which he dwelt on the
influence Scotland had on him in early life and how he had sought in
the *Excursion* to bring out the spiritual life of Scotland which he
thought had never been adequately sung by any of her poets, who had
mainly confined themselves to the humanities.[55]

Between Wordsworth and Archdeacon Hare, also at Cambridge in November 1844, was a closer bond of sympathy
than between the poet and Macmillan or the Master of Trinity.
A contemporary of Whewell's, Julius Charles Hare had been
undergraduate, fellow, and tutor at Trinity. Later, he was
vicar of Hurstmonceaux, and, from 1840 on, archdeacon of
Lewes. He was of the Broad Church party—according to
Crabb Robinson, 'certainly . . . not a Church Christian—
he may be something better.'[56]

When Hare was editor of the *Philological Museum*, Wordsworth
had allowed him to print in 1832 a part of his fragmentary
translation of the *Aeneid*, an 'experiment begun for amusement.'[57] Hare dedicated the second edition of *Guesses at
Truth by Two Brothers* to Wordsworth.[58] The mutual regard
between the Archdeacon of Lewes and Wordsworth lasted
throughout the poet's life. 'I am glad you are so much pleased
with Mr Hare's Works,' wrote Wordsworth to Henry Reed,
in March 1842, 'he is an old and valued friend of mine.'[59]
Crabb Robinson saw the archdeacon in London in December
1843, and wrote to Mrs Wordsworth: 'Only a few minutes
ago I parted from Julius Hare who heard with great delight
of the report Qu: gives of the bards high health.'[60]

The Hares were friends of the Arnolds, and on 18th July
1844 Archdeacon Hare and his sister, Maria Leycester Hare,
their nephew, and Esther Maurice arrived at Fox How to
visit the Arnolds. The Wordsworths called immediately, and

Q

Miss Hare was pleased with both of them. In the evening
Mrs Arnold took her guests to Rydal Mount, where, after a
little general conversation, the poet escorted the whole party
to the terrace, 'along his garden-walks,' and to Rydal Falls.[61]
The engagement of Esther Maurice to Julius Hare probably
took place at Fox How.[62] Mrs Twining, one of Dr Arnold's
daughters, said of Archdeacon Hare: 'He says he has five
Popes, *Wordsworth, Niebuhr*, Bunsen, *Fred[eric]k Maurice*, and
Archdeacon Manning.' [63]

Frederick Maurice, John Sterling, and Richard Chenevix
Trench were a decade younger than Julius Hare, all undergraduates at Trinity College in the twenties when Hare was
tutor, and probably led by him to an appreciation of Wordsworth. 'Frederick Maurice,' said Rannie, 'upheld Wordsworth against utilitarianism at Cambridge.' [64]

A Cambridge man himself, Wordsworth enjoyed a friendship
with many Oxonians a generation younger than he, and was
influential in sending Hartley Coleridge and later sent his own
son to Oxford.   The elder Thomas Arnold was elected a Fellow
of Oriel in 1815, four years after John Keble had won the same
distinction, and four years before Hartley Coleridge. Hartley's
first cousin, John Taylor Coleridge, was a contemporary of
Arnold's and Keble's at Oxford, and a friend of both throughout their lives.   Arnold recalled in 1839 how 'old Coleridge
inoculated a little knot of us with the love of Wordsworth.' [65]
When Hartley proceeded from Merton to Oriel, John Henry
Newman was an undergraduate.   Hartley forfeited the Fellowship in 1820, and Newman became a Fellow of Oriel in 1822.
Keble, Arnold, Pusey, Newman—all were Fellows of Oriel about
1820.

But the exciting time at Oxford was not the twenties.   On
Sunday, 14th July 1833, Keble, then Poetry Professor, preached
his famous assize sermon on National Apostasy. Then, for
more than a decade, Oxford was a hot-bed of religious strife—
the Low Church Party trying to direct the Church of England
toward Methodism, the High Church toward Catholicism.

Low Churchmen became High; High Churchmen became Roman Catholics and agnostics. Keble, Pusey, and Newman were the leaders of the Oxford Movement; its principal antagonist was Dr Arnold. The *Tracts for the Times* began to appear shortly after Keble's sermon in 1833, and continued until 1841, culminating in Newman's 'Tract 90.' Newman, originally affiliated with the Low Church Party, became in the thirties the most eloquent and influential of the Tractarians, and in October 1845 a convert to Roman Catholicism. Pusey's name was given to the group. But it was the Poetry Professor who had started the Oxford Movement, the Rev. John Keble.

Frederick W. Faber and his brother went to Oxford in the thirties, when Newman and Keble were inciting the younger men. Faber became a Fellow of University College in 1837, spending his vacations in Westmorland. Arthur Hugh Clough became a tutor at Balliol, and took reading parties to the Lakes, especially in 1843, when 'Matt' Arnold and John Campbell Shairp were with him. Shairp said of Clough: 'Often, too, I have remembered that, by his taste, I was first led to read and take pleasure in Wordsworth.' [66] Henry Fletcher went up to Balliol from Grasmere in 1844, with Wordsworth's blessing. Matthew Arnold was elected a Fellow of Oriel in 1845, exactly thirty years after his father. Many of these younger men the aged poet regarded as his personal friends, and some of the others were ardent Wordsworthians.

The men of the Oxford Movement considered Wordsworth their poet. It is true, he had read only one of their tracts,[67] and he did not go the whole way with the Puseyites, but he was in sympathy with what most of them were attempting. In his *Ecclesiastical Sonnets* he felt that he had anticipated the movement by a decade.[68]

In 1839, when the influence of Newman was at its height, before the reaction had begun, or the Tractarians had started going 'over to Rome,' Oxford conferred on Wordsworth the honorary degree of Doctor of Civil Law. It was a happy time both for Wordsworth and for the enthusiastic Oxonians. Clough had written to a friend at Cambridge:

> You must really come to Oxford, overcoming circumstances and cacoëthes and everything else. . . . You should see the Arch-Oxford-Tractator before you leave this part of the world . . . on your return to England perhaps you will find Newman Archbishop of Canterbury and Father Confessor to the Queen. . . . Again, you will see Chevalier Bunsen, Poet Wordsworth, and Astronomer Herschel metamorphosed into doctors of civil law; a sight worthy, especially in the second case, of all contemplation.[69]

Wordsworth was accompanied by his son, William, and joined by his nephew, Christopher, then Fellow of Trinity College, Cambridge. Dr Arnold went to Oxford to do honour to his old friend.[70] Faber was there, as Fellow of University College. John Peace went from Bristol.

The poet's nephew states that Wordsworth was introduced for the degree by Keble, but Sir John Taylor Coleridge says that this is a mistake, that Wordsworth was introduced by the Regius Professor of Civil Law, as is the custom at Oxford, and that Keble eulogized Wordsworth in his Creweian Oration.[71] Professor Knight and Elizabeth Wordsworth corroborate Justice Coleridge's statement. After comparing the Church and the University, and pointing out the difference that the University was not open to the poor, Keble closed his oration:

> Verum huic loco satis superque me fecisse arbitrabar, Academici, si semel vobis eum in memoriam revocarem: cum praesertim is praesto sit nobis in nobili hac corona, qui unus omnium maxime poetarum, mores, studia, religiones pauperum collocaverit non dicam bono verum etiam coelesti lumine. Ad ejus itaque viri carmina remittendos esse hoc tempore putabam, si qui ex intimo animo sentire vellent arcanam illam necessitudinem honestae Paupertatis cum Musis severioribus, cum excelsa Philosophia, immo cum sacrosancta Religione.[72]

'Wordsworth was exceedingly gratified,' said Sir John Taylor Coleridge, 'by this unexpected tribute, which was received in the crowded Theatre with hearty and general applause, according well with the universal shout with which his name was received, when announced by the Professor in presenting him.'[73] Crabb Robinson felt that the 'reception from the Undergraduates at Oxford' was more significant than the conferring of the degree. Eye-witnesses told him: 'The Shouting was universal and continuous.' [74] A Fellow of University College, probably Frederick W. Faber, told Wordsworth 'that he had never witnessed such an outburst of enthusiasm in that place, except upon the occasions of the visits of the Duke of Wellington.' [75] And Serjeant Talfourd wrote a sonnet:

> O never did a mighty truth prevail
> With such felicities of place and time,
> As in those shouts sent forth with joy sublime
> From the full heart of England's Youth, to hail
> Her once neglected Bard, within the pale
> Of Learning's fairest Citadel! . . .[76]

The personal friendship between Keble and Wordsworth dates from this commemoration, though Keble had long been a Wordsworthian, and it is likely that the elder poet was already interested in the famous Tractarian and anonymous author of *The Christian Year*. Dr Arnold had probably talked to Wordsworth of his old friend, his present theological opponent. Faber, becoming more and more absorbed in the Oxford Movement, would hardly fail to tell Wordsworth of the Rev. John Keble. It was probably through Faber that the greater and the lesser poet met in the rooms of Faber's brother, the Rev. F. A. Faber, in Magdalen College.[77] The admiration was mutual: 'Wordsworth's admiration for the author of "The Christian Year," and the volume itself, was in after life very warm.' [78]

Keble visited in the Lake District for a short time in July 1842. This was after 'Tract 90' had raised such a storm in Oxford that Keble, sharing the responsibility for the tract, had resigned his professorship. Now, he enjoyed the quiet of the Lakes, the kindly people, and the society of Wordsworth. Not realizing, perhaps, that the old poet was suiting his conversation to his company, Keble wrote to Professor Wilson that it was good 'to hear old Wordsworth, how he kept falling back on Church matters, whatever other subject was started.' [79]

In 1844, when Keble published his *Praelectiones Academicae*, the Latin lectures on poetry which he had been delivering at Oxford from 1832 to 1841, he dedicated the volume to Wordsworth. The long Latin dedication pleased Wordsworth, especially the line: 'Legentium animos semper ad sanctiora erigeret.' [80] Now his aim in poetry was understood. When he received the dedication he told Mrs Davy 'that he had never seen any estimate of his poetical powers, or more especially of his aims in poetry, that appeared to him so discriminating and so satisfactory.' [81] To Henry Reed he wrote in similar vein.[82]

To the end of his life Wordsworth was in sympathy with the Oxford Movement. When Ellis Yarnall broached the subject, the last summer of Wordsworth's life, the old man 'replied deliberately that his opinion was unchanged. "I foresaw," said he, "that the movement was for good, and such I conceive it has been beyond all question."' [83]

Throughout England Wordsworth had many friends. In Ireland, too, he had made some warm friendships, particularly with persons who had first appreciated his poetry. 'I may at least hope to be named hereafter among the friends of Wordsworth.' So wrote Sir Aubrey de Vere, father of the better-known poet, dedicating to Wordsworth in 1842 his volume, *A Song of Faith, Devout Exercises, and Sonnets*.[84] 'Wordsworth greatly admired the modest little volume,' said Grosart.[85] And the younger Aubrey was proud to recall the Laureate's comment on his father's poetry.

But the Irishman whom Wordsworth valued most, 'the only man like Coleridge whom I have known,' [86] was really no Irishman, but a Scot born in Dublin, Sir William Rowan

Hamilton. When Wordsworth first met him in 1827, Hamilton was only twenty-two years old, but he was no ordinary youth of twenty-two. 'Hamilton,' says Miss Batho, 'provides one of the rare instances of an infant prodigy who developed into a great man. One of the greatest of mathematical physicists, he was also an extraordinary linguist and had an indubitable literary gift.'[87] He had studied before he was fourteen Latin, Greek, Hebrew, Italian, French, Arabic, Sanskrit, 'several Indian languages,' Syriac, and Persian—many with great proficiency. He had also shown 'marked originality and power in mathematics and physics before he was twenty, and in 1827, when he was only twenty-two and still an undergraduate at Trinity College, Dublin, he was appointed Professor of Astronomy there and, in the same year, Astronomer Royal for Ireland.'[87]

That Wordsworth and Hamilton should have formed a strong bond of friendship seems remarkable. Wordsworth was fifty-seven, Hamilton twenty-two. Both had been much fêted, and in different circles. But when they met in the Lake District, and when two years later Wordsworth visited Hamilton at Dunsirk, the intellectual stimulus to both was immediate and lasting. Each felt humbled by the greatness of the other.

Putting Hamilton in the class with Coleridge was the greatest tribute Wordsworth could pay him. Though he considered Hamilton's verses creditable, he recognized in the young man a greater scientist than poet, and urged him in November 1831 to sacrifice his lesser talent for his greater.[88]

When Hamilton became President of the Royal Irish Academy in 1837, he wanted the poet's advice on patronage of genius and on 'better canons of criticism and general improvement of scholars.' Most of these questions Wordsworth felt incompetent to answer,[89] but he found it 'mortifying' to disappoint Hamilton.

The young President of the Academy did not readily accept Wordsworth's refusal to give advice, and wrote again, this

time offering to publish any criticism Wordsworth would
write.   The old poet's regret at disappointing his young friend
is patent.   He did, however, advise Hamilton to disseminate
his criticism, as Coleridge had done, to 'a few select and
superior minds, that might each become a centre for illustrating it in a popular way.' [90]

More important than as stimulus to literary criticism was
the impelling influence of this young man who reminded
Wordsworth of Coleridge.   It is likely that Sir William Rowan
Hamilton actually quickened the poet to the creation of two
beautiful lines in *The Prelude*:

> The marble index of a mind for ever
> Voyaging through strange seas of Thought, alone.[91]

Wordsworth continually revised *The Prelude* from its completion in 1805 until almost the last decade,[92] and some of
the best corrections were made toward the end.

Wordsworth retained his critical acumen [says Mr de Selincourt]
far longer than his creative energy; and some of his best corrections,
in *The Prelude* as in other poems, are among the last.   And to the
end he was capable of writing a superb line.   Those who accept with
too much literalness the obvious truth that what is great in Wordsworth belongs to a single decade (1798–1807), will do well to note
that two lines on the statue of Newton . . . were written when he
was over sixty years of age.[93]

Miss Batho has suggested that this tribute to Newton was
added as a result of Wordsworth's friendship with Sir William
Rowan Hamilton.[94]   Without pointing the evidence, she gives
passages which might support her theory.   Wordsworth and
Hamilton often discussed the intellectual and the imaginative
faculties, Wordsworth putting the imaginative higher.   Once
when Wordsworth was visiting the brilliant young mathematician, physicist, astronomer, the latter objected to lines in
some of Wordsworth's poems belittling scientists.   The poet
'then defended himself,' wrote Hamilton's sister, 'with a
beautiful mixture of warmth and temperateness, from the
accusation of any want of reverence for Science. . . . "What,"

he said, "would have been the use of my praising such men as Newton? They do not need my insignificant praise, and therefore I did not allude to such sons of Science."' [95]   To Hamilton's suggestion that the abstract forms of mathematics were a connecting link between man and the Divine, 'Wordsworth smiled kindly, but said *that* reminded him of the Platonic doctrine of the internal existence in the marble of those beautiful forms from which the sculptor was supposed only to withdraw the veil.' [95]

The lines in *The Prelude* refer, of course, to the statue of Newton in Trinity College, Cambridge. And yet it seems more than coincidence that Wordsworth asked Hamilton why he should praise such giants as Newton and, in the same conversation, referred to the Platonic concept of idea behind matter, illustrating by the form of a statue within the marble —and later added to his description of Newton's 'silent face' the words 'the marble index of a mind . . .'

Just at the time Wordsworth was revising *The Prelude* in 1838,[96] Sir William Rowan Hamilton visited him in the Lakes. On his way to the meeting of the British Association at Newcastle, Hamilton stopped for one day with the poet, spending Sunday with him. In a letter to Sir Henry Taylor Miss Fenwick writes that Wordsworth is revising *The Prelude*, and that Sir William Rowan Hamilton has been at Rydal, and is to return after the meeting at Newcastle.[97] Hamilton returned to Rydal about the end of the month. There, on Thursday evening, 30th August, he read to Mrs Wordsworth at tea some lines, *To the Elysian Fields of Lowther*, in which he dwelt on the fraternity of minds:

> Mind meeting mind, heart heart, and every hour
> Melting away reserve's estranging power,

and also employed the common metaphor of a ship sailing.[98] Possibly, in conversation with Wordsworth Hamilton spoke of this fraternity of great minds, poet and scientist, and suggested to the poet, by contrast,

> Voyaging through strange seas of Thought, alone.

To Hamilton Wordsworth wrote freely on many subjects. He explained, in 1843, his acceptance of the Laureateship. He gave him permission 'to print when and where you like any verses which you may do me the honour of writing upon, or addressing to, me.'[99] And it was to Hamilton that he called Landor 'a mad-man, a bad-man, yet a man of genius, as many a mad-man is.' But the old man showed no bitterness, for he ended his letter in a lighter vein:

Your godson, his sister, and four brothers are all doing well. He is a very clever boy . . . and his heart appears to be not inferior to his head, so that I trust he will as a man do you no discredit.[100]

Hamilton visited Robert Perceval Graves at the Windermere rectory in 1844, arriving with his eldest son on 18th July, the same day that Archdeacon Hare came to Fox How; and many were the dinners, walks, and rowing parties.[101] One of the walks over Loughrigg Fell produced the poem, *So fair, so sweet, withal so sensitive*.[102] Hamilton remained till the end of July, and he, too, was stimulated to verse. On 30th July he went to Rydal Mount to bid Wordsworth farewell, and wrote in Dora Quillinan's album a sonnet to her father.[103]

Shortly after becoming President of the Royal Irish Academy, Hamilton had suggested Wordsworth's name for honorary membership. Wordsworth had declined the honour, 'believing the Royal Irish Academy to be almost exclusively a scientific Society,'[104] and fearing that Hamilton had been over-influenced by his feeling of friendship. Later, the Royal Society of Edinburgh conferred on him a similar honour, which he accepted. Now in 1845 he was afraid there might be a misunderstanding, and therefore asked Graves to write to Hamilton for him.

The clergyman assured the President of the Royal Irish Academy that the poet did not value the Scottish honour more than the Irish.[105] Dublin had been the first to offer Wordsworth such a distinction. Then in 1838 Durham conferred on him an honorary degree. In 1839 Oxford did the same;

'then some American learned Society, and lastly the Edinburgh Royal Society offered similar marks of respect.'[106] As an Irishman Graves was proud that Dublin had been the first to offer Wordsworth 'such a mark of honour,' and he expressed the hope that the membership would be again offered. The honour was conferred again on 29th November 1845, and this time the poet gladly accepted.

Wordsworth's letter of appreciation to Hamilton refers graciously to the academy and to Ireland. But his chief gratification seemed to be that he owed this honour to his friend,[107] the brilliant mathematician and astronomer who was so versatile that he reminded Wordsworth of 'the rapt One, of the godlike forehead.'

Only one man in the United States could, strictly speaking, be called the friend of Wordsworth, and that man the poet never saw; but many Americans sought a glimpse of the old poet at Rydal Mount, and to most of them he was graciously hospitable. Unlike many Englishmen of his day Wordsworth had a kindly, almost paternal feeling for the daughter-country. As early as 1809 he had expressed a sympathy for the former colony, calling the American Revolution one of the two wars England had waged *against* Liberty.[108] Apparently he had long cherished the hope of going some day to the United States, for when he was almost eighty he said to James T. Fields: 'Ah, . . . I shall never, never see your country,—that is impossible now; but . . . John shall go, please God, some day.'[109]

America was not slow to appreciate him, either. Mrs Wordsworth told Ellis Yarnall 'that they had visitors constantly, and from various quarters—more Americans by far than all other foreigners put together.'[110] Wordsworth told Edwin Paxton Hood: 'I think I have almost more from America than from England.'[111] The window in St Mary's Church at Ambleside is inscribed:

Gulielmi Wordsworth Amatores et Amici
partim Angli, partim Anglo-Americani.[112]

William Cullen Bryant went to Rydal Mount during the summer of 1845, introduced by Crabb Robinson. Robinson met him at Twyford on 19th June, and liked the man better than his poetry. 'Bryant is rather reserved than modest,' he said on 20th June, 'but I liked him sufficiently to give him my card and desire him to call on Wordsworth.'[113] In September Robinson asked Mrs Wordsworth: 'Have you seen the Yankee-poet Bryant?'[114] 'We have, THRO THE SEASON been beset by strangers,' answered Mrs Wordsworth. 'Among these we liked best was the Poet Bryant he was an agreeable modest person—and my husband enjoyed his society.'[115]

Bryant, then fifty-one, 'often recurred in conversation to this pleasant visit to Wordsworth,' said John Bigelow,

but one always suspected that, much as he reverenced the poet, he was not very strongly impressed by the man. Wordsworth had a way of talking of himself and his poetry which must have seemed strange if not ludicrous to one so habitually reticent. . . . Mr Bryant sometimes amused his more intimate friends with imitations of Wordsworth's reverent manner of repeating his own verses—not, however, in a way that lessened respect for the venerable bard.[116]

Emerson went to see Wordsworth, too, when he was visiting Harriet Martineau in 1848. Emerson and his hostess called on the poet one Sunday afternoon and found him asleep on a sofa. 'He was at first silent and indisposed,' wrote the American, 'as an old man suddenly waked before he had ended his nap; but soon became full of talk on the French news.'[117] Emerson told Crabb Robinson later 'that Wordsworth spoke highly of Longfellow and regretted his name.'[118]

Jane Wordsworth shared her grandfather's interest in Longfellow, and asked Ellis Yarnall about him when he visited them in 1849. Jane was only sixteen then; and after Wordsworth's death Professor Reed sent her Longfellow's note accompanying his contribution. 'It has occurred to me,' he said, 'that possibly she would be interested by the inclosed note which I received from that gentleman—the more so from the feeling it shows for her grand-father's memory.'[119]

Washington Alston, the South Carolina painter who had once lived in England, and had painted a portrait of Coleridge, was recalled to Wordsworth by Henry Reed. Through Coleridge Wordsworth had met the painter years before, and he considered Alston's portrait of Coleridge 'so admirable a likeness of what that great and good man then was, both as to person, feature, air, and character . . . [that] there is not one in the least to be compared to that by Mr Alston.' [120] Alston now lived in Boston, and he encouraged Reed in his hope of crossing the Atlantic, saying 'with the emphasis of an earnest sincerity —"I want you to see Wordsworth."' [121]

Reed copied out for the painter Wordsworth's remarks on the portrait of Coleridge, along with friendly personal comment, and Alston was of course gratified. 'To be numbered among the friends of the "Great Poet," by himself,' he wrote in September 1843, 'is indeed an honour; yet not less do I prize this mark of regard from the *man*.' [122]

When the relationship between Wordsworth and his American editor had advanced to a warm personal friendship of eight years' duration, Henry Reed had an opportunity of seeing vicariously the man whom he so much admired and loved. Henry Inman, the portrait painter, was going to England, and Professor Reed engaged him to paint Wordsworth's portrait in the Lake District.[123]

Inman went first to Rydal Mount on 20th August 1844:

Mr Wordsworth's reception of me, and the brief professional and social intercourse I enjoyed with him and his excellent family, furnish me with none but the most pleasing recollections. He seemed to be much gratified with your request for his portrait; and though his house teems with tokens of regard from his countrymen, he evidently had a peculiar value for this transatlantic compliment to his genius. . . . He told me he had sat twenty-seven times to various artists, and that my picture was the best likeness of them all.[124]

Between the poet and the painter was a kind of freemasonry which each recognized instantly. Inman talked to Wordsworth about his own art, and enjoyed Wordsworth's breathing out his poems. He remembered his manner long afterward.

The portrait arrived in Philadelphia about the 1st November 1844, and was hung in Henry Reed's parlour, where it was admired by many American Wordsworthians. Bishop Doane and, later, Reed's own brother assured the professor that the picture was a faithful likeness.

The Wordsworths liked the portrait so much that they wanted a copy of it for themselves. Inman had said something to Mrs Wordsworth about making a copy for her after he returned to America, and the poet wrote to Professor Reed. Before the letter arrived, however, Inman and Reed had made arrangements to have the picture copied as a present to Mrs Wordsworth. While it was in New York being copied, Reed missed its almost living presence. And the painter felt so deeply the force and charm of Wordsworth's personality that he asked Professor Reed to let him share in making the gift. It was finished about the middle of November 1845, and the duplicate portraits were sent to Reed.[125]

Reed's joy in his own Inman portrait was heightened by a feeling that America had contributed a little to Wordsworth's honour.[126] The poet wrote to Professor Reed on 23rd January 1846:

Mrs W—returns her grateful thanks to you and Mrs Reed for a Present on which she sets so high a value, both for its own sake, and as coming from Friends for whom she entertains a high respect. In these thanks we beg Mr Inman may be included—[127]

Wordsworth's thanks came too late. About the time the picture arrived in England Inman died of enlargement of the heart. The portrait of Wordsworth was the last picture he completed, and he was doing a picture of Rydal Mount for Professor Reed when he died.[128]

The summer after Inman went to Rydal Mount Professor Reed introduced his brother to the poet. William B. Reed was a lawyer, former Attorney-General of the State of Pennsylvania and Chairman of the Committee of Finance in the State Senate. It was he who, in 1841, had provided Reed with information on the State debt for Miss Fenwick. He was a man of culture, and was interested in meeting the poet, but his special reason for calling on Wordsworth was to represent Henry Reed.

Reed's brother was received graciously by the Wordsworths both in London and in their own home, and the Philadelphia professor was grateful. 'As a piece of kindness to me,' he wrote to Wordsworth, 'I feel it sensibly and have peculiar pleasure in thinking of a brother of mine having met you.' [129] After Dora's death, he wrote to the bereaved father of the graciousness and kindness with which Dora Quillinan had greeted his brother in London.

William B. Reed realized the depth of friendship between Henry Reed and the great Englishman. He wrote to Wordsworth's family when Reed was lost at sea in 1854, knowing that they would feel a sympathy for him and for Reed's widow.[130] And shortly afterwards he set himself the task of editing his brother's lectures, particularly those on Wordsworth. In 1855 he published in two volumes a series of lectures delivered by Henry Reed from 3rd January 1850 to 20th March 1851: *Lectures on English Literature from Chaucer to Tennyson*. These volumes are full of references to Wordsworth, Reed illustrating his criticism of other poets by drawing parallels to Wordsworth or quoting from him. In 1857 he published two volumes of earlier lectures: *Lectures on the British Poets*.

Ellis Yarnall had attended Professor Reed's course of public lectures in 1841, and had felt the charm of the young teacher. During the next decade Reed gave several courses of lectures, and Yarnall attended all of them. Reed shared his great enthusiasm with his student, and showed him the letters he had received from Wordsworth. 'I felt at once their high importance,' said Yarnall. '. . . Wordsworth had from the beginning a clear discernment of the right-mindedness of his American correspondent; his heart seemed to go out to him.' And in 1849, when Yarnall was making his first trip to England, Professor Reed gave him, unasked, a letter to Wordsworth.[131]

Ellis Yarnall visited Wordsworth on 18th August 1849, arriving at two in the afternoon. He had made ample preparation for this visit, and had anticipated it with the greatest excitement. He called on Sara Coleridge in London before approaching the bard himself:

The lady I was soon to see was the one in all England who best represented Wordsworth, her mind being in part a creation of his own.[132]

Arriving in the Lake District, Yarnall spent the night at Bowness, and at noon drove from there to Ambleside with friends. The rest of the way he went on foot alone.

He noted every detail: the wicket gate, the gravel path leading through shrubbery, the flower-beds, and then the drawing-room. 'It was with a curious emotion,' he said, 'that I felt myself in the house of the great poet and awaiting his coming.'[133] The young man continued to observe closely: the low ceiling, the two windows giving a view of the shrubbery, the Dresden Madonna over the fireplace, and the Inman portrait of Wordsworth.

Then Wordsworth entered, an old man weighed down by sorrow. He welcomed Yarnall cordially, gave him his hand, and led him to the dining-room, where he presented him to Mrs Wordsworth and three of the grandchildren. The party soon returned to the drawing-room, and Wordsworth discussed many subjects with his American guest.

He inquired after George Ticknor, 'who had visited him a few months before, and for whom he expressed much regard.' As he and Yarnall talked of the settling of California, Wordsworth looked up and Yarnall 'noticed a fixing of his eye as if on some remote object. He said that considering this extension of our language it behoved those who wrote to see to it that what they put forth was on the side of virtue.' Yarnall felt that in Wordsworth 'a deep sense of responsibility had ever been present; to purify and elevate had been the purpose of all his writings.'

They discussed the Inman portrait and the Pickersgill portrait, made for St John's College, Cambridge, and the honorary degrees conferred by Oxford and Durham. Wordsworth said that 'Cambridge would have done the same had he not declined,' and Mrs Wordsworth smiled silently as if he were boasting too much—'but there was perfect simplicity and naturalness in his way of saying this.'

The discussion of Cambridge led to Henry VIII, founder of Trinity College: 'Of that king he spoke in terms of the strongest abhorrence . . . "I loathe his very memory."'' Wordsworth regretted Prince Albert's election to the Chancellorship of Cambridge, for he felt that the election was merely to please the queen, not based on any qualifications of the prince consort:

He said Prince Albert's German education, his training at Bonn, was in itself a disqualification. He was supposed to entertain opinions opposed to classical study as pursued at the English Universities, and to have intimated a wish for extensive changes. This Wordsworth deprecated strongly: he spoke with great animation of the importance of the study of the classics—Greek especially.

Wordsworth and Yarnall discussed also the Oxford Movement and the French Revolution. Wordsworth spoke of having been at Orleans at the time of the September massacres, and then turned to Mrs Wordsworth and said: 'I wonder how I came to stay there so long, and at a period so exciting.' Unlikely as it is that Wordsworth had actually forgotten his romance with Annette Vallon, apparently the principles of the French Revolution were more exciting to him than his personal experience. It was of the time *after* his return to England that he had written:

> Bliss was it in that dawn to be alive,
> But to be young was very Heaven.[134]

Wordsworth's disappointment in the French Revolution was still a vivid memory in 1849. Yarnall wrote to Professor Reed, though omitting it from his book:

He seemed to feel deep commiseration for the sorrows of that unhappy country. It was evidently the remembrance of hopes which

R

in his youth he had ardently cherished, and which had been blighted, on which his mind was dwelling.[135]

When Yarnall rose to go Wordsworth urged him to sit down again, and when he stood up a second time Wordsworth took him once more into the dining-room to see the ancestral cabinet,[136] and then outside to see the views. 'Wordsworth pulled aside the shrubbery or hedge in places,' he said, 'that I might see to better advantage. He accompanied me to the gate, and then said, if I had a few minutes to spare, he would like to show me the waterfall which was close by—the lower fall of Rydal.'[137]   For another forty-five minutes the two wandered about together. Yarnall took from his pocket a tiny volume of Wordsworth's selected poems, edited by Professor Reed in 1841. The old man was much interested, and began reading the preface aloud. After a little while he offered to autograph the book. His attitude was simple and unaffected. Then he walked with Yarnall to the main road, gave him his hand in parting, sent messages to the Reeds, and wished him a safe return to America.

Yarnall liked Wordsworth's attitude toward his own poetry: 'It seemed almost as if he was awed by the greatness of his own power, the gifts with which he had been endowed.'[138]

Ellis Yarnall became a great Wordsworth devotee. He made successive visits to England, stayed with Mrs Wordsworth at Rydal Mount, and saw William Wordsworth the third at his father's rectory at Cockermouth. He bought some of Wordsworth's books in 1859, and 'a pair of Wordsworth's spectacles!'[139]   When he was eighty-two years old he published his own book about Wordsworth and the Coleridges. But when he was only thirty-two and had just taken leave of Wordsworth on the Ambleside road, he was thrilled by the vital personality:

I went on my way happy in the recollection of this to me memorable interview. My mind was in a tumult of excitement, for I felt that I had been in the familiar presence of one of the noblest of our race. The sense of Wordsworth's intellectual greatness had been with me

during the whole interview. I may speak, too, of the strong perception of his moral elevation which I had at the same time. He
seemed to me a man living as in the presence of God by habitual
recollection. A strange feeling almost of awe had impressed me
while I was thus with him.[140]

Henry Reed was only two years older than Wordsworth's
youngest child. He began the friendship diffidently, but
Wordsworth responded so warmly that there was soon an
intimate understanding. Though Reed became the chief
American exponent of Wordsworth's poetry, both as lecturer
and as editor, he remained to the end of his life the humble
disciple. Wordsworth valued the criticism of Henry Reed,
often took his advice about alterations of poems, and even
wrote a good many verses in the last decade at his suggestion.
But the Professor of English Literature at the University of
Pennsylvania never ceased to wonder at his high privilege of
calling Wordsworth friend. Each invited the other repeatedly
to visit in his home. Despite an intimate correspondence of a
decade (possibly the fullest and most intimate correspondence
of Wordsworth's later years), his closest American friend never
saw him.

Through Henry Reed Wordsworth came to have a broader
understanding of, and a deeper affection for, the daughtercountry, and with the deeper affection for America came a
sense of increased responsibility. Wordsworth wrote religious
and political sonnets about the United States, showing in both
the continuity of British tradition. In political matters he
rebuked America as he had previously rebuked England.

On 25th April 1836 Henry Reed began the correspondence.
He had long known Wordsworth's poetry, and had felt a personal attachment to the writer. He considered, too, that his
own character had been elevated and his own patriotism
strengthened by the study of Wordsworth's poetry. His
natural reticence was finally overcome by the persistence of a
woman friend who was going to England and offered to take
Wordsworth a message from Reed.

The first letter is long and elaborate in its formality, and yet beneath the almost fulsome phrases glows a warmth of genuine appreciation which Wordsworth was not slow to feel.

It may appear to you strange or perhaps presumptuous [begins the shy young teacher], that the address of familiarity should be thus assumed by one personally an utter stranger and a citizen of a distant country.   [He explained that he felt himself addressed in Wordsworth's poems and was now replying.]   I have felt my nature elevated—I have learned to look with a better spirit on all around me.   You cannot be indifferent to hearing that by your agency your fellow-beings at the distance of thousands of miles are thus benefitted. . . . I feel that I have unconsciously been taught by you a warmer and more filial attachment to old England.   But what is more, in your example I have discovered the best elements of a true and rational patriotism, and guided most safely by the light of your feeling, I have a deeper love for my own country. [141]

Though Wordsworth accepted the friendship warmly, and indicated it in numerous ways, Reed continued to use terms of excessive formality.

In 1837 Henry Reed made a one-volume edition of the complete poetical works of Wordsworth, a beautiful piece of editing done in the spirit of reverence and affection.   With the copyright laws as ineffective as they were, Reed felt that this was the best way to prevent pirating and mangling of Wordsworth's poetry.   He sent the book to Wordsworth, and the latter expressed his appreciation.   Then Reed waited more than a year before writing again, 'studiously anxious to avoid even the appearance of intruding a correspondence.'   On 3rd January 1839 he admitted that he had another motive also for editing the poems, the desire to have his name associated with the poems of Wordsworth.[142]

Professor Reed had recently contributed to the *New York Review*, by special request of the editor, a philosophical analysis of Wordsworth's poetry.   This article he now sent to the poet, explaining his reasons for accepting the task and the enjoyment he felt in executing it.   With Wordsworth's reception of the article he was delighted.[143]   He sent Wordsworth the first

American edition of the *Lyrical Ballads*, published in Philadelphia in 1802. 'It occurred to me,' he wrote to the poet in
May, 'that probably you had never seen it and might feel an
interest in possessing it as an evidence of the early regard of
your American friends.' [144]   He also kept a copy for himself.

Reed's devotion was such that he was sedulous to make no
demands of Wordsworth. Again and again he begged him
not to apologize for any delay in writing. 'While it is one of
my chief gratifications to enjoy the privilege of your correspondence,' he wrote, after eight years, 'especially as there
has been so much unreserved and cordial friendliness to me in
it—I cannot for an instant indulge anything approaching a
feeling of impatience at delays such as, I can well understand,
your convenience may require.' [145]

On Wordsworth's seventieth birthday Professor Reed all
but 'canonized' him. Bishop White, one of the two American
bishops first consecrated in England after the Revolution,[146]
was Mrs Reed's grandfather, and had lived for many years in
Reed's home. After Bishop White's death Reed transferred to
Wordsworth the veneration he had felt for the old patriarch.[147]

Wordsworth's first letter to Reed, written on 19th August
1837, after he had found on his return from Italy the beautiful
one-volume edition of his poems and two letters from Reed,
is cordial. The new edition delighted him. He took it
around and showed it to 'several persons of taste' in London,
the fastidious Rogers in particular, and reported that it was
'far the handsomest specimen of printing in double columns'
that they had seen.

Allow me to thank you [he wrote] for the pains you have bestowed
upon the work. Do not apprehend that any difference in our several
arrangements of the poems can be of much importance; you appear
to understand me far too well for that to be possible.[148]

When he thanked Reed for the article in the *New York
Review* Wordsworth said:

In respect to one particular, both in your letter and critique, I can

speak without diffidence or hesitation: I mean the affectionate tone
in which you give vent to your feelings of admiration and gratitude.
          'Grant me thy love, I crave no other fee,'
is the concluding line of a valedictory sonnet at the close of a volume
. . . consisting of my sonnets only. This sentiment is, I assure you,
predominant in my mind and heart.[149]

Wordsworth was an infrequent correspondent; therefore, to
put his young American friend at his ease he assured him of
his 'affectionate regard and sincere esteem.'[150] On another
occasion he told him: 'I shall be very glad to hear from you at
any time, being truly grateful for all your kindness, and sensible
I trust of the claims you have upon my sincere esteem.'[151]
Two years later he ended a letter: 'But, weak or strong in
body, I shall ever remain, in heart and mind, Faithfully, your
much obliged friend.'[152]

The idea of Reed's visiting at Rydal Mount was early mentioned and often repeated. Wordsworth was already *repeating*
the invitation in his third letter. By 18th July 1842 he was
indulging the high hope that Reed and Mrs Reed would make
the trip that summer. Again on 18th November 1844 he
wrote: 'I need not say what pleasure it would give us to see
you and Mrs Reed in our beautiful place of abode.'[153] But
Reed's duties at the University of Pennsylvania and the
financial condition of the State kept him from making the
long-anticipated trip during the poet's lifetime. Only in 1854
did he finally go to England.

It was to Henry Reed that the poet wrote of the departure
of his only daughter to Portugal and her seizure with rheu-
matic fever, of the illness of his daughter-in-law in Italy, and
of his own temporary loss of his four grandsons, who were
being taken to their mother. Wordsworth knew that he had
the sympathy of his unseen American friend. To Reed he
wrote again of his troubles: of the continued illness of his
daughter-in-law, of the fever caught by three of the children,
and the death of the youngest, of the severe illness of his only
living brother, and of the approaching death of John Wordsworth, only son of his eldest brother.

Reed knew unfailingly which was the source of greatest distress. Three times he expressed the hope that Wordsworth's daughter had returned from Oporto with her health restored. He was so distressed at the poet's suffering that he hesitated to write, for fear of intruding on a more recent grief. He urged his friend to give him more information.[154] Reed's sympathy was deepened by his own suffering, and he wrote to the poet of the death of his own father.

When Dora Quillinan died Reed knew that the burden was almost more than the aged father could bear, and refrained for a time from adding even his sympathy.[155] Wordsworth never wrote again to Henry Reed, but the latter understood. He, too, wrote only occasionally afterwards, but he assumed that his letters were welcome. Sometimes, when an American visited at Rydal Mount, Wordsworth would send a message to his friends in America.

Reed entered into Wordsworth's thought, and studied his poetry and his prose that he might understand him better. He interpreted him to readers and audiences in America— and occasionally even to the poet himself.

After the poet's death Reed edited *The Prelude* in America simultaneously with the English edition. And in 1851 he brought out the American edition of Christopher Wordsworth's *Memoirs* of his uncle.[156] Also in 1851 Reed published his final octavo edition of Wordsworth's Poetical Works, inserting the poems of the last years in their respective groups, and giving in his own notes personal interpretation hardly suitable while the poet was still living. Of Reed's one-volume edition Ellis Yarnall said:

> Professor Reed had prepared an admirable single-volume edition of Wordsworth's poetry—to this day the best double-column issue which has appeared, whether in England or America. Professor Reed had to take the responsibility of a rearrangement of some of the poems, and the classification he made was commended by Wordsworth, and adopted by him in his own subsequent editions. . . .[157]

Professor Reed delivered several courses of public lectures, two of which his great poet-friend largely dominated. But his most intimate criticism of Wordsworth was expressed in letters to him, sprinkled between financial advice and personal sympathy, between introductions of friends and comments on public affairs.

Reed was interested in Wordsworth's prose, and the consistency between it and the poetry. He noticed, also, the continuance of Wordsworth's principles from youth to old age. The tract on the Convention of Cintra he particularly admired, and he urged Wordsworth to preserve it by printing it with his poems. He pointed out the harmony between the tract and Wordsworth's poetry.[158] It may have been partly due to Reed's urgent request, that this tract and the other prose pieces were finally edited by the Rev. Alexander B. Grosart in 1876, for the poet wrote in September 1840:

I am much pleased by what you say in your letter of the 18th May last, upon the Tract of the 'Convention of Cintra,' and I think myself with some interest upon its being reprinted hereafter along with my other writings.[159]

Reed wrote again to Wordsworth in October, pointing out a parallel between *The Convention of Cintra* and Milton's *Samson Agonistes*. He felt that the tract illuminated Wordsworth's political sonnets,[160] and was rejoiced that Wordsworth also felt its permanent value.[161] Three years after the poet's death Reed repeated his request to Mrs Wordsworth that the Prose Works should be published in one or two volumes. 'It is important,' he wrote, 'were it only to give to its proper place in English literature the Tract on the Convention of Cintra—which is so rare that, besides my own copy I do not know of another in this country.'[162]

The new volume of Chaucer modernized, produced by R. H. Horne, Elizabeth Barrett, Leigh Hunt, and others in 1841, the poet discussed with Henry Reed. Wordsworth had started the publication by modernizing *The Prioress's Tale*, but had given up his connection with the volume—except for three contributions.

So great is my admiration of Chaucer's genius [he wrote, however, after the book was out] and so profound my reverence for him as an instrument in the hands of Providence for spreading the light of literature thro' his native land that notwithstanding the defects and faults in this Publication, I am glad of it, as a mean for making many acquainted with the original, who would otherwise be ignorant of every thing about him, but his name.[163]

Professor Reed anticipated eagerly the new volume of Wordsworth's poetry, *Poems, chiefly of Early and Late Years*, looking forward especially to the unpublished tragedy. When the volume came out in 1842 he noticed alterations in the poems previously published, and urged the restoration of the opening stanza of *Dion*.[164] He asked Wordsworth to tell him more about 'that dear old schoolmaster Mathew—who has strangely fascinated me in the several pieces of which he is the *hero*.' Though unable to give Reed exactly the information requested, Wordsworth answered:

The character of the School Master about whom you inquire, had like the Wanderer in the Excursion a solid foundation in fact and reality, but like him it was also in some degree a Composition. . . .[165]

In 1845 Wordsworth brought out his own one-volume edition, patterning it after the 1837 American edition. While the book was still in the press Wordsworth wrote to Reed:

In the Heading of the Pages I have followed the example of your Edition by extending the classification of imagination far beyond what it has hitherto been except in your Edition. The Book will be by no means so well-looking as your's; as the Contents will be more crowded. The new matter is not of much consequence but will amount to about 300 lines.[166]

Wordsworth saw that Reed's arrangement was better than his own, and was glad to acknowledge his indebtedness to his American friend. He wrote again in September and explained in more detail how Reed's idea had helped him:

I do not remember whether I have mentioned to you that, following your example, I have greatly extended the class entitled 'Poems of the Imagination,' thinking, as you must have done, that if imagination were predominant in the class, it was not indispensable that it should pervade every poem which it contained. Limiting the class as I had done before, seemed to imply . . . that the faculty, which is the *primum mobile* in poetry, had little to do, in the estimation of the author, with the pieces not arranged under that head. I, therefore, feel much obliged to you for suggesting by your practice the plan which I have adopted.[167]

This is substantially the plan used to-day in the Oxford edition.

Reed was happy when he realized that his own arrangement of the poems had guided Wordsworth, and again when Wordsworth sent him as a present the new volume, with an 'affectionate inscription' in his own handwriting. 'It will be preserved,' wrote Reed, 'as a most valued memorial of the friendship it has been my privilege to enjoy. . . . It is a book which I shall be happy to preserve for my children after me.' [168] He thought that the one-volume edition would have a considerable American circulation, and asked Wordsworth to suggest the possibility to Moxon.

Henry Reed suggested the themes of a good many of Wordsworth's later sonnets, not great as poetry, but interesting biographically. In April 1841 he asked Wordsworth to introduce into his Ecclesiastical Sonnets a link between the English Church and that in America: 'the transmission of the spiritual functions of the Church in England to the *daughter* Church in this Western Continent, by *the consecration of the American Bishops.*' [169]   To support his suggestion Reed sent to Wordsworth his published article on Bishop White.

During the summer the Right Rev. George Washington Doane, Bishop of New Jersey, visited at Rydal Mount and made the same suggestion, lending Wordsworth his funeral sermon on Bishop White. Wordsworth and the Bishop of New Jersey got along very well.

He is a man of no ordinary powers of mind and attainments [said Wordsworth], of warm feelings and sincere piety. Indeed, I never saw a person of your country, which is remarkable for cordiality, whose manner was so thoroughly cordial. He had been greatly delighted with his reception in England, and what he had seen of it both in art and nature. By the by, I heard him preach an excellent sermon in London.[170]

Bishop Doane told the following anecdote to the writer's grandfather.[171] The bishop and Wordsworth went for a long walk and were overtaken by a thunderstorm. As soon as they reached home Wordsworth supplied his guest with dry clothing, especially with dry shoes. When Bishop Doane was all dressed he stood up and said: 'Think of being in Wordsworth's shoes!'

Early in 1842 Wordsworth wrote not one sonnet but three on the aspects of Christianity in America, the third of which mentions Bishop White by name — *Patriots informed with Apostolic light.* He sent the sonnets to Reed on 1st March,[172] and asked him to transcribe them for Bishop Doane. When the sonnets were published, the poet appended a note acknowledging his indebtedness both to Henry Reed and to Bishop Doane.[173]

Reed was emboldened by this success to make in April another suggestion: that Wordsworth should add to the sonnets on the rites and ceremonies of the Church one on Matrimony and one on the Burial Service.[174] Wordsworth complied in September, writing the two sonnets suggested, two others on special services,[175] and two on the Roman Catholic Church, 'for the services which she did actually render to Christianity and humanity in the Middle Ages.'[176] Poor as these sonnets are, Reed was deeply grateful for what he considered 'one of the highest compliments that could be paid to me—that on resuming poetical composition after some interval, you should have taken up the subjects of my suggestion.'[177]

Some of Reed's suggestions Wordsworth did not follow. In 1842, for instance, the professor of literature urged Wordsworth to write a series of sonnets on the English poets of the past: 'to record in verse your judgment and gratitude to the poets who have enriched our language with their inspirations!' Citing the stanzas on Burns, 'the several tributes to Milton—that matchless memorial by a poet of his contemporaries in the "Lines on the Ettrick Shepherd" so full of truth and feeling—the exquisite allusions to Scott—the elegy on Charles

Lamb etc. etc.,' Reed was convinced that Wordsworth could not only give 'fit homage' to the greatest English poets, but also pay tribute to 'such as the world has too much neglected, . . . George Wither, Drayton, Daniel, the Beaumonts and others.' He felt that such a series would be to the history of literature what the ecclesiastical series was to the history of the Church of England.[178]

Another barren suggestion was that Wordsworth should publish a separate volume of his Church poems.[179] 'What you advise . . .' answered Wordsworth, 'I have often turned in my own mind; but I have really done so little in that way compared with the magnitude of the subject, that I have not courage to venture on such a publication.'[180] Wordsworth had good business sense, too. 'Besides,' he added, 'it would not, I fear, pay its expenses.' He had published his sonnets in a separate volume six years before, and some of the edition was still on Moxon's hands.

Wordsworth used to enclose in letters to Reed poems recently composed even when they were not suggested by the American. *Grace Darling* he sent him on 27th March 1843, requesting Reed not to publish it.[181] Two years later he sent *The Westmoreland Girl*, and asked Reed to send it to an abolitionist in Boston, William P. Atkinson, for publication, 'if you think this little piece would serve his cause indirectly.'[182] Reed, though opposed to slavery himself, was more temperate than the Bostonian, and was unwilling to have Wordsworth's name appear to sanction 'a species of lawless, undisciplined philanthropy that takes counsel neither from sober reason, nor even legitimate enthusiasm, much less from the word of God.'[183] He, therefore, did not send the poem, and Wordsworth relied on his judgment.[184]

In January 1846, after the death of his little grandson in Italy, Wordsworth eased his troubled spirit with two sonnets: *Why should we weep or mourn, Angelic Boy*, and *Where lies the truth ? has Man, in wisdom's creed*. These he asked Mrs Wordsworth to transcribe for Henry Reed, 'as the best acknowledgment she can make for Mrs Reed's and your kindness.' [185]

Wordsworth's feeling for America was a mixture of affection and severity. He chastened her, but had faith in her inherent good. Toward the end of 1839, 'reading an account of mis-doings in many parts' of the United States, he wrote the sonnet, *Men of the Western World! in Fate's dark book.* [186] When the sonnet was published in the 1842 volume, Wordsworth somewhat softened the rebuke by appending a note.

Meanwhile the State of Pennsylvania was defaulting in the payment of interest on its bonds, and Wordsworth was concerned for his friend, Miss Fenwick, and for others. To Henry Reed he wrote of 'the cloud under which the American good name, including that of the ancient State of Pennsylvania, lies.' [187] The next year he wrote:

After all, much as I am interested in this matter on account of my Friends, it is for the reproach which has justly come upon the American name from these proceedings that I am chiefly moved.[188]

In the 1845 edition he published the sonnet *To the Pennsylvanians,* a severe rebuke to those who had 'ruthlessly betrayed' the principles on which the state was founded.

Henry Reed was distressed that the sonnet should stand as a permanent indictment of his state. He wrote to Wordsworth in April 1849 that the bonds had never been repudiated, that the interest was now resumed, and that the rebuke was no longer merited. He urged his friend either to write a sequel to the sonnet or to add an explanatory note.[189] Again in December, when Wordsworth's final six-volume edition was going through the press, Reed repeated his request:

I can perfectly understand your strong indignation at the bare apprehension of broken public faith. But the apprehension has proved unfounded, and no such state dishonour rests upon Pennsylvania. It was a temporary embarrassment . . . and since effectually removed.[190]

He urged the poet in the forthcoming edition to modify the sonnet by a note: 'I grieve that a stern rebuke, happily undeserved, should stand unqualified and unexplained.'

Wordsworth complied with this last request, composing the qualifying note shortly before his death, and inserting it at the end of the fourth volume, some of the earlier volumes having been already published. Professor Reed wrote afterwards to the poet's nephew:

> It was very gratifying to me on receiving a copy of the new Edition —which was not till after his death—to find the 'additional note' at the close of the 5th volume showing by its being printed in the unusual place of a fly leaf that he was anxious to attend to such a request. It was characteristic of that *righteousness* which distinguished him as an author—and it has this interest that it was probably . . . the last sentence, which he composed for the press.[191]

Wordsworth cherished his old friends in the Lake District, in London, and in other parts of England. He befriended the children of his friends and the friends of Dorothy and of Coleridge. In middle life and even in old age he made new friendships, which lasted to the end. Throughout his life he was interested in young men, and valued their admiration and affection. His admitted scorn of trivialities did not preclude his real interest even in those whom he had not long known.

> I am very sure [wrote Crabb Robinson] that your declaration against 'personal talk' has deterred many a would-be correspondent from writing—Knowing the deep interest you take in the welfare of others, I never scruple writing when I have any fact to relate that will gratify your kind Sympathies even with mere acquaintances.[192]

Possibly indifferent to 'critical praise and censure,' Wordsworth was far from indifferent to affection and gratitude.[193]

His friendships went back to his earliest memory and forward to the rising poets and scientists in London and in Ireland. His sense of responsibility extended as far as the English language was spoken, and his feeling of kinship to America

was like his love for England. But with all his breadth of
interest Wordsworth was still centred in the land of his
childhood, where he had

> learned the meaning of all winds,
> Of blasts of every tone; and, oftentimes,
> When others heeded not, He heard the South
> Make subterraneous music. . . .

There, the different aspects of nature

> summoned him
> Up to the mountains: he had been alone
> Amid the heart of many thousand mists,
> That came to him, and left him, on the heights.

NOTES

FOREWORD

[1] Henry Crabb Robinson, *The Correspondence of Henry Crabb Robinson with the Wordsworth Circle* (1808–66), edited by Edith J. Morley, ii, p. 728. 16th Nov. 1847.

[2] Ibid. p. 729. H. C. R. to T. R. 3rd/4th May 1850. Not in Sadler.

[3] Ibid. p. 754. H. C. R. to T. R. 17th Aug. 1850. Not in Sadler.

[4] Ibid. p. 731. Q. to H. C. R. 11th May 1850. Not in Sadler.

[5] Ibid. p. 739. Q. to H. C. R. 21st May 1850. Not in Sadler.

[6] Ibid. p. 770. 16th Jan. 1851.

[7] Ibid. *Diary*. Transcript. 22. 338 C. The Diaries of Henry Crabb Robinson, in Dr Williams's Library in Gordon Square, London. 22, p. 310. 21st Apr. 1851.

[8] Ibid. p. 316. 27th Apr. 1851.

[9] Ibid. p. 340. 21st May 1851.

[10] Ibid. *Correspondence*, ii, p. 784. H. C. R. to T. R. 3rd Oct. 1851.

[11] Ibid. p. 793. 20th Apr. 1853.

[12] Letter in British Museum, 30, 262. f. 96. 18th Dec. 1860. W. W. jun. to Mrs Gordon, daughter of Professor Wilson.

[13] Edwin Paxton Hood, *Wordsworth—a Biography*, pp. 410–12.

[14] Wiltshire Stanton Austin and John Ralph, *The Lives of Poets-Laureate*, p. 404, footnote.

CHAPTER I

[1] Thomas Powell, *Living Authors of England*, p. 28.

[2] William Jerdan, *Men I Have Known*, p. 476.

[3] Thomas Cooper, *Life, written by himself*, 1872, p. 289.

[4] John Duke Coleridge, *Life and Correspondence*, i, p. 134. 3rd Aug. 1843.

[5] Wordsworth, *Prose Works*, edited by Alexander Grosart, iii, p. 428. Personal Reminiscences (1836) by the Hon. Justice Coleridge.

[6] Christopher Wordsworth, *Memoirs of William Wordsworth*, ii, p. 353. Letter to Professor Henry Reed, 1839.

[7] R. P. Graves, *Life of Sir William Rowan Hamilton*, ii, p. 487.

[8] James T. Fields, *Yesterdays with Authors*, p. 258.

[9] Arthur P. Stanley, *Life and Correspondence of Thomas Arnold*, Fourth edition, 1845, ii, p. 249. 3rd Jan. 1841.

[10] Ibid. 15th Jan. 1841.

[11] Henry Taylor, *Notes from Books*, Second edition, 1849, 'Wordsworth's Sonnets,' 1841, p. 164.

S

[12] Crabb Robinson, *Correspondence*, i, p. 532; also Sadler, iii, pp. 234-5. 9th Dec. 1843.

[13] Wordsworth, *Prose Works*, iii, pp. 166-7. No. 441.

[14] Edith C. Batho, *The Later Wordsworth*, p. 324, identifies him as F. M. Reynolds.

[15] 27, 925: f. 109.

[16] Ibid. f. 105.

[17] Henry Taylor, *Correspondence*, p. 1. 26th Dec. 1823.

[18] Christopher Wordsworth, *Memoirs*, ii, p. 223. 10th Jan. 1830.

[19] Mrs Fletcher, *Autobiography*, 1876, p. 243.

[20] Edith C. Batho, *The Later Wordsworth*, pp. 318-31.

[21] Christopher Wordsworth, *Memoirs*, ii. p. 364. 21st Feb. 1840, to Henry Alford.

[22] Ibid. p. 367. July 1840.

[23] William Knight, *Letters of the Wordsworth Family*, iii, p. 316. 30th June 1845.

[24] Thomas Carlyle, *Reminiscences*, edited by Froude, 1881, ii, Appendix, p. 339.

[25] Christopher Wordsworth, *Memoirs*, edited by Henry Reed, ii, p. 325, footnote.

[26] Crabb Robinson, *Correspondence*, ii, p. 636. Q. to H. C. R. 30th Aug. 1846. Not in Sadler.

[27] Ibid. p. 551. M. W. to H. C. R. 7th April 1844. Not in Sadler.

[28] Ibid. p. 602. H. Martineau to H. C. R. 24th June [1845]. Not in Sadler.

[29] Ibid. p. 639. H. C. R. to T. R. 17th Jan. 1847. Not in Sadler.

[30] Ibid. pp. 639-40. H. C. R. to T. R. 5th Feb. 1847. Not in Sadler.

[31] Ibid. *Diaries*, 20, p. 631. 18th Nov. 1846. Not in Sadler.

[32] Ibid. *Correspondence*, i, p. 446. 28th Oct. 1841. Not in Sadler.

[33] Ibid. p. 448. 29th Nov. 1841. Not in Sadler.

[34] Ibid. *Diaries*, 18, p. 427. 13th June 1841.

[35] Ibid. *Correspondence*, ii, p. 783.

[36] Thomas Cooper, *Life, written by himself*, p. 290.

[37] Henry Taylor, *Autobiography*, i, pp. 180-1.

[38] Ralph W. Emerson, *English Traits*, Boston, 1896, p. 21. 1833.

[39] Ibid. p. 280.

[40] Egerton 2075: ff. 118-19. 21st June 1844, probably to Abraham Cooper, R.A.

[41] Ellis Yarnall, *Wordsworth and the Coleridges*, p. 45.

[42] Leigh Hunt, *Autobiography*, ii, p. 167.

[43] Thomas Arnold, *Passages in a Wandering Life*, pp. 40-1.

[44] Ibid. p. 43.

[45] Ellis Yarnall, *Wordsworth and the Coleridges*, p. 46.

[46] Thomas Carlyle, *Reminiscences*, ii, pp. 333-4.

[47] Crabb Robinson, *Diaries*, 19, p. 88. 29th May 1842. Also Sadler, ii, p. 294.

[48] Ibid. 20, pp. 262–3. 3rd May 1845. Not in Sadler.

[49] Ibid. *Correspondence*, i, p. 523. [4th Sept. 1843.] Not in Sadler.

[50] Ibid. *Diaries*, 19, p. 84. 24th May 1842.

[51] Ibid. *Correspondence*, ii, p. 621. 8th Feb. 1846. Not in Sadler.

[52] Ibid. *Diaries*, 21, pp. 473–4. 4th Oct. 1848. Not in Sadler.

[53] Ibid. *Correspondence*, i, p. 301. [27th Apr. 1836.] Not in Sadler.

[54] Ibid. p. 303. 4th May 1836. Not in Sadler.

[55] Mary Russell Mitford, *Life*, iii, pp. 52–3. 31st May 1836.

[56] Crabb Robinson, *Correspondence*, i, p. 316. 12th Sept. 1836. Not in Sadler.

[57] Christopher Wordsworth, *Memoirs*, ii, p. 309. 7th Oct. 1836.

[58] Thomas Powell, *Living Authors*, p. 28.

[59] John Morley, *Life of William Ewart Gladstone*, iii, p. 483.

[60] Mary Russell Mitford, *Life*, iii, p. 44. To Dr Mitford, 26th May 1836.

[61] Ibid. p. 53. To Miss Jephson. 19th June 1836.

[62] Mrs Fletcher, *Autobiography*, p. 246. 4th June 1840.

[63] Crabb Robinson, *Correspondence*, ii, p. 561. 4th July 1844. Not in Sadler.

[64] Ibid. *Diaries*, 18, p. 449. 10th July 1841.

[65] Ibid. *Correspondence*, i, p. 462. 21st May 1842. Also Sadler, iii, p. 200.

[66] Ibid. *Diaries*, 19, p. 80. 20th May 1842.

[67] Ibid. *Correspondence*, ii, p. 626. 21st May [1846]. Not in Sadler.

[68] Henry Taylor, *Correspondence*, p. 221. De Vere to Taylor. 17th Dec. 1856.

[69] Christopher Wordsworth, *Memoirs*, ii, p. 260. 25th June 1832.

[70] Leigh Hunt, *Autobiography*, ii, p. 164.

[71] Thomas Powell, *Living Authors*, p. 240.

[72] Thomas Carlyle, *Reminiscences*, ii, pp. 338–40 and p. 333.

[73] Crabb Robinson, *Diaries*, 19, pp. 58–9. 29th Apr. 1842. Also Sadler, ii, p. 294.

[74] Mrs Anne Grant, *Memoir and Correspondence*, p. 59. 3rd Nov. 1814.

[75] Thomas Carlyle, *Reminiscences*, ii, p. 332. About 1840.

[76] Wordsworth, *Prose Works*, iii, p. 437. 28th Aug. 1841.

[77] Caroline Fox, *Memories of Old Friends*, Philadelphia, 1882, p. 143. 28th June 1841.

[78] Ibid. p. 173. 4th June 1842.

[79] Ibid. pp. 213 and 217. 6th and 8th Oct. 1844.

[80] Crabb Robinson, *Correspondence*, i, p. 472. [29th Dec. 1842.] Also Sadler, iii, p. 210.

[81] Augustus J. C. Hare, *Memorials of a Quiet Life*, ii, p. 273. 18th July 1844.

[82] Christopher Wordsworth, *Memoirs*, ii, pp. 445–6. 11th July 1844.

[83] J. M. Sutherland, *William Wordsworth, the Story of his Life*, p. 169.

[84] Crabb Robinson, *Diaries*, 18, p. 240. 28th Oct. 1840.

[85] Ibid. pp. 562–3. 2nd Jan. 1842.

[86] Ibid. 19, p. 92. 1st June 1842. Partly in shorthand.

[87] Ellis Yarnall, *Wordsworth and the Coleridges*, p. 42. 18th Aug. 1849.

[88] Crabb Robinson, *Correspondence*, ii, p. 562. 9th July [1844]. Not in Sadler.

[89] Ibid. p. 606. 7th Aug. [18]45. Not in Sadler.

[90] Ibid. p. 544. 6th Feb. [1844.] Not in Sadler.

[91] Sara Coleridge, *Memoir and Letters* (Harper, 1874, p. 182). To her husband. 13th Oct. 1841.

[92] Christopher Wordsworth, *Memoirs*, ii, p. 439. 22nd Dec. 1843.

[93] Henry Taylor, *Correspondence*, pp. 133–4. 11th May 1842.

[94] Calvert, *Wordsworth*, p. 169.

[95] Christopher Wordsworth, *Memoirs*, ii, pp. 384–5. W. W. to John Peace, 4th Sept. 1841.

[96] Ibid. ii, pp. 32–3. MSS. I. F.

[97] Crabb Robinson, *Correspondence*, i, p. 499. 1st June 1843. Not in Sadler.

[98] Ibid. p. 345. 5th June 1837.

[99] Mrs Fletcher, *Autobiography*, pp. 227–8. From M. F.'s notebook. 19th Aug. 1837.

[100] Henry Taylor, *Correspondence*, p. 134. To Miss Fenwick. 11th May 1842.

[101] Wordsworth, *Prose Works*, iii, p. 159. No. 425. 'To my Sister.'

[102] Mrs Fletcher, *Autobiography*, p. 228.

[103] Christopher Wordsworth, *Memoirs*, ii, pp. 242–3. W. W. to Lady Frederick Bentinck. 9th Nov. [1831].

[104] Ibid. p. 451. Lady Richardson's notes. 6th Sept. 1844.

[105] Ibid. p. 370. W. W. to Lady F. Bentinck. 26th Sept. 1840.

[106] Ibid. edited by Henry Reed, pp. 428–9. Reed's footnote. 'This Lawn, a carpet all alive.'

[107] Ibid. pp. 427–8. New York. 23rd June 1845.

[108] Wordsworth, *Prose Works*, iii, p. 468. 'Reminiscences of the Rev. R. P. Graves . . .'

[109] Christopher Wordsworth, *Memoirs*, ii, p. 301.

[110] Ernest Hartley Coleridge, *Life and Correspondence of John Duke Lord Coleridge*, i, p. 45.

[111] Mrs Fletcher, *Autobiography*, pp. 243 et seq.

[112] Crabb Robinson, *Correspondence*, ii, p. 608. 9th Sept. 1845. Not in Sadler.

[113] Wordsworth, *Prose Works*, iii, p. 436. 2nd May 1842.

[114] John Morley, *Critical Miscellanies*, iii, pp. 239–40.

[115] Crabb Robinson, *Correspondence*, i, pp. 220–1. 22nd Apr. 1830. Not in Sadler.

[116] It was Gordon who copied the earlier Waverley Novels for the press, to preserve their anonymity, and was compensated for his labour by a sermon composed by Sir Walter.

[117] Christopher Wordsworth, *Memoirs*, ii, p. 224. 6th Apr. 1830.

[118] Wordsworth, *Prose Works*, iii, p. 180. No. 466.

[119] The quotations from Mr Wordsworth, though substantially true, may not be verbally exact.

[120] Arthur H. Clough, *Poems and Prose Remains*, i, 'Lecture on the Poetry of Wordsworth,' pp. 324-5.

[121] Crabb Robinson, *Diaries and Correspondence*, edited by Sadler, Macmillan, 1869, iii, p. 275.

[122] Andrew Lang, *Poet's Country*. Article by E. H. Coleridge, p. 44.

[123] H. D. Rawnsley, *Literary Associations of the English Lakes*, p. 124.

[124] Ibid. p. 127.

[125] Christopher Wordsworth, *Memoirs*, ii, p. 55. MSS. I. F. Also Grosart, iii, pp. 122-3.

[126] James Russell Lowell, *Among my Books*, second series, 1882, p. 245.

[127] Christopher Wordsworth, *Memoirs*, ii, p. 302. Personal Reminiscences.

[128] William Ellery Channing, *Memoirs*, ii, p. 218.

[129] James T. Fields, *Yesterdays with Authors*, p. 257.

[130] Mrs Fletcher, *Autobiography*, p. 243. 'Extract from M. F.'s Notes. Fox How, Aug. 1839.'

[131] Christopher Wordsworth, *Memoirs*, ii, pp. 448-9. Reminiscences, Lady Richardson's notes. 6th Sept. 1844. Also Grosart, iii, p. 445.

[132] Mrs Fletcher, *Autobiography*, p. 264. Letter to daughter, Mary. 24th Nov. 1847.

[133] Margaret Fuller-Ossoli, *Memoirs*, iii, p. 84.

[134] Harriet Martineau, *Autobiography*, p. 508.

[135] Mrs Fletcher, *Autobiography*, p. 259.

[136] Ibid. p. 245. Dora W. to Mary F. 21st Oct 1839.

[137] Christopher Wordsworth, *Memoirs*, ii, p. 303. Personal Reminiscences, footnote.

[138] Thomas Arnold, *Passages in a Wandering Life*, p. 41.

[139] Mrs Fletcher, *Autobiography*, p. 249.

[140] Charles Mackay, *Forty Years' Recollections*, i, pp. 244-5.

[141] H. D. Rawnsley, *Literary Associations*, ii, p. 138.

[142] Ibid. pp. 136-7.

[143] Crabb Robinson, *Correspondence*, ii, p. 602. H. Martineau to H. C. R. 24th June [1845]. Not in Sadler.

[144] Ibid. *Diaries*, 18, pp. 555 and 559. 27th and 30th Dec. 1841.

[145] Ibid. *Correspondence*, i, p. 448. [Oct. 1841.] Not in Sadler.

[146] Ibid. *Diaries*, 18, pp. 296, 297-8, 300, and 301.

[147] Mary Russell Mitford, *Correspondence*, pp. 48-9. To Charles Boner, Feb.-Mar. 1846.

[148] Crabb Robinson, *Correspondence*, ii, p. 787. 21st Feb. 1852.

[149] Christopher Wordsworth, *Memoirs*, ii, p. 458. Lady Richardson's notes, c. 21st Dec. 1846.

[150] Rawnsley, *Literary Associations*, p. 137. An eye-witness told the canon this story.

[151] Christopher Wordsworth, *Memoirs*, ii, p. 450. Lady Richardson's notes. 6th Sept. 1844.

[152] Wordsworth, *Prose Works*, iii, pp. 152-3. No. 402. 'Tynwald Hill.'

[153] Ibid. p. 434. Recollections of Tour in Italy by H. C. Robinson. 18th Oct. 1850.

[154] Crabb Robinson, *Correspondence*, ii, p. 832. H. M.'s obituary notice (from *Daily News*) of Mrs Wordsworth, Jan. 1859. Also Harriet Martineau, *Biographical Sketches*, p. 92.

[155] Ibid. i, p. 496. Quillinan to H. C. R. [19th] April 1843. Not in Sadler.

[156] Wordsworth, *Prose Works*, iii, pp. 443–4. Lady Richardson.

[157] Crabb Robinson, *Correspondence*, i, p. 90. H. C. R. to W. W. [Oct. 1816], footnote. Not in Sadler, cf. Ernest de Selincourt, *Dorothy Wordsworth*, pp. 303–4.

[158] William Jerdan, *Men I Have Known*, p. 480.

[159] Thomas Cooper, *Life, written by himself*, p. 295.

[160] Christopher Wordsworth, *Memoirs*, ii, p. 457. Reminiscences. Lady Richardson's Notes. 8th Nov. 1845.

[161] Austin and Ralph, *Lives of Poets-Laureate*, p. 410.

[162] January Searle, *Memoirs of William Wordsworth*, p. 208.

[163] Ernest de Selincourt, *Dorothy Wordsworth*, p. 145.

[164] Ibid. p. 302.

[165] Searle quotes de Quincey to the effect that Wordsworth received later the distributorship for Cumberland with an annual stipend of £400. He further mentions Dorothy's legacy of £100 and a vague inheritance of 'thousands of pounds' by Mrs Wordsworth from an uncle, pp. 210, 120, 208.

[166] Crabb Robinson, *Diaries*, 19, p. 86. 26th May 1842. Italicized part originally in shorthand.

[167] Ibid. *Correspondence*, i, p. 466. Mrs Clarkson to H. C. R. June 1842.

[168] William Knight, *Letters of the Wordsworth Family*, iii. pp. 247–8.

[169] Crabb Robinson, *Diaries*, 19, p. 64. 4th May 1842.

[170] Ibid. pp. 107–8. 16th June 1842.

[171] Ibid. *Correspondence*, i, p. 436, footnote. Stephen Spring-Rice.

[172] William Knight, *Letters*, iii, p. 246.

[173] *Sir Robert Peel, from his Private Papers*, edited by Charles Stuart Parker, pp. 437–8. 10th Oct.

[174] Ibid. p. 438. 11th Oct. 1842.

[175] Christopher Wordsworth, *Memoirs*, ii, p. 389.

[176] Crabb Robinson, *Diaries*, 19, pp. 194, 202, and 206. 18th and 29th Oct. and 2nd Nov. 1842.

[177] Ibid. *Correspondence*, i, pp. 468–9. 19th Oct. 1842. Not in Sadler.

[178] Charles Mackay, *Forty Years' Recollections*, i, p. 245.

[179] James Montgomery, *Memoirs*, vi, p. 160.

[180] Matthew Arnold, Preface to his edition of *William Wordsworth's Poems*, London, 1888, p. v.

[181] Christopher Wordsworth, *Memoirs*, ii, pp. 207–8. W. W. to Wrangham.

[182] Wilfrid Ward, *Aubrey de Vere—a Memoir*, p. 70.

[183] Crabb Robinson, *Correspondence*, i, p. 448. Not in Sadler.

[184] Ibid. *Diaries*, 18, p. 543. 15th Dec. 1841.

[185] Ibid. 19, p. 79. 19th May 1842.

[186] Crabb Robinson, *Correspondence*, i, pp. 243–4. H. C. R. to T. R. 4th July 1833. Not in Sadler.

[187] Ibid. p. 290. H. C. R. to T. R. 7th Jan. 1836. Not in Sadler.

[188] Henry Taylor, *Notes from Books*, 'Wordsworth's Sonnets,' 1841, p. 170.

[189] Crabb Robinson, *Correspondence*, i, p. 408. H. C. R. to W. W. Not in Sadler.

[190] Christopher Wordsworth, *Memoirs*, edited by Henry Reed, ii, pp. 474-6. 1830.

[191] Crabb Robinson, *Correspondence*, i, p. 335. W. W. to H. C. R. 28th Jan. [1837]. Not in Sadler.

[192] Thomas Powell, *Living Authors*, p. 29.

[193] Crabb Robinson, *Correspondence*, ii, p. 643. Sara Coleridge to H. C. R. [28th Mar. 1847.] Not in Sadler.

[194] Ibid. i, p. 368. W. W. to H. C. R. 28th July 1838. PS. Misplaced in Sadler, iii, p. 157, as parenthesis of letter of Dec. 1838.

[195] Ibid. i, p. 322. H. C. R. to M. W. 27th Oct. 1836. PS. Not in Sadler.

[196] William Jerdan, *Men I Have Known*, p. 480.

[197] Austin and Ralph, *Lives of Poets-Laureate*, p. 421.

[198] William Charles Macready, *Diaries*, edited by William Toynbee, ii, p. 291, footnote.

[199] Charles Mackay, *Forty Years' Recollections*, i, p. 232.

[200] Ibid. p. 236.

[201] Henry Taylor, *Autobiography*, ii, p. 57. 24th May 1850.

[202] Mary Russell Mitford, *Life*, ii, pp. 10-11. To Sir Wm. Elford. 13th Sept. 1817.

[203] Thomas Cooper, *Life, written by himself*, p. 290.

[204] Crabb Robinson, *Correspondence*, ii, p. 779. Q. to H. C. R. 15th May 1851.

[205] Ibid. p. 621. 'Extract [copied by H. C. R.] from a letter of H. Martineau.' 8th Feb. 1846. Not in Sadler.

[206] Edith C. Batho, *The Later Wordsworth*, pp. 70-1.

[207] Crabb Robinson, *Diaries*, 18, pp. 577-8. 17th Jan. 1842.

[208] Henry Taylor, *Notes from Books*, 'Wordsworth's Sonnets,' 1841, p. 105.

[209] Thomas Carlyle, *Reminiscences*, ii, p. 336.

[210] Christopher Wordsworth, *Memoirs*, ii, pp. 212-13.

[211] Crabb Robinson, *Diaries*, 18, p. 183. 26th June 1840.

[212] Ibid. *Correspondence*, ii, pp. 563-4. W. W. to H. C. R. 14th July 1844. Also Sadler, iii, p. 254.

[213] Samuel Taylor Coleridge, *Biographia Epistolaris*, edited by A. Turnbull, 1911, i, p. 152. S. T. C. to Cottle. 8th Mar. 1798.

[214] Ibid. ii, p. 2. S. T. C. to J. Tobin. 10th Apr. 1804.

[215] Crabb Robinson, *Diaries*, 18, p. 315. 1st Feb. 1841.

[216] Ibid. *Correspondence*, i, p. 451. H. C. R. to T. R. Rydal. 6th Jan. 1842. Not in Sadler.

[217] Ibid. *Diaries*, 21, pp. 799-800. 3rd Jan. 1850.

[218] Wordsworth, *Poems—1807*, edited by Helen Darbishire, Introduction, p. xxvi.

[219] Crabb Robinson, *Correspondence*, i, p. 421. H. C. R. to T. R. 12th Jan. 1841.

CHAPTER II

[1] Crabb Robinson, *Correspondence*, i, p. 233. W. W. to H. C. R. 5th Feb. 1833.

[2] Ibid. pp. 211 and 213. D. W. to H. C. R. 2nd May 1829.

[3] Ibid. p. 206. W. W. to H. C. R. 26th Apr. 1829.

[4] Christopher Wordsworth, *Memoirs*, ii, p. 260. 25th June 1832.

[5] Professor de Selincourt gives 27th June—*Dorothy Wordsworth*, p. 393.

[6] Crabb Robinson, *Correspondence*, i, p. 277. W. W. to H. C. R. [24th June 1835.]

[7] Ibid. p. 279. 6th July 1835.

[8] Ibid. p. 283. 25th Nov. 1835.

[9] Ibid. p. 290. H. C. R. to T. R. Rydal Cottage. 7th Jan. 1836.

[10] Coleridge, *Biographia Epistolaris*, i, p. 249. S. T. C. to Godwin. 23rd June 1801.

[11] Crabb Robinson, *Correspondence*, i, p. 325. M. W. to H. C. R. Not in Sadler.

[12] Ibid. p. 351. W. W. to H. C. R. Not in Sadler.

[13] Ibid. *Diaries*, 18, pp. 288–9. 31st Dec. 1840. Not in Sadler.

[14] Ibid. *Correspondence*, i, p. 421. H. C. R. to T. R. Rydal Mount. 12th Jan. 1841. Not in Sadler.

[15] Ibid. *Diaries*, 18, p. 494. 11th Oct. 1841.

[16] Ibid. *Correspondence*, i, p. 444. M. W. to H. C. R. Not in Sadler.

[17] Ibid. p. 470. Q. to H. C. R. 28th Nov. 1842. Not in Sadler.

[18] Ibid. ii, p. 713. Q. to H. C. R. Christmas Night, 1849. Not in Sadler.

[19] Ibid. i, p. 282. H. C. R. to M. W. 22nd Nov. 1835.

[20] Elizabeth Wordsworth, *William Wordsworth*, p. 168.

[21] Crabb Robinson, *Correspondence*, ii, p. 830. Jan. 1859.

[22] William Wordsworth, *Prose Works*, iii, p. 70. No. 256. 'Yarrow Visited.'

[23] Christopher Wordsworth, *Memoirs*, ii, pp. 439–40. 22nd Dec. 1843.

[24] Ibid. p. 451. 7th Sept. 1844.

[25] Crabb Robinson, *Correspondence*, ii, p. 601. 21st June 1845. Not in Sadler.

[26] Charles Mackay, *Forty Years' Recollections*, i, pp. 242–3.

[27] Thomas Cooper, *Life, written by himself*, p. 295.

[28] Crabb Robinson, *Correspondence*, ii, p. 676. Q. to H. C. R. 12th Aug. 1848.

[29] Ibid. p. 685. 15th Jan. 1848. Also Sadler, iii, p. 340.

[30] Ibid. p. 725. Loughrigg Holme. Tuesday, 23rd Apr. 1850.

[31] Crabb Robinson, *Correspondence*, ii, p. 829. Jan. 1859. Obituary in *Daily News*.

[32] Ibid. p. 654. Mrs Montagu to H. C. R. 10th Dec. 1847. Not in Sadler.

[33] Ibid. p. 800. M. W. to H. C. R.

[34] Thomas Arnold, *Passages in a Wandering Life*, pp. 43–4.

[35] Ellis Yarnall, *Wordsworth and the Coleridges*, pp. 36 and 40.   Aug. 1849.

[36] Augustus J. C. Hare, *Memorials of a Quiet Life*, ii, p. 274.

[37] Crabb Robinson, *Correspondence*, ii, pp. 643 and 644.   S. C. to H. C. R. Not in Sadler.

[38] Ibid. p. 685.   15th Jan. 1849.

[39] Hattie Griswold, *Home Life of Great Authors*, p. 44.

[40] Crabb Robinson, *Correspondence*, ii, p. 632.   Q. to H. C. R.   30th July 1846.   Not in Sadler.

[41] Ibid. p. 637.   W. W. to H. C. R.   Not in Sadler.

[42] Eleanor A. Towle, *A Poet's Children*, p. 257.

[43] Margaret Fuller-Ossoli, *Memoirs*, iii, pp. 83–4.

[44] Crabb Robinson, *Correspondence*, ii, p. 832.   Obituary notice.

[45] Thomas Carlyle, *Reminiscences* (Froude), ii, p. 338.

[46] Thomas Carlyle, *Reminiscences*, edited by Norton, 1887, ii, p. 306. Note: 'According to Sir Henry Taylor, Mrs Wordsworth was "rather tall," and was in all respects so unlike this description that he says, "I cannot but think there was simply a mistake of one person for another."— *Nineteenth Century* for June 1881.'

[47] Crabb Robinson, *Correspondence*, ii, pp. 829–30.   Jan. 1859.

[48] Ibid. p. 643, Sara Coleridge to H. C. R.   [28th Mar. 1847.]   Not in Sadler.

[49] Ibid. p. 621.   8th Feb. 1846.

[50] Henry Reed, *Poetical Works of Wordsworth*, 1851, p. vii.   Probably William B. Reed, brother of the editor.

[51] James T. Fields, *Yesterdays with Authors*, pp. 256–7.

[52] Crabb Robinson, *Correspondence*, i, p. 305.   4th July [1836].   Not in Sadler.

[53] Ibid. p. 317.   [28th Sept. 1836.]   Not in Sadler.

[54] Ibid. p. 318.   30th Aug. 1836.   Not in Sadler.

[55] Ibid. ii, p. 540.   M. W. to H. C. R.   5th Feb. [1844].   Not in Sadler.

[56] Mrs Fletcher, *Autobiography*, p. 213.

[57] Mary Russell Mitford, *Correspondence*, p. 73.   2nd July 1847.

[58] Crabb Robinson, *Correspondence*, ii, pp. 652, 657, and 666.   Miss F. to H. C. R., 12th Aug. 1847; H. C. R. to T. R., 7th Jan. 1848; H. C. R. to Miss F., 10th Jan. 1848; and Q. to H. C. R., 6th June 1848.

[59] William Knight, *Letters*, iii, 342.   23rd Feb. 1848.

[60] Christopher Wordsworth, *Memoirs*, ii, p. 368.   July 1840.

[61] Harriet Martineau, *Biographical Sketches*, p. 99.

[62] Crabb Robinson, *Correspondence*, i, p. 502.   Sara Coleridge to H. C. R. 29th June 1843.   Not in Sadler.

[63] Christopher Wordsworth, *Memoirs*, edited by Henry Reed, ii, p. 427, note.   23rd June 1845.

[64] Christopher Wordsworth, *Memoirs*, ii, pp. 444–5.   Reminiscences, Mrs Davy's notes.   11th July 1844.

[65] Wordsworth, *Prose Works*, iii, p. 169.   No. 446.   'Humanity.'

[66] Henry Taylor, *Correspondence*, p. 118.   Miss F. to H. T.   28th Mar. 1839.

[67] Christopher Wordsworth, *Memoirs*, i, pp. 183-4. W. W. to Wrangham, 4th Nov., and note.

[68] Wordsworth, *Prose Works*, iii, p. 39. No. 136. 'I wandered lonely as a cloud.'

[69] He has perpetuated the 'lovely apparition sent to be a moment's ornament' in *To a Highland Girl*, 1803, and in the last two stanazs of *The Three Cottage Girls*, 1820. He says in the Fenwick notes: 'This delightful creature and her demeanour are particularly described in my Sister's Journal . . . and now, approaching the close of my seventy-third year, I have a most vivid remembrance of her and the beautiful objects with which she was surrounded.' Wordsworth, *Prose Works*, iii, p. 67. No. 244.

[70] Crabb Robinson, *Correspondence*, i, pp. 463-4. Not in Sadler, except Robinson's note.

[71] Ibid. *Diaries*, 19, p. 72. 12th May 1842.

[72] Cited by A. J. George, in Wordsworth, *Complete Poems*, Cambridge students' edition, 1904, p. 841, as referring to Mary Hutchinson.

[73] Wordsworth, *Poetical Works*, edited by Reed, 1851, p. 129, note.

[74] Christopher Wordsworth, *Memoirs*, ii, p. 232.

[75] Crabb Robinson, *Correspondence*, i, p. 226. D. W. to H. C. R. 1st Dec. [1831]. This part of letter not in Sadler.

[76] Ibid. p. 500. Q. to H. C. R. 1st June 1843. Not in Sadler.

[77] Ibid. p. 521. 1st Sept. 1843. Not in Sadler.

[78] Ibid. *Diaries*, 19, p. 451. 28th Aug. 1843.

[79] Ibid. *Correspondence*, i, p. 258. W. W. to H. C. R. 3rd April [1834]. Not in Sadler.

[80] Wordsworth, *Prose Works*, iii, p. 170. No. 448. 24th Jan. 1843.

[81] Ellis Yarnall, *Wordsworth and the Coleridges*, p. 44.

[82] Crabb Robinson, *Correspondence*, i, p. 295.

[83] Ibid. p. 371. M. W. to H. C. R. 19th Aug. Not in Sadler.

[84] Ibid. p. 379. [19th Feb. 1839.] Written by M. W. Not in Sadler.

[85] Ibid. p. 417. W. W. to H. C. R. 4th Sept. 1840. Not in Sadler.

[86] Ibid. *Diaries*, 21, p. 791. 24th Dec. 1849. Not in Sadler.

[87] Ibid. *Correspondence*, i. pp. 516-17. Q. to H. C. R. 25th Aug. 1843. Also Sadler, iii, pp. 225-6.

[88] Ibid. p. 520. Q. to H. C. R. 1st Sept. 1843. Not in Sadler.

[89] Ibid. ii, p. 562. M. W. to H. C. R. 9th July 1844. Not in Sadler.

[90] Wordsworth and Reed, *Correspondence*, pp. 144-5 and 147. W. W. to Reed. 1st July and 31st July 1845.

[91] Crabb Robinson, *Correspondence*, ii, p. 610. M. W. to H. C. R. 16th Sept. 1845.

[92] Wordsworth and Reed, *Correspondence*, p. 161. W. W. to Reed. 23rd Jan. 1846.

[93] Ibid. pp. 161-2.

[94] Crabb Robinson, *Correspondence*, ii, p. 619. W. W. to H. C. R. 2nd Feb. 1846. Not in Sadler.

[95] Ibid. pp. 674–5. Q. to H. C. R. 23rd July 1848. Not in Sadler.

[96] Ibid. pp. 677–9. Q. to H. C. R. 2nd Oct. 1848. Not in Sadler.

[97] Eleanor A. Towle, *A Poet's Children*, p. 81.

[98] Crabb Robinson, *Correspondence*, i, p. 135. H. C. R. to D. W. 13th Dec. 1824. Not in Sadler.

[99] Ibid. p. 429. D. W. to H. C. R. [2nd Feb. 1841.] Not in Sadler.

[100] Letter at Dove Cottage, No. 12. 14th Nov. 1829.

[101] Crabb Robinson, *Correspondence*, i, p. 171. D. W. to H. C. R. 18th Dec. 1826. Not in Sadler.

[102] Ibid. p. 218. D. W. to H. C. R. 22nd Apr. 1830. Not in Sadler.

[103] Thomas Arnold, *Passages in a Wandering Life*, p. 44.

[104] Crabb Robinson, *Correspondence*, i, p. 291. M. W. to H. C. R. 20th Feb. [1836]. Not in Sadler.

[105] Ibid. pp. 356–7. H. C. R. to M. W. 12th Mar. 1838. Not in Sadler.

[106] Ibid. ii, p. 842. J. C. Richmond to H. C. R. 5th Mar. 1863.

[107] Christopher Wordsworth, *Memoirs*, ii, p. 379.

[108] Crabb Robinson, *Correspondence*, i, p. 119, note.

[109] Letter at Dove Cottage, No. 12. 14th Nov. 1829.

[110] Christopher Wordsworth, *Memoirs*, ii, p. 347.

[111] Ibid. p. 348.

[112] Robinson, *Correspondence*, i, p. 352. W. W. to H. C. R. 15th Dec. [1837]. Not in Sadler.

[113] Ibid. p. 208. W. W. to H. C. R. 26th Apr. 1829. Also Sadler, ii, p. 414.

[114] Ibid. p. 510. Q. to H. C. R. 28th July 1843. Not in Sadler.

[115] Ibid, p. 397.

[116] Ibid. *Diaries*, 18, pp. 87–9. 21st and 22nd Feb. 1840.

[117] Wordsworth, *Prose Works*, iii, p. 99. No. 319.

[118] Ibid. p. 65. No. 235.

[119] *Sketch of an Ascent to the Top of Helvellyn*, 31st Aug. 1840.

[120] Crabb Robinson, *Diaries*, 18, p. 365. 3rd Apr. 1841.

[121] Henry Taylor, *Autobiography*, i, p. 337.

[122] Wordsworth, *Poetical Works*, edited by William Knight, Edinburgh: William Paterson, 1889, xi, p. 379. 6th May 1841.

[123] Ibid. p. 383.

[124] Crabb Robinson, *Correspondence*, i, p. 432. M. W. to H. C. R.

[125] Ibid. p. 434. Dora Quillinan to H. C. R. 19th May [1841]. Not in Sadler.

[126] Ibid. *Diaries*, 18, pp. 552–3 and 578.

[127] Ibid. 19, p. 202. 29th Oct. 1842.

[128] Edward Quillinan, *Poems*, edited by William Johnston, p. xxxi: 'Mr Quillinan's letters in the winter of 1842–3 appear to have been written in Ambleside and it was there that he wrote the dialogue between Walter Savage Landor and the Editor of Blackwood's Magazine which was published in Blackwood for April 1843.'

[129] Crabb Robinson, *Diaries*, 19, pp. 27, 71, and 202.

[130] Ibid. *Correspondence*, i, p. 496. Q. to H. C. R. [19th] Apr. 1843. Not in Sadler.

[131] *Wordsworthiana*, edited by William Knight, p. 88.

[132] Crabb Robinson, *Correspondence*, ii, p. 562. M. W. to H. C. R. 9th July 1844. Not in Sadler.

[133] Ibid. pp. 573 and 576. W. W. to H. C. R. 29th Sept. 1844, and M. W. to H. C. R. 4th Nov. 1844. Not in Sadler.

[134] Ibid. p. 594. Q. to H. C. R. 4th Apr. 1845. Not in Sadler.

[135] Ibid.

[136] Ibid. p. 597. Q. to H. C. R. 8th Apr. 1845. Not in Sadler.

[137] Ibid. p. 598. Q. to H. C. R. 18th Apr. 1845. Not in Sadler.

[138] Ibid. *Diaries*, 20, p. 263. 3rd May 1845.

[139] Ibid. *Correspondence*, ii, pp. 599–600. H. C. R. to T. R. 5th May 1845. Not in Sadler.

[140] Ibid. p. 607. M. W. to H. C. R. [7th Aug. 1845.] Not in Sadler.

[141] Ibid. p. 608. M. W. to H. C. R. [16th Sept. 1845.] Extract from Dora's letter. Not in Sadler.

[142] Ibid. p. 612. H. C. R. to M. W. 11th Nov. 1845. Reported by Kenyon. Not in Sadler.

[143] Ibid. p. 631. Sara Coleridge to H. C. R. 27th June 1846. Not in Sadler.

[144] Ibid. p. 636. Q. to H. C. R. 30th Aug. 1846. Not in Sadler.

[145] Ibid. pp. 636–7. Dora Quillinan to H. C. R. 21st Sept. [1846].

[146] Dora Wordsworth, *Journal of a Few Months' Residence in Portugal*, edited with memoir by Edmund Lee, p. xxxv.

[147] Crabb Robinson, *Diaries*, 21, p. 72. 10th Apr. 1847. Not in Sadler.

[148] Ibid. p. 73. 12th Apr. 1847. Not in Sadler.

[149] Ibid. p. 85. 26th Apr. 1847. Small part in Sadler, iii, p. 291.

[150] Ibid. *Correspondence*, ii, p. 645. Q. to H. C. R. 30th Apr. 1847. Not in Sadler.

[151] Ibid. *Diaries*, 21, p. 90. 1st May 1847. Not in Sadler.

[152] Sara Coleridge, *Memoir and Letters*, p. 313. 31st May 1847.

[153] Crabb Robinson, *Correspondence*, ii, p. 648. Mrs Arnold to H. C. R. 1st June 1847. Part in Sadler, iii, p. 294, slightly altered.

[154] George McLean Harper, *William Wordsworth—his Life, Works, and Influence*, ii, pp. 432–3.

[155] Christopher Wordsworth, *Memoirs*, ii, p. 434.

[156] Crabb Robinson, *Diaries*, 21, p. 153. 16th July 1847. Not in Sadler.

[157] St John, vi, 37.

[158] Crabb Robinson, *Correspondence*, ii, p. 654. 23rd Dec. 1847. H. C. R. to T. R. Not in Sadler.

[159] Ibid. pp. 656 and 657. H. C. R. to T. R. 31st Dec. 1847 and 7th Jan. 1848. Not in Sadler.

[160] Ibid. pp. 657–8. 10th Jan. 1848. Not in Sadler.

[161] Ibid. p. 659. H. C. R. to T. R. 14th–15th Jan. 1848. Not in Sadler.

[162] Christopher Wordsworth, *Memoirs*, ii, p. 435. 29th Dec. 1847.

[163] Crabb Robinson, *Correspondence*, ii, p. 656. H. C. R. to Miss F. 24th Dec. 1847. Not in Sadler.

[164] Ibid. p. 658. H. C. R. to Miss F. 10th Jan. 1848.

[165] Ibid. p. 660. Miss F. to H. C. R. Bath. 17th Jan. 1848. Not in Sadler.

[166] Ibid. p. 663. 1st Feb. 1848. Not in Sadler.

[167] Ibid. p. 669. 7th June 1848. Not in Sadler.

[168] Letter in British Museum. 33, 515. b. 19. f. 100. R. W. Emerson, Ambleside. 29th Feb. 1848.

[169] Crabb Robinson, *Correspondence*, ii, p. 666. 6th June 1848. Not in Sadler.

[170] Ibid. p. 637. 23rd July 1848.

[171] Mary Russell Mitford, *Correspondence*, p. 102. 25th Aug. 1848.

[172] Ibid. p. 94.

[173] Crabb Robinson, *Correspondence*, ii. p. 671. 8th June [1848]. Not in Sadler.

[174] Christopher Wordsworth, *Memoirs*, edited by Henry Reed, ii, p. 503, note, quoting Hilliard's letter of Apr. 1849.

[175] Crabb Robinson, *Correspondence*, ii, p. 680. 28th Dec. 1848. Also Sadler, iii, p. 335, slightly altered.

[176] Ibid. p. 683. 12th Jan. 1849.

[177] Ibid. p. 685. 15th Jan. 1848 [1849]. Also Sadler, iii, p. 340. Last part not in Sadler.

[178] Ibid. p. 682. 12th Jan. 1849. Also Sadler, iii, p. 339.

[179] William Knight, *Letters*, iii, p. 347. To John Taylor Coleridge. 19th Feb. 1849.

[180] Crabb Robinson, *Correspondence*, ii, p. 706. 14th Oct. 1849. Also Sadler, iii, p. 348.

[181] Ibid. *Diaries*, 19, p. 64. 4th May 1842.

[182] Ibid. *Correspondence*, i, pp. 476–7. 7th Feb. 1843. Not in Sadler.

[183] Ibid. p. 478. 15th Feb. 1843.

[184] Ibid. *Diaries*, 19, p. 309. 16th Feb. 1843.

[185] Ibid. *Correspondence*, i, p. 492. 10th Apr. 1843. Not in Sadler.

[186] Ibid. *Diaries*, 19, pp. 354–5. 10th Apr. 1843.

[187] Ibid. 20, pp. 469–78. 4th–15th Mar. 1846. Not in Sadler.

[188] Ibid. *Correspondence*, ii, p. 635. 17th Aug. [1846]. Not in Sadler.

[189] Ibid. *Diaries*, 20, p. 642. 30th Nov. 1846. Not in Sadler.

[190] Ibid. *Correspondence*, ii, pp. 638–9. H. C. R. to M. W. Bury. 19th Dec. 1846. Not in Sadler.

[191] Ibid. *Diaries*, 20, p. 644. 1st Dec. 1846. Not in Sadler.

[192] Christopher Wordsworth, *Memoirs*, ii, p. 433.

[193] Crabb Robinson, *Diaries*, 21, p. 32.

[194] Ibid. *Correspondence*, ii, p. 784. H. C. R. to T. R. 25th–26th Sept. 1851. Rydal Mount.

[195] Ibid. *Diaries*, 22, pp. 285, 287, 290, and 291. 18th–27th Mar. 1851.

[196] Ibid. p. 296. 2nd Apr. 1851.

197 Ernest de Selincourt, *Dorothy Wordsworth*, pp. 147–8.

198 Ibid. pp. 290 ff.

199 Ibid. p. 290.   9th Oct. 1814.

200 Ibid. pp. 296–7.

201 Ibid. p. 342.

202 Crabb Robinson, *Correspondence*, i, p. 102.   H. C. R. to D. W.   6th July 1821.   Not in Sadler.

203 Ibid. p. 105.   H. C. R. to D. W.   19th Nov. 1831.   Not in Sadler.

204 Ibid. pp. 358–9.   [16th Mar. 1838.]   Not in Sadler.

205 Ibid. p. 369.   [July or Aug. 1838.]   Not in Sadler.

206 Edith C. Batho, *The Later Wordsworth*, pp. 390–3.

207 Crabb Robinson, *Diaries*, 19, p. 129.   8th Aug. 1842.

208 Ibid. p. 130.   9th Aug. 1842.

209 Ibid. p. 139.   19th Aug. 1842.

210 Ibid. 22, pp. 73–4.   Not in Sadler.

211 Ibid. p. 136.   29th Aug. 1850.   Not in Sadler.

212 Ibid. *Correspondence*, ii, pp. 756–7.   Grasmere.   31st Aug. 1850.   Not in Sadler.

213 Ibid. *Diaries*, 22, p. 357.   17th July 1851.

214 Edwin Paxton Hood, *Wordsworth—a Biography*, p. 471.

215 Christopher Wordsworth, *Memoirs*, ii, pp. 301–2.   Personal Reminiscences of the Hon. Justice Coleridge.

216 Crabb Robinson, *Correspondence*, i, pp. 535–6.   Christmas, 1843.

217 Ibid. *Diaries*, 20, p. 171.   23rd Dec. 1844.   Not in Sadler.

218 Ibid. *Correspondence*, ii, p. 616.   H. C. R. to T. R.   20th Dec. 1845.   Not in Sadler.

219 Though early orphaned and in extreme poverty when the Wordsworths found him, James regarded himself as particularly blessed by fortune.

220 Crabb Robinson, *Correspondence*, ii, p. 661.   H. C. R. to Miss Fenwick, 24th Jan. 1848.   Different version in Sadler, iii, p. 309.   8th Jan.

221 Ibid. pp. 685–6.   H. C. R. to Miss F.   15th Jan. [1849].   Also Sadler, iii, pp. 340–1.

222 Ellis Yarnall, *Wordsworth and the Coleridges*, pp. 72–3.   15th Aug. 1855.

223 Crabb Robinson, *Correspondence*, i, pp. 529–30.   24th Oct. 1843.   Also Sadler, iii, p. 233.

224 Mrs Fletcher, *Autobiography*, p. 248.   M. F.'s notebook.   [1st Aug. 1840.]

225 Crabb Robinson, *Diaries*, 18, pp. 554 and 560.

226 Ibid. *Correspondence*, i, p. 84, footnote.

227 Ibid. *Diaries*, 21, p. 439.   18th Aug. 1848.   Not in Sadler.

228 Ibid. *Correspondence*, ii, p. 572.   M. W. to H. C. R.   23rd Sept.   Not in Sadler.

229 Christopher Wordsworth, *Memoirs*, ii, p. 360.   To Lady Frederick Bentinck.   3rd Jan. 1840.

230 Ibid. p. 358.   11th Dec. 1838.

231 Crabb Robinson, *Diaries*, 20, p. 129.   5th Nov. 1844.   Not in Sadler.

[232] Ibid. p. 452.   9th Feb. 1846.
[233] Ibid. 21, p. 282.   26th Jan. 1848.   Not in Sadler.
[234] Ibid., *Correspondence*, i, pp. 209–10 and 221.   Not in Sadler.
[235] Elizabeth Wordsworth, *Glimpses of the Past*, p. 1.
[236] Crabb Robinson, *Diaries*, 20. pp. 111–14.   Not in Sadler.
[237] Ibid. *Correspondence*, i, pp. 209–10.   Not in Sadler.
[238] Elizabeth Wordsworth, *Glimpses of the Past*, p. 157.
[239] F. V. Morley, *Dora Wordsworth—her Book*, p. 171.
[240] Elizabeth Wordsworth, *Glimpses of the Past*, pp. 10–11.
[241] Wordsworth, *Prose Works*, iii, p. 181.   No. 468.
[242] Ibid. p. 152.   No. 400.
[243] Wordsworth and Reed, *Correspondence*, p. 154.   27th Sept. 1845.
[244] Ibid. p. 153.
[245] Ibid. p. 49.   15th May 1841.
[246] Ibid. p. 153.
[247] Crabb Robinson, *Correspondence*, i, p. 505.   H. C. R. to T. R.   21st–22nd July 1843.   Not in Sadler.
[248] Ibid. p. 506.   Q. to H. C. R.   23rd July 1843.   Not in Sadler.
[249] Ibid. p. 520.   Q. to H. C. R.   1st Sept. 1843.   Not in Sadler.
[250] Ibid. p. 529.   H. C. R. to T. R.   28th Sept. 1843.   Not in Sadler.
[251] Ibid. ii, p. 698.   Q. to H. C. R.   9th July 1849.   Not in Sadler.
[252] Edwin Paxton Hood, *Wordsworth—a Biography*, p. 7.
[253] Wordsworth, *Prose Works*, iii, p. 219.   'Autobiographical Memoranda,' Nov. 1847.
[254] Robert Perceval Graves, *Life of Sir William Rowan Hamilton*, iii, p. 171. To Miss Alcock, 29th Apr. 1864.
[255] Crabb Robinson, *Correspondence*, i, p. 418.   4th Sept. 1840.   Not in Sadler.
[256] Wordsworth, *Prose Works*, iii, p. 219.
[257] Ellis Yarnall, *Wordsworth and the Coleridges*, p. 44.

CHAPTER III

[1] Crabb Robinson, *Correspondence*, i, p. 403.   H. C. R. to W. W.   19th Mar. 1840.   Also Sadler, iii, p. 184.
[2] Henry Taylor, *Autobiography*, i, p. 52.
[3] Ibid. p. 333.
[4] Crabb Robinson, *Diaries*, 19, p. 251.   26th Dec. 1842; and *Correspondence*, ii, p. 617.   To T. R.   25th Dec. 1845.   Not in Sadler.
[5] Ibid. *Correspondence*, i, p. 485.   Q. to H. C. R.   Rydal Mount, 4th Apr. 1845.   Not in Sadler.
[6] Wilfrid Ward, *Aubrey de Vere—a Memoir*, p. 69.   6th Mar. 1845.
[7] Henry Taylor, *Correspondence*, pp. 155–6.   9th Mar. 1845.
[8] Ibid. *Autobiography*, i, p. 336.
[9] Ibid. *Correspondence*, pp. 86–7.   Rydal Mount.   29th June 1838.

[10] Ibid. p. 93. Rydal Mount. 18th Aug. 1838.

[11] Ibid. p. 94.

[12] Ibid. p. 95.

[13] Ibid. pp. 95-6.

[14] Ibid. pp. 109-10. Ambleside, 4th Jan. 1839.

[15] Crabb Robinson, *Correspondence*, i, pp. 378-9. W. W. to H. C. R. [19th Feb. 1839] Not in Sadler.

[16] Henry Taylor, *Correspondence*, p. 117. Ambleside. 28th Mar. 1839.

[17] *Wordsworth's Prelude*, edited by Ernest de Selincourt, p. xix.

[18] Henry Taylor, *Correspondence*, p. 97. Rydal. 18th Aug. 1838.

[19] Ibid. p. 123. 9th June 1839.

[20] Ibid. p. 124. [July or Aug. 1839.]

[21] Ibid. *Autobiography*, i, pp. 335 and 336.

[22] Crabb Robinson, *Correspondence*, i, p. 496. Q. to H. C. R. 9th [19th] Apr. 1843. Not in Sadler.

[23] Ibid. ii, p. 597. Q. to H. C. R. 7th Apr. 1845. Not in Sadler.

[24] Wordsworth and Reed, *Correspondence*, pp. 45-6 and 48. H. R. to W. W. 25th Feb. and 14th Apr. 1841.

[25] Ibid. p. 33. H. R. to W. W. 28th Sept. 1840.

[26] Ibid. p. 56. W. W. to H. R. 16th Aug. 1841.

[27] Ibid. p. 62. W. W. to H. R. 1st Mar. 42.

[28] Ibid. pp. 62-138.

[29] Ibid. p. 95. W. W. to H. R. Rydal Mount. 27th Mar. 1843.

[30] Ibid. p. 146. W. W. to H. R. Rydal Mount. 31st July 1845.

[31] Wordsworth, *Prose Works*, iii, p. 49. No. 176. 'The Cuckoo-Clock.'

[32] Henry Taylor, *Correspondence*, p. 295, footnote.

[33] Crabb Robinson, *Correspondence*, i, p. 503. Q. to H. C. R. 7th July 1845. Not in Sadler.

[34] Ibid. p. 436. M. W. to H. C. R. Lyme, Monday night. 31st May 1841. Not in Sadler.

[35] Ibid. *Diaries*, 21, p. 50. 4th Mar. 1847. Not in Sadler.

[36] These notes, though quoted largely in Christopher Wordsworth's *Memoirs* of his uncle, were never printed in their entirety until 1876, when Alexander B. Grosart edited the *Prose Works*; they occupy 213 pages of vol. iii.

[37] Henry Taylor, *Autobiography*, i, pp. 334-5.

[38] Ibid, *Correspondence*, p. 114. 26th Jan. 1839.

[39] Ibid. *Autobiography*, i, p. 281.

[40] Ibid. p. 336.

[41] Wordsworth, *Prose Works*, iii, p. 162. No. 431. 'Personal Talk,' xiii.

[42] Wilfrid Ward, *Aubrey de Vere—a Memoir*, p. 70. De Vere's diary, 9th Mar. 1845.

[43] Crabb Robinson, *Diaries*, 21, p. 207. 30th Sept. 1847. Much of it in Sadler, iii, p. 298, slightly altered. Shorthand insertion italicized.

[44] Ibid. *Correspondence*, ii, p. 653. 1st Oct. 1847. Not in Sadler.
[45] Ibid. p. 673. 9th–10th June 1848. Not in Sadler.
[46] Henry Taylor, *Autobiography*, i, p. 336.
[47] Ibid. ii, p. 56. 25th Apr. 1850.
[48] Crabb Robinson, *Correspondence*, ii, p. 754. 'At Rydal—17th Augt. 1850.' Not in Sadler.
[49] Henry Taylor, *Autobiography*, ii, p. 57. 3rd June 1850.
[50] Ibid. p. 58.
[51] Wordsworth and Reed, *Correspondence*, p. 196, footnote. I. F. to H. R. 'The Uplands — East Sheen — Surrey — England — 31 August, 1853.' [Written by Henry Taylor.]
[52] Sara Coleridge, *Memoir and Letters*, pp. 278–9.
[53] Ibid. pp. 521–2. To Aubrey de Vere. 1st Oct. 1851.
[54] Henry Taylor, *Correspondence*, pp. 220–2. 17th Dec. 1856.
[55] Neither was published until after his death, in the *Memoirs*.
[56] Henry Taylor, *Correspondence*, pp. 110–11. Miss F. to H. T. 4th Jan. 1839.
[57] Crabb Robinson, *Correspondence*, i, pp. 45–6. 25th July 1802.
[58] Ibid. p. 114. 3rd Mar. 1822.
[59] Ibid. p. 247. H. C. R. to T. R. Bath. 6th Oct. 1833. Not in Sadler.
[60] Ibid. *Diaries*, 20. p. 419. 1st Dec. 1845. Not in Sadler.
[61] Ibid. 18, p. 95. 1st Mar. 1840.
[62] Ibid. 21, p. 558. 30th Jan. 1849. Not in Sadler.
[63] Ibid. *Correspondence*, i, p. 447. [29th Oct.] 1841. Not in Sadler.
[64] Henry Taylor, *Correspondence*, pp. 115–16. Miss F. to H. T. 26th Jan. 1839.
[65] Crabb Robinson, *Diaries*, 20, p. 383. 28th Sept. 1845. Not in Sadler.
[66] Ibid. *Correspondence*, i, p. 311. [17th July 1836.]
[67] Ibid. *Diaries*, 19, p. 511. 23rd Nov. 1845.
[68] Ibid. p. 629. 13th May 1844.
[69] Ibid. p. 46. 15th Apr. 1842.
[70] Ibid. pp. 191 and 256. 14th Oct. and 30th Dec. 1842.
[71] Henry Taylor, *Correspondence*, p. 116. 26th Jan. 1839.
[72] Crabb Robinson, *Diaries*, 18, p. 282. 25th Dec. 1840.
[73] Ibid. p. 306. 21st Jan. 1841.
[74] Ibid. *Correspondence*, i, p. 536. 26th and 28th Dec. 1843.
[75] Ibid. *Diaries*, 18, pp. 421 and 449. 6th June and 10th July 1841.
[76] Ibid. 20, p. 261. 2nd May 1845.
[77] Ibid. 18, pp. 599–600. 11th Feb. 1842. Ibid. 19, pp. 12–13. 7th Mar.
[78] Ibid. pp. 316 and 322. 24th Feb. and 13th Mar. 1843. Also *Correspondence*, i, p. 479. Miss F. to H. C. R. 9th Mar. 1843. Not in Sadler.
[79] Ibid. *Diaries*, 19, p. 541. 30th Jan. 1844.
[80] Ibid. *Correspondence*, ii, p. 544. 6th Feb. [1844]. Not in Sadler.
[81] Ibid. p. 550.

T

[82] Ibid. p. 589. 29th Jan 1845. Not in Sadler.

[83] Ibid. *Diaries*, 20, pp. 186 and 188. 6th and 8th Feb. 1845. Not in Sadler.

[84] Ibid. 18, p. 405. 15th May 1841.

[85] Ibid. 22, p. 340. 22nd May 1851.

[86] Ibid. p. 396. 10th Sept. 1851.

[87] Ibid. 21, p. 580. 24th Feb. 1849. Not in Sadler.

[88] Ibid. *Correspondence*, i, p. 403. 19th Mar. 1840. Also Sadler, iii, pp. 184–5.

[89] Ibid. p. 436. 29th May 1841. H. C. R. to T. R.

[90] Ibid. *Diaries*, 19, p. 279. 15th and 16th Jan. 1843.

[91] Ibid. *Correspondence*, ii, p. 605. Rydal Mount. 7th Aug. [18]45. Not in Sadler.

[92] Ibid. *Diaries*, 18, pp. 188 and 190. 2nd and 6th July 1840.

[93] Ibid. p. 570. 9th Jan. 1842.

[94] Ibid. 19, p. 160. 9th Sept. 1842.

[95] Ibid. *Correspondence*, ii, p. 836. 'List of Wordsworth Poems recommended by H. C. R. as the best to begin with.' 17th May 1861.

[96] Ibid. p. 576. 4th Nov. [1844]. Not in Sadler.

[97] Courtenay had died since this change was made, possibly by his own hand.

[98] Crabb Robinson, *Diaries*, 18, p. 554. 26th Dec. 1841. Shorthand passages italicized.

[99] Ibid. *Correspondence*, ii, p. 650. 11th June 1847. Not in Sadler.

[100] Ibid. *Diaries*, 22, p. 387. 30th Aug. 1851.

[101] Ibid. 18, p. 421. 6th June 1841.

[102] Ibid. p. 592. 2nd Feb. 1842.

[103] Ibid. 21, pp. 775–6. 3rd Dec. 1849. Not in Sadler.

[104] Ibid. *Correspondence*, ii, p. 636. Loughrigg Holme. 30th Aug. 1846. Not in Sadler.

[105] Ibid. p. 663. Loughrigg Holme. 1st Feb. 1847. [1848.]

[106] Ibid. *Diaries and Correspondence*, edited by Sadler, iii, pp. 370–1. 30th Dec. 1850.

[107] Wordsworth, *Prose Works*, i, p. ix.

[108] Personal letter from the late Mr Gordon Wordsworth, 13th Nov. 1932.

[109] Crabb Robinson, *Correspondence*, i, p. 431. 18th Apr. [1841]. Not in Sadler.

[110] Ibid. *Diaries*, 18, p. 553. 24th Dec. 1841.

[111] Ibid. pp. 563–4. 3rd Jan. 1842.

[112] Ibid. p. 578. 17th Jan. 1842.

[113] Ibid. *Correspondence*, i, p. 452. 19th Jan. 1842.

[114] Ibid. *Diaries*, 18, p. 606. 17th Feb. 1842.

[115] Ibid. *Correspondence*, i, p. 454. H. C. R. to Mrs Q. 7th Mar. 1842. Not in Sadler.

[116] Ibid. 21st Feb. 1842. Not in Sadler.

[117] Ibid. p. 457. 15th Mar. 1842. Not in Sadler.

118 Ibid. pp. 458–9. 23rd Apr. 1842. Not in Sadler.

119 Ibid. ii, p. 760. H. C. R. to T. R. 25th Oct. 1850. Not in Sadler.

120 James Dykes Campbell, *Samuel Taylor Coleridge—a Narrative of the Events of his Life*, pp. 179–80; and George McLean Harper, *William Wordsworth—his Life, Works, and Influence*, ii, pp. 192–3.

121 By Coleridge's own admission, Mrs Wordsworth and Dorothy had sat up with him alternately night after night, and Wordsworth had 'forced' on him a hundred pounds when he went south. Coleridge, *Biographia Epistolaris*, i, p. 288. Jan. 1804.

122 Ernest de Selincourt, *Dorothy Wordsworth*, pp. 178–9.

123 *Wordsworth's Prelude*, edited by Ernest de Selincourt, pp. xxxv–xxxvi.

124 Ibid. pp. 80 and 382. (1805) iii, 200, and x, 373, cited by Ernest de Selincourt, *Dorothy Wordsworth*, p. 174.

125 To Sir George Beaumont, quoted by Ernest de Selincourt, *Dorothy Wordsworth*, p. 188.

126 Ernest de Selincourt, *Dorothy Wordsworth*, pp. 208–9.

127 Wordsworth, *Prose Works*, iii, p. 23. No. 57. 'A Complaint.'

128 Dean Sperry, in *Wordsworth's Anti-Climax*, pp. 40–7, *passim*, puts the break as far back as 1803, and even hints that it began in Germany. His conclusions, however, are different from those in this book.

129 Ernest de Selincourt, *Dorothy Wordsworth*, pp. 210–11.

130 Coleridge, *Sibylline Leaves*, 1817, pp. 197–203. Cited by Ernest de Selincourt, *Dorothy Wordsworth*, pp. 211–12.

131 Ernest de Selincourt, *Dorothy Wordsworth*, pp. 211–12.

132 Ibid. pp. 217–18.

133 Ibid. pp. 218–19.

134 Ibid. pp. 240–9.

135 *To a Gentleman*, Coleridge, *Sibylline Leaves*.

136 Ernest de Selincourt, *Dorothy Wordsworth*, p. 254.

137 Crabb Robinson, *Correspondence*, i, pp. 66–7 and 71. 15th May and 7th Dec. 1811, and 29th May 1812.

138 'The Estrangement Between Coleridge and Wordsworth,' *Blake, Coleridge, Wordsworth, Lamb, etc.—Selections from the Remains of Henry Crabb Robinson*, edited by Edith J. Morley, pp. 146–56.

139 Ernest de Selincourt, *Dorothy Wordsworth*, p. 257.

140 'The Estrangement Between Coleridge and Wordsworth,' op. cit., p. 155.

141 Crabb Robinson, *Diaries*, 20, p. 393. 26th Oct. 1845. Italicized part originally in shorthand.

142 He had written to Cottle in June 1797: 'I speak with heart-felt sincerity, and I think, unblinded judgment, when I tell you that I feel myself a little man by his side, and yet I do not think myself a less man than I formerly thought myself'; and to Godwin in Mar. 1801: 'If I die, and the booksellers will give you anything for my life, be sure to say, "Wordsworth descended on him like the γνῶθι σεαυτόν from heaven; by showing to him what true poetry was, he made him know that he himself was no Poet."'—*Biographia Epistolaris*, i, pp. 135 and 229–30.

[143] 8th Oct. 1822. Coleridge, *Biographia Epistolaris*, ii, p. 262.

[144] Ibid. p. 296. Also Ernest de Selincourt, *Dorothy Wordsworth*, p. 375.

[145] 24th Jan. 1831. Robert Perceval Graves, *Life of Sir William Rowan Hamilton*, i, p. 425.

[146] 22nd Nov. 1831. Ibid. p. 492.

[147] 'On the Death of Coleridge,' Wordsworth, *Prose Works*, iii, pp. 469–70.

[148] Crabb Robinson, *Correspondence*, i, p. 402. 10th Mar. 1840.

[149] Wordsworth, *Prose Works*, iii, pp. 441–2. Reminiscences of Mrs Davy, 11th July 1844.

[150] Wilfrid Ward, *Aubrey de Vere—a Memoir*, p. 70. 9th Mar. 1845.

[151] Wordsworth, *Prose Works*, iii, p. 492. 'Recollections of Wordsworth by Aubrey de Vere, Esq., Part. I.

[152] Coleridge, *Biographia Epistolaris*, i, p. 240. Southey to Coleridge. 11th July 1801, footnote.

[153] Henry Reed, *British Poets*, ii, Miscellaneous Essays, 'Hartley Coleridge,' p. 284.

[154] Letter from Gordon Wordsworth, 17th Aug. 1933.

[155] Harriet Martineau, *Autobiography*, i, p. 511.

[156] Wilfrid Ward, *Aubrey de Vere—a Memoir*, p. 97. 29th Oct. 1845.

[157] Crabb Robinson, *Correspondence*, ii, p. 684. H. C. R. to T. R. 12th Jan. [18]49. Not in Sadler.

[158] Thomas Arnold, *Passages in a Wandering Life*, pp. 46–7.

[159] Towle, *A Poet's Children*, p. 205.

[160] Henry Taylor, *Correspondence*, p. 157. 9th Mar. 1845.

[161] Ibid.

[162] Hallam Tennyson, *Tennyson and his Friends*, 'Fragmentary Notes of Tennyson's Talk,' p. 266.

[163] Hallam Tennyson, *Tennyson—a Memoir*, i, p. 154.

[164] Caroline Fox, *Memories of Old Friends*, pp. 20 and 23.

[165] Ibid. pp. 21 and 22.

[166] Ibid. p. 211. 1st Oct. 1844.

[167] Towle, *A Poet's Children*, p. 255.

[168] Hallam Tennyson, *Tennyson—a Memoir*, i, pp. 153–4.

[169] Wilfrid Ward, *Aubrey de Vere—a Memoir*, p. 69. 8th Mar. 1845.

[170] Caroline Fox, *Memories of Old Friends*, p. 212. 5th Oct. 1844.

[171] Coleridge, *Biographia Epistolaris*, i, p. 201. S. T. C. to Davy. 25th July 1800.

[172] *To H. C., Six Years Old*, Wordsworth, *Poetical Works*, Oxford, 1926, p. 88, ll. 11–14 and 21–4.

[173] Coleridge, *Biographia Epistolaris*, ii, pp. 124–5. Cottle to S. T. C. 25th Apr. 1814.

[174] Ibid. p. 189, and Ernest de Selincourt, *Dorothy Wordsworth*, p. 258. 8th Apr. 1813.

[175] Towle, *A Poet's Children*, pp. 113 and 115.

[176] Ibid. p. 167.

[177] Crabb Robinson, *Correspondence*, i, p. 411. Also Sadler, iii, p. 187.

[178] William Knight, *Letters*, iii, p. 255. 13th Dec. 1842.

[179] Caroline Fox, *Memories of Old Friends*, pp. 174-5. Hampstead, 4th June 1842.

[180] Ibid. p. 21. 9th Sept. 1837.

[181] Ibid. p. 212. 1st Oct. 1844.

[182] Letter at Dove Cottage. Dora Wordsworth to Edward Quillinan, 1822.

[183] Wordsworth and Reed, *Correspondence*, pp. 183-4. H. R. to Mrs W. Philadelphia. 27th Oct. 1852.

[184] Coleridge, *Biographia Literaria*, 1847, i, Preface, p. lxxxiv.

[185] Towle, *A Poet's Children*, p. 259.

[186] Ibid. p. 260.

[187] Sara Coleridge, *Memoir and Letters*, p. 369. Derwent's letter quoted by Sara to Miss Fenwick, 7th Jan. 1849.

[188] Crabb Robinson, *Diaries*, 21, p. 543. Not in Sadler.

[189] Sara Coleridge, *Memoir and Letters*, p. 371. Letter to the Rev. Edward Coleridge, quoting letter from Derwent. Jan. 1849.

[190] Ibid. The same letter to the Rev. Edward Coleridge, but quoting another letter from Derwent.

[191] Crabb Robinson, *Correspondence*, ii, p. 681. Q. to H. C. R. 12th Jan. 1849. Also Sadler, iii, p. 338.

[192] Ibid. p. 682. Q. to H. C. R. 12th Jan. 1849. Also Sadler, iii, p. 339.

[193] Sara Coleridge, *Memoir and Letters*, p. 371.

[194] Ibid. pp. 371-2.

[195] Ellis Yarnall, *Wordsworth and the Coleridges*. 'A Visit to Wordsworth.' 18th Aug. 1849, p. 47.

[196] Crabb Robinson, *Correspondence*, ii, p. 681. H. C. R. to T. R. Ambleside. 4th-5th Jan. 1849. Not in Sadler.

[197] Sara Coleridge, *Memoir and Letters*, p. 64. Letter to her daughter, Edith Coleridge.

[198] Henry Taylor, *Correspondence*, p. 336. 27th July 1874.

[199] Personal letter, 17th Aug. 1933.

[200] Sara Coleridge, *Memoir and Letters*, 'Recollections of the Early Life of Sara Coleridge,' written by herself. 8th Sept. 1851. pp. 44-5.

[201] Ibid. p. 49.

[202] Ibid. pp. 50-1. Account by her daughter, Edith.

[203] Towle, *A Poet's Children*, p. 124.

[204] Sara Coleridge, *Memoir and Letters*, p. 57. Account by her daughter, Edith.

[205] Towle, *A Poet's Children*, pp. 123-4.

[206] Sara Coleridge, *Memoir and Letters*, p. 53.

[207] Ibid. p. 54. Also Crabb Robinson, *Correspondence*, i, p. 131. D. W. to H. C. R. 13th Dec. 1824, footnote by Miss Morley.

[208] Crabb Robinson, *Correspondence*, i, p. 173.

[209] Ibid. p. 207. 26th Apr. 1829. The last part not in Sadler, but omission not indicated.

[210] *Oxford Wordsworth*, p. 220.

[211] Sara Coleridge, *Memoir and Letters*, p. 59.

[212] Crabb Robinson, *Correspondence*, i, p. 233. W. W. to H. C. R. 5th Feb. 1833. This part not in Sadler.

[213] Sara Coleridge, *Memoir and Letters*, p. 66. Aubrey de Vere to Edith Coleridge.

[214] Ibid. pp. 64–5.

[215] Crabb Robinson, *Diaries*, 19, p. 88. 29th May 1842. Not in Sadler.

[216] William Knight, *Letters*, iii, p. 254.

[217] Crabb Robinson, *Diaries*, 19, p. 280. 17th Jan. 1843. Not in Sadler.

[218] Ibid. *Correspondence*, i, p. 502. 29th June 1843. Not in Sadler.

[219] Sara Coleridge, *Memoir and Letters*, p. 287. To Rev. Henry Moore. 5th Sept. 1846.

[220] Ibid. p. 61, footnote.

[221] Crabb Robinson, *Diaries*, 21, p. 649. 16th May 1849. Not in Sadler.

[222] Ibid. *Correspondence*, ii, p. 766. 7th Jan. 1851.

[223] Ibid. *Diaries*, 19, p. 418. 18th July 1843.

[224] Coleridge, *Poetic and Dramatic Works*, Boston, 1854, p. v Advertisement, by Derwent Coleridge.

[225] Crabb Robinson, *Diaries*, 21, p. 485. 18th Oct. 1848. Not in Sadler. 'Wordsworth' in shorthand.

[226] Coleridge, *Poetic and Dramatic Works*, pp. lxviii–lxxvi and lxxxii, Memoir of the Author.

[227] Coleridge, *Biographia Literaria*, ii, pp. 7–8, footnote: 'Poetry is not now the *fashion*. We bestow our "*ignorance, incapability* and *presumption*," or at least our superficiality, incompetence, and hastiness on the religious tract or controversial pamphlet, and poetry is resigned to those who have a true taste for it and study it in earnest.'

[228] Crabb Robinson, *Diaries*, 19, p. 411. 11th June 1843. Also Sara Coleridge, *Memoir and Letters*, pp. 470–1. To Miss Fenwick. 19th Nov. 1850.

[229] Crabb Robinson, *Diaries*, 19, p. 517. 29th Nov. 1843.

[230] Ibid. pp. 516–17. 29th Nov. 1843.

[231] Ibid. 21, p. 239. 10th Nov. 1847.

[232] Expressed in *Man's Nature and Development*, written in collaboration with H. G. Atkinson.

[233] Crabb Robinson, *Diaries*, 22, pp. 412–13. 17th Oct. 1851.

[234] William Knight, *Letters*, iii, p. 325. 29th Sept. 1845.

[235] Sara Coleridge, *Memoir and Letters*, p. 240. 26th Sept. 1845.

[236] Crabb Robinson, *Diaries*, 21, p. 547. 16th Jan. 1849. Not in Sadler.

[237] Sara Coleridge, *Memoir and Letters*, p. 315. 7th July 1847.

[238] Ibid. pp. 492–3. 19th May 1851.

[239] Ibid. p. 301. To the Hon. Mr Justice Coleridge, 20th Mar. 1847.

[240] Crabb Robinson, *Correspondence*, ii, p. 644. 28th Mar. P. S. Not in Sadler.

[241] Sara Coleridge, *Memoir and Letters*, pp. 305–6. Apr. 1847.

[242] Ibid. p. 307. To Miss Erskine. Apr. 1847.

[243] Ibid. p. 309. To Miss Fenwick. 26th Apr. 1847.

[244] Ibid.

[245] Ibid. p. 427. To E. Quillinan, Esq. Good Friday, 1850.

[246] Ibid. p. 435. To E. Quillinan, Esq.

[247] Ibid. p. 437. To Mrs H. M. Jones. Apr. 1850.

[248] F. V. Morley, *Dora Wordsworth—her Book*, p. 168. 17th Sept. 1850.

[249] Sara Coleridge, *Memoir and Letters*, p. 498. To Miss Fenwick.

[250] Ibid. p. 224. To Hartley Coleridge, Esq. 20th Jan. 1845.

[251] Ibid. pp. 253–4. To Aubrey de Vere, Esq. 1846.

[252] Ibid. pp. 256–7. To Mrs Richard Townsend. 17th June 1846.

[253] Coleridge, *Biographia Literaria*, ii, pp. 178–9, footnote.

[254] Sara Coleridge, *Memoir and Letters*, p. 439. 13th June 1850.

[255] Ibid. p. 495. 19th May 1851.

[256] Ibid. pp. 455 and 457.

[257] Ibid. p. 300. She wrote to Miss Fenwick: 'The trouble I have taken with this book is ridiculous to think of—it is a filial phenomenon; nobody will thank me for it, and no one will know or see a twentieth part of it. But I have done the thing *con amore*, for my father's book.'

[258] Crabb Robinson, *Correspondence*, ii, p. 630. W. W. to H. C. R. 22nd June 1846. Not in Sadler.

[259] Cf. p. 119, *supra*, for Wordsworth on this charge in *Blackwood's* for Mar. 1840.

[260] Crabb Robinson, *Diaries*, 20, p. 594. 31st July 1846. Not in Sadler.

[261] Ibid. p. 638. 26th Nov. 1846.

[262] Sara Coleridge, *Memoir and Letters*, p. 300.

[263] Coleridge, *Biographia Literaria*, 1847, Dedication.

[264] Henry Taylor, *Notes from Books*, pp. 114–18, footnote.

[265] Ellis Yarnall, *Wordsworth and the Coleridges*, pp. 106–7.

[266] Ibid. p. 125. Derwent Coleridge gave Yarnall this information shortly after his sister's death.

[267] Crabb Robinson, *Diaries*, 22, p. 292. 28th Mar. 1851.

[268] Sara Coleridge, *Memoir and Letters*, p. 522. 13th Oct. 1851.

[269] Towle, *A Poet's Children*, p. 308.

CHAPTER IV

[1] Austin and Ralph, *Lives of Poets-Laureate*, p. 411. Also William Knight, *Letters*, iii, p. 327. M. W. to S. C.

[2] William Taylor, *Memoir of Life and Writings*, ii, p. 78. R. S. to W. T.

[3] Ibid. p. 428. R. S. to W. T. Keswick, 27th Dec. 1814.

[4] Crabb Robinson, *Correspondence*, i, p. 93. 24th June 1817.

⁵ Ibid. p. 328. H. C. R. to Landor. 7th Dec. [1836]. Copy. Also Sadler, iii, p. 107.

⁶ Ibid. pp. 480–1. H. C. R. to Q. Not in Sadler.

⁷ Cottle, *Reminiscences of Coleridge and Southey*, p. 307. Southey to Cottle, 9th May 1837.

⁸ Crabb Robinson, *Correspondence*, i, p. 423. W. W. to H. C. R. [28th Jan. 1841].

⁹ Ibid. p. 373. [Dec. 1838.] Not in Sadler.

¹⁰ Thomas Carlyle, *Reminiscences* (Norton), ii, p. 293: 'Miss Bowles was twelve years younger than Southey.'

¹¹ Thomas Carlyle, *Reminiscences* (Froude), ii, p. 326.

¹² Ibid. (Norton), ii, p. 295.

¹³ William Jerdan, *Men I have Known*, pp. 413–14.

¹⁴ Crabb Robinson, *Correspondence*, i, pp. 392–3. Aug. 1839. Not in Sadler.

¹⁵ Ibid. *Diaries*, 18, pp. 19–20. 21st Nov. 1839.

¹⁶ Thomas Arnold, *Passages in a Wandering Life*, p. 45.

¹⁷ Crabb Robinson, *Correspondence*, i, p. 416. [July 1840.] Not in Sadler.

¹⁸ Christopher Wordsworth, *Memoirs*, ii, pp. 368–9. To Lady Frederick Bentinck. July 1840.

¹⁹ Joseph Cottle, *Reminiscences*, p. 310. To John Foster. 6th July 1842.

²⁰ Crabb Robinson, *Diaries*, 18, pp. 256–7. 20th Nov. 1840.

²¹ Ibid. pp. 284–5. 28th Dec. 1840.

²² Ibid. p. 292. 4th Jan. 1841.

²³ Ibid. *Correspondence*, i, pp. 426–7. W. W. to H. C. R. [28th Jan. 1841.]

²⁴ Ibid. *Diaries*, 18, p. 330. 19th Feb. 1841.

²⁵ Ibid. *Correspondence*, i, p. 428. W. W. to H. C. R. 26th Jan. 1841; and pp. 444–5. M. W. to H. C. R. 14th Oct. 1841. Not in Sadler.

²⁶ Ibid. *Diaries*, 18, p. 321. 9th Feb. 1841.

²⁷ Ibid. *Correspondence*, i, pp. 427–8. W. W. to H. C. R. [28th Jan. 1841.]

²⁸ Ibid. *Diaries*, 18, pp. 309–10. 25th Jan. 1841.

²⁹ Ibid. *Correspondence*, i, p. 477. Q. to H. C. R. 15th Feb. 1843. Not in Sadler.

³⁰ Ibid. p. 479. H. C. R. to T. R. 29th Mar. 1843. Not in Sadler.

³¹ Ibid. p. 485. Q. to H. C. R. 4th Apr. 1843. Not in Sadler.

³² Robert Southey, *Life and Correspondence*, edited by his son, C. C. Southey, p. 563.

³³ Christopher Wordsworth, *Memoirs*, ii, p. 394. 27th Mar. 1843.

³⁴ Ibid. p. 395. W. W. to H. R. 27th Mar. 1843.

³⁵ Crabb Robinson, *Correspondence*, i, pp. 497–8. Q. to H. C. R. 12th May 1843. Not in Sadler.

³⁶ Thomas Cooper, *Life, written by himself*, pp. 292–3.

³⁷ Crabb Robinson, *Correspondence*, i, p. 494. Q. to H. C. R. 9th Apr. 1843. Not in Sadler.

[38] Ibid. ii, p. 607. [7th Aug. 1845.] Not in Sadler.

[39] Ibid. p. 671. 8th June [1848]. Not in Sadler.

[40] Ibid. i, p. 503. Q. to H. C. R. 7th July 1843; and *Diaries*, 19, pp. 417–18. 18th July 1843.

[41] Ibid. *Diaries*, 20, p. 37. 12th July 1844.

[42] Ibid. pp. 13–14. 17th June 1844.

[43] William Knight, *Letters*, iii, p. 342. 23rd Feb. 1848.

[44] Mrs Fletcher, *Autobiography*, pp. 246–7.

[45] Ibid. p. 221.

[46] Ibid. pp. 227–9.

[47] Ibid. p. 243. Aug. 1839.

[48] Ibid. p. 247.

[49] Ibid. p. 249.

[50] Ibid. p. 250.

[51] Cf. Chapter I, pp. 18–19.

[52] Mrs Fletcher, *Autobiography*, p. 254.

[53] He and Dorothy had come on 21st Dec. 1799.

[54] Christopher Wordsworth, *Memoirs*, ii, p. 441. Reminiscences—Mrs Davy's notes. 22nd Jan. 1844. Also Wordsworth, *Prose Works*, iii, p. 440.

[55] Ibid. p. 452. Reminiscences—Lady Richardson's notes. 21st Nov. 1844.

[56] Crabb Robinson, *Diaries and Correspondence* (Sadler), iii, pp. 259–60. 26th Dec. 1844.

[57] Mrs Fletcher, *Autobiography*, pp. 255–6.

[58] Crabb Robinson, *Diaries and Correspondence* (Sadler), iii, p. 259.

[59] Ibid. *Diaries*, 20, p. 190. 11th Feb. 1845. Not in Sadler.

[60] Mrs Fletcher, *Autobiography*, p. 260.

[61] Ibid. p. 262.

[62] Crabb Robinson, *Diaries*, 21, p. 307. 26th Feb. 1848. Not in Sadler.

[63] Mrs Fletcher, *Autobiography*, pp. 268–9. Letter to Mrs Stark from Mrs Fletcher. 26th Mar. 1848.

[64] Ibid.

[65] Crabb Robinson, *Correspondence*, ii, p. 690. [24th Feb. 1849.] Not in Sadler.

[66] Mrs Fletcher, *Autobiography*, p. 282. Apr. 1850.

[67] Ibid. p. 283. 26th Apr. 1850.

[68] Ibid. p. 284. Letter to Mary. 1st May 1850.

[69] Wordsworth and Reed, *Correspondence*, i, p. 35. W. W. to H. R. 14th Sept. 1840.

[70] Crabb Robinson, *Diaries*, 18, p. 562. 1st Jan. 1842.

[71] Ibid. *Correspondence*, ii, p. 825. William Wordsworth [grandson] to H. C. R. Jan. 1858.

[72] Ibid. *Diaries*, 18, p. 291; and 19, pp. 261 and 269.

[73] Thomas Arnold, *Passages in a Wandering Life*, p. 11.

[74] Ibid. pp. 39–40.

[75] Mrs Humphry Ward, *A Writer's Recollections*, i, pp. 101–2.

[76] Mary Russell Mitford, *Life*, iii, p. 193.

[77] Crabb Robinson, *Diaries and Correspondence* (Sadler), iii, p. 193. 5th Jan. 1842, footnote.

[78] Mrs Humphry Ward, *A Writer's Recollections*, i, p. 102.

[79] Mrs Fletcher, *Autobiography*, p. 221.

[80] Crabb Robinson, *Correspondence*, ii, p. 704. H. C. R. to T. R. 15th Sept. 1849. Not in Sadler.

[81] Thomas Arnold, *Passages in a Wandering Life*, p. 39.

[82] Stanley, *Life and Correspondence of Thomas Arnold*, ii, p. 249. 15th Jan. 1841.

[83] Crabb Robinson, *Diaries*, 18, p. 303. 16th Jan. 1841.

[84] Ibid. p. 305. 19th Jan. 1841.

[85] Stanley, *Life and Correspondence of Thomas Arnold*, ii, pp. 274-5.

[86] Crabb Robinson, *Correspondence*, i, p. 445. [14th Oct. 1841.] Not in Sadler.

[87] Worboise, *Life of Dr Arnold*, p. 210.

[88] Crabb Robinson, *Diaries*, 18, p. 573. 12th Jan. 1842.

[89] Matthew Arnold, *Poems, Rugby Chapel.*

[90] Mrs Fletcher, *Autobiography*, p. 251. M. F.'s notes.

[91] Crabb Robinson, *Diaries*, 19, pp. 104-5. Also Sadler, iii, p. 198, slightly altered.

[92] Ibid. p. 105.

[93] Ibid. pp. 126-7. 5th Aug. 1842.

[94] Mrs Fletcher, *Autobiography*, pp. 252-3. 1844.

[95] Crabb Robinson, *Correspondence*, ii, p. 565. 14th July 1844.

[96] Ibid. p. 574. 11th Oct. 1844.

[97] Ibid. p. 547. 19th Mar. 1844. Not in Sadler.

[98] Harper, *William Wordsworth—his Life, Works, and Influence*, ii, p. 436.

[99] Clough, *Poems and Prose Remains*, i, pp. 96-7. 2nd Apr. 1845.

[100] Wordsworth, *Poems*, edited by Matthew Arnold, p. xxvi.

[101] Crabb Robinson, *Correspondence*, ii, pp. 695-6. Q. to H. C. R. 20th June 1849. Not in Sadler.

[102] Ibid. p. 769. 16th Jan. 1851. Not in Sadler.

[103] Bowden, *Life and Letters of Frederick William Faber*, p. 70.

[104] Crabb Robinson, *Diaries*, 18, p. 291. 3rd Jan. 1841.

[105] Ibid. p. 305. 20th Jan. 1841.

[106] Bowden, *Life and Letters of Frederick William Faber*, p. 89.

[107] Crabb Robinson, *Diaries*, 18, pp. 556-7. 27th Dec. 1841.

[108] Ibid. p. 557. 28th Dec. 1841.

[109] Ibid. p. 565. 5th Jan. 1842.

[110] Bowden, *Life and Letters of Frederick William Faber*, p. 168.

[111] Ibid. p. 170.

[112] Crabb Robinson, *Correspondence*, i, pp. 472-3. [29th Dec. 1842.] Also Sadler, iii, p. 210. Dated 29th Jan. 1843.

[113] Ibid. *Diaries*, 19, p. 250. 25th Dec. 1842.

[114] Ibid. p. 251. 26th Dec. 1842.

[115] Ibid. p. 254. 30th Dec. 1842.

[116] Ibid. p. 256.

[117] Ibid. pp. 266-7. 5th Jan. 1843. Also Sadler, iii, pp. 209-10.

[118] Ibid. p. 269. 7th Jan. 1843. Not in Sadler.

[119] Ibid. pp. 270-1.

[120] Ibid. *Correspondence*, i, p. 474. Rydal, 12th Jan. 1843. Not in Sadler.

[121] Bowden, *Life and Letters of Federick William Faber.*

[122] Clough, *Poems and Prose Remains*, i, p. 102. 21st Sept. 1845.

[123] Ibid. p. 105. 23rd Nov. 1845.

[124] Crabb Robinson, *Correspondence*, ii, p. 616. H. C. R. to T. R. 30th Dec. 1845. Not in Sadler.

[125] Especially *O Paradise, O Paradise; Hark! hark, my soul! Angelic songs are swelling*; and *Faith of our Fathers, living still.*

[126] David Watson Rannie, *Wordsworth and his Circle*, pp. 307-8.

[127] Mary Russell Mitford, *Life*, p. 154. 23rd July 1842.

[128] Crabb Robinson, *Diaries*, 20, p. 155. 4th Dec. 1844. Not in Sadler.

[129] Ibid. *Correspondence*, i, p. 531. H. C. R. to M. W. 4th Dec. [1843]. Not in Sadler.

[130] Ibid. *Diaries*, 20, p. 200. 24th Feb. 1845.

[131] Ibid. p. 177. 27th Jan. 1845. Not in Sadler.

[132] Clayden, *Rogers and his Contemporaries*, ii, p. 261.

[133] Crabb Robinson, *Correspondence*, i, p. 471. Q. to H. C. R. 28th Nov. 1842. Also Miss Morley's footnote. Not in Sadler.

[134] Ibid. *Diaries*, 19, pp. 282, 323, 353, and 447. 19th Jan., 2nd Mar., 8th Apr., and 23rd Aug. 1843.

[135] Ibid. p. 528. 12th Dec. 1843.

[136] Harriet Martineau, *Autobiography*, i, p. 490.

[137] Crabb Robinson, *Diaries*, 20. p. 147. 27th Nov. 1844. Not in Sadler.

[138] Harriet Martineau, *Autobiography*, i, p. 481.

[139] Crabb Robinson, *Diaries*, 20, p. 172. 24th Dec. 1844 (26th Jan. a.m.). Not in Sadler.

[140] Ibid. *Correspondence*, ii, p. 584. H. C. R. to T. R. 16th Jan. 1845. Rydal Mount. Not in Sadler.

[141] Ibid. *Diaries*, 20, p. 172. Not in Sadler.

[142] Ibid. *Correspondence*, ii, p. 585. H. C. R. to T. R. 24th Jan. 1845. Not in Sadler.

[143] Harriet Martineau, *Autobiography*, i, p. 506.

[144] Crabb Robinson, *Correspondence*, ii, p. 590. W. W. to H. C. R. 2nd Feb. 1845. Not in Sadler.

[145] Harriet Martineau, *Autobiography*, i, p. 482.

[146] Ibid. p. 495.

[147] Crabb Robinson, *Correspondence*, ii, pp. 605-6. 7th Aug. 1845. Not in Sadler.

[148] Harriet Martineau, *Autobiography*, i, pp. 500-1.

[149] Crabb Robinson, *Correspondence*, ii, pp. 608-9. [16th Sept. 1845.] Not in Sadler.

[150] Ibid. p. 611. M. W. to H. C. R. 7th Nov. [1845]. Not in Sadler.

[151] William Knight, *Letters*, iii, p. 328.

[152] Crabb Robinson, *Correspondence*, ii, p. 617. H. C. R. to T. R. Rydal Mount. 25th Dec. 1845. Not in Sadler.

[153] Ibid. p. 618. H. C. R. to T. R. 2nd Jan. 1846. Not in Sadler.

[154] Harriet Martineau, *Autobiography*, i, p. 507.

[155] Crabb Robinson, *Correspondence*, i, p. 421. 8th Jan. 1841. Not in Sadler.

[156] Ibid. ii, p. 622. 'Extract from a letter of H. Martineau.' 8th Feb. 1846. Not in Sadler.

[157] Mary Russell Mitford, *Correspondence*, p. 48. Feb.–Mar. 1846.

[158] Harriet Martineau, *Autobiography*, i, p. 505.

[159] William Howitt, *Homes of the Poets*, ii, pp. 121–2.

[160] Crabb Robinson, *Diaries*, 21, p. 125. 13th June 1847. Not in Sadler.

[161] Mary Russell Mitford, *Life*, iii, p. 214. Sept. 1848.

[162] Crabb Robinson, *Correspondence*, ii, p. 670. 7th June 1848. Not in Sadler.

[163] Ibid. p. 667. Loughrigg Holme. 6th June 1848. Not in Sadler.

[164] Ibid. p. 697. [Endorsed 21st June 1849.] Not in Sadler.

[165] Ibid. p. 686. 15th Jan. [1849]. Sadler, iii, p. 341.

[166] Wordsworth, *Prose Works*, iii, p. 27. No. 78. 'The Widow on Windermere Side.'

[167] D. Masson, *The Collected Writings of T. de Quincey*, ii, p. 432, cited by Alan Lang Strout, 'William Wordsworth and John Wilson,' *Publications of the Modern Language Association of America*, xlix, Mar. 1934, p. 153.

[168] Alan Lang Strout, 'William Wordsworth and John Wilson,' p. 149.

[169] Ibid. pp. 150–62.

[170] Wordsworth, *Prose Works*, i, pp. 297–308.

[171] MS. letter in British Museum. 30, 262: f. 96. W. W. jun. to Mrs Gordon, daughter of Wilson. 'St Ann's Hill, Carlisle, 18th Dec. 1860.' The late Mr Gordon Wordsworth also confirmed this.

[172] Mrs Anne Grant, *Memoir and Correspondence*, ii, p. 224. 23rd Jan. 1819.

[173] Alan Lang Strout, 'William Wordsworth and John Wilson,' pp. 179–80.

[174] Edith J. Morley, *Blake, Coleridge, Wordsworth, Lamb, etc.—Selections from the Remains of Henry Crabb Robinson*, p. 50. 13th May 1812. Cited by Strout, op. cit., p. 173.

[175] N. P. Willis, *Prose Works, Pencillings by the Way*, p. 199.

[176] Ibid. p. 200.

[177] Alan Lang Strout, 'William Wordsworth and John Wilson,' pp. 180–1.

[178] Crabb Robinson, *Correspondence*, i, pp. 200–1. 27th Jan. [1829]. Not in Sadler.

[179] Alan Lang Strout, 'William Wordsworth and John Wilson,' p. 182, note.

[180] Crabb Robinson, *Correspondence*, i, p. 516. 25th Aug. 1843.

[181] Alan Lang Strout, 'William Wordsworth and John Wilson,' p. 182, note.

[182] Coleridge, *Biographia Literaria*, 1847, ii, p. 374. S. T. C. to Poole. 24th Sept. 1796.

[183] H. D. Rawnsley, *Literary Associations of the English Lakes*, p. 101.

[184] Wordsworth, *Prose Works*, iii, pp. 187–8. No. 499. 'Epitaph in the Chapel-yard of Langdale, Westmoreland.'

[185] Crabb Robinson, *Correspondence*, i, p. 411. W. W. to H. C. R. 3rd June 1840. Not in Sadler.

[186] It is erroneously dated 1824 in Macmillan's Globe Edition.

[187] Christopher Wordsworth, *Memoirs*, ii, p. 244. 9th Nov. [1831?].

[188] Ibid. p. 407. 31st Mar. 1844.

CHAPTER V

[1] Thomas Powell, *Living Authors*, p. 34.

[2] Crabb Robinson, *Diaries*, 18, p. 179. 21st June 1840.

[3] Ibid. pp. 277–8. 22nd Dec. 1840.

[4] Wordsworth, *Prose Works*, iii, pp. 496–7. Aubrey de Vere, 'Recollections of Wordsworth.'

[5] Crabb Robinson, *Diaries*, 18, pp. 179 and 277; 20, pp. 434 and 590; 21, p. 246.

[6] Ibid. 18, p. 104. 13th Mar. 1840.

[7] Ibid. p. 210. 3rd Aug. 1840.

[8] Henry Taylor, *Autobiography*, i, p. 321.

[9] R. E. Roberts, *Rogers and his Circle*, pp. 165–6.

[10] Christopher Wordsworth, *Memoirs*, edited by Henry Reed, ii, p. 234. H. R.'s footnote.

[11] Crabb Robinson, *Correspondence*, i, p. 373. W. W. to H. C. R. [Dec. 1838.] Not in Sadler.

[12] Henry Taylor, *Autobiography*, i, p. 320. Through Aubrey de Vere.

[13] The name by which Henry Taylor was known, from his dazzling success in 1834.

[14] Rowland E. Prothero and G. G. Bradley, *The Life and Correspondence of Arthur Penrhyn Stanley, D.D.*, i, p. 298.

[15] Crabb Robinson, *Diaries*, 18, p. 597. 8th Feb. 1842.

[16] Ibid. p. 612. 24th Feb. 1842.

[17] Ibid. *Correspondence*, i, p. 455. H. C. R. to M. W. 7th Mar. 1842. Not in Sadler.

[18] Ibid. *Diaries*, 19, pp. 58–9. 29th Apr. 1842. Also Sadler, iii, pp. 196–7.

[19] Wordsworth, *Prose Works*, iii, p. 498. Aubrey de Vere, 'Recollections of Wordsworth.'

[20] Charles Robert Leslie, *Autobiographical Recollections*, 1860, p. 159.

[21] Crabb Robinson, *Correspondence*, i, p. 470. Q. to H. C. R. 28th Nov. 1842. Not in Sadler.

[22] For this letter I am indebted to Professor Ernest Hunter Wright, of Columbia University.

[23] William Knight, *Letters*, iii, p. 313. 10th Apr. 1845.

[24] Wilfrid Ward, *Aubrey de Vere—a Memoir*, p. 72.

[25] Crabb Robinson, *Diaries and Correspondence* (Sadler), iii, p. 263.

[26] Benjamin Robert Haydon, *Autobiography*, ii, pp. 278–9.

[27] Christopher Wordsworth, *Memoirs*, ii, p. 415. To Professor Reed. 1st July 1845.

[28] Wilfrid Ward, *Aubrey de Vere—a Memoir*, p. 73. 4th May 1845.

[29] P. W. Clayden, *Rogers and his Contemporaries*, pp. 323–4. 16th Mar. 1848.

[30] Crabb Robinson, *Correspondence*, i, p. 304. H. C. R. to W. W. 8th May 1836. Not in Sadler.

[31] William Knight, *Letters*, iii, p. 350. 29th Oct. 1849.

[32] Crabb Robinson, *Correspondence*, i, p. 280, Miss Morley's footnote.

[33] Thomas Powell, *Living Authors*, pp. 226–7. Review by Croker.

[34] The teacher of Gray, Pitt, and Wordsworth.

[35] Christopher Wordsworth, *Memoirs*, edited by Henry Reed, i, p. 14. Reed's footnote.

[36] Crabb Robinson, *Diaries*, 19, p. 101.

[37] Mary Russell Mitford, *Letters*, i, p. 213. 21st Mar. 1843.

[38] Ibid. *Life*, iii, p. 4. 22nd Oct. 1833. Also Crabb Robinson, *Correspondence*, i, p. 351. W. W. to H. C. R. 15th Dec. [1837]. Not in Sadler.

[39] Crabb Robinson, *Correspondence*, i, p. 362.

[40] Percy Lubbock, *Elizabeth Barrett Browning in her Life and Letters*, p. 68.

[41] Mary Russell Mitford, *Correspondence*, p. 77. To Boner. 11th Oct. 1847.

[42] Cf. *Anecdote for Fathers*.

[43] Christopher Wordsworth, *Memoirs*, ii, pp. 411–12. 1st Oct. 1844.

[44] Crabb Robinson, *Correspondence*, i, p. 374. W. W. to H. C. R. [6th Dec. 1838.] Not in Sadler.

[45] Ibid. *Diaries*, 18, p. 452. 14th July 1841.

[46] Ibid. 19, p. 604. 13th Apr. 1844; and 20, p. 169. 21st Dec. 1844.

[47] Cf. p. 180, *supra*.

[48] Crabb Robinson, *Diaries*, 19, p. 71. 11th May 1842.

[49] Ibid. pp. 142–3. 23rd Aug. 1842. Also Sadler, iii, p. 200.

[50] Ibid. 20, p. 169. 21st Dec. 1844. Not in Sadler.

[51] Ibid. *Correspondence*, i, p. 501. 1st June 1843. Not in Sadler.

[52] William Knight, *Letters*, iii, p. 328. 25th Nov. 1845.

[53] Crabb Robinson, *Correspondence*, ii, p. 614. 9th [8th] Dec. [1845]. Not in Sadler.

[54] Ibid. p. 616. H. C. R. to T. R. 13th Dec. 1845. Not in Sadler.

[55] Sara Coleridge, *Memoir and Letters*, p. 315. To Miss Fenwick. 6th July 1847.

[56] Crabb Robinson, *Diaries*, 21, pp. 111–12. 28th May 1847. Substance but not the words in Sadler, iii, pp. 292–3.

[57] Ibid. *Correspondence*, i, p. 222. H. C. R. to T. R. 25th Sept. 1830. Not in Sadler.

[58] Ibid. p. 223. 27th Oct. 1831. Not in Sadler.

[59] Ibid. p. 254. Landor to H. C. R. Dec. 1833. Not in Sadler.

[60] Ibid. p. 304. H. C. R. to W. W. 8th May 1836. This part not in Sadler.

[61] Mary Russell Mitford, *Life*, iii, p. 44. 25th May 1836.

[62] Thomas Hughes, *Memoir of Daniel Macmillan*, pp. 105-6. 10th Dec. 1842.

[63] Walter Savage Landor, *Letters and Unpublished Writings*, p. 156.

[64] Crabb Robinson, *Correspondence*, i, pp. 326-7 and 329-33. 7th and 17th Dec. 1836. Copy.

[65] Ibid. p. 383. H. C. R. to W. W. [*Circa* 30th Apr. 1839.] Not in Sadler.

[66] Ibid. *Diaries*, 18, p. 99. 8th Mar. 1840.

[67] Ibid. 19, p. 245. 19th Dec. 1842.

[68] Ibid. p. 247. 21st Dec.

[69] Ibid. *Correspondence*, i, pp. 475-6. 7th Feb. 1843. Not in Sadler.

[70] Ibid. pp. 480-1. H. C. R. to Q. [3rd Apr. 1843.] Not in Sadler.

[71] Ibid. pp. 481-2 and 488. H. C. R. to Q. 3rd and 7th Apr. 1843. Not in Sadler.

[72] Ibid. *Diaries*, 19, p. 400. 30th May 1843.

[73] Ibid. *Correspondence*, i, p. 500. Q. to H. C. R. 1st June 1843. Not in Sadler.

[74] Ibid. *Diaries*, 19, p. 569. 4th Mar. 1844: 'On my return to the omnibus fell in with *Moxon*. He tells me that Landor has given all his Dialogues to Forster who is going to publish them at his own risque. But he will not allow the attack on Wordsworth to be among them.'

[75] Ibid. *Correspondence*, ii, p. 844. John Forster to H. C. R. 26th Mar. 1866.

[76] Mary Russell Mitford, *Life*, ii, pp. 10-11. To Sir Wm. Elford. 13th Sept. 1817.

[77] Thomas Noon Talfourd, *Critical and Miscellaneous Writings*, p. 47.

[78] Mary Russell Mitford, *Life*, iii, pp. 49-50 and 52. 30th and 31st May 1836.

[79] Thomas Noon Talfourd, *Critical and Miscellaneous Writings*, 'Speeches on the Law of Copyright,' p. 163.

[80] Crabb Robinson, *Correspondence*, i, p. 349. W. W. to H. C. R. 15th Dec. [1837].

[81] Ibid. p. 296. 26th Mar. [1838].

[82] Ibid. p. 379. [19th Feb. 1839.]

[83] Thomas Noon Talfourd, *Critical and Miscellaneous Writings*, 'Speeches on the Law of Copyright,' p. 174.

[84] Crabb Robinson, *Correspondence*, i, p. 296, footnote.

[85] Ibid. *Diaries*, 18, p. 168. 6th June 1840.

[86] Ibid. *Correspondence*, i, pp. 438-9. M. W. to H. C. R. 28th June [1841].

[87] Mrs Mary Gordon, '*Christopher North*'—a *Memoir of John Wilson*, p. 416.

[88] Crabb Robinson, *Correspondence*, ii, p. 587. H. C. R. to M. W. 27th Nov. 1845, and footnote. Not in Sadler.

[89] Ibid. *Diaries*, 20, pp. 170-1. 22nd Dec. 1844. Not in Sadler.

[90] Mary Russell Mitford, *Correspondence*, p. 102. To Boner. 25th Aug. 1848.

[91] Crabb Robinson, *Diaries*, 21, pp. 278, 279, 290, 291, 356, and 374. 20th and 21st Jan, 4th and 6th Feb., 27th Apr., and 17th May 1848. Not in Sadler, except item of 6th Feb., given as 5th Feb. in Sadler, iii, pp. 311–12.

[92] Ibid. *Correspondence*, ii, p. 674. Not in Sadler.

[93] Ibid. *Diaries*, 21, p. 441. 21st Aug. 1848. Not in Sadler.

[94] Mary Russell Mitford, *Correspondence*, p. 102. 25th Aug. 1848.

[95] Crabb Robinson, *Diaries*, 21, p. 538. 19th Dec. 1848. Not in Sadler.

[96] Ibid. *Correspondence*, ii, p. 683. 12th Jan. 1849. Not in Sadler.

[97] Ibid. *Diaries*, 21, pp. 699–700. 26th July 1849. Also Sadler, iii, p. 343.

[98] Ibid. p. 738. 20th Sept. 1849. Not in Sadler.

[99] MS. letter in British Museum 38, 110—Leigh Hunt Correspondence, vol. iii, f. 339. Letter from Leigh to Leigh Hunt, 4th Jan. 1850. PS.: 'Is not Judge Talfourd Wordsworth's happy Warrior?'

[100] Crabb Robinson, *Diaries*, 22, p. 77. 10th May 1850. Not in Sadler.

[101] Mary Russell Mitford, *Life*, iii, p. 248. 1st Dec. 1852.

[102] Ibid. p. 39. 19th Oct. 1835.

[103] Ibid. p. 64. 17th Oct. 1836.

[104] *Bookman*, Feb. 1913. Article by Louis A. Holman: 'Old Pigments and New Found Faces,' pp. 608–14.

[105] Ibid. p. 612. Also Benjamin Robert Haydon, *Autobiography*, i, pp. 356–7.

[106] Edith C. Batho, *The Later Wordsworth*, pp. 79–86.

[107] Ibid. p. 85. Also Benjamin Robert Haydon, *Autobiography*, ii, pp. 274–5. 12th Apr. 1831.

[108] Ibid. Also William Knight, *Letters*, ii, p. 449. W. W. to Haydon, June 1831. PS.

[109] He had received the freedom of Plymouth for his painting, 'The Judgment of Solomon.'

[110] William Knight, *Poetical Works of William Wordsworth*, xi, p. 389.

[111] William Knight, *Letters*, iii, p. 206.

[112] Benjamin Robert Haydon, *Autobiography*, iii, p. 146.

[113] Wordsworth and Reed, *Correspondence*, p. 37. W. W. to Reed. 14th Sept. 1840.

[114] Ibid. p. 42. W. W. to Reed. 13th Jan. 1841.

[115] Benjamin Robert Haydon, *Autobiography*, iii, pp. 199–200.

[116] Ibid. pp. 203–4.

[117] Benjamin Robert Haydon, *Correspondence and Table-Talk*, i, p. 434.

[118] Ibid. ii, p. 54. 16th Oct. 1842.

[119] Christopher Wordsworth, *Memoirs*, ii, p. 252.

[120] Benjamin Robert Haydon, *Correspondence and Table-Talk*, ii, p. 56. 30th Mar. 1843.

[121] Ibid.

[122] F. V. Morley, *Dora Wordsworth—her Book*, pp. 72–3. Henry Taylor described Wordsworth's poise: '. . . He met Jeffrey the other day at Sir J. Mackintosh's and at Jeffrey's request they were introduced. Lockhart beheld the ceremony, and told me that Wordsworth played the part

of a man of the world to perfection, much better than the smaller man, and did not appear to be conscious of anything having taken place between them before.'

[123] Crabb Robinson, *Diaries*, 19, p. 520. 3rd Dec. 1843. Also *Correspondence*, i, p. 532. 4th Dec. 1843. Not in Sadler.

[124] Ibid. *Correspondence*, ii, p. 838. List of Wordsworth's poems, etc. 17th May 1861.

[125] Benjamin Robert Haydon, *Correspondence and Table-Talk*, i, p. 461. 3rd Mar. 1843.

[126] Ibid. p. 460. 20th May 1845.

[127] Ibid. ii, pp. 57–8. 5th July 1843.

[128] Ibid. pp. 58–9. 5th May 1844.

[129] Ibid. *Autobiography*, iii, p. 276.

[130] Ibid. p. 279. 22nd May 1845.

[131] Ibid. p. 301. 6th Feb. 1846.

[132] Ibid. *Life, Letters and Table-Talk*, edited by Stoddard. Preface, p. xxii. Bayard Taylor's Reminiscences.

[133] Mary Russell Mitford, *Correspondence*, p. 54. July 1846.

[134] Ibid. pp. 53–4. Letter from Elizabeth Barrett enclosed in letter to Boner.

[135] Wife of the poet's youngest brother, Dr Christopher Wordsworth, and mother of John, Charles, and Christopher.

[136] Elizabeth Wordsworth, *Glimpses of the Past*, pp. 3–5.

[137] Crabb Robinson, *Diaries*, 18, p. 444. 5th July 1841. Not in Sadler.

[138] Cf. p. 214, *infra*.

[139] Ernest de Selincourt, *Dorothy Wordsworth*, pp. 57 and 213.

[140] Crabb Robinson, *Diaries*, 18, p. 422. 7th June 1841.

[141] Ibid. 19, p. 98. 8th June 1842.

[142] Edith C. Batho, *The Later Wordsworth*, p. 10.

[143] Henry Taylor, *Autobiography*, i, p. 83.

[144] Ibid. *Correspondence*, p. 38. May 1831.

[145] Coleridge, *Biographia Epistolaris*, ii, p. 290. [1825.]

[146] Wilfrid Ward, *Aubrey de Vere—a Memoir*, pp. 32–3. 1838.

[147] Henry Taylor, *Autobiography*, i, pp. 192–3 and 196.

[148] Ibid. p. 210.

[149] Ibid. p. 190.

[150] William Knight, *Letters*, iii, p. 188.

[151] Christopher Wordsworth, *Memoirs*, ii, p. 365.

[152] Caroline Fox, *Memories of Old Friends*, p. 151. 6th Sept. 1841.

[153] Henry Taylor, *Autobiography*, i, p. 201, note.

[154] Ibid. *Correspondence*, p. 129. 8th Nov. 1841.

[155] Ibid. *Autobiography*, p. 324.

[156] Crabb Robinson, *Diaries*, 18, p. 560. 31st Dec. 1841.

[157] Ibid. 19, p. 441. 14th Aug. 1843.

[158] Ibid. 21, p. 671. 11th June 1849. Not in Sadler.

[159] Cf. p. 15, *supra*.

[160] Wilfrid Ward, *Aubrey de Vere—a Memoir*, p. 73. 28th Apr. 1845.

U

[161] The baby was only twelve days old at the time, having been born on 16th Apr. Henry Taylor, *Autobiography*, ii, p. 25.

[162] Henry Taylor, *Autobiography*, ii, p. 57. 24th May 1850.

[163] Crabb Robinson, *Diaries*, 22, p. 145. 16th Sept. 1850. Part in Sadler, iii, p. 366.

[164] Ibid. *Correspondence*, ii, p. 759. 20th Sept. 1850.

[165] Ibid. Miss Morley's footnote.

[166] Wilfrid Ward says it was the sixteenth earl and gives the date as 1831. *Aubrey de Vere—a Memoir*, p. 1, note, and p. 3.

[167] Eleanor A. Towle, *A Poet's Children*, p. 221.

[168] Wilfrid Ward, *Aubrey de Vere—a Memoir*, p. 392.

[169] John P. Gunning, *Aubrey de Vere—a Memoir*, p. 17.

[170] Sara Coleridge, *Memoir and Letters*, p. 65.

[171] Ibid. pp. 263 and 348.

[172] Ibid. p. 286. 31st Aug. 1846.

[173] Ibid. p. 263.

[174] Ibid. pp. 319–20.

[175] Ibid. p. 392.

[176] Ibid. p. 236. 8th Sept. 1845.

[177] Ibid. p. 235. 1845.

[178] Ibid. pp. 318–19. 1847.

[179] Eleanor A. Towle, *A Poet's Children*, p. 305.

[180] Wilfrid Ward, *Aubrey de Vere—a Memoir*, pp. 64 and 95. John Marshall's sister and brother had married Spring-Rices, first cousins of Aubrey de Vere.

[181] Ibid. p. 64.

[182] Ibid. p. 65.

[183] Ibid. p. 66.

[184] John P. Gunning, *Aubrey de Vere—a Memoir*, p. 36.

[185] Wordsworth, *Prose Works*, iii, p. 486. Aubrey de Vere, 'Recollections of Wordsworth.'

[186] This was almost certainly Miss Fenwick, whom de Vere visited.

[187] Wordsworth, *Prose Works*, iii, p. 498. Aubrey de Vere, 'Recollections of Wordsworth.'

[188] Ibid. p. 488.

[189] Ibid. p. 492.

[190] Robert Perceval Graves, *Life of Sir William Rowan Hamilton*, ii, pp. 402–3. 10th Jan. 1843.

[191] Wordsworth, *Prose Works*, iii, p. 491. Aubrey de Vere, 'Recollections of Wordsworth.'

[192] Miss Martineau had been visiting Greg in January and February, and had departed only a fortnight before.

[193] Wilfrid Ward, *Aubrey de Vere—a Memoir*, p. 68.

[194] Hallam Tennyson, *Alfred Lord Tennyson—a Memoir*, p. 209. Also John P. Gunning, *Aubrey de Vere—a Memoir*, pp. 119–20.

[195] Wilfrid Ward, *Aubrey de Vere—a Memoir*, p. 69.

[196] Henry Taylor, *Correspondence*, p. 157. Ambleside. 9th Mar. 1845.

[197] Wilfrid Ward, *Aubrey de Vere—a Memoir*, p. 392.

[198] Ibid. pp. 69–70.

[199] Henry Taylor, *Correspondence*, p. 156. 9th Mar. 1845.

[200] Wilfrid Ward, *Aubrey de Vere—a Memoir*, p. 71.

[201] Hallam Tennyson, *Alfred Lord Tennyson—a Memoir*, i, pp. 71–2.

[202] Thomas R. Lounsbury, *The Life and Times of Tennyson*, p. 354.

[203] Hallam Tennyson, *Alfred Lord Tennyson—a Memoir*, i, p. 179. 19th Sept. 1841.

[204] F. V. Morley, *Dora Wordsworth—her Book*, p. 165.

[205] Wilfrid Ward, *Aubrey de Vere—a Memoir*, p. 73.

[206] Hallam Tennyson, *Alfred Lord Tennyson—a Memoir*, i, p. 209.

[207] Wilfrid Ward, *Aubrey de Vere—a Memoir*, pp. 73–4.

[208] Hallam Tennyson, *Alfred Lord Tennyson—a Memoir*, i, p. 210.

[209] Wilfrid Ward, *Aubrey de Vere—a Memoir*, pp. 73–4.

[210] Hallam Tennyson, *Alfred Lord Tennyson—a Memoir*, i, p. 265. Report of Dr Ker, Tennyson's brother-in-law.

[211] F. V. Morley, *Dora Wordsworth—her Book*, p. 164.

[212] Wordsworth and Reed, *Correspondence*, p. 144. 1st July 1845.

[213] Thomas Cooper, *Life, written by himself*, p. 292.

[214] Wilfrid Ward, *Aubrey de Vere—a Memoir*, p. 99.

[215] Ibid. p. 155. 9th Apr. 1850.

[216] John P. Gunning, *Aubrey de Vere—a Memoir*, p. 62.

[217] Wordsworth, *Prose Works*, iii, p. 494. Aubrey de Vere, 'Recollections of Wordsworth.'

CHAPTER VI

[1] Ernest de Selincourt, *Dorothy Wordsworth*, pp. 123 and 137.

[2] Ibid. p. 146.

[3] Ibid. pp. 290–7.

[4] Crabb Robinson, *Correspondence*, i, p. 430. Mrs C. to H. C. R. 25th Feb. 1841. Not in Sadler.

[5] William Knight, *Letters*, iii, pp. 335–6. 2nd Oct. 1846.

[6] Crabb Robinson, *Correspondence*, i, p. 456. Mrs C. to H. C. R. 13th Mar. 1842. Not in Sadler.

[7] Ibid. ii, p. 546. Mrs C. to H. C. R. 21st Feb. 1844. Not in Sadler.

[8] Ernest de Selincourt, *Wordsworth's Prelude*, p. xxxvi.

[9] Crabb Robinson, *Correspondence*, ii, p. 732. Mrs C. to H. C. R. [13th May 1850.] Not in Sadler.

[10] Ernest de Selincourt, *Wordsworth's Prelude*, p. 499.

[11] Ibid. *Dorothy Wordsworth*, p. 399, footnote.

[12] Wordsworth, *Prose Works*, iii, p. 237.

[13] Ernest de Selincourt, *Dorothy Wordsworth*, p. 85.

[14] Ibid. p. 86, and footnote.

[15] Wordsworth, *Prose Works*, iii, p. 237. No. 20.

[16] Ibid. p. 45. No. 154, 'Tintern Abbey.'

[17] Ernest de Selincourt, *Dorothy Wordsworth*, p. 90.

[18] Ibid. p. 106. Also Wordsworth, *Prose Works*, iii, p. 237.

[19] Coleridge, *Biographia Epistolaris*, ii, pp. 121–6. 25th Apr. 1814.

[20] Mary Russell Mitford, *Life*, iii, p. 177; June 1843; and *Notes of a Literary Life*, pp. 9–11.

[21] Crabb Robinson, *Diaries*, 18, pp. 387–8 and 390–1. 28th and 30th Apr. 1841.

[22] Wordsworth, *Prose Works*, iii, pp. 394–5. W. W. to Joseph Cottle. 6th Dec. 1845.

[23] Ibid. p. 357. 30th Aug. 1839.

[24] Ibid. p. 368. 19th Jan. 1841.

[25] Ibid. pp. 174–5. 23rd Feb. 1842.

[26] Ibid. p. 373. 12th Dec. 1842.

[27] Ibid. ii, p. 23. 8th Apr. 1844.

[28] Ibid. p. 174. 23rd Feb. 1842.

[29] Ibid. p. 400. Nov. 1848.

[30] Crabb Robinson, *Diaries*, 18, p. 392. 1st May 1841.

[31] Joseph Cottle, *Reminiscences of Coleridge and Southey*, p. 351.

[32] Wordsworth, *Prose Works*, iii, p. 359. 21st May 1840.

[33] Ernest de Selincourt, *Dorothy Wordsworth*, pp. 158 ff.

[34] Ibid. p. 182.

[35] Ibid. pp. 208–12.

[36] Wordsworth, *Prose Works*, iii, pp. 59 and 183.

[37] Ibid. pp. 44 and 71.

[38] Ibid. pp. 59–60.

[39] Ibid. p. 71. No. 261.

[40] Ibid. pp. 23, 39, 40, and 59.

[41] Ibid. p. 178. No. 460.

[42] Ibid. p. 126. No. 332.

[43] Ibid. pp. 187 and 189.

[44] Edwin Paxton Hood, *Wordsworth—a Biography*, p. 124.

[45] Christopher Wordsworth, *Memoirs*, ii, p. 162.

[46] Wordsworth, *Prose Works*, iii, pp. 63 and 190. Nos. 227 and 507.

[47] *Inscriptions in the Grounds of Coleorton*, 'The embowering rose . . .'

[48] Cf. p. 180, *supra*.

[49] Charles Robert Leslie, *Autobiographical Recollections*, pp. 159–60.

[50] Elizabeth Wordsworth, *Wordsworth*, p. 166.

[51] Crabb Robinson, *Diaries*, 18, p. 423. 8th June 1841.

[52] Christopher Wordsworth, *Memoirs*, ii, p. 412. To Professor Reed. 18th Nov. 1844.

[53] Professor J. M. Purcell, of Marquette University, Milwaukee, where the poet's own copies of the Camden Society publications are in the Public Library, says in *The Times Literary Supplement*, 31st Dec. 1933: 'Wordsworth was a member of the Camden Society from its founding in 1838, or shortly thereafter, until his death in 1850.'

[54] Crabb Robinson, *Correspondence*, ii, p. 577. 18th Nov. 1844. Not in Sadler.

[55] Thomas Hughes, *Memoir of Daniel Macmillan*, p. 26, and footnote.

[56] Crabb Robinson, *Diaries*, 21, p. 610. 30th Mar. 1849. Not in Sadler.

[57] Wordsworth, *Poetical Works*, edited by Henry Reed. 1851. p. 439.

[58] Christopher Wordsworth, *Memoirs*, edited by Henry Reed, ii, p. 68, footnote.

[59] Wordsworth and Reed, *Correspondence*, p. 64. 1st Mar. 1842.

[60] Crabb Robinson, *Correspondence*, i, p. 534. 16th Dec. 1843. Not in Sadler.

[61] Augustus J. C. Hare, *Memorials of a Quiet Life*, ii, pp. 273–4.

[62] Ellis Yarnall, *Wordsworth and the Coleridges*, p. 97. 6th July 1873.

[63] Crabb Robinson, *Diaries*, 21, p. 130. 19th June 1847. Also Sadler, iii, p. 295.

[64] David Watson Rannie, *Wordsworth and his Circle*, p. 327.

[65] Wordsworth, *Poetical Works*, edited by Henry Reed. 1851. Biographical note, p. viii.

[66] Arthur Hugh Clough, *Poems and Prose Remains*, i, p. 35.

[67] Crabb Robinson, *Correspondence*, i, p. 396. W. W. to H C. R. 23rd Jan. 1840. Not in Sadler.

[68] Wordsworth, *Prose Works*, iii, pp. 127–8. No. 333.

[69] Arthur Hugh Clough, *Poems and Prose Remains*, i, pp. 82–3. 30th May 1839.

[70] Arthur Penrhyn Stanley, *Life and Correspondence of Thomas Arnold*, ii, p. 162. 6th July 1839.

[71] John Taylor Coleridge, *Memoir of the Rev. John Keble*, p. 285.

[72] Christopher Wordsworth, *Memoirs*, ii, pp. 355–6.

[73] John Taylor Coleridge, *Memoir of the Rev. John Keble*, pp. 286–7.

[74] Crabb Robinson, *Correspondence*, i, p. 391. H. C. R. to W. W. 10th July 1839. Not in Sadler.

[75] Wordsworth, *Prose Works*, iii, p. 357. W. W. to Peace. 30th Aug. 1839.

[76] Wordsworth, *Poetical Works*, edited by Henry Reed. 1851. p. x.

[77] John Taylor Coleridge, *Memoir of the Rev. John Keble*, p. 285.

[78] Ibid. p. 35.

[79] Ibid. p. 395. 29th July 1842.

[80] Christopher Wordsworth, *Memoirs*, ii, p. 356.

[81] Wordsworth, *Prose Works*, iii, p. 441. Reminiscences of Mrs Davy. 5th Mar. 1844.

[82] Wordsworth and Reed, *Correspondence*, p. 128. 5th July 1844.

[83] Ellis Yarnall, *Wordsworth and the Coleridges*, p. 42. 18th Aug. 1849.

[84] Wordsworth, *Prose Works*, iii, p. 495 and note. Aubrey de Vere, 'Recollections of Wordsworth.'

[85] Ibid. p. 509.

[86] Ibid. p. 492. Aubrey de Vere, 'Recollections of Wordsworth.'

[87] Edith C. Batho, *The Later Wordsworth*, p. 24.

[88] Wordsworth, *Prose Works*, iii, pp. 318–19.   22nd Nov. 1831.

[89] Ibid. p. 351.   21st Dec [1837].

[90] Ibid. pp. 352–3.   4th Jan. 1838.

[91] Bk iii, ll. 62–3.

[92] *Wordsworth's Prelude*, edited by Ernest de Selincourt, pp. xli ff.

[93] Ibid. p. xlvi.

[94] Edith C. Batho, *The Later Wordsworth*, pp. 26–7.

[95] Robert Perceval Graves, *Life of Sir William Rowan Hamilton*, i, pp. 313–14. Cited by Batho, pp. 29–31.

[96] Cf. p. 93, *supra*.

[97] Henry Taylor, *Correspondence*, pp. 97–8.   18th Aug. 1838.

[98] Robert Perceval Graves, *Life of Sir William Rowan Hamilton*, ii, p. 270.

[99] Ibid. p. 410.

[100] Hamilton was godfather to Wordsworth's grandson and namesake, John Wordsworth's second son.   Wordsworth, *Prose Works*, iii, pp. 352 and 354.   21st Dec. 1837 and 4th Jan. 1838.

[101] Robert Perceval Graves. *Life of Sir William Rowan Hamilton*, ii, pp. 459–60.

[102] F. V. Morley, *Dora Wordsworth—her Book*, pp. 45–6.

[103] Ibid. p. 46.   Also Robert Perceval Graves, *Life of Sir William Rowan Hamilton*, ii, p. 460.

[104] Robert Perceval Graves, *Life of Sir William Rowan Hamilton*, ii, p. 488. 14th May 1845.

[105] Ibid. p. 487.   7th Apr. 1845.

[106] Ibid. p. 488.

[107] William Knight, *Letters*, iii, p. 335.   14th Mar. 1846.

[108] *The Convention of Cintra*, Wordsworth, *Prose Works*, i, p. 136.

[109] James T. Fields, *Yesterdays with Authors*, p. 258.

[110] Ellis Yarnall, *Wordsworth and the Coleridges*, p. 42.   Aug. 1849.

[111] Edwin Paxton Hood, *Wordsworth—a Biography*, p. 470.

[112] Ellis Yarnall, *Wordsworth and the Coleridges*, p. 57.

[113] Crabb Robinson, *Diaries*, 20, p. 303.   20th June 1845.   Not in Sadler.

[114] Ibid. *Correspondence*, ii, p. 607.   9th Sept. 1845.   Not in Sadler.

[115] Ibid. p. 609.   16th Sept. 1845.   Not in Sadler.

[116] Godwin's *Life*, ii, p. 9.   *William Cullen Bryant*, by John Bigelow, p. 184.   Boston, 1890 (Am. Men of Letters Series). Cf. Bradley, *William Cullen Bryant*, New York, 1905, p. 155.

[117] Ralph Waldo Emerson, *English Traits*, p. 279.

[118] Crabb Robinson, *Diaries*, 21, p. 398, 17th June 1848.   Not in Sadler.

[119] Wordsworth and Reed, *Correspondence*, p. 187.   27th June 1853.

[120] Ibid. p. 95.   27th Mar. 1843.

[121] Ibid. p. 83.   15th Nov. 1842.

[122] Ibid. p. 112.   28th Sept. 1843.

[123] Ibid. pp. 124–6.   28th June 1844.

[124] Christopher Wordsworth, *Memoirs*, edited by Henry Reed, ii, pp. 427–8, note.   Inman to Reed, 23rd June 1845.   Not in Broughton.

[125] Both portraits are extant—the original in the Library of the University of Pennsylvania, and the copy in the possession of the Rev. Christopher W. Wordsworth, great-grandson of the poet.

[126] Wordsworth and Reed, *Correspondence*, p. 159.   H. R. to Mrs W. 27th Nov. 1845.

[127] Ibid. p. 160.   23rd Jan. 1846.

[128] Ibid. p. 163.   H. R. to W. W.   26th Feb. 1846.

[129] Ibid. p. 147.   28th Aug. 1845.

[130] Ibid. pp. 274-5.   W. B. Reed to W. W. jun.   12th Oct. 1854.

[131] *The Alumni Register*, University of Pennsylvania, vol. v, No. 8, May 1901, pp. 257-64.

[132] Ellis Yarnall, *Wordsworth and the Coleridges*, p. 106.

[133] Ibid. pp. 34 ff.

[134] *Prelude*, Bk XI, ll. 108-9.

[135] Wordsworth, *Prose Works*, iii, p. 479.   Letter to Professor Henry Reed, Sept. 1850.

[136] The cabinet now hangs in the room pointed out to me, in Aug. 1931, as Wordsworth's study.

[137] Ellis Yarnall, *Wordsworth and the Coleridges*, pp. 44-5.

[138] Ibid. p. 49.

[139] E. H. Coleridge, *Life and Correspondence of John Duke Coleridge*, i, p. 306.

[140] Ellis Yarnall, *Wordsworth and the Coleridges*, pp. 50-1.

[141] Wordsworth and Reed, *Correspondence*, pp. 1-3.   25th Apr. 1836.

[142] Ibid. pp. 5-7.   3rd Jan. 1839.

[143] Ibid. p. 8.   7th May 1839.

[144] Ibid. p. 12.

[145] Ibid. p. 130.   14th Oct. 1844.

[146] Before friendly relations between England and the United States were restored, Bishop Seabury was consecrated in Scotland.   On 4th Feb. 1787, Bishop White and Bishop Provoost were consecrated at Lambeth.

[147] Wordsworth and Reed, *Correspondence*, pp. 19-20.   7th Apr. 1840.

[148] Wordsworth, *Prose Works*, iii, p. 345.   Only in abridged form in Wordsworth and Reed, *Correspondence*.

[149] Wordsworth and Reed, *Correspondence*, p. 7.   22nd Feb. 1839.

[150] Ibid. p. 13.   23rd Dec. 1839.

[151] Ibid. p. 57.   16th Aug. 1841.

[152] Ibid. p. 110.   Aug. 1843.

[153] Ibid. p. 137.

[154] Ibid. p. 163.   26th Feb. 1846.

[155] Ibid. pp. 173-4.   28th Oct. 1847.

[156] This edition is more interesting than the better-known English edition, because of the illuminating notes by Professor Reed.

[157] *The Alumni Register*, University of Pennsylvania, vol. v, No. 8, May 1901, p. 259.

[158] Wordsworth and Reed, *Correspondence*, p. 16.   18th Mar. 1840.

[159] Wordsworth, *Prose Works*, i. Preface, viii.   14th Sept. 1840.

[160] Cf. Ernest de Selincourt, *English Poets and the National Ideal*, pp. 61–88, for the development of a similar idea.

[161] Wordsworth and Reed, *Correspondence*, p. 40. 30th Oct. 1840.

[162] Ibid. p. 187. 27th June, 1853.

[163] Ibid. p. 43. Also Wordsworth, *Poetical Works*, edited by Reed, 1851, p. 441, footnote. 13th Jan. 1841.

[164] Wordsworth answered this request in the Fenwick notes.

[165] Wordsworth and Reed, *Correspondence*, p. 96. Also Christopher Wordsworth, *Memoirs*, edited by Henry Reed, i, p. 138. 27th Mar. 1843.

[166] Wordsworth and Reed, *Correspondence*, pp. 146–7. 31st July 1845.

[167] Ibid. p. 152. 27th Sept. 1845.

[168] Ibid. p. 168. 30th July 1846.

[169] Ibid. p. 51. 28th Apr. 1841.

[170] Ibid, pp. 56–7. 16th Aug. 1841.

[171] The late George Augustus Mayhew, of Newark, New Jersey, a great friend and admirer of Bishop Doane.

[172] Wordsworth and Reed, *Correspondence*, pp. 63–4. Also Christopher Wordsworth, *Memoirs*, edited by Henry Reed, ii, pp. 395–6, note. Letter to Henry Reed, 1st Mar. 1842.

[173] Wordsworth, *Prose Works*, iii, p. 135. No. 355.

[174] Wordsworth and Reed, *Correspondence*, pp. 68–9. 29th Apr. 1842.

[175] Visitation of the Sick and Thanksgiving of Women after Child-birth.

[176] Wordsworth and Reed, *Correspondence*, p. 81. W. W. to H. R. 4th Sept. 1842.

[177] Ibid. pp. 83–4.

[178] Ibid. pp. 84–5.

[179] Ibid. pp. 123–4. 29th May 1844.

[180] Ibid. p. 129. 5th July 1844.

[181] Ibid. pp. 96–7. 27th Mar. 1843.

[182] Ibid. pp. 144–5. 1st July 1845. Poem dated 6th June 1845.

[183] Ibid. pp. 149–50. 28th Aug. 1845.

[184] Ibid. p. 152. 27th Sept. 1845.

[185] Ibid. pp. 161–2. 23rd Jan. 1846.

[186] Ibid. pp. 14–15. 23rd Dec. 1839.

[187] Ibid. p. 76. 18th July 1842.

[188] Ibid. p. 94. 27th Mar. 1843.

[189] Ibid. pp. 175–6. 2nd Apr. 1849.

[190] Ibid. pp. 177–8. 10th Dec. 1849.

[191] Ibid. p. 181. H. R. to C. W. 28th Oct. 1850. It is at the end not of the fifth but of the fourth volume.

[192] Crabb Robinson, *Correspondence*, i, p. 353. 9th Jan. 1838. Not in Sadler.

[193] Cf. pp. 245–6, *supra*, letter to Henry Reed, 22nd Feb. 1839.

INDEX

MADE AT THE
TEMPLE PRESS
LETCHWORTH
GREAT BRITAIN

1. error -

a good book for schools - first
paragraph gives the measure - not a
subtle book & not intended to be so.